LORDS OF THE DESERT

Britain's Struggle with America to Dominate the Middle East

JAMES BARR

SIMON & SCHUSTER

London · New York · Sydney · Toronto · New Delhi

A CBS COMPANY

First published in Great Britain by Simon & Schuster UK Ltd, 2018
This edition published in Great Britain by Simon & Schuster UK Ltd, 2019
A CBS COMPANY

1 3 5 7 9 10 8 6 4 2

Simon & Schuster UK Ltd
1st Floor
222 Gray's Inn Road
London WC1X 8HB

www.simonandschuster.co.uk
www.simonandschuster.com.au
www.simonandschuster.co.in

Simon & Schuster Australia, Sydney
Simon & Schuster India, New Delhi

A CIP catalogue record for this book
is available from the British Library

Paperback ISBN: 978-1-4711-3980-2
eBook ISBN: 978-1-4711-3981-9

Typeset in the UK by M Rules
Printed and bound by CPI Group (UK) Ltd, Croydon, CR0 4YY

For Anna

CONTENTS

Part Three: Descent to Suez – 1953–58

Part Four: Clinging On – 1957–67

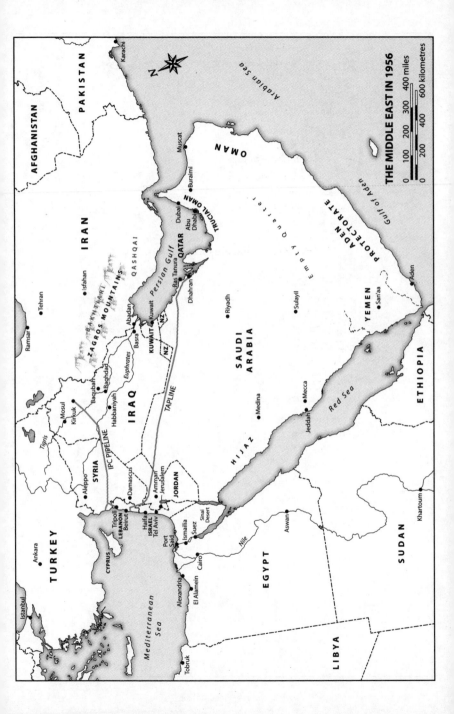

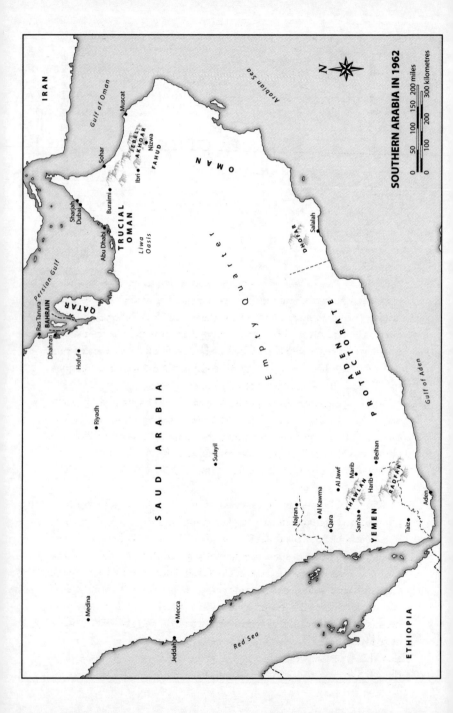

INTRODUCTION

'Ah Enoch, dear Enoch! He once said something to me I never understood,' Anthony Eden admitted in retirement. The former British prime minister was recalling a conversation that he and Enoch Powell had had during the late 1940s. The Conservative Party was then in opposition; Eden, at that stage widely regarded as the best foreign secretary Britain had ever had, had been picking his formidably intelligent colleague's brains about housing policy before giving a speech.

'I've told you all I know about housing, and you can make your speech accordingly,' said Powell. 'Can I talk to you about something that you know all about and I know nothing?' he continued. 'I want to tell you that in the Middle East our great enemies are the Americans.'

'You know, I had no idea what he meant,' Eden reflected all those years later. 'I do now.'

With his chilly stare Powell came across as slightly unhinged, an impression that his incendiary later prophecy about immigration would only reinforce. But on this, at least, there is no question that Enoch was right. Powell had spent the pivotal years of the war in the Middle East. He had witnessed the fraught Casablanca conference between Churchill and Roosevelt in 1943 where, the president's chief of staff admitted, 'There was too much anti-British feeling on our side.' And he was by no means the only man to see Britain and the United States as rivals in the region. His political opponent Richard Crossman wrote that the Americans represented 'the greatest danger to British rule in the Middle East today' after visiting Palestine in 1946. Nor was the feeling confined to the British. Two years later the American spy Kim Roosevelt, who had also served in Cairo in the war, remembered 'times when British representatives on the spot were, in defiance of London's instructions, doing all in their power to knife their American opposite numbers and . . . Americans on the scene whose every act was inspired by a desire to "do the British in".' A further, post-war tour of the area reinforced his view that 'actually Americans and British in the Middle East get along rather badly'.

All this is now forgotten history. During the Cold War Britain and the United States tried not to draw attention to their differences, and to this day the British government retains over 100m worth of files about its ally that it would rather not declassify. It is clearly best not to let too much light in upon the magic. This policy of secrecy and the Anglo-American coalitions in the Gulf in 1991 and in Iraq again after 2003 have helped obscure a fact that was once common knowledge: from 1942, until Britain's exit from the Gulf in 1971, Britain and the United States were invariably competitors in the Middle East, and often outright rivals. As this book will show, the joint Anglo-American effort to oust the Iranian prime minister Mohammad Mosaddeq in 1953 – so often produced as evidence of Anglo-American collusion – was the exception, not the rule.

* * *

This is a fascinating chapter in a long-running story, because the Middle East has served as an arena for Great Power conflict since the beginning of recorded time. In the first half of the twentieth century, Britain and France were the great powers of the day. Midway through the First World War they carved up the Ottomans' Arab territory between them and, once they had won the war, then subdivided it into mandates which they went on to rule for the best part of thirty years. The French left in 1946, chased out by Lebanese and Syrian nationalists who had had surreptitious British help. Any British sense of victory was short-lived, because a new contest, with the United States, then followed.

Britain's original motive for wanting to control the Middle East was primarily strategic: by dominating a belt of territory stretching from Egypt to Iran she could control the route between Europe and India.

Yet, by the time that Indian independence in 1947 rendered that rationale redundant, another justification had already taken its place – oil. British companies' domination of Middle Eastern oil production generated vital revenues for the Crown, improved Britain's perennially poor balance of payments, and would enable the country to defend itself in the event of a war with Soviet Russia. The belief that oil was, as one minister put it, a 'wasting asset' that would run out by about the end of the century – if it had not already been superseded by atomic energy (which many people at that time expected would be powering cars by now) – encouraged short-term thinking, and one hope in particular: the British might manage to resist mounting nationalist pressures for longer than the oil flowed out the ground.

Oil and the vast profits that it generated influence almost everything that happens after 1947 in this story: they were a constant source of tension between Washington and London. Compared to the British government – which owned a majority of the biggest oil company operating in the region and, through it, held a stake in another, the United States seemed far less organised. The goals of its government and oil industry were frequently at odds. Once the Americans had realised the sheer scale of likely regional oil reserves, the speculative concession won by a US company, Aramco, to hunt for oil in Saudi Arabia acquired a new, strategic significance.

Whereas short-termism led the British to defend their own interests aggressively, the Americans' prime interest was initially commercial, which made them more realistic and flexible. Aramco came under pressure from the Saudis from the late 1940s onwards but, knowing it could count on the United States government's support, agreed to split its profits fifty-fifty with the Saudi king. Not only did this suddenly increase the money that the Saudis could spend to advance their own regional ambitions – which caused huge political instability – but it also set a precedent that the American company's British rivals refused to follow. That miscalculation triggered a series of events, starting with Iran's nationalisation of Anglo-Iranian, that first stripped Britain of that crucial imperial asset, prestige, and left the region's once great and now denuded power fighting increasingly desperately to cling on.

The Americans knowingly abetted this process, a fact that Eden – despite his later claim of ignorance – knew full well at the time. Six months after the crucial battle of El Alamein – at a time when the British still directly ruled Palestine and occupied half of Persia, and whispered in the ears of the kings of Egypt, Jordan and Iraq – the foreign secretary wrote a memorandum in which he acknowledged how difficult the Anglo-American relationship in the Middle East had become. In it, he summed up the threat to Britain's position in the region as being 'a major nationalistic revival . . . of two contending forces, Arabism and Zionism' stoked by 'Zionist propagandists in the United States'. As Eden's use of the word 'revival' implied, the British had seen both before. What was new – and ominous, in the foreign secretary's eyes – was how the Zionists were now successfully courting the support of the United States. And in due course the leading Arab nationalist of the era, Eden's nemesis Gamal Abdel Nasser, would as well.

The British intended to enlist the Americans to deal with both these threats. They hoped to thwart Zionist ambitions by persuading the US government to recognise their privileged position in Palestine. If they could also convince Washington to support the post-war economic system for the region that they had dreamed up, they reasoned that they might prolong their dominance of the Middle East as a whole.

Today this strategy seems obviously flawed, but in 1945 the British did not have the advantage of hindsight. They expected their counterparts to lapse into their pre-war state of isolation, just as they had done after the First World War. When this did not happen, the British found themselves in competition with a formidable rival – the very ally they had assumed would be their closest friend. This is the story of their struggle.

PART ONE

Heading for Trouble
1941–48

I

THE BEGINNING OF THE END

Flanked by the Lord Mayor of London and the archbishop of Canterbury, Winston Churchill stood up in the Mansion House on 10 November 1942 to deliver some good news: Britain had at last won a decisive victory in the Middle East. Rightly, the prime minister sensed that the war had reached a turning point, but he was determined that his words should not encourage complacency. 'Now this is not the end,' he went on to warn, before turning the phrase for which his speech is famous. 'It is not even the beginning of the end. But it is, perhaps, the end of the beginning.'[1]

Whatever the moment represented, it had certainly been a long time coming. For three whole years the news had invariably been bad. 'In our wars the episodes are largely adverse, but the final results have hitherto been satisfactory,' Churchill reflected, before reminding his audience, 'In the last war we were uphill almost to the end.' Then he quoted a former Greek prime minister who had once observed that Britain always won one battle – the last. 'It would seem to have begun rather earlier this time,' he suggested, to laughter. It was the sound not of hilarity, but relief.

For 'largely adverse' was a typically British understatement, when used to describe a war in which disaster had pursued disaster. After Norway and Dunkirk in 1940, and Greece and Crete in 1941, there was no hiding the fact that 1942 had also been calamitous so far. In February the German pocket battleships *Gneisenau* and *Scharnhorst* had steamed through the Straits of Dover unopposed. A few days later Singapore surrendered, and the Japanese marched 85,000 British Empire troops into a captivity many of them would not survive. Churchill had depicted the 33,000-strong garrison of the Libyan port of Tobruk as the linchpin of British resistance to Hitler. But in June, while he was in Washington to confer with Franklin D. Roosevelt, it too had capitulated. He would not forget how the president had wordlessly passed him a pink slip of paper bearing the news before solicitously enquiring if there was anything he could do to help. 'Defeat is one thing;' Churchill wrote in his memoirs, 'disgrace is another.'[2]

The beleaguered prime minister had returned from Washington to London to face down criticisms that his strategy was failing as well as calls to resign his role as minister of defence – a tactic that he reckoned was the first step along the road to forcing him out altogether. He was a man who 'wins debate after debate and loses battle after battle', claimed one sceptic during a parliamentary debate on his direction of the war. Although Churchill easily survived the vote of confidence that followed it, and set off soon afterwards to see the situation in Egypt for himself, it was hard to deny that his critics had a point, not least when the Dieppe Raid proved a fiasco that August.[3]

At the Mansion House, Churchill now finally had something he could brandish at his critics. 'Now we have a new experience. We have victory – a remarkable and definite victory,' he announced, to cheers. At the end of October a predominantly British force had attacked the Germans at El Alamein; a few days later, once the mid-term elections had passed, United States troops landed at the other end of North Africa. The German army, now in a headlong retreat to avoid being pinched between the Americans and British, had been 'very largely destroyed as a fighting force', the prime minister declared.

If, in the first half of his speech, Churchill sounded cautiously optimistic, in the second half he bristled with defiance, because he knew what would come next. Having been a minister during the previous war, he knew from personal experience that the prospect of the end of the current one – no matter how long the final victory might be in coming – would again trigger a debate between Britain and the United States about the shape of the peace.

The signs were that history was repeating itself. From the safety of the other side of the Atlantic Roosevelt was already arguing that there was no room for empire in the post-war world, just as his predecessor

Woodrow Wilson had done during and after the last war, resisted by the British all the way. When, at the armistice in 1918, Churchill's private secretary declared that he was so grateful for the American contribution to the victory that he wanted to kiss Uncle Sam 'on both cheeks', Churchill had retorted, 'But not on all four.'[4]

By November 1942 Churchill must have feared that, were Uncle Sam to present his other two cheeks to him, it might be difficult to say no. Over a year earlier, after Britain allied herself to Stalin following Hitler's invasion of the Soviet Union, he had received a summons to a meeting off Newfoundland from Roosevelt: he crossed the ocean half-hoping that the president might declare war there and then. He was to be disappointed. For, over dinner on 9 August 1941, Roosevelt, who was wondering what secret deal the British might have stitched up with the Russians, instead asked him to commit to a joint declaration respecting the principles of self-determination and free trade for 'all peoples'. Churchill knew that both concepts had ominous implications for Britain and her empire, but he did not dare annoy the man on whom his hopes of victory depended. He and his advisers hurriedly drafted the declaration, which Roosevelt then significantly rewrote, but Churchill managed to dilute it somewhat by deleting the president's reference to trade 'discrimination' – an attack on the tariff system imposed across the British Empire – known as 'imperial preference' – that left American companies trying to sell goods in this enormous market at a significant disadvantage. But he had no choice but to agree to what would become known as the 'Atlantic Charter' and it was clear the issues that it broached were not going to go away, particularly once the United States started footing the bill for Britain's war effort, and then – after Pearl Harbor – joined battle herself.

Knowing that he could not win the war singlehandedly, Churchill had tried from the outset to 'drag the Americans in'. Now that he had managed to do so, he was having to confront the consequences of that strategy's success. It was only at the Mansion House after the victory at El Alamein that he felt strong enough to mount a sturdy public defence of the Empire against the incoming American assault. Although he readily acknowledged that it was American weapons and equipment that had finally enabled a fight with the Germans at El Alamein on equal terms, he emphasised that the battle had been 'fought throughout almost entirely by men of British blood'. For a year the British Empire had provided the only resistance to Hitler, he argued, and he had no plans to acquiesce to its break-up now. Britain was not fighting 'for profit or expansion', he insisted, rebutting an accusation that was regularly made – and not just by the enemy – and the time had come to make something else very clear. 'We mean to hold our own,' he stated, to cheers. 'I have not become the King's First Minister in order to preside over the liquidation of the British Empire ... I am proud to be a member of that vast commonwealth and society of nations and communities gathered in and around the ancient British monarchy, without which the good cause might well have perished from the earth. Here we are, and here we stand, a veritable rock of salvation in this drifting world.' It is often assumed that these pointed remarks were aimed at Roosevelt. But in fact Churchill had another American in mind.

*   *   *

Nine weeks earlier, when the victory proclaimed by Churchill was a distant and uncertain prospect, a four-engine American bomber had landed at Cairo airport with an important passenger aboard. Once it had taxied to a halt, its padded side door swung open to reveal a large, familiar-looking man dressed in a rumpled suit and pith helmet, who then half raised a hand to acknowledge the small crowd that had turned out to greet him.

Wall to wall press coverage of the US presidential election two years earlier made Wendell C. Willkie instantly recognisable: he was the Republican candidate, the dark horse from Ellwood, Indiana, with the booming voice and seismic handshake who had challenged Roosevelt for the presidency but lost. Now made a special envoy by the very man who had defeated him, he had come to Egypt on a 31,000-mile odyssey around the world.

This journey was to be a formative experience for Willkie – and that had dramatic implications for Britain. For when the American politician set out from the East Coast at the end of August 1942 he was one of the most energetic American supporters of Britain. But by the time he reached the West Coast, forty-nine days later, he had turned into one of her most outspoken critics. With hindsight it is clear that Willkie helped to trigger the beginning of the end of Britain's empire in the Middle East.

After posing for press photographs beside his aircraft Willkie left for the American embassy where the ambassador briefed him on the fragile situation. Ten weeks had passed since the German general Erwin Rommel captured Tobruk and chased the British back to their prepared defences at El Alamein, just 75 miles west of Alexandria. Until that point Cairo had escaped the rigours of the conflict. The atmosphere of easy-going calm was shattered on 1 July. On what was soon dubbed 'Ash Wednesday', the British embassy and military headquarters incompetently burned their files, scattering charred fragments of secret information, and seeding panic, across the city.

It was soon after this that Churchill had appeared in Cairo. Having survived the vote of confidence in parliament he then flew to Egypt so that he could visit the front, fire the general in command and insist that his order to fight to the last man must if necessary be carried out. All the same, the American ambassador was 'not hopeful about the future', Willkie recollected. He blamed 'British bungling'.[5]

The precarious military situation was made worse by the fact that relations between the British and the Egyptians were awful. The British had invaded Egypt in 1882 in order to take over the Suez Canal and safeguard the route to India, and they had never left. 'We do not govern Egypt,' Britain's first consul-general in the country would claim, 'we only govern the governors of Egypt.' It was a subtlety lost on the general population. The British let Egypt remain part of the Ottoman Empire, run by a khedive who paid homage to the Ottoman sultan, an arrangement that lasted until the Ottomans declared war on Britain in November 1914. At that point the British dismissed the khedive, declared his uncle sultan and made Egypt a protectorate. That lasted until 1922, when the sultan declared himself king and the country independent.[6]

Egyptian independence had come at a cost that made it meaningless, however. To gain their freedom the Egyptians were obliged to acquiesce to a treaty that granted Britain the right to station 10,000 troops along the Suez Canal and made her responsible for defending the country in the event of an attack, an arrangement that sowed the seeds of the 1956 Suez crisis. The outbreak of war in 1939 brought hundreds of thousands of British imperial troops back to Egypt, and with them roaring inflation and food shortages. The invasiveness of the measures required to defend the country would cause endless friction between the Egyptians and the British.

The man at the centre of this trouble, whom Willkie met after his briefing from the United States ambassador, was the current British ambassador to Egypt, Sir Miles Lampson. A 6ft 5in bully who had long believed Egypt should simply be sucked into the British Empire, he operated out of an office, at 10 Sharia Tolumbat in the city, which was known for short as 'Number Ten'. Willkie soon realised why. Although nominally the most senior diplomat in Egypt, Lampson was 'for all practical purposes its actual ruler'.[7]

What riled Lampson most was the way in which Egypt's king, Farouq, allowed pro-Axis sentiment in his country to flourish. Six months earlier, on 4 February 1942, he had tried unsuccessfully to lance the boil, causing an incident that had only made the situation worse. Following the resignation of the then Egyptian prime minister the ambassador had issued an ultimatum to Farouq to ask a more compliant politician to take charge, or else to abdicate. When, at six o'clock that evening, the king declined to do as he was told, the burly British pro-consul paid a visit to the royal residence, the Abdin Palace, with soldiers, tanks and a letter of resignation which he presented to Farouq for signature.

Farouq backed down and Lampson confessed in his diary at the end of a long evening that he 'could not have more enjoyed' the confrontation, but the cathartic effect of what would become known as the 'Abdin Palace incident' was brief. The following day he noted, 'We are still faced with the fact that we have a rotter on the Throne and if things go badly with us he will be liable to stab us in the back.' His relationship with the king was a write-off.[8]

Willkie met both Lampson and Farouq and then headed to the front to see General Montgomery, who had just taken charge. Given the American ambassador's views on British military prowess, Willkie's own expectations were low, but he found Montgomery's 'wiry, scholarly, intense, almost fanatical personality' most impressive. Egged on by the British general, who had repelled an attack by Rommel six days earlier, he declared to the reporters who were accompanying him that they were witnessing 'the turning point of the war'.[9]

For Willkie the burning question was what the British thought would happen once the war was won. Between Cairo and the frontline, he broached it with a group of British officials over dinner in Alexandria. 'I tried to draw out these men ... on what they saw in the future, and especially in the future of the colonial system and of our joint relations with the many peoples of the East,' he later wrote. Their answers unsettled him. 'What I got was Rudyard Kipling, untainted even with the liberalism of Cecil Rhodes ... these men, executing policies made in London, had no idea that the world was changing ... The Atlantic Charter most of them had read about. That it might affect their careers or their thinking had never occurred to any of them.' It was just as he had feared and he was in no doubt that the British prime minister was to blame.[10]

* * *

Willkie had been sceptical about Winston Churchill ever since his first encounter with the British prime minister in early 1941, ten months before the United States entered the war. His defeat by Roosevelt was recent but his presidential ambitions were undimmed. After all, he reminded himself, he had won more votes than any previous Republican candidate; he might now be president were it not for 600,000 voters spread across ten states. Although he was already hoping to stand again in 1944, he was an outsider with no political office: he needed to find other ways to stay in the public eye. That was why, in January 1941, he had decided to make sending military aid to Britain his next cause.

By doing so, Willkie threw himself into the greatest political controversy of the moment in the United States. When isolationism was at its height during the 1930s, Roosevelt had been obliged by public pressure to pass a series of Neutrality Acts which aimed to make America's embroilment in another world war less likely. The laws stopped the administration from selling arms or lending money to belligerent foreign states. Following the outbreak of war, Roosevelt managed to persuade Congress to dilute the restrictions, allowing arms purchases on cash and carry terms, but he was unable to end the veto on loans. By the end of 1940 this was a pressing problem. 'The moment approaches', Churchill warned the president in a letter, 'when we shall no longer be able to pay cash for shipping and other supplies.'[11]

While Churchill regarded the Atlantic as the bond uniting Britain and

America, Willkie and Roosevelt each saw it as a rather useful moat. They knew that the longer Britain held out, the later America would have to enter the conflict, if at all. Churchill's letter therefore alarmed Roosevelt: at the end of December 1940 the president declared his country 'the arsenal of democracy', and proposed a workaround to Congress. Under 'Lend-Lease', the United States would lend Britain the equipment she needed to fight, in expectation not of payment but the return of the materiel, or a like-for-like replacement, at the end of the war. Willkie came out in support of this measure midway through the following month and announced that he was going to London to investigate. 'Appeasers, isolationists, lip-service friends of Britain will seek to sabotage the program', he warned, 'behind the screen of opposition to this bill.'[12]

Ever searching for consensus, Roosevelt thoroughly approved of Willkie's mission. The passage of Lend-Lease through Congress was no foregone conclusion, as isolationism was widespread and cut across party lines; the president was keen to show that there were Republicans who felt the same way that he did. He also wanted his old rival to deliver an encouraging message to Churchill. The prime minister had been seeking reassurance since late December, but until very recently Roosevelt had been reluctant to give it.

That delay reflected an uncomfortable fact. Not only were there political grounds for Roosevelt's silence, there were personal ones as well. Churchill's behaviour at a dinner in 1918 (when, said Roosevelt, he had 'acted like a stinker ... lording it over us') and several hostile articles that he had then written about the New Deal in the 1930s had left the president with the impression that the prime minister profoundly disliked him. It took a visit to London by his trusted, spiky, adviser Harry Hopkins to convince him that this was not the case. Finally, on 20 January Roosevelt wrote a letter for Willkie to give to Churchill, including in it some lines of Longfellow, which, he offered, applied 'to you people as it does to us':

> Sail on, Oh Ship of State
> Sail on, Oh Union strong and great
> Humanity with all its fears
> With all the hope of future years
> Is hanging breathless on thy fate.

On 26 January 1941 Willkie flew in to London; he handed over the missive when he had lunch with the prime minister the following day.

Here was the assurance Churchill had been longing for. In a reply to Roosevelt the next day, he wrote that he was 'deeply moved' by the president's letter, which he interpreted as 'a mark of our friendly relations, which have been built up telegraphically but also telepathically under all the stresses'.[13]

* * *

For Churchill, who was trying to draw the United States into the war, Willkie's appearance in London in the midst of the Blitz presented a fantastic opportunity. His mother Jennie was a New Yorker and he believed there was a visceral connection between Britain and America. Oblivious to the waves of Irish, Jewish and Eastern European immigration that had transformed the United States in recent years, he felt sure that nothing would 'stir them [the Americans] like fighting in England', and that 'the heroic struggle of Britain' represented the 'best chance of bringing them in'. With this in mind, on Willkie's arrival, he later recollected, 'every arrangement was made by us, with the assistance of the enemy, to let him see all he desired of London at bay'. The press followed the American everywhere he went: 'Veni, vidi, Willkie,' wrote one newspaper of his visit.[14]

Having spent the week in London, on Saturday night Willkie was driven out into the countryside to stay at Chequers with Churchill, who had rather theatrically told him he would be safer there. The prime minister enjoyed entertaining foreign guests, not least because the government hospitality fund would then foot the bill, and the two men passed a convivial eight hours together. 'He is the most brilliant conversationalist and exchanger of ideas,' Willkie reported of his host. 'He can thrust. He can take, appreciate and acknowledge your thrusts.'[15]

With the British taxpayer rather than the cash-strapped Churchill paying, there had been plenty to drink, Willkie reflected afterwards, and he had drunk more than the prime minister, whose own capacity for alcohol was fabled. Despite one similarity – both had switched parties in their pursuit of power – the two men did not have a great deal in common. They came from different generations – Churchill was being

shot at on India's North-West Frontier before Willkie was even five years
old – and the prime minister's romantic conception of the blood-ties
that linked Britain and America must have sounded strange to the son
of German immigrants to Indiana. There is no question that Willkie
detested imperialism; what Churchill made of Willkie's views on race
and empire we do not know. The prime minister only recorded 'a very
long talk with this most able and forceful man'.[16]

Back in London, Willkie praised the prime minister's 'dauntless
courage' and 'inspirational leadership' in public, but in private he was
critical. While it was clear that the British people were fully behind
Churchill, the late-night conversation at Chequers had revealed that
the prime minister was 'subject to no doubts about his own greatness
and importance – his supreme importance as the greatest man in the
British Empire' and Willkie suspected that he did not listen to advice.
At a dinner the following Thursday, Willkie admitted that, while the
prime minister might be the right man for the country at that moment,
he was 'not so sure, however, that Mr Churchill would be so valuable a
leader when it came to the post-war period and economic adjustments
and reconstruction that were necessary'. Churchill could speak 'like
a Demosthenes and write like an angel', he told vice-president Henry
Wallace on his return to Washington, but he was altogether 'too self-
assured'. It was clear, thought Wallace, that Willkie 'had no confidence
in Churchill'.[17]

While there was no political advantage in making these doubts public,
Willkie kept his counsel. After being feted for ten days in Britain, he was
dramatically summoned home by the US secretary of state to testify on
his experience in the Senate. When he arrived back at La Guardia airport
four days later, he immediately reassured waiting reporters that 'What
the British desire from us is not men, but materials and equipment.'
That same day Churchill, whom he had fully briefed on the sensitivities
of the American debate, made a radio broadcast. In it, he quoted from
Roosevelt's letter and responded to it. Echoing Willkie, he made no
mention of needing American manpower to help fight the war. 'Give us
the tools and we will finish the job,' he growled instead.[18]

Before the Senate Foreign Relations Committee in Washington on 11
February Willkie faced one of the men he had beaten to the nomination
the year before. When Arthur Vandenberg, a prominent isolationist,

asked him whether his proposal to supply Britain destroyers to safeguard its convoys would not embroil the United States in the war, Willkie argued, 'The odds on America keeping out of the war come from aiding Britain.' Having taken the measure of Churchill, he then added an important further argument for American intervention. 'If American aid was effective the United States could dominate what happens afterward and influence the type of peace that is finally written.' A day later, following the hearing – in which one of Vandenberg's colleagues accidentally called Willkie 'Mr President' – the committee voted decisively in favour of Lend-Lease. The Senate passed the bill the following month. The uses to which Britain then put Lend-Lease would become a bone of contention forever after.[19]

Although Willkie was not directly involved in Roosevelt's effort to bind Churchill into the Atlantic Charter that August, the Charter was a manifestation of Willkie's desire that the United States should shape the peace. Willkie did not see Churchill again until the prime minister paid a hasty visit to Washington after Roosevelt had declared war following Pearl Harbor. Willkie may not have liked Churchill, but he did not dislike him so much that he did not want to be seen with him. With an eye on 1944, Willkie spied a photo opportunity that would reinforce his image as the president-in-waiting and asked for a meeting.

* * *

A meeting between Churchill and his ally Roosevelt's main political rival was always going to be sensitive. When, earlier that year, the president had found out that Willkie was trying to establish a direct channel of communication with Churchill, he was furious and asked his ambassador in London to frustrate it. 'I think the Prime Minister should maintain the friendliest of relations with Mr Willkie,' said Roosevelt, 'but direct communication is a two-edged sword.'[20]

Churchill was, however, very keen to see Willkie. By the time that Churchill arrived in Washington for Christmas it was apparent that leading Republicans preferred Willkie to any other potential candidate for 1944; a Gallup poll showed that American voters thought that he was the man most likely to succeed Roosevelt, who was in visible decline. Aware that relations between the president and Willkie were tense and probably not wishing to look as if he were anticipating the president's retirement, Churchill decided not to broach the issue with Roosevelt. Instead, unwisely, he tried to call Willkie from Palm Beach, where he was having a few days' rest, in order to arrange a clandestine meeting. A mistake by the switchboard operator meant that he was, without realising it, put through to Roosevelt instead.

'I am so glad to speak to you,' gushed Churchill, before asking whether the man he thought was Willkie might join him on his train for part of his return journey to Washington.[21]

'Whom do you think you are speaking to?' the voice came back.

'To Mr Wendell Willkie am I not?'

'No,' came the answer. 'You are speaking to the President.'

'Who?' asked Churchill, not quite believing his ears.

'You are speaking to me, Franklin Roosevelt,' came the reply.

After some small talk, Churchill brought the conversation to a close. 'I presume you do not mind my having wished to speak to Wendell Willkie?' enquired Churchill. 'No,' Roosevelt responded.

Churchill was not convinced by Roosevelt's answer. Caught red-handed trying to contact his host's rival secretly, he had no desire to embarrass himself further. Without explaining why, he denied Willkie the photograph he wanted, by insisting that their meeting take place inside the White House in private. Willkie, who like many politicians was thinner-skinned than he pretended, leapt to the wrong conclusion. Believing that the prime minister's refusal was an indication that he had been written off politically by Churchill, he took umbrage. Left sceptical of Churchill by their first encounter, and slighted by the second, it would take only one more altercation, during 1942, to shatter their relationship permanently.

* * *

The Christmas visit revealed other important points of tension between Roosevelt and Churchill, who had already begun to renege on the Atlantic Charter, recasting it as 'a simple, rough and ready wartime statement' which was relevant to the countries conquered by Germany rather than 'the regions and peoples which owe allegiance to the British Crown'. When, during their talks that Christmas, the president returned to the important question of trade discrimination, which Churchill had managed to excise from the Atlantic Charter, the prime minister refused point-blank to discuss it. And the two men had to agree to differ over India to avoid a heated argument.[22]

Thanks to Churchill's backsliding, by early 1942 Roosevelt was fending off questions from the press about the Atlantic Charter's significance and scope. Behind the scenes the president warned Churchill that he would not release Lend-Lease aid until the British government abandoned imperial preference; the fall of Singapore that February revealed tensions between Britain and her dominions that Roosevelt then exploited to force the beleaguered prime minister to concede. On the same day that the deal was signed – committing Britain and America to the 'elimination of all forms of discriminatory treatment in international commerce and to the reduction of tariffs and other trade barriers' – Roosevelt made a broadcast. In it he insisted that the Atlantic Charter applied not just to the countries bordering that ocean, but worldwide. That was the basic message that members of his administration would hammer home throughout that summer.[23]

In July 1942 Roosevelt approached Willkie to undertake another foreign mission, starting in the Middle East. His motives for doing so were mixed. He wanted Willkie to spread the word that America was determined to win the war, and to shape a lasting, post-imperial peace. But it also suited him to have his charismatic old rival out of the way in the run-up to the mid-term elections due that November. The Democrats were divided. Roosevelt hoped that this new mission would again show that the Republicans were divided too.

The offer was a godsend for Willkie. By mid-1942 he was convinced that Roosevelt was a spent force; if only he could win the Republican primary a second time, he felt confident of succeeding him in 1944. The mission appealed philosophically and politically to his instincts. It would give him a platform to speak his mind, six weeks' continuous press coverage, and the material to write a book that would burnish his credentials as an international statesman.

2

THE OLD IMPERIALISTIC ORDER

'Cairo ... was the crossroads of the free world, the Clapham Junction of the war,' recalled one man based there at the moment when Wendell Willkie arrived on the first leg of his trip round the world. 'No one could get from America or Britain to India, the Far East, or indeed Russia, without passing through it.' The city was the furthest Willkie had ever gone from the United States, and it gave him his first glimpse of the disturbing squalor that he would witness throughout the Middle East, which reminded him uncomfortably of the Deep South. 'Cripples, deformities, ophthalmia, goitre, amputations, lice, flies,' recalled another resident of that time. 'In the streets you could see horses cut in half by careless drivers or obscene black men with flies hanging like a curtain over their wounds.'[1]

The experience would profoundly affect Willkie, who blamed the British for the situation. The British in turn blamed the Egyptians. According to Willkie they claimed that the 'Arabs actually prefer to die young', and that 'their religion prevents them from accumulating the capital with which to make the improvements they need in their way of life'. The Arabs' fatalism was certainly an obstacle, but for the British the bigger problem was that – because of their tortured relationship with Egypt – the Egyptians would brook no interference by them in domestic policy, which might have alleviated these problems.

Willkie did not accept these excuses. And an encounter when he went on to Lebanon convinced him that these problems went unsolved because the energies of the British and French officials whom he met were diverted elsewhere. From the moment that he met Charles de Gaulle in

Beirut it was apparent that the betterment of the Lebanese and Syrian people was not what drove the Free French leader. In a room in which 'every corner, every wall, held busts, statues and pictures of Napoleon', de Gaulle described 'his struggle of the moment with the British as to whether he or they should dominate Syria and the Lebanon'.[2]

The Napoleonic décor was entirely apt because the struggle was hardly 'of the moment'. The French had in fact been vying with the British to dominate that part of the world since the end of the eighteenth century. In a bid to stop this rivalry poisoning their alliance during the Great War, the two powers had secretly agreed to divide the Middle East between them. But the Sykes-Picot agreement of 1916 only succeeded in aggravating the problem, when it then shaped the post-war settlement and made the two old rivals unhappy neighbours who blamed their problems on each other. The French had taken over Syria four years later, carving Lebanon from it to form a predominantly Christian bridgehead, and spent much of the second half of the 1920s fighting an insurgency that they became convinced the British were supporting. Such was the bad blood that, when France fell in 1940, the French administration in Beirut sided not with Britain but with Vichy. When the Vichy administration then let Germany use Syria as a base to make trouble in Iraq in 1941, British and Free French forces invaded Syria and Lebanon and took over.

In an effort to win local support, shortly before the invasion the Free French had promised that they would make Syria and Lebanon 'free and independent'. Once installed in Beirut, however, de Gaulle backpedalled. Although he was happy to behave like La France personified when he felt like it, the moment that Willkie asked him when France would give up her mandate he became most evasive. 'I hold it in trust,' he answered. 'I cannot close out that mandate or let anyone else do so. That can be done only when there is a government again in France.'[3]

By that point relations between the French and British were close to rupture over the issue of Lebanese and Syrian independence. The British had effectively guaranteed the Free French promise and were under pressure from Lebanese and Syrian nationalists to hold de Gaulle to account. That same day Willkie met the British man who had come to Beirut determined to do so. Sir Louis Spears was an old mate of Churchill's who had championed de Gaulle until realising that British and French interests in the Middle East were irreconcilable. 'I have created a Frankenstein's monster', Spears privately admitted. 'Can I strangle it or will it strangle me?'[4]

Having met both main protagonists in the Anglo-French struggle over the Levant, Willkie went south to Palestine, then under British control. In Jerusalem he was taken on a tour of the notoriously squalid old city by the man who ruled the country, the British high commissioner, Sir Harold MacMichael. As the two men picked their way past underfed and scrawny children playing in the dirty streets, Willkie listened incredulously as MacMichael explained, apparently without irony, that 'here was the centre of Christianity and, in a metaphorical sense, the core of all the things for which we are fighting'. The American politician was momentarily lost for words. 'There is only one thing I can think of to say in reply, and that is something I heard way back in Indiana,' he eventually replied. 'Here I am in the land where Christ was born, and I wish to Christ I was back in the land where I was born.'[5]

By then tensions were rising in Palestine. Almost exactly twenty-five years earlier, in the hope of creating what it called 'a buffer Jewish state' to guard the eastern approaches to the Suez Canal and keep the French at bay, the British government of the day had issued the Balfour Declaration, named after the then foreign secretary, Arthur Balfour. This pledged support for a Jewish national home in Palestine so long as it did not impinge on the civil and religious rights of the existing non-Jewish communities there. It helped Britain secure the mandate to rule Palestine in 1920.[6]

The British had imagined that they would reap Jewish gratitude for this manoeuvre and appreciation from the Arab population for the economic gains brought by Jewish capital. Both hopes proved naïve. 'The problem of Palestine', one British general decided, was 'the same as the problem of Ireland, namely, two peoples living in a small country hating each other like hell.' After soaring Jewish immigration triggered an Arab uprising in 1936, the British first mooted partition and then, when that idea only produced uproar, bought an uneasy peace with a White Paper in early 1939 that most controversially limited the number of Jewish immigrants to Palestine to 15,000 a year for the following five years. After war broke out, the policy was justified as necessary to ensure stability in Palestine and to keep German agents provocateurs out of the Mandate. But, as evidence of Nazi atrocities against the Jews mounted, the draconian British curb on immigration was fuelling Jewish support in both the Middle East and the United States for extremism. In Palestine, there had already been a wave of terrorist attacks by Jewish extremists earlier that year. It was a taste of what was to come.[7]

Whether the British liked it or not, the question of Palestine now demanded an urgent answer. Late that summer afternoon, Willkie met a woman who thought she had one. Originally from Baltimore and now in her eighties, Henrietta Szold had emigrated to Palestine at the turn of the twentieth century. Earlier that summer, with several others, she had set up a moderate political party that encouraged fellow Jews to form personal friendships with Arabs as the first step in the establishment of a bi-national, Jewish–Arab state. Convinced by Szold that 'goodwill and simple honesty' might yet resolve the Arab–Jewish question, Willkie also used the opportunity to ask her what was getting in the way. 'I asked her if she thought it true that certain foreign powers were deliberately stirring up trouble between the Jew and the Arab to help sustain their own control.'

'With a sad heart I must tell you it is true,' said Szold.[8]

* * *

After barely twenty-four hours in Palestine Willkie flew to Iraq, which had been ruled by the British-backed Hashemite dynasty since 1921. As the king was then just seven years old, Willkie dined the first night in private with the smooth and scheming regent, Abdul Ilah, before he and his colleagues were feted the next night by the pro-British prime minister, Nuri Said, who would play a central role in the events that followed. Nuri was one of the earliest Arab nationalists, a former Ottoman army officer who had rallied to fight for the present king's grandfather, Feisal, alongside Lawrence of Arabia and then helped Feisal establish himself as the first king of modern Iraq. A firm believer that the ends justified the means, he had once come to parliament brandishing a hand-grenade in expectation of trouble from his opponents. At the dinner the American party raised eyebrows when Willkie's aircrew asked if it might be possible to see the city's famous dancing girls in action. Willkie's public relations man recalled what happened next. 'At least eight of the best whorehouses in town were represented. The madam of each house introduced her girls one by one, who did a little dance, waved to the customers they recognized, and trotted off.'[9]

Despite Baghdad's exotic reputation, the boy king and his advisers lived less extravagantly than King Farouq did in Cairo: one visitor to the royal palace remembered 'a good deal of brown paint' and thought Farouq's carpets were rather better. Like Egypt, Iraq was in theory independent but in practice the British pulled the strings. A 1930 treaty, rammed through the Iraqi parliament by Nuri, had given Britain two airbases. Shaiba was outside Basra; Habbaniyah, west of Baghdad, had a church, cinema and a foxhunt. 'All very Poona', remarked a British visitor. In Baghdad, the ambassador and a clique of British advisers steered decision-making; 'C', the chief of Britain's intelligence service, MI6, boasted that his organisation knew of the outcome of one meeting held in the palace within half an hour. Britain owned the majority of the Iraq Petroleum Company where British personnel dominated the management. 'Mutual distrust and dislike' between the company's Arab, Kurdish, Assyrian, Turkoman and Armenian employees ensured that there was 'never . . . any labour trouble'.[10]

By now oil generated a fifth of Iraq's national income, but it had barely changed the country. Nineteen out of twenty Iraqis were illiterate; life expectancy at birth was thirty because of high infant mortality. The fundamental problem was becoming familiar to Willkie. As in Egypt and Syria, most of Iraq belonged to a small group of wealthy landowners. 'I met a number of them', he wrote, 'and found them largely disinterested in any political movement, except as it affects the perpetuation of their own status.'[11]

Before Willkie headed on to Moscow and then China, the last leg of his route through the Middle East took him eastwards over the mountains that formed the eastern frontier of the Arab world to the Iranian capital, Teheran. There he met the country's 22-year-old ruler, Shah Mohammed Reza Pahlavi, a Swiss-schooled princeling who was at that point married to King Farouq's sister. The two men lunched outdoors, on the first anniversary of the shah's accession to the throne. For the shah it was no occasion to celebrate. A year earlier his father had been forced out after the British and the Soviets invaded to secure a supply route across the country following Hitler's invasion of Russia, carving the country into spheres of influence. The British government had a massive financial interest in the south of the country through its stake in the oil company that owned the concession, Anglo-Persian. Some Americans suspected that they would be quite happy to prolong the partition of the country with the Soviets indefinitely. Not surprisingly the young shah detested the British. Before continuing to Moscow himself, Willkie gave the young man a ride in his aeroplane – the first time that the shah had been airborne in his life.

* * *

Willkie would spend nineteen days of his forty-nine-day mission aloft. The long hours in the air gave him the chance to brood over the causes of what he had seen and heard. By the time he reached Teheran he had made up his mind. 'The veil, the fez, the sickness, the filth, the lack of education and modern industrial development, the arbitrariness of government' that he had witnessed across the Middle East were symptoms of a failure resulting from 'a combination of forces within their own society and the self-interest of foreign domination'.[12]

Willkie was alarmed that the colonial powers' dependence on the United States meant that he and his fellow countrymen were seen across the Middle East as complicit in a situation over which, in reality, they had no control. 'Again and again', he recalled later, he had been asked if America intended 'to support a system by which our politics are controlled by foreigners, however politely, our lives dominated by foreigners, however indirectly, because we happen to be strategic points on the military roads and trade routes of the world.' His answer to that question was always going to be 'No'. Days later it would be Winston Churchill who needled him into stating it.[13]

* * *

The third and final episode of Willkie's fraught relationship with Churchill began when Willkie, under heavy pressure from Joseph Stalin from the moment he arrived in Moscow, called for the opening of a second front in Western Europe to take the pressure off the Russians as soon as possible. By doing so he reopened an issue that Churchill hoped he had just buried.

After his emergency visit to Cairo that summer the British prime minister had gone on secretly to Moscow to see Stalin. In an attempt to persuade the Soviet leader to stop calling for a second front, he told him that a major offensive was planned in Europe in 1943 and that the British and American governments agreed that any earlier action to divert the Germans from the eastern front would only end in disaster. Willkie's call was profoundly unhelpful because it undid Churchill's effort to convince Stalin that there was Anglo-American unity on the question.

After Willkie's intervention made the headlines, Churchill was asked a mischievous question in parliament. Would he 'impress upon all persons with access to inside information, the need to exercise greater restraint than hitherto in any public statements or published speculation about Second Front possibilities', an MP from his own party asked. The prime minister readily agreed that such comments were undesirable. There, he should have stopped. Instead, in a clumsy attempt to pour oil on troubled waters, he went on to reassure his colleague that the remarks were based on 'inferences, and not . . . on inside information'. To laughter, the MP stood up to deliver his punchline: 'Will my right honourable friend convey this to Mr. Wendell Willkie?'[14]

The exchange was picked up by the press: for Willkie, already annoyed that the British had stopped him from visiting India, and were censoring what he said, it was the final straw. Churchill's poor choice of words reinforced Willkie's assumption that the British leader believed he was unlikely to succeed Roosevelt as president and that there was therefore no harm in belittling him. By now in China, Willkie reacted with a direct and public attack on British imperialism. 'The colonial days are past,' he declared. 'We believe this war must mean an end to the empire of nations over other nations.' British censors struck out the first of these two phrases.[15]

Willkie reached home on 13 October 1942, three weeks before the mid-term elections. He met Roosevelt a day later. Warning the president that he had 'not a pleasant report to make', he said that British rule in the Middle East was kindling discontent that Axis propaganda was exploiting. As Britain's ally, the United States was being damaged by association. Roosevelt, said Willkie, needed to work harder to give the people of the Middle East 'a feeling that they do not have: that we are not committed to an indefinite perpetuation of British imperialism in this area, but rather to the establishment of political freedom and economic liberty'.[16]

A fortnight later Willkie broadcast a half-hour 'Report to the People' expanding on this theme. In it he described his travels and his conversations with people he had met and argued that a long legacy of American philanthropy overseas meant that the world looked to the United States with a 'mixture of respect and hope'. However, he continued, this 'gigantic reservoir of goodwill toward the American people' was now threatened by the United States' failure to define clear war aims. 'Besides giving our Allies in Asia and in eastern Europe something to fight with we have got to give them the assurance of what we are fighting for.'[17]

The answer to this rhetorical question was 'freedom', but Willkie said that the United States had so far avoided confronting the implications of that aim. 'In Africa, in the Middle East, and throughout the Arab world, as well as in China and in the Far East, freedom means orderly but scheduled abolition of the colonial system,' he declared. 'The rule of the people by other peoples is not freedom and not what we must fight to preserve.'

Though Willkie denied that he was attacking Britain, in his broadcast he invited constant, and negative, comparison between the United States and her transatlantic ally. People round the world were aware, he said, that America was 'not fighting for profit, or loots, or territory or mandatory power over the lives or governments of other people'. They liked 'our works' because 'American business enterprise, unlike that of most industrial nations, does not necessarily lead to political control or imperialism.' In 1940 Willkie had won 22 million votes. Two years after his defeat, an estimated 36 million Americans – about a quarter of the entire population – tuned in to hear him speak.

With the mid-term elections now imminent, however, Willkie was increasingly interested in a subsection of the electorate: the Jewish vote. In 1942 there were about 5 million Jews living in the United States. The states of Illinois, Michigan, New Jersey, New York and Ohio, where Willkie had closely tailed Roosevelt in the 1940 elections and which he would need to win to secure victory in 1944, all had significant Jewish populations. The twenty-fifth anniversary of the Balfour Declaration, which fell on the eve of the mid-term election, offered Willkie an opportunity to address them. An entire Friday spent in Palestine seven weeks earlier made him feel qualified to do so.[18]

As he had over Lend-Lease, Willkie was again deliberately courting controversy. Growing awareness of the Nazis' systematic efforts to exterminate the Jews of Eastern Europe had endowed the Balfour Declaration's vision of a Jewish homeland with a talismanic importance. Earlier that year the American weekly, *Life*, had reported a 'methodical massacre' of Polish Jews, backing up the allegation with a series of grim photographs. Then came the news of the sinking of a ship called the *Struma*. The vessel, an unseaworthy hulk that was crammed with Jewish refugees fleeing Romania and a similar fate, had spent eight weeks anchored off Istanbul after the British government refused it entry to Palestine. Towed out of port the *Struma* either hit a mine or was struck by a torpedo in the Black Sea. All but one of its 769 passengers died.[19]

Extremists within the Zionist movement in the United States exploited the anger generated by the *Struma* disaster. Known as the Revisionists, they had been campaigning for over twenty years for the establishment of an independent Jewish state that stretched east of the Jordan. Since the beginning of the war, they had been pressing for the relaxation of the immigration limits imposed by the British government and for a Jewish army – ostensibly to take part in the Allied war effort, but ultimately to advance their own expansionist agenda. Until the *Struma*'s sinking, they had made little headway, however. Thereafter they started to attract significant political support.

A conference of American Zionists in New York, which took place in May, not long before Willkie set off on his odyssey, showed that opinion had swung in the Revisionists' favour. After five days' discussion at the art deco Biltmore Hotel in the city, the delegates issued a landmark statement. Known afterwards as the 'Biltmore Declaration', this condemned the British government's immigration restrictions as 'cruel and indefensible' and called for the transfer of responsibility for immigration policy to the Jews in Palestine, as the prelude to the establishment of a 'Jewish Commonwealth integrated into the structure of the new democratic world' – in other words, an independent Jewish state. It also backed the Revisionists' call for a Jewish army.[20]

In deference to the problems any intervention would inevitably cause Churchill, Roosevelt had so far studiously avoided talking about Palestine. But this was becoming increasingly difficult to do. The Zionists had started funding a stream of angry full-page advertisements in the press, calling on him to take action. The two Republicans he had co-opted to his cabinet had both broken ranks and were now openly backing the Jewish army movement. As if to counter them, so too was Roosevelt's wife Eleanor.

With silence no longer an option, the administration released a statement to mark the Balfour Declaration's anniversary. But it was a guarded acknowledgement that evaded the great questions of Jewish statehood and the immigration limits, both of which were rapidly becoming burning political issues. It probably did more harm than good.

Unbound by the diplomatic considerations that constrained Roosevelt, Willkie could exploit the anniversary to the full. On the eve of the mid-term elections he issued a statement that repeated the Revisionists' demands. In it he argued that 'Hitler's program of exter-mination of the Jewish people' meant that the 'doors of Palestine' would 'have to be opened for the homeless Jews of Central and Eastern Europe who survive the war'. The Jews – and not the British – should control the numbers, he continued, and 'the establishment of a Jewish national home in Palestine in fulfilment of the promise contained in the Balfour Declaration must find its rightful place in the new world order of tomorrow.'[21]

In London, Churchill and the foreign secretary, Anthony Eden, argued over what to do about Willkie. Eden, already annoyed by Willkie's radio broadcast, suggested that the best way to silence him was to invite him back to Britain, where he could be muzzled by the censors. But Churchill disagreed. His relationship with Roosevelt remained del-icate and, still mortified by his Christmas phone call, he did not want to give the president further grounds to think that he was waiting for Willkie to succeed him, even though he was. 'My whole system is based on friendship with Roosevelt,' he replied to Eden. 'We must not seem to be in too great a hurry to hail the rising sun.'[22]

The success of Willkie's isolationist rivals in November's mid-term elections, and the victory at El Alamein a week afterwards, soon emboldened Churchill to take a much more forthright approach, however. Thinking that Willkie now had no chance of winning the nomination in 1944, the prime minister decided to make it clear that he would not accept American attempts to bring down the British Empire without a fight.

In the United States, Willkie rightly appreciated that Churchill's Mansion House speech – with its point-blank denial that Britain was fighting 'for profit or expansion' – was a rebuke aimed squarely at him. In a speech six days later the former presidential candidate claimed that the world was 'shocked' by Churchill's defence of the 'old imperialistic order'. When his comments were reported in the London press, he received a visit from the British ambassador in Washington, and the two men had a row. After being accused by the ambassador of being 'vague and libellous', he retorted that he had been the victim of 'sharp digs' from Churchill and said that he had the impression that, as the prime minister began to think that he was winning the war, he 'attached less importance to keeping step with American opinion than before'. The ambassador accused him of trying in his broadcast 'to smear the whole colonial system' and asked if it had occurred to him that it was thus 'bound to be very offensive and provocative to British thought'. If it had, it became clear that Willkie no longer cared. The American, the ambassador reported, replied, 'We were running a bad show and the sooner we got out the better.'[23]

There is perhaps no better summary of American thinking and policy towards Britain in the Middle East in the years that were to follow.

3

HEADING FOR TROUBLE

Willkie's call for the 'gates of Palestine' to be opened to Jewish refugees reflected the growing strength of the Zionists in the United States. When shortly it was followed by the American landings in northwest Africa and the British victory at El Alamein, it triggered euphoria in Palestine and then a tremendous sense of urgency that would spread across, and then destabilise, the Middle East.

Even before Churchill advised caution at the Mansion House, in Palestine the leading Zionist David Ben Gurion had latched onto the feeling that the war would soon be over. He urged the Jewish people to organise themselves, because a peace conference, at which the Palestine question would undoubtedly be raised, was in the offing.

Ben Gurion was head of the Jewish Agency, which represented the Jewish population of Palestine in its dealings with the British, and he had long felt that the Zionists needed to be more demanding. He had been in America when the *Struma* sank, saw which way the wind was blowing, and encouraged American Zionists to hold the Biltmore conference, which then proved there had been a sea change in Jewish opinion that favoured the Revisionists. Now back in the Mandate, he urged his colleagues on the executive of the Jewish Agency to accept the Biltmore Declaration. Although this was a move that they had previously rejected because they disliked the Revisionists, the shift of Jewish opinion in the Revisionists' favour was so obvious that they gave in to Ben Gurion's demand on 10 November – the same day that Churchill spoke at the Mansion House.

A fortnight later Ben Gurion announced that the Biltmore Declaration would form the Agency's 'main demand' at the peace conference. To this end, he said, the Agency would press for the establishment of a Jewish army and promote Palestine's ability to accommodate 'large masses of Jews'. This prospect caused Arab uproar and British alarm, but Ben Gurion did not care. 'There will be disturbances,' he would acknowledge later. 'The weeks and months following the collapse of the Hitler regime will be a time of uncertainty in Europe and even more so in Palestine, and we must exploit this period in order to confront Britain and America with a *fait accompli*.'[1]

The Arabs soon reacted to Ben Gurion's proposal. Days later, the Iraqi prime minister, Nuri Said, unveiled a plan of his own, which he dubbed the 'Fertile Crescent' scheme. In it he called on the Allies to reunite Syria, Lebanon, Palestine and Transjordan and guarantee the Jews only a degree of autonomy in Palestine. This state would then link up with Iraq to form an Arab League, which other Arab states could also later join. It was, he claimed, 'the only fair solution . . . the only hope of securing permanent peace'.[2]

The British, from Lawrence of Arabia onwards, had long encouraged dreams of Arab unity, partly as a way to make up for the fact that the territory that the Hashemites had acquired after the previous war – Transjordan and Iraq – fell far short of the much larger empire which the British had promised them in order to secure their help against the Ottomans in the war. Once more, British officials in Cairo ranged themselves behind their old ally Nuri Said's scheme. They feared that Ben Gurion's announcements would provoke an Arab backlash in Palestine and destabilise the entire region. For them the 'Fertile Crescent' plan represented a way to bolster the moderate Jews who distrusted Ben Gurion, reconcile the Arabs to a permanent Jewish presence and so prolong Britain's role in the Middle East long beyond the end of the war.

The man who took on the responsibility of trying to turn this idea into a reality was Lord Moyne. Quiet, slight and self-effacing, with steel-grey hair and turquoise eyes, Moyne was another old friend of Churchill's, a millionaire with a distinguished war record who had ditched a career in politics to indulge a love of adventure in the 1930s. 'He had a passion for the sea, and for long expeditions to remote places,' a contemporary recorded. 'He collected yachts, fish, monkeys and women.' The British foreign secretary Anthony Eden recollected a less frivolous side to the adventurer, which he had witnessed during the Great War. Moyne was, he said, one of those men 'who could discipline themselves to be insensitive to danger and who lacked neither brains nor imagination'. It was for precisely that reason that Churchill dragged his old friend back into government in 1940, and then sent him to Cairo in August 1942 to serve as deputy to the top British official in the Middle East, the minister of state. Moyne's true task was to ensure that, if Rommel broke through, the British followed the prime minister's order to fight to the last man.[3]

Moyne was spared this fiery denouement by the decisive victory at El Alamein. Briefly, he felt 'definitely under employed', but the sensation was short-lived. Having served as colonial secretary in Churchill's government in London he understood the Palestine question well enough, and he appreciated that the victory would unbottle long-standing tensions that Rommel's nearness to Palestine had previously stilled. In a series of letters to a friend he confided 'grave anxieties as to the future' as 'fears of the Axis die down and animosities revive'. That sense of foreboding proved to be entirely justified, for Moyne would ultimately be murdered by Zionist extremists.[4]

* * *

Moyne soon realised that turning the Fertile Crescent scheme – or Greater Syria, as the British often called it – from a dream into reality was no easy task. Not only could he expect to encounter opposition from Ben Gurion, but in addition the Arab world was by no means united behind Nuri's scheme. He soon discovered that the plan's association with the Hashemites alarmed one man in particular. No sooner had Nuri spoken out, than he received an invitation from Ibn Saud, the king of Saudi Arabia, to come to see him. He was to meet the king in the Red Sea port of Jeddah at the very end of 1942.

Ibn Saud had long regarded Nuri's Hashemite patrons as his main rivals. After capturing the city of Riyadh – where, legend had it, he had thrown the city governor's severed head into the waiting crowd – he had then turfed the Hashemite ruler Sharif Hussein out of the holy city of Mecca in 1924. By then, however, thanks to the British, Hussein's son Feisal had become king of Iraq, while Feisal's brother Abdullah was emir of Transjordan. What that meant was that Ibn Saud was boxed into the

Arabian peninsula by two neighbours who he was certain still wanted to avenge their father's overthrow. They would be more threatening still if, as Nuri Said envisaged, they were able to unite.

The Hashemite threat would obsess Ibn Saud for the remaining eleven years of his life. Already by 1942 it was a menace that he felt ill equipped to meet. Though, at over 6ft tall, he towered over Moyne, the legendary warrior was a shadow of his terrifying former self. Now in his early sixties, he was half-blind from a cataract and an old war wound meant he could no longer climb the stairs. He tried to quash rumours of his declining virility by descending on the tribe where the gossip was prevalent, selecting a bride, marrying her, and then consummating the marriage behind the woollen walls of the royal tent.

Frailty was one weakness. A desperate shortage of money was another. In 1933 the king had granted exclusive rights to drill for oil within his kingdom to an American firm, the California Arabian Standard Oil Company, but the company did not strike oil until 1938. The outbreak of war the following year disrupted the embryonic market for Saudi oil and, more importantly, the pilgrimage, which still provided Ibn Saud with the vast majority of his income, plunging the kingdom into a financial crisis. A drought made matters worse. The crisis had dire implications for the ageing king, because he bought the loyalty of his Bedu subjects.

Fearing that his Hashemite rivals would exploit his weakness, Ibn Saud leant on the British and the oil company for funds. The company feared the British, who had helped him out during the previous war, might try to extract a quid pro quo for their support. And so it rashly promised a $3 million advance against future royalties in early 1941, before asking the US government to reimburse it. When Roosevelt refused – on the grounds that Saudi Arabia seemed 'a little too far afield for us' – a compromise was reached whereby the British government funnelled both American money it had borrowed and Lend-Lease aid to Ibn Saud. In 1942 the British would pass on £3 million in this way.[5]

If Moyne hoped that this money might influence Ibn Saud's reaction to the Fertile Crescent scheme, he was to be disappointed. 'Our talk ranged over many subjects', he recalled afterwards, before the conversation reached the matter he had been summoned 600 miles to discuss.

Speaking in a hoarse whisper, the old warlord used his audience to register his hostility to Nuri's plans. The king was not averse to closer economic ties between his northern Arab neighbours but, when Moyne raised the prospect of an Arab Federation uniting them, 'He gave no encouragement to this idea.' It was a disappointing answer from a man the British still regarded as their client, who – they were always glad to see – wore socks with 'Pure Wool – Made in England' printed on their soles.[6]

* * *

The Jeddah meeting confirmed Moyne's suspicion that a more gradual and innocuous approach was needed. It was probably no coincidence that another British ally, the prominent and moderate Zionist Judah Magnes, made just such a proposal the next month. Writing in the American journal *Foreign Affairs*, Magnes, who was president of the Hebrew University in Jerusalem, proposed the establishment of a bi-national Palestine within a broader Arab federation exactly like the one that Nuri Said had already described. Since that was 'delicate and complicated', he suggested that the first step was an economic union. 'One way of forming this very desirable economic union', he ventured, 'might be to develop the Middle East Supply Center to its full capacity for usefulness.'[7]

In theory a joint Anglo-American agency, but in practice British-dominated, the Middle East Supply Centre had been set up in 1941 after the war closed the Mediterranean to merchant shipping, which now had to go round the Cape to reach Egypt. At a time when ships were in very short supply and when the Middle East imported 5 million tons of food each year, the Centre's task was to keep the local population and the armies that were based there fed, using as little shipping as possible. When its officials quickly realised that the best way to do this was to increase the region's self-sufficiency, they wrote their organisation a licence to interfere. They were soon setting import quotas and redistributing American Lend-Lease aid to the countries of the region; by 1943 the Centre also controlled all internal transport, and advised on agricultural techniques, irrigation and industry. It even ran an anti-locust unit which had acquired the right to roam across the Middle East, because, as its director was known to say, 'the political troubles, when the locusts copulate, are immense'. While Magnes made the case for using the Centre in public, in private Moyne was arguing for exactly the same extension of its powers beyond the war's end. The Centre would form the executive agency of a Middle East Economic Council, comprising representatives of the region's states, and delegates from the United States and Britain naturally, whose task would be to manage a glacially paced transition from war to peace.[8]

American involvement was crucial for this plan to work. From the battle of El Alamein onwards the British began trying to convince their American counterparts that the Middle East Supply Centre was the answer to the problems that Willkie had identified. Briefed by the centre's director the British weekly, *The Economist*, suggested that 'a revised MESC, representing the United Nations, could provide the capital, the machinery, the experts, the advisers, the educationalists without which there can be no speedy raising of Middle East living standards, no end to the recurring crises of want, little genuine political cooperation and little hope of the area being withdrawn finally from the struggle for predominant influence between the Great Powers'. It was only in private that Moyne and his colleagues admitted why they were actually so keen to keep the Centre going. Britain's control of this obscure yet powerful bureaucracy offered 'one of the most hopeful means of keeping the general initiative in the Middle East in our hands'.[9]

* * *

A long-term British strategy was taking shape and might succeed – that was, if the Zionists did not seize the initiative first. By April 1943 the British had enough intelligence to convince them that the Zionists were going to use force to get what they wanted. Ben Gurion's Jewish Agency was devoting 15 per cent of its annual budget to 'internal security' which, they believed, meant arming the Haganah, an 80,000-strong, illegal, paramilitary organisation, partly with weaponry it was buying secretly from the French in Syria, partly through well-organised and large-scale theft from British forces based in Palestine. In one month alone, 600 rifles, twenty machine guns, ammunition and three tons of explosive disappeared from British depots in the Mandate. A bug or an informer enabled the British to eavesdrop on a meeting at which the head of the Haganah spoke. 'We all know that the Zionist problem will have to be solved one day by force of arms,' he said. 'It can never be solved by political argument; only by a fight.'[10]

After seeing an intelligence report which suggested the Haganah was reconciling its differences with more extreme Jewish terrorist groups, Moyne's boss, the minister resident Richard Casey, decided that it was time to alert London. In April 1943 he warned the British government that Palestine was 'heading for the most serious outbreak of disorder and violence which it has yet seen ... as soon as the War ends in Europe, or possibly a few months earlier.' There were differences of opinion over exactly what would trigger renewed violence, he admitted, 'But of the certainty of the outbreak, unless it can be averted by some action of the British Government, there is no doubt.'[11]

Casey's own view was that the most likely cause of war would be a Zionist attempt to engineer Ben Gurion's 'fait accompli', and he now put forward an idea to pre-empt it. In his view, the Zionists' noisy public-relations campaign was designed to win over, or at least divide, public opinion in the United States and Britain so that the governments of both countries would have to acquiesce when finally the Zionists struck. To disrupt this strategy, Casey proposed that the British and the American governments should both state publicly as soon as possible that they would not tolerate any 'forceful changes' to the administration of Palestine, and in particular the 'forcible establishment of a Jewish State'.[12]

There was no guarantee that either government would want to make such a statement – both had done their utmost to say as little as possible on the subject. In an attempt to end this silence, Casey and his colleagues had already decided to work on the Americans first of all, using a devious and roundabout approach.

Reckoning that the Americans would pay more attention to secret intelligence they had received from one of their own agents than shrill warnings from London, the British decided to feed what they knew to an American spy in Cairo. Colonel Harold Hoskins of the Office of Strategic Services had appeared in the Egyptian capital at the end of 1942, tasked with writing an appraisal of political developments in the Middle East and establishing a base for his organisation in the region.

The British had never wanted him to come, but after trying and failing to stop him from doing so, they realised that he might have his uses. For Hoskins was extremely well connected, counting President Roosevelt and the number two at the State Department, Sumner Welles, among his friends. The son of American missionaries to Syria and a fluent Arabic speaker, he was also no friend of the Revisionists.

Given how the British had strained to stop Hoskins from coming, the access to Cairo's secret world that they now gave him is striking. Within four days of his arrival he was introduced by Casey to the heads of MI6's and Special Operations Executive's regional operations, and the local representatives of the Political Warfare Executive and the Ministry of Information. Casey then gave him a lift to Beirut on his plane.

The upshot of these efforts was that on 20 April 1943 Hoskins informed Welles, in terms that parroted Casey's own warning to London, that a 'renewed outbreak of fighting' in Palestine was likely. To make Roosevelt take notice, he warned that renewed Arab–Jewish conflict in Palestine had important implications for the United States, domestically because it might lead to a massacre of Jews living in the neighbouring Arab states, and militarily because it might destabilise Arab North Africa, threatening the security of Eisenhower's forces, which were now based there ahead of the invasion of Europe.

Hoskins went on to suggest that the best way to avoid violence in the short run was for the Allies to issue a statement promising that 'no final decisions' regarding Palestine would be taken until after the war's end, and then 'only after full consultation with both Arabs and Jews'. As for the longer term, he proposed a solution that was a hybrid of Judah Magnes's and Nuri Said's schemes: a bi-national Arab–Jewish state, within a broader Levant Federation. Hoskins' recommendations had British fingerprints all over them.[13]

A few days later, Casey and his top officials met and confirmed their plan to prolong the lifespan of the Middle East Supply Centre, preferably in concert with the US government, beyond the war's end. The Americans were not invited to this secret conference, but they knew it was taking place. Immediately afterwards Casey was buttonholed by the American ambassador to Cairo. He 'asked me straight out what we had been discussing,' the minister resident reported. 'In the circumstances I could tell him nothing more than generalities.'[14]

* * *

Richard Casey's evasiveness only fortified American suspicions about British activity in the Middle East. These had been growing since the moment earlier that year when it dawned on the Americans that the British were using Lend-Lease aid to bolster their own standing in the region, at American expense. In January 1943, soon after Ibn Saud was heard observing that while 'America can supply nearly everything . . . if we want anything we go to the British and the King of England sees that we get it', the American ambassador to Cairo decided that it was time to find out what the Middle East Supply Centre was up to. After a visit to Jeddah he reported that the United States had 'lost considerable prestige in the eyes of Saudi Arabians who have been given increasingly to feel that the British were their only friends in need'.[15]

While American diplomats fretted about prestige, American oilmen were more worried about money. CASOC's executives and owners both feared that the king might cancel the company's concession and award it to the British if he could not afford to pay them back. In February the president of CASOC and its two shareholders approached the Roosevelt administration with a plan. If the US government picked up the Saudi kingdom's debt to Britain, the company would give the government oil of an equivalent value.

This idea appealed instantly to the secretary of the interior, Harold Ickes, whose concurrent role as petroleum administrator for war made him responsible for husbanding US oil resources. A paternalist who practised what he preached – he was married to a woman forty years his junior – Ickes had long argued that the United States government should follow Britain's example in taking strategic stakes in companies with foreign oil concessions because oil was a finite resource and oil production in the US would shortly start to fall. CASOC's proposal was a significant step in the direction of his own philosophy.

Over lunch with Roosevelt on 16 February Ickes warned the president that the British, who 'never overlooked the opportunity to get in where there was oil', were 'trying to edge their way into' Saudi Arabia – 'probably the greatest and richest oil field in the world'. Roosevelt's in-tray already contained a request to extend direct Lend-Lease aid to Saudi Arabia in order to stop British middlemen taking credit for disbursing

American generosity, and following the lunch the president promptly signed it off. 'I hereby find the defense of Saudi Arabia vital to the defense of the United States,' he declared two days later. It was a calculation that has underpinned the American relationship with the Saudis ever since.[16]

With American forces now stationed in North Africa, Roosevelt was suddenly paying much closer attention to the politics of the Arab world. At the end of March he despatched another envoy to the region. Patrick Hurley was a Republican who had been Hoover's secretary of war before becoming an enthusiastic supporter of the New Deal; since the beginning of the war he had performed a number of diplomatic missions for Roosevelt. On this latest, Hurley would be the president's personal representative in the Middle East. Following in Willkie's footsteps, that spring Hurley spent two days in Palestine, ten days in Lebanon and Syria and then flew on to Baghdad and Teheran. In early May he reported his impressions to the president from Cairo.

Hurley was an Anglophobe but in Washington his report was taken at face value because it corroborated existing suspicions. On his travels he had heard numerous people say that British officials were encouraging the perception that the Americans were insisting on the establishment of a sovereign Jewish state in Palestine – a 'line of propaganda' that, he noted, was 'distinctly helpful to British prestige with the Arabs'. Another rumour he had heard was that Churchill, during a private conversation when he was last in Cairo, had said that he was in favour of a Jewish state, and that Roosevelt would 'accept nothing less'. Hurley's conclusion was that the British were no longer able to settle this increasingly acrimonious issue on their own: like Hoskins, whose own report had by now reached Roosevelt, he believed that it was time for the United States to intervene.[17]

*   *   *

Roosevelt was soon able to broach the matter face to face with Churchill, who arrived in the United States on 11 May 1943 for what would prove an ill-tempered conference on future strategy. A week later, when both men were having breakfast at the presidential retreat at Shangri-La, they saw that the Zionists had paid for another large advert in the *New York Times*. 'Mr Churchill DROP THE MANDATE!' it demanded. This

gave Roosevelt the opportunity to broach the subject. He also showed
Hurley's report to Churchill. Its comments 'make me rub my eyes', the
prime minister is reported to have said.[18]

Roosevelt favoured making a statement along the lines that Hoskins
had suggested but the prime minister had an alternative idea. Encouraged
by the president of the Zionist Organization, Chaim Weizmann, who
had tried to reach a deal with the Hashemites over Palestine at the end
of the Great War, Churchill had long thought that Ibn Saud – to his
mind 'the greatest living Arab' – might be capable of reaching a grand
bargain with the Zionists.[19]

This idea was a simplistic fantasy, but its appeal grew when, towards
the end of May, the president received an unsettling letter from the Saudi
king himself. The message turned out to be a bitter complaint about the
effect that Zionist propaganda was having in the United States, news of
which had clearly reached Riyadh. Even if this campaign succeeded in
convincing the Allies to turn Palestine over to the Jews, the king said, it
would not solve 'the Jewish problem' because the country was not large
enough. He called on Roosevelt to help stop the flow of Jewish refugees
to Palestine, by finding other places for them to go, and to ban the sale
of land in Palestine to Jews. Given Hurley's observations, and the fact
that the British knew before anybody else that Ibn Saud was writing
to the president, Roosevelt must have suspected that it was they who
had inspired the king to write. The news that the British were insisting that American Lend-Lease aid should continue to be channelled
through the Middle East Supply Centre only reinforced the impression
in Washington that they were being deliberately obstructive.[20]

Ibn Saud's letter had taken a month to make its way to Washington,
and caused alarm when it arrived. Roosevelt replied immediately, asking
the king to stay quiet before putting the gist of Churchill's idea to him.
It would be 'highly desirable' if 'the interested Arabs and Jews' could
reach 'a friendly understanding' over Palestine before the war's end,
the president suggested. He then reassured the king that 'no decision
altering the basic situation of Palestine should be reached without full
consultation with both Arabs and Jews'.[21]

Roosevelt's reply would prove to be an important assurance, but it
reached Ibn Saud too late to do any immediate good. Although in April
the king had promised to say nothing in public that would embarrass

the president, he had since evidently changed his mind. On 31 May 1943, *Life* magazine ran a cover story about Ibn Saud following an interview with the king. It was a sympathetic portrait, which included a statement by him dismissing the Zionists' claim to Palestine and, again, calling for a ban on land sales to the Jews. 'If the Jews are imperilled to seek a place to live, Europe and America as well as other lands are larger and more fertile than Palestine, and more suitable to their welfare and interests,' Ibn Saud was quoted as saying.[22]

Hurley flew to see Ibn Saud, to try to establish what had caused the king's change of heart. He found the king particularly exercised about the fact that the British were using Lend-Lease aid to improve their own oil facilities in Iran and Iraq, while CASOC's, on the Gulf coast, denied similar investment, were largely dormant. The report rang alarm bells in Washington, because it made it clear that two separate issues – the future of the American oil concession in Saudi Arabia and the Arab–Jewish conflict in Palestine – were, at least in Ibn Saud's mind, now intertwined. On his return to Cairo Hurley recommended to Roosevelt that, to ensure investment in the oil concession and to bypass Lend-Lease altogether, the US government now create a military oil reserve in Saudi Arabia and take a direct stake in CASOC. American investment would enable the company to increase output, generating royalties for Ibn Saud, and – most important – reducing the king's unwelcome dependence on the British.

Ickes had been thinking along similar lines to Hurley since his February lunch with Roosevelt. He now urged the president to back the creation of a state-owned Petroleum Reserves Corporation that would buy up not just CASOC's oil but also a controlling stake in the company itself. As he told Roosevelt, his aim was to 'counteract certain activities of a foreign power which presently are jeopardizing American interests in Arabian oil reserves'. Knowing precisely which power Ickes meant, Roosevelt agreed. That both men were willing to take such an extra-ordinary, unprecedented step shows just how great a threat they thought they faced from Britain.[23]

At the same time the Americans were working to bind the British government into a public statement on Palestine that would stop British officials from claiming that the United States was pursuing a Jewish state, and so pacify Ibn Saud. On 11 June Roosevelt met Weizmann himself, telling him that during the prime minister's recent visit he had 'gotten Mr Churchill to agree to the idea of calling together the Jews and the Arabs' – the idea that had been Weizmann's in the first place. Roosevelt's protégé, Sumner Welles, was also present at this meeting. At Welles's suggestion Roosevelt and Weizmann agreed that Harold Hoskins should be sent to Riyadh to sound out Ibn Saud.[24]

* * *

More than a month passed before the British answered the American request for a joint statement, mainly because neither Churchill nor Eden wanted to make one. Churchill, a Zionist since his first visit to Palestine in 1921, loathed the restrictions on immigration and land sales imposed by the 1939 White Paper and feared that any announcement about Palestine would only draw attention to his failure to abandon it. Eden, who had read Arabic and Persian at Oxford and was instinctively pro-Arab, worried that it would simply create yet another contentious document that would be parsed by each side, and then used by both against the British. Although he acknowledged that they were 'witnessing the first, but rapidly developing symptoms of a major nationalistic revival in the Middle East of two contending forces, Arabism and Zionism', he held Zionist propagandists in the United States responsible for stoking the problem. In his view it was up to Roosevelt to deal with them, starting with the pro-Zionist members of his cabinet, including Henry Stimson, secretary of war.[25]

It seems that it was Casey who changed both Churchill's and Eden's minds. On a visit from Cairo to London to seek cabinet approval of new Palestine and Middle Eastern strategies, he joined the cabinet for a discussion of Palestine on 2 July. New thinking on this issue was urgent, to replace the controversial policies established by the 1939 White Paper, which was due to lapse in nine months' time. At that meeting he ran through a series of proposals that he had come up with to try to keep the peace in the country while a new cabinet subcommittee devised a new policy for the Mandate. Again, he urged a joint statement with the Americans.

While Churchill felt that it was 'not a good time for statements on long-term policy', Casey assured him that it was a stopgap. Eden was supportive, seeing how the statement might discourage the Revisionists from seeking to achieve violent change while the British government was groping around for a new policy on Palestine. After Churchill relented and said that he would tolerate an 'anodyne Declaration' provided that there was no further public discussion of the matter until the war had turned more in the Allies' favour, the cabinet agreed to respond positively to the American overture. It required a further cabinet meeting on 14 July for Churchill and his colleagues to discuss Britain's broader Middle Eastern strategy.[26]

'Our only chance of projecting our influence post-war is through the economic side,' Casey declared when he opened the discussion on 14 July, before he explained the purpose of the Middle East Supply Centre and the Middle East Economic Council. The Centre would be in a position to offer the expert guidance and material help, which were 'likely to be more acceptable than political tutelage', while the Council would help integrate the Middle East into whatever 'world commodity and monetary control arrangements may be adopted at the peace settlement'.[27]

This was an obscure but extremely important point for the governors of a country that had incurred vast debts to fight the war. To the great surprise of those who said that empire paid for itself, defending countries like Egypt was enormously expensive: by the end of that year Britain would owe Egypt alone over a quarter of a billion pounds for goods that British forces had bought from the Egyptians but not yet paid for. By prolonging currency controls and offering guidance, the British hoped to monopolise post-war trade with countries like Egypt in order to repay what they owed. If only the British could get American buy-in to the British-dominated Middle East Supply Centre and the Economic Council, Casey continued, Britain would be able to encourage her creditors to buy British. Why the Americans might acquiesce to this, he did not say.

Casey also broached the question of oil. He wanted to seek an understanding with Washington to avoid further friction on the issue. Churchill, however, was not convinced. He had only reluctantly agreed to the review of Palestine policy, the Allies had just invaded Sicily, and to his mind the Middle Eastern war was over. 'Why open up these wide questions?' he asked during the discussion. 'At the peace we'll know how much each of us counts. We don't need US help in this area, and aren't likely to see many of them there from now on.'[28]

The Palestine statement was scheduled to be issued on both sides of the Atlantic on 27 July but it never went out. After the US secretary of state, Cordell Hull, had given the green light for the announcement, he then appears to have got cold feet, perhaps because the British had in the meantime beefed up the wording to include a much clearer warning that neither government was willing to tolerate the Zionists' use of force. Hull referred the issue to the secretary of war Henry Stimson on the grounds that it had been army officers like Hoskins who had first warned that violence in Palestine was likely. He must have known what this would mean, because Stimson openly supported the Zionists, and on 30 July the *New York Times* reported that a statement was imminent. On 5 August Stimson rang up Hull to tell him that the situation in Palestine was less serious than was previously thought, giving Hull the excuse he needed to abandon the statement. The British ambassador reported afterwards that it had been scuttled by Zionist lobbying.

Over six months' patient work by Casey to tie the Americans in to British policy on Palestine had been for naught. And in Cairo, Harold Hoskins was about to show that Churchill's complacent assumption that American interest in the Middle East would now die away could not have been more wrong.

4

SHEEP'S EYES

It has often been said it was either God or gold that first brought Americans to the Middle East. The earliest American visitors to the region tended to be missionaries or merchants, who came after the final victory against the pirates in the Barbary wars in 1815 made it safe at last to ply the Mediterranean. The first businessmen traded rum for Turkish figs and opium, and then, following the end of the civil war, surplus weapons and machinery for a broadening range of commodities that included liquorice and tobacco. Oil also mattered. In 1879 the American consul in Constantinople boasted that the lamps surrounding the Prophet's tomb in Medina burned paraffin that came from Pennsylvania. By the time of the American spy Harold Hoskins' mission to Saudi Arabia, midway through 1943, a major reason why the Middle East mattered was because oil was now beginning to flow in the opposite direction.[1]

The missionaries included Hoskins' own father Franklin. Driven by millenarian beliefs or guilt at Christianity's anti-Semitism, they originally set out to help the Jews restore their ancient state of Israel, but many of them ended up working among the Armenian and Alawite populations in the Ottoman Empire. It was incredibly slow work: the first Alawite convert to Protestantism was baptised in 1860; four years passed before there was another.

Education was key to the missionaries' strategy. The best known of the schools that the Americans set up was the Syrian Protestant College in Beirut, at which Franklin Hoskins taught. Renamed the American University of Beirut, by 1940 it had 2,000 students on its roll, meaning that the Americans had overtaken the French as the most significant providers of education in the region. It, and the American University in Cairo, which was established just after the end of the First World War, reinforced the Americans' reputation as disinterested philanthropists. Writing a few years later, a British politician reckoned that these two institutions had 'done more to promote American interests in the Middle East than all the British diplomats and armies put together'.[2]

While God had brought Franklin to the Middle East, it was gold that drew his son Harold back there on his mission to see Ibn Saud in the summer of 1943. For although his ostensible remit was to find out whether Ibn Saud might be willing to meet the Zionist leader Chaim Weizmann, by the time that he set out for Riyadh, this job had effectively become cover for a far more important and sensitive task – one which the Americans were desperately keen to keep secret, so that the British could not spike it. Indeed it is possible that this was the real reason for Hoskins' mission all along.

* * *

The moment that Roosevelt's secretary of state, Cordell Hull, heard about Harold Ickes's idea to buy a controlling stake in CASOC, the company that held the concession in Saudi Arabia, he realised that the administration would first need to square Ibn Saud. Although there appeared to be nothing in the agreements between the company and the king that stopped the American government from doing what Ickes was suggesting, Hull thought that the company should notify the king at least out of courtesy. Moreover, given that the king enjoyed telling Americans that one reason why he had given them the concession was because 'you are very far away', no one knew quite how he might react to a proposal that would inevitably increase American involvement in his country. And so Hull suggested sending 'a special representative' to the Middle East to confer with the American ambassadors in Cairo and Jeddah. Then, together, these men would approach Ibn Saud.[3]

The day after Hull put this plan to Roosevelt, he told Hoskins to 'proceed at once to Saudi Arabia'. His instruction to Hoskins told him, rather theatrically, to confine himself exclusively to establishing whether Ibn Saud would meet Weizmann. But if that was really all Hoskins was expected to do, it was a pointless quest. When the American ambassador in Saudi Arabia was posed precisely that question only eight weeks earlier, he informed the State Department that there was 'little likelihood' that Ibn Saud would meet Weizmann. Since then, the *Life* magazine interview, and the tenor of the king's comments to the president's envoy Patrick Hurley both tended to confirm that judgement. Eden was himself bemused by Hoskins' mission. He did not share Churchill's enthusiasm for Weizmann's plan and knew – and knew that the Americans knew – that it was implausible that the king would ever agree to it. And yet he appears to have suspected nothing.[4]

The mission only makes sense if Hoskins had a further, clandestine purpose. Certainly once he had reached Cairo he behaved exactly like the 'special representative' Hull had envisaged, disclosing the CASOC plan to the American ambassador. What no one in Washington appears to have anticipated was the ambassador's reaction, which was one of horror. The Saudis had repeatedly told him that the reason they had chosen CASOC in the first place was because they felt the Americans, unlike the British, nursed no ulterior political agenda. 'Overt American Government intervention', the American ambassador now warned Washington, 'would tend to tar us with the same brush.'[5]

The diplomat was not the only man to raise doubts about the plan. So too did the presidents of Texaco and SoCal, CASOC's two shareholders, when they were let into the secret by Ickes in Washington at the start of August.

Hull realised that the purchase was not going to be plain sailing and ordered Hoskins not to say another word about the scheme. Unsure whether his envoy had obeyed this instruction and worried that the British were intercepting his communications, the secretary of state went on to warn him not to telegraph details of his conversation with the king, but instead to send his written report in the diplomatic bag to Washington. Ickes's scheme to buy CASOC hobbled on until October when details of it leaked to the press, forcing American diplomats in Saudi Arabia to brief the king on the plan. Although Ibn Saud was surprisingly unbothered by the idea, back home in the United States the news alarmed many of the small independent oil companies, which feared the emergence of a government-backed rival. Their pressure forced Ickes to water down, and then abandon, his plan.

* * *

Days after Hoskins met Ibn Saud and discovered that the king had no desire whatsoever to see Weizmann, another American party arrived in Cairo. The Five Senators, as they were known, were partway through a round-the-world trip to investigate the progress of the war. On 18 August they dined with the British ambassador Miles Lampson and his American counterpart.

Two of the delegation, James Mead and Ralph Brewster, were departing the following morning to spend the day in Palestine and 'It was soon clear both ... were abysmally ignorant of the Palestine question', the British ambassador complained. The brevity of this side-trip broke one of Brewster's golden rules. 'I don't think one day is enough to really give you the hang of a country. And if you spend much more than a day or two there, you're likely to become a prejudiced native,' he once told a fellow American. 'But two days is just about right to make you a real expert,' he had said.[6]

Casey appeared before the end of the dinner to tell both men more about the Zionists' preparations to fight for independence, but it is unlikely that either senator was interested, for they were visiting for a different reason. The two men were nominees of Harry S. Truman, a fellow senator who was making a name for himself for curbing the waste that bedevilled the war effort. They had been asked by Truman to investigate the United States' 'administrative activities in foreign fields' and the distribution of American supplies abroad – in other words, how the British were using Lend-Lease. Although Roosevelt would later deny any involvement, the Five Senators' mission was a typical Rooseveltian ruse: it would raise difficult issues that the president did not want to confront Churchill over, creating a political storm to which he would then be obliged to respond.

The Five Senators returned to Washington in late September 1943 to report back to their colleagues. At a press conference soon after their return Brewster and Mead announced that Britain's diplomatic and economic activity was outpacing the Americans' and warned that the British were building oil installations and airfields using Lend-Lease money. Meanwhile, said Brewster, the United States possessed a quarter of the world's known oil reserves, but was supplying two-thirds of the fuel necessary to fight the war. 'If that goes on, and we have another war in ten or fifteen years, we may have to go out with a tin dipper and ask somebody for oil,' he said.[7]

A day in the mandate may not have left Brewster with a profound understanding of the simmering Arab–Jewish conflict, but his grasp of domestic politics in America was faultless. Oil was a sensitive issue at home because at that very moment the East Coast was facing an acute fuel shortage. The following week Roosevelt was asked by journalists if Britain had been deliberately avoiding supplying the Allies with oil in order to conserve its own reserves for future use. The president explained that it was a far more efficient use of shipping tonnage to ship American oil across the Atlantic than it was to transport Middle Eastern oil from the Persian Gulf round the Cape and back north to Europe.

True as it was, Roosevelt's explanation did not convince the senators. They issued a statement calling on the British to pull their weight over the supply of oil, and delivered their conclusions to their colleagues in a secret session of the Senate. Selective leaking of what they said produced a political firestorm which dragged in Roosevelt and then Churchill. On 28 October the leading senator of the Five, Richard Russell, decided to go public with his views. 'I came home with a healthy respect bordering on envy for the efficiency of the British in administration', he told the Senate. While the British were pursuing 'a definite foreign policy with respect to every corner of the globe', the Americans he had encountered were disorganised, short-sighted and naïve. The United States' willingness to allow the British to buy good-will internationally using Lend-Lease aid, and to supply the lion's share of the oil, both had to cease. 'With the opening of the Mediterranean and the great increase in the construction of shipping, there is no longer any valid reason for not giving our oil deposits a rest, and tapping those of other areas,' he said.[8]

A week later Truman's committee made a suggestion. If the British could not afford American petroleum and did not have the shipping to transport it from the oilfields they did control, the United States government should consider demanding the transfer of 'ownership of an equivalent value of foreign petroleum reserves or of English-held securities of corporations having a title to such reserves'. This was an incendiary proposal, and it provoked a barbed response. The British government briefed the press that, in order to do as the Truman Committee proposed, they would need to use Lend-Lease aid to upgrade their refinery at Abadan so that it could produce more aviation fuel, and build another pipeline from Iraq to the Mediterranean.[9]

From the State Department Hull looked on alarmed. On the day that the failure of the government's plan to take control of CASOC was reported in the press, he wrote a tetchy letter to Ickes, warning him that the events of the previous few weeks could not help but undermine the Saudis' confidence in the US government and CASOC. The British were already trying to exploit the fiasco, he told Ickes. American officials had found out that the British ambassador to Saudi Arabia was furtively trying to get hold of a copy of CASOC's concession agreement – so that his government could make the king a better offer, Hull assumed. He asked his colleague urgently to come up with a new idea to develop American oil facilities in the Middle East. 'We believe that strong criticism will develop if British petroleum facilities in the Middle East are further expanded ... with American materials,' he finished, 'for to do so will retard the development of American enterprises, jeopardize their holdings, and so tend to make this country dependent on British oil in the future.'[10]

* * *

As Ickes well knew, what Hull was asking for was easier said than done. If the last few months had proved anything, it was the substantial advantage the British enjoyed in matters that related to oil. The fact that the British government owned a significant percentage of the country's oil companies ensured that its, and the oil industry's, interests largely coincided. By contrast, in the United States, where the government had no stake in any oil company, and there was the added complication of a large domestic oil industry, government and industry were at odds. The US government wanted to conserve domestic oil stocks, while the domestic oil companies wanted to produce. And, as the reaction to his proposal to buy CASOC had amply demonstrated, these domestic producers would fight any attempt by the government to help the bigger companies exploit foreign oilfields, because they feared a glut of oil would drive down the market price.

The alternative to government intervention was private investment, but in CASOC's case this was not straightforward either. The two companies that were the most likely sources of capital, Jersey Standard and Socony, were precluded from investing in Saudi Arabia because they held minor stakes in the rival Iraq Petroleum Company. In 1928, they and the IPC's other shareholders had signed a deal, known as the Red Line Agreement, that prevented each of them investing in most of the other oil fields in the Middle East if any of the other shareholders objected. Since one of these was the Anglo-Iranian Oil Company, in which the British government owned a controlling stake, the British effectively had a veto on private American investment in CASOC, for as long as the Red Line Agreement was in place.

It was now clearly in the United States' interest to abandon the Red Line Agreement and in late November 1943 the State Department's Middle East expert, Wallace Murray, wrote that it was time to press the British to scrap the fifteen-year-old deal. The Foreign Office had recently been in touch, proposing talks about the future of the Middle East, when it hoped to win American support for the Middle East Supply Centre and a new Middle East Economic Council, the linchpins of its strategy to perpetuate British influence in the region. As a quid pro quo, the Americans now demanded a discussion on Middle Eastern oil.

When the British prevaricated over the scope and level of the talks, the United States government retaliated. First Ickes unveiled what he described as a 'blunderbuss shot' – a new proposal for the Petroleum Reserves Corporation to finance a pipeline from Saudi Arabia to the Mediterranean coast, which would allow the Arabian American Oil Company, or Aramco – as CASOC had now been diplomatically renamed – to compete directly with the British-dominated Iraq Petroleum Company, which also piped oil to the Mediterranean. Then on 11 February 1944 (before the precise scope of the talks had been agreed) the *New York Times* reported that the British government was sending a delegation to Washington for discussions on how best to develop Middle Eastern oil. The State Department ramped up the pressure. First it threatened to argue in public that the Red Line Agreement breached the clause in the Atlantic Charter in which Churchill had committed to endeavour to further 'the enjoyment . . . of access, on equal terms . . . to the raw materials of the world'. Then, when this failed to move the British, it threatened to announce that the conference would be opened by the president and the American delegation led by Cordell Hull, a choice that made it clear that the Americans expected the proceedings to be decisive and binding. 'Roosevelt is jumping us into a conference on oil in the Middle East – rather outrageously,' wrote Eden's private secretary. 'We cannot bear anyone to touch us in that part of the world – even our friends.'[11]

The British ambassador to Washington demanded a meeting with Roosevelt, which took place on 18 February. The president wanted to allay British fears and showed him a rough map he had drawn of the Middle East. Iran's oil belonged to Britain, he said. Britain and the United States shared Iraqi and Kuwaiti oil. Saudi oil was America's.[12]

The report of this meeting did not reassure Churchill. Still bruised by how dismissively Roosevelt had treated him at the Teheran conference with Stalin late in 1943, he now telegraphed the president directly, starting a fortnight-long spat between the two men.

Blaming the Five Senators, Churchill noted 'apprehension in some quarters here that the United States has a desire to deprive us of our oil assets in the Middle East', a fear that the threatened announcement about Roosevelt's and Hull's involvement in a Middle Eastern oil conference only reinforced. If Roosevelt took part, 'the whole question will become one of the first magnitude in Parliament', he warned. 'It will be felt that we are being hustled.' When Roosevelt responded in kind, revealing his own worry 'about the rumor that the British wish to horn in on Saudi Arabian reserves', and rejecting Churchill's proposal of technical talks, the prime minister resisted, threatening the danger of 'a wide difference opening' in the run-up to D-Day if the Americans made their announcement regardless. A week passed before Roosevelt responded to tell Churchill that 'we are not making sheep's eyes at your oil fields in Iraq or Iran', but that the conference could not be held off much longer. Churchill, gratified by Roosevelt's commitment, replied to give the US president 'the fullest assurance that we have no thought of trying to horn in upon your interests or property in Saudi Arabia'.[13]

Two days later the British cabinet confirmed that it was ready to send a delegation to Washington for preliminary talks. In exchange the State Department agreed that its Middle East expert, Wallace Murray, would come to London to talk about the future of the Middle East simultaneously.[14]

By the end of February 1944, it looked briefly as if both governments might reconcile their differences over the Middle East. The British hoped for American endorsement of their plans for the Middle East Supply Centre. The Americans expected an agreement on oil that would allay their fear that the British were attempting to usurp their privileged position in Saudi Arabia. Between London and Washington, a fragile truce existed. In the Middle East, however, their representatives on the spot had other plans.

A PRETTY TOUGH NUT

While Churchill and Roosevelt were trading accusations about each other's ambitions in the Middle East, Lord Moyne returned to Egypt in February 1944 as Britain's new minister resident in the Middle East.

Moyne had spent the last six months in Britain sitting on the cabinet committee charged by Churchill with devising a long-term strategy for Palestine, which had instead led to a fudge. The committee had once again recommended partition but Churchill's instinctive dislike of the idea and Eden's doubts about the feasibility of the broader Greater Syria scheme, which was supposed to reconcile the Arabs to the division of Palestine, led the cabinet to agree that more work was needed on the detail before the new policy could be openly pursued. Moyne returned to Cairo that spring with the unenviable task of trying to make surreptitious headway on a project that had cabinet approval in principle, but lacked either Churchill's or Eden's endorsement in practice.[1]

To add to Moyne's difficulties, both policies would need American support to succeed, but here the omens were not good either. In Moyne's absence in London an abrasive new American representative had arrived in Cairo, to whom the British ambassador Miles Lampson, newly ennobled Lord Killearn for his efforts, had taken an instant and profound dislike. James Landis had been appointed the United States' director of economic operations in the Middle East, in the wake of the Five Senators' criticisms of American disorganisation. Killearn accused him of taking 'a hectoring and bullying attitude towards the Egyptians', an activity where he had previously exercised a monopoly himself. He recognised the new director of economic operations as 'a pretty tough nut', and now briefed Moyne on his new opponent.[2]

Landis was certainly a controversial appointment. The son of a carping missionary, he was the dean of Harvard Law School, a zealous, heavy-drinking, rather tortured workaholic whose low self-esteem drove him ceaselessly to prove himself. On the opposite side of the New Deal to Willkie, he had made his name drafting tough financial market regulation in the wake of the Wall Street Crash, and then serving as a commissioner, then chairman of the Securities Exchange Commission in the second half of the 1930s. To make a point, he once entertained the pompous chairman of the New York Stock Exchange to a 45-cent luncheon brought up from the canteen to his office. Trapped in a dead-end wartime job and looking to escape a marriage that he was deliberately allowing to fail, he jumped at the opportunity to work abroad when Roosevelt offered it to him in September 1943. 'Forgive me for running out again', he wrote to the acting dean of Harvard Law School, after his appointment was announced, 'but I honestly think there is a job to do there and that I may make some contributions toward our general future.'[3]

When Landis set out for Cairo, there was a danger that the 'general future' might be bleak. The Roosevelt administration was becoming increasingly concerned about the economic challenge that peace would pose. The war effort absorbed 60 per cent of industrial output in the United States: on victory, that demand would fall away, threatening mass unemployment. The answer to that problem was for the country to export itself out of trouble. It did not take long for Landis to realise, once he had reached Egypt, that such an economic strategy would place the Americans on a collision course with their British allies, because the biggest obstacle to a successful American export drive in the region was the organisation in which the British had invested their hopes of postwar economic revival and influence, the Middle East Supply Centre.

'I stuck my nose into it,' Landis said later. The more he looked, the more he thought that the British Empire resembled one of the great holding companies that the Roosevelt administration had tried to break up in the 1930s. One way that the British were using the Middle East Supply Centre to perpetuate their influence in the region was to handicap American exporters. On the grounds of shipping shortages, the

Centre limited – among many other things – the import of machine and hand tools. These restrictions not only denied American manufacturers export sales opportunities, but also made the region more dependent on manufactured imports than it might otherwise have been. Again using shipping as its justification, the Centre ensured that what imports it did allow into the region came mainly from Britain rather than more distant America. That explained why Ibn Saud wore English socks.[4]

For Landis, the trading framework established by the British presented not just an economic but also a moral challenge to the United States. A country like Palestine, he noted, had accumulated a dollar trade surplus (principally by exporting oranges to the United States) but its inhabitants' ability to spend those dollars on luxury American goods was constrained by the currency controls imposed by the British which affected every country in the sterling area – those countries that either used, or pegged their currencies to, sterling – of which Palestine was part. Americans could either acquiesce to this or speak out, he said, and it was abundantly clear that he favoured the latter option. For acquiescence made the United States complicit in a system whereby the British knowingly depressed living standards in the countries of the sterling area in order to protect their imperial economic system as a whole.

Landis realised that he could not resolve this problem while he was in Cairo. It was a matter of high policy that could only be settled by direct talks between senior British and American officials. Since the American ambassador seemed more interested in 'the evanescent building of goodwill through tea and cocktail parties, dinners and ceremonies', Landis decided to take up the matter himself. Flying home to Washington he argued that it was time for the United States to question the basis of Britain's Middle Eastern economic policy because the excuse of shipping and supply shortages which were the Supply Centre's raison d'être were 'no longer plausible'. But there he found that there was little appetite inside the government for such a confrontation in the run-up to D-Day and he was forced to return to Egypt empty-handed.[5]

'Landis, in spite of everyone's best efforts, insisted in regarding the British, not the Germans, as his principal enemy,' recalled a colleague. On his return to Cairo, he decided that his best bet was to starve the Middle East Supply Centre of personnel. Although his staff grew rapidly to fifty, and although he was the United States' representative in the Centre, just thirteen of those fifty staff worked there. Of the rest, half worked with the British on economic warfare against Germany, while the others – some of whom were OSS men working undercover – were engaged in promoting American trade. These last were the most talented, the British noticed, and their zeal was obvious. The general manager of the Egyptian State Railway said that they were badgering him for details of the railway's current and future procurement plans. They were also adept at finding Egyptian businessmen space on flights back to the United States at a time when seats on aeroplanes were still in very short supply. 'They have just flown a local agent for textile machinery to the USA with high priority and have offered to do the same for the Egyptian manager of one of the principal local cotton textile mills,' a panicky-sounding Killearn reported, midway through March.[6]

While Killearn had woken up to the fact that Landis and his colleagues threatened the British strategy of trying to corner the Middle Eastern market, Moyne was more complacent, perhaps because the Americans he had worked with during the previous war had been – in his view – inflexible and poorly organised. 'We can reasonably count upon our greater experience, our superior connections and the goodwill and prestige that I believe we shall continue to enjoy for seeing us through,' he felt.[7]

This assumption blinded Moyne to what was actually going on. When he met Landis to discuss the Americans' understaffing of the Middle East Supply Centre, the American, who was clearly reluctant to confront his British counterpart directly, blamed the State Department for denying him the staff he needed to support the Centre. Disingenuously he said that unless he received more personnel, he would be obliged to end American participation in the venture. Taken in by this, Moyne endorsed Landis's request in a telegram to London.

The long-heralded Anglo-American talks about the Middle East, which opened a day later in London on 11 April 1944, provided the British with the opportunity to raise this issue. After receiving Moyne's message, the head of the Foreign Office's Middle East department, Maurice Peterson, gingerly raised the matter with his opposite number Wallace Murray on 18 April. He had heard that 'Mr Landis might be compelled to change the status of American participation in the Middle

East Supply Centre to that of a mere liaison mission,' he said. 'This would be a deplorable development.'[8]

Murray was infamous for his explosive temper, while his open contempt for British Middle Eastern policy convinced one British official that he 'hates our guts ... his policy is merely to frustrate our policy'. But before departing for London that spring he had been told not to rock the boat ahead of D-Day and he was temporarily on his best behaviour. 'American views ran along the same lines', he replied vaguely to Peterson's query about his country's attitude towards the Supply Centre. Then he added an important caveat. While the Centre was 'useful in the war period ... we should not want to perpetuate the barriers and restrictions of the system into the post-war period'. The British seized on Murray's more positive noises to deceive themselves that 'the development through MESC of an autonomous and social services institution for the ME is now agreed Anglo-American policy'. It was only six weeks later – after American manpower to support the Centre's work had failed to materialise – that the penny dropped with Moyne. 'Landis ... takes every opportunity offered by his position to forward American trade interests,' he wrote. 'American cooperation in MESC is indeed a mere pretence.'[9]

* * *

By then, events in Saudi Arabia had convinced the Americans of their British counterparts' bad faith. The Americans had not forgotten the attempt by the British ambassador, Stanley Jordan, the previous October to filch a copy of Aramco's concession agreement, and they were now watching the British envoy with a mixture of interest and alarm. Jordan was a career diplomat who had last served in Jeddah in the 1920s. A rather strait-laced character, he had been struck on his return to the port after a decade and a half's absence that the condition of the ordinary Saudi had not changed at all. The only visible difference was the number of palaces that the Saudi royal family had constructed in the meantime. 'Bribery and corruption are everywhere,' he reported back to London. The dependability of the British subsidy was not encouraging efforts to address the problem.[10]

Having shelled out £4.5 million in 1943, the Foreign Office took little persuading that it was time to trim how much it paid Ibn Saud, not least because the king's main source of revenue, the pilgrimage, was now recovering. Since the subsidy was only ever supposed to make up for the king's loss of revenues during wartime, in early 1944 the British took the step of withholding tariffs paid by pilgrims that they would ordinarily have passed on to the king on the grounds that they were recouping some of their previous year's subsidy. The Saudis broke the news of this move to the American embassy, portraying the measure as a hostile act. The Americans, having long agonised about Ibn Saud's growing reliance on the British, now feared that the British were using the threat of the withdrawal of their subsidy to coerce the king. Their discovery soon afterwards that Jordan seemed to have orchestrated the sacking of one of Ibn Saud's pro-American advisers only deepened their concern.

At the London talks in April 1944 Peterson raised Saudi Arabia on day two, before his American opposite number Wallace Murray could do so. When Murray commented that Ibn Saud was upset that the British were withholding his money, Peterson, shifting the subject, said that the king had asked Stanley Jordan if he could recommend a Sunni Muslim financial adviser. This clearly came as news to Murray, who immediately appreciated that whoever filled this role would wield great influence and, if the king really was seeking a Muslim, that the British would find it much easier than his own government to supply a suitable candidate.

The Americans queried whether the king had been so specific, insinuating that Jordan had suggested a Muslim in order to put them at a disadvantage. From Washington, the secretary of state Cordell Hull insisted that any such adviser must be an American, to reflect the 'preponderant American economic interests in Saudi Arabia', but conceded that the leader of a military mission, which was also being mooted, might be a British officer, in an attempt to satisfy the Foreign Office. Peterson, however, refused to give ground. In a response to Hull he asserted that the finance expert had to be a Muslim since the king's treasury was situated in Mecca, a city that no non-Muslim was allowed to enter.[11]

That response triggered an angry spat between Washington and London. Such was the collapse in trust that when Hull answered Peterson he suggested that Jordan and his American counterpart visit Ibn Saud together and offer him a white British military adviser and an

American financial adviser, and see what the king said. He threatened to send his own representative to see Ibn Saud alone if the British would not go along with this proposal. The warning elicited an angry reply from Peterson, who questioned Hull's assertion that American economic interests outweighed British in Saudi Arabia, by observing that the revenues from the pilgrimage were far greater than those from oil and would continue to be for the foreseeable future.

The two allies were at loggerheads. Although, in Cairo, Landis and Moyne managed to reach agreement that their governments would share the burden of the subsidy in future years, the dispute over the current year's subsidy meant that payment had still not been made. By now the Americans were receiving increasingly desperate calls for money from the Saudis. The British, however, refused to budge. They had it on good authority from the Saudi ambassador to London that several of the king's advisers, including his finance minister, habitually exaggerated the country's problems in order to line their own pockets. By now their lack of faith in the Americans was such that they felt they could not share this information with Washington because they feared that its source would be identified and dry up.

When Moyne and Landis proved unable to break the deadlock, Landis again returned to Washington for talks. At the end of July Hull decided to act unilaterally. Earlier that year he had intimated that his government would be willing to supply 10 million silver riyals in order to keep the Saudis solvent. He now confirmed that the United States would do this. The American calculation was that the sums involved in keeping the king happy were peanuts compared to the profits that would ultimately accrue from the oil concession, as long as they hung onto it. By doing so they wrecked British hopes of imposing some financial discipline in Saudi Arabia, where the royalties from Aramco still passed through the finance minister's personal New York bank account. It was, sighed Moyne, 'another of the many cases we have had in the Middle East where the local American idea of cooperation is that we should do all the giving and they all the taking'.[12]

On 1 September 1944 a new American minister took up residence in Jeddah. Bill Eddy was, like Harold Hoskins, the son of missionaries to Lebanon: the two men were in fact cousins. Before the war he had been a teacher at the American University in Cairo, where he translated the rules of basketball into Arabic. Like Hoskins, he had then been drawn into the OSS. He would later refer to the moment he arrived in Jeddah as the beginning of the 'American invasion of the Near East'.[13]

Eddy was as forceful as Landis, and it soon became obvious to Stanley Jordan that his new American counterpart meant business. The American diplomat made it clear that in the future his government was not going to allow the British to restrict the sums that the United States would pay to Ibn Saud. Jordan backed away. Following his first encounter with Eddy he wrote to Eden arguing that it was time for the British to extract themselves from any ongoing financial obligation to the Saudis. 'The position of a junior partner being towed along in the wake of the Americans is ... a very undignified one for His Majesty's Government to accept,' he commented, and the advantages of sharing the subsidy with Washington were 'few or none'. From Cairo Moyne agreed. 'Conversations with Colonel Eddy have clearly shown that the American conception of what should be given to Saudi Arabia goes far beyond anything which we have had in mind,' he wrote within a fort-night of Eddy's appointment. It was an early sign of how the Americans would outgun the British financially in the years to come.[14]

* * *

Landis left Washington to return to Cairo that autumn determined to finish off the Middle East Supply Centre. The Americans insisted that the Atlantic Charter and, more definitely, the original Lend-Lease agree-ment had committed Britain to ending trade discrimination. Then, at the Bretton Woods conference that summer, the British had accepted a system that envisaged multilateral free trade. All this was at odds with the restrictions that the Middle East Supply Centre continued to police. When, en route for Egypt, Landis paused in London, he told British officials that his prime objective was 'to cut out the red tape' that impeded American exporters selling in the Middle East. While he was willing to accept ongoing exchange controls that limited the amount of sterling that could be exchanged for dollars, he proposed deregulating the import of all but a select list of commodities in very short supply. In fact, 'the only control would be a shipping tonnage programme within which the exporters would have to keep'. Twisting another British

argument, that the restrictions were necessary to prevent post-war inflation, he reassured the British that 'within the present shipping situation
these new proposals might mean only a small increase in imports into
the Middle East'.[15]

The question was, what kind of imports? This was what bothered
the British, and it was a legitimate concern. Although the Middle East
Supply Centre had dramatically improved the region's self-sufficiency,
imports of basic commodities were still necessary. British officials
wondered what would happen when American importers realised that
'200 radio sets' were 'a better paying proposition than their equivalent
shipping space in grain or nitrates'. What was to stop Egyptian importers
spending their dollar allowances entirely on luxury goods?[16]

Initially, the British felt that there was not too wide a gap between
their position and Landis's. That gap rapidly became a chasm when
the British circulated a list of nearly 100 wildly differing imported
goods – from specific industrial and agricultural chemicals to entire
categories of manufactured products including 'trucks', 'passenger cars'
and 'furniture' – that they wanted the Middle East Supply Centre to
continue to regulate. The items on the list that produced the most immediate discord were tyres and inner tubes. The British, whose Malayan
rubber plantations were still in Japanese hands, wanted to prevent the
Americans – who had created a large synthetic rubber industry – from
breaking into the Middle Eastern market where a set of four re-treaded
tyres could change hands for as much as $3,000. When Landis refused
to play ball there was nothing that the British could do about it. By the
time he left the British capital, an agreement to relax import controls
was in place.[17]

Moyne, who had been grappling with a special economic mission
sent by the State Department to investigate the controls imposed by the
Middle East Supply Centre, was pleased to see Landis reappear in Cairo
at the end of October. At lunchtime on 6 November 1944 he offered his
counterpart a lift, which the American official declined. On his return
to his residence Moyne was shot, fatally, by a pair of Jewish assassins
who had been waiting for him.

Moyne did not live to see the verdict of the State Department's mission, which sealed the Centre's fate with its conclusions that the seas
were now safe enough to make import controls unnecessary and that,

while Anglo-American collaboration had been real enough, it had 'not at any time transformed MESC into a genuine joint undertaking'. Nor did he witness the barely veiled attack on British policy that his American counterpart made that December in what turned out to be a valedictory speech, before he resigned the following month. 'Peace to me is a vision of free seas, free skies, free trade and freedom in the development of ideas,' Landis declared. 'It is not mercantilism, uneconomic or political subsidies, narrow nationalism, group preferences or the fascist conception of one race entitled to dominance over another.'[18]

Although Moyne's efforts to encourage Arab unity would lead to the creation of the Arab League, the Middle East Supply Centre, through which the British peer had hoped to prolong British dominance of the region, was dissolved on 1 November 1945. By that time British ambitions for it were a distant memory.

'THE JEWISH PROBLEM'

Wendell Willkie never lived to see, let alone contest, the 1944 presidential election, which took place on the day after Lord Moyne was murdered in Cairo. The man once tipped to succeed Roosevelt that November had died suddenly from a heart attack, aged fifty-two, the previous month, having failed to win the Republican nomination in the summer. Contrary to the assumption he had made two years earlier – the calculation that had led him to the Middle East in the first place – the election had demonstrated that Roosevelt was not 'through'. On 7 November 1944 the president defeated his opponent, Thomas Dewey, overwhelmingly.

Under fire from the Zionists for failing to do more for Jewish refugees, Roosevelt had gone further than he had ever done before to court the Jewish vote during the campaign. Three weeks before the poll he had announced that he favoured 'the opening of Palestine to unrestricted Jewish immigration'. A day later he declared that he knew 'how long the Jewish people have worked and prayed for the establishment of Palestine as a free and democratic Jewish Commonwealth'. Were he re-elected, he continued, 'I shall help to bring about its realisation.'[1]

* * *

While statements like these helped Roosevelt to a fourth successive win, they endangered his relationship with Ibn Saud at a time when his administration needed the support of the king to advance two vital projects. One was the trans-Arabian pipeline that Harold Ickes had floated earlier that year. The other was an airbase on the limestone plateau at Dhahran, in eastern Saudi Arabia.

As Willkie's airborne odyssey had demonstrated, a new era of long-distance international flight was approaching. Although the Americans enjoyed a technological advantage because they had been developing and building bombers while encouraging the British to make fighter planes, the British controlled more landing rights, particularly in the Middle East where the main route between Cairo and Karachi hopped via Habbaniyah, Abadan and Bahrain. A runway at Dhahran – the only spot in northern Saudi Arabia where the geology could cope with heavy air-craft – would enable the Americans to bypass these British staging posts, establishing a new trans-Middle Eastern route that enjoyed the distinct advantage of being 200 miles shorter. Since British air force officers had also recently been spotted prospecting the site, the Americans knew they had no time to lose.

If only for these immediate reasons, the president needed to mend fences with Ibn Saud. But it seems that he thought a meeting might achieve something far greater. If he could reconcile the king to the Jews' presence in Palestine he might permanently resolve a tension that his country's domestic politics created. Months earlier he had written to Ibn Saud, expressing his disappointment that they had never met. In February 1945 the opportunity now arose to do so, as the president returned home via Cairo from the summit at Yalta, where he, Churchill and Stalin had met to discuss the end of the war and the arrangements for Europe in the peace. Roosevelt hoped that, by force of personality in a meeting, he might be able to bring the king around. Once again, he was pursuing a consensus.

On 12 February Ibn Saud boarded an American destroyer at Jeddah, together with a retinue that included an astrologer, a food taster, serv-ants, bodyguards, slaves and six sheep. Two days later, on the Bitter Lake on the Suez Canal, he met Roosevelt for the first – and only – time. When Ibn Saud compared their age and infirmity, the grey-faced presi-dent gave him his spare wheelchair, and then asked him how they might resolve the question of Palestine. The king repeated his opposition to Jewish immigration to Palestine: 'The Arabs', he stated, 'would choose to die rather than yield their lands to the Jews.'[2]

'We talked for three hours and I argued with the old fellow up hill and down dale, but he stuck to his guns,' Roosevelt said afterwards. 'There was nothing I could do with him.'[3]

* * *

Roosevelt ruffled feathers when, on his return, he told Congress that he had 'learned more about the whole problem, the Moslem problem, the Jewish problem, by talking with Ibn Saud for five minutes than I could have learned in an exchange of two or three dozen letters.' But by far the most important outcome of the conversation was the incendiary minute it produced. Written by the American ambassador, Bill Eddy, who translated, this revealed that Roosevelt, in his effort to win over Ibn Saud, had suggested Poland – and not Palestine – might provide 'space ... for the resettlement of many homeless Jews', that 'as Chief Executive of the United States Government' he would 'do nothing to assist the Jews against the Arabs', and that he thought an Arab mission to the United States would be 'a very good idea' because many people in America were 'misinformed'.[4]

Three weeks later Ibn Saud tried to drive home his victory by seeking to extract in writing what the president had said during the meeting. On 10 March he wrote Roosevelt a long letter that set out his opposition to the Zionists' claim to Palestine and asked the president to prevent the Jews from consolidating their position in the mandate any further.

Once the king's letter reached Washington, the minute of the Bitter Lake meeting was retrieved from the State Department files and, on 5 April Roosevelt replied to Ibn Saud. In his letter he reminded the king of the even-handed promise he had made back in May 1943, that no decision on Palestine would be taken 'without full consultation with both Arabs and Jews'. Not only had this policy not changed, he continued, but he was happy to renew the assurance that he had given him during their meeting. As president he would 'take no action ... which might prove hostile to the Arab people'. This, as the minute showed, was not what he had said, but Roosevelt would never have to account for the difference. A week later he was dead.[5]

The man obliged to pick up where Roosevelt had abruptly left off was Roosevelt's running mate and vice-president of twelve weeks, Harry Truman. Whereas Roosevelt was a natural leader, Truman was the perfect sidekick: an earnest, bespectacled details man who gave the ticket the sense of being in touch with ordinary Americans' concerns. A former farmer and failed businessman before he was elected to the Senate, Truman had made his name as chairman of a committee investigating the war effort – the committee that had sparked outrage in London at the end of 1943 with its proposal that the British government might turn over its stakes in foreign oilfields to the United States government. The Truman Committee, as it became known, had made him the champion of the taxpayer against fraud and waste, inept bureaucrats and politicians, big businessmen and union barons.

Throughout his first term Truman was acutely aware of the fact that it had been Roosevelt, not he, who had been elected. 'I don't feel that I am,' Truman said, when he was once asked what it felt like being president. 'I feel that I am trying to carry on for someone else.' While he felt his way into the job he followed Roosevelt's equivocal policy on Palestine. In response to a query about the issue, from Ibn Saud's Hashemite rival and neighbour Abdullah of Transjordan, he signed off a letter drafted by the State Department that stuck to Roosevelt's 'no decision . . . without full consultation' script. But this ran counter to the pro-Zionist manifesto that he and Roosevelt had stood on and he soon decided it was not tenable. The end of the war in Europe in May that year finally made the scale of the refugee crisis apparent. An estimated quarter of a million 'displaced people' needed to be found a home. For the estimated 138,000 of them who were Jewish, the Zionists were adamant that it should be Palestine.[6]

This issue mattered because, from the moment Truman was sworn in, he knew that his first electoral test would be for the New York mayoralty on 6 November 1945. New York had the largest Jewish population of any city in the country: there were nearly four times more Jews in New York than in the whole of Palestine. And unlike his own party, which had picked a candidate with Irish roots, the Republicans' contender was Jewish too.

That election made Truman peculiarly sensitive to American Jews' interest in the Palestine question. 'I'm sorry, gentlemen,' he would tell a group of American diplomats who disliked that fact, 'but I have to answer to hundreds of thousands who are serious for the success of Zionism; I do not have hundreds of thousands of Arabs among my constituents.' To show the Zionists that he was taking action that June he asked the US representative on the Inter-Governmental Committee on Refugees, Earl Harrison, to go to the American-occupied zone in Europe to investigate. But he did not wait for Harrison to report. At a press conference in mid-August, in answer to a question that had been planted with a reporter, he said that his aim was 'to let as many Jews into Palestine as possible and still maintain civil peace'. Crucial to this plan was the acquiescence of both the British and the Arabs, since Truman had no desire to send half a million American soldiers to Palestine to keep the peace.[7]

Eight days later, Harrison reported the terrible conditions he had found in the American zone, where Jewish survivors of the Holocaust were trapped in limbo, still living in the concentration camps, clad in their camp pyjamas or discarded German uniforms, because they had nowhere else to go. Aware that winter would cause many deaths, he highlighted a 'persuasive' proposal made by the Jewish Agency. This was for the British government to create 100,000 extra immigration visas to enable 'the quick evacuation of all non-repatriable Jews in Germany and Austria, who wish it, to Palestine'.[8]

This large round number appealed to Truman. A week later he forwarded the report to Britain's new prime minister, Clement Attlee, under a letter pressing him to accept 100,000 Jewish refugees in Palestine. With his eye firmly on the forthcoming mayoral election, he also allowed a former Democratic senator-turned-Zionist lobbyist, Guy Gillette, to reveal what he had privately asked Attlee for.

This gambit did nothing to improve Truman's relationship with Attlee, which had got off to a bad start. On becoming prime minister, Attlee found a letter from the president that left no doubt that Truman had assumed Churchill would win. Truman's willingness to let Gillette spread the message suggested that he took Attlee's approval of his demand for granted. It was presumptuous, but not entirely unreasonable. Attlee was a quiet and modest man, and perhaps Truman mistook these qualities for weakness. Perhaps equally he could not understand how his request could possibly be contentious. After all, like the Democrats the previous November, the British Labour Party had just won that summer's election on a pro-Zionist platform. As Harrison had noted in his report, the Labour politician Hugh Dalton, now Attlee's chancellor

of the exchequer, had said publicly that the 'unspeakable horrors perpe-
trated upon the Jews' in occupied Europe made it 'morally wrong and
politically indefensible' to bar entry to Palestine to any Jew who wished
to go there.

What neither Truman nor Harrison had allowed for was the fact
that a key member of the new government had since changed his mind.
'Clem,' the new foreign secretary Ernest Bevin said to Attlee one day,
'about Palestine. According to the lads in the Office, we've got it wrong.
We've got to think again.'[9]

It took Truman's letter eleven days to reach Attlee and, in the meantime, Bevin had been reviewing British Middle Eastern policy. An earthy
bruiser who had started out in life as a farmhand, Bevin had briefly
caused consternation in the Foreign Office when it transpired that he
ate food off his knife. That disquiet evaporated as he revealed himself
a robust defender of the country's interests. Critical of the Atlantic
Charter from the outset and an implacable anti-communist, he believed
that an ongoing British presence in the Middle East would assure the
country's continued international relevance and prevent the expansion
of Soviet influence southwards into Africa and beyond.

As there was mounting opposition in Egypt to the continued presence
of British forces, Bevin hoped to switch Britain's military base from one
bank of the Suez Canal to the other. His plan was to negotiate an exit
from Egypt that would improve Britain's reputation in the wider Arab
world enough to permit a deal with the Jews that gave Britain an ongoing right to base her forces in Palestine. Until such an agreement could
be worked out, the government would allow a low level of immigration
to Palestine. Following military advice that it would require far fewer
British troops to deal with 'localized trouble with the Jews in Palestine'
than with 'widespread disturbances among the Arabs throughout the
Middle East', ministers hoped to do just enough 'to appease Jewish
sentiment', but not so much as to provoke Arab uproar.[10]

Maintaining this finely calibrated piece of prevarication might have
been possible had Britain been acting in a vacuum. But it was immediately upset by Truman's demand to Attlee to accept a large number of
Jewish refugees to Palestine. When, four days after delivering the letter,
Truman's secretary of state James Byrnes told Bevin that the president
intended to endorse Harrison's conclusions that very evening, the foreign

secretary threatened to demand publicly that American soldiers police the situation that Truman's intervention would cause. Attlee echoed this, warning the president that his policy might 'set aflame the whole Middle East' and do 'grievous harm' to transatlantic relations.[11]

Truman backed off; his demand had also produced opposition on two other fronts. At home his own administration was ganging up against him. Prompted by the State Department, which feared he was damaging relations with the Saudis, the War Department warned him that his all-important demobilisation plans would be delayed indefinitely if he persisted with his support for Jewish immigration. This was because more American troops would be needed in Germany if British forces based there were redeployed to the Middle East to quell an Arab backlash. Abroad, thanks to Guy Gillette, news of his support for large-scale Jewish immigration to Palestine had reached Baghdad and Cairo. There, the secretary-general of the Arab League said that the president's insistence that 100,000 Jews be let into the mandate conflicted with Roosevelt's pledge to Ibn Saud in February that year, that the United States would 'never support the Zionists' fight for Palestine against the Arabs'.[12]

This first hint of what had passed between Roosevelt and Ibn Saud at that February's meeting on the Bitter Lake immediately intrigued journalists. Asked at a press conference whether Roosevelt had indeed said this, Truman answered reflexively 'with a flat "no"' – which was untrue. Digging himself deeper and deeper, he went on to claim 'that he had looked through the records of the foreign conferences very carefully and had found no such commitment', then, 'that since there was no official or other record of any such pledge having been made by his predecessor in the White House, he would not feel bound by any such understanding'. It all sounded very fishy.[13]

Truman's performance was a red rag to Ibn Saud and his advisers, who were avid listeners to radio news. After hearing reports of what the president had said, they told the American ambassador, Bill Eddy, that the king would be asking Truman for clarification. They knew – and so did Eddy – that the minute of the king's meeting with Roosevelt clearly contradicted what the president had just claimed. In a letter to Truman, Ibn Saud now threatened to publish it. That prospect left the administration aghast because the record of the meeting was dynamite.

Not only would it show that the president had lied, but, as a senior State Department official observed, the publication of Roosevelt's candid views 'would have unfortunate consequences both in this country and abroad.'[14]

Desperate to stop Ibn Saud from carrying out his threat before the election, Truman wrote a grovelling letter to the king. In it he claimed his remarks had been inaccurately reported and said that he was willing to publish Roosevelt's letter of 5 April, but not the original minute of the meeting as its release 'just now . . . would not be in the common interest of our two countries'. After Ibn Saud had accepted this suggestion, the letter was published on 18 October. That same day Truman tried to regain the initiative ahead of the election by saying that he hoped that Attlee would accept his proposal.[15]

As the British realised, Truman was now relying on a positive response from Attlee, and they immediately tried to exploit the president's vulnerability. Bevin, under pressure to set out the new government's policy on Palestine, had wanted to establish a joint Anglo-American Committee of Enquiry. Mindful of his broader strategic objective to maintain a British base in Palestine, his aim was to rope the Americans into finding a permanent solution that would enable Britain to remain there. Time was short. Although, in the absence of a new policy on Palestine the government was allowing the remaining immigration permits from the White Paper regime to continue to be used, these would soon run out. MI6, meanwhile, had just reported that the two main Jewish terrorist groups in Palestine, the Stern Gang and the Irgun, had both placed themselves at the disposal of the Haganah for a coordinated onslaught on the British. On the day after Truman's press conference, the British ambassador went to see Byrnes with a memorandum outlining Bevin's proposal, which he said the foreign secretary wanted to announce on 25 October. 'That is next Thursday,' the secretary of state spluttered. More importantly, it was twelve days before the New York mayoral election.[16]

For the next fortnight Bevin and Byrnes haggled over whether the Committee's remit would include a specific reference to Palestine. Bevin felt that to do so would preclude the consideration of other potential safe havens; Byrnes, with one eye on the New York election, insisted that it must. Fearing that Bevin might jump the gun and make an announcement before the poll had taken place, Byrnes withdrew his offer of involvement in the Committee altogether. It was only on the day after the election that Truman overruled his secretary of state's decision. His price for doing so was that Palestine must be the focus of the Committee's investigation. But he had now also accepted a reference that the Committee might also investigate the possibility that the refugees might go to other countries.

The terms of reference were not as Bevin wanted, but he was in no position to argue. On the night of 31 October, a chain of 150 coordinated attacks on the rail network across Palestine had killed four people and confirmed the accuracy of MI6's intelligence. A new, more violent era in the mandate had begun. Moreover, Attlee had by then arrived cap in hand in Washington to request a $3.75 billion loan from the United States that would enable the Labour government to fund its ambitious welfare state. The American government was insisting on tough terms, including the free convertibility of sterling for dollars by the summer of 1947. 'We are in Shylock's hands,' Bevin grumbled during a cabinet meeting. He would not make further efforts to rewrite the Committee's mandate, he explained, since he had no wish 'to make our political relations with the United States any worse'. And, at bottom, he had got what he had wanted. His announcement on 13 November in the House of Commons that the United States government had accepted his invitation to join the Committee was met by cheers.[17]

* * *

The twelve members of the Committee of Enquiry met in Washington in January 1946. The British party had a dreary respectability – three members of parliament, a judge, the economist of the Midland Bank and an expert on industrial disputes. Their American counterparts were more varied. Since no congressman dared get involved for fear of crossing the Zionist lobby their delegation comprised a Texan judge, a former head of the State Department, a newspaper editor, the former League of Nations High Commissioner for Refugees and a successful Californian lawyer. 'We had one common characteristic,' said one of the British MPs, Richard Crossman, 'a total ignorance of the subject.'[18]

After hearings in Washington, where the witnesses included Albert Einstein, and the British delegates felt like the accused at a show trial, and then in London, where the Americans correctly realised they were under surveillance, the Committee split and fanned out across continental Europe. Its members were all shocked by what they saw. When they reconvened in Vienna they discussed their shock at the prevalence of anti-Semitism. 'They all should be killed! We want none of them!' a German hotel porter had spat at the Californian lawyer, whose name was Bartley Crum. 'It's too bad this war didn't last another two or three months,' a red-faced British officer had told Crum and Crossman. 'They'd all have been done away with by then. We'd have had no problem.' The stories of the survivors they had met were no less appalling. Some had returned home – as Roosevelt had thought they would – only to find that every other member of their community had been wiped out. Some of these had then committed suicide. One young man produced a photograph of his school class. Out of the forty-three children in it, only the ten who went to Palestine had survived. The moral of that story was obvious.[19]

The Committee proceeded, via Cairo, to Palestine. 'This is Texas,' the American judge declared when he stepped off the train at Lydda, in the south of the country. The landscape reminded Crum of California. It was early spring. The Jews they met were happy and healthy; the Arabs visibly better off than their Egyptian cousins. And briefly there was peace. Apart from a raid on an arms depot, there were no significant attacks while the Committee was in Palestine because the Haganah, the Irgun and the Stern Gang had decided it was in their interests for there not to be. The tight security the British organised around the party then looked to the Americans like a theatrical charade.[20]

The seemingly pointless security reinforced Crum's growing conviction that the problem was not the Jewish but the British presence. The lawyer had been a friend of Willkie's and he had been re-reading his copy of Willkie's memoir of his 1942 mission, *One World*, in which Willkie quoted Henrietta Szold implying that the British were the root of the tension. In Washington Einstein had said exactly the same thing: Palestine's problems had been 'artificially created' by the British. If there were a 'really honest government for the people there which would get the Arabs and Jews together', the theoretical physicist insisted, then 'there would be nothing to fear'. Three weeks in Palestine left Crum convinced that Zionism would benefit the Arabs as well. Remove the British – whose alliance with the landowners held the Middle Eastern countries back – and there could be 'freedom and progress', he felt sure.[21]

One day Crum and another American member of the panel had a drink in La Régence, the basement bar of the King David Hotel, where they were staying in Jerusalem and which also housed the British administration up above. 'I felt like getting down on my knees before these people,' Crum's colleague admitted. 'I've always been proud of my own ancestors who made farms out of the virgin forest. But these people are raising crops out of rock!' During the hearings the Zionists worked this parallel hard. 'The leaky boats in which our refugees come to Palestine are their Mayflowers,' said Chaim Weizmann, 'the Mayflowers of a whole generation.' Crossman thought history explained a lot. While the Americans empathised with the Zionists as pioneers, the pro-Arabism of the majority of his British colleagues derived from 'our deepest national fear ... invasion by a foreign conqueror'. At the end of March 1946 the Committee repaired to Lausanne in Switzerland to write its report. The Irgun resumed hostilities with another spectacular attack on the railway system on 3 April.[22]

By now the Committee members' tempers were fraying. The Americans felt that Bevin had outwitted Truman. Under constant pressure from Washington they were determined to do no more than endorse their president's demand on immigration and avoid entangling their country further. That attitude exasperated their British counterparts, because it meant that the administration in Palestine would have to deal alone with the violence that the arrival of 100,000 Jewish immigrants was bound to cause.

On the other hand, the British Committee members knew that Bevin wanted unanimity: Crossman feared that disagreement might even lead the United States government to pull the all-important multi-billion dollar loan. They had also heard evidence in camera from senior British soldiers who now told them that it would be far more costly to impose a pro-Arab settlement than one that was pro-Jewish. This was the opposite of what the military had said a few months earlier but it was entirely plausible: a funeral for two Jews killed during an attack, which took place during their stay in Palestine, had attracted perhaps 60,000 mourners.

When it started to look like the Committee might have to produce two or three conflicting reports, the fear of an open split with the Americans drove the Committee's British members to compromise. In exchange for their acceptance of the proposal that 100,000 Jews be allowed entry into Palestine, the Americans agreed that the report should include a detailed statement of Jewish terrorism and a recommendation that the Jewish Agency resume cooperation with the British authorities, so that terrorism could be 'resolutely suppressed'. Together the Committee's members, hamstrung by their realisation that they would trigger violent upheaval if they endorsed partition, could only recommend that the mandate should continue, pending the involvement of the United Nations. It fell far short of the permanent solution that they had been asked to find.[23]

In London, the report went down extremely badly. Although Bevin defended his brainchild when it was discussed in Cabinet, even he admitted that it would be impossible to implement without American support, which he now proposed to ask for. The potential cost of continuing to police the mandate alone was astronomical. The chancellor – once a fervent pro-Zionist – estimated this at £100 million upfront and £5–10 million a year thereafter, at a time when the government was straining to cut military spending. 'We can't contemplate that,' was his verdict. Attlee agreed. The Committee had 'ignored everybody's responsibility but ours', he said. While he supported Bevin's effort to make the United States say what share of the financial burden she would take, he clearly did not expect the foreign secretary to succeed. 'The truth is', he told his cabinet, 'the United States wants her interests at our expense.'[24]

Attlee's pessimism was well founded. When the report was published on both sides of the Atlantic on 30 April 1946, Truman seized on its endorsement of his immigration proposal. 'The transfer of these unfortunate people should now be accomplished with the greatest dispatch,' he stated. But he refused to engage with the other recommendations that the British had insisted on, beyond saying they raised questions that merited 'careful study'.[25]

Annoyed by Truman's cherry-picking, on 1 May Attlee drew the House of Commons' attention to the section of the report the president had ignored and refused to accept the entry of so many immigrants until the illegal armies disbanded and surrendered their weapons. It was, he added pointedly, a process in which the Jewish Agency had an important part to play.[26]

* * *

The Jewish Agency had originally been established to represent the interests of the Jewish inhabitants of Palestine to the British mandate authorities. But by May 1946 it had long outgrown its advisory role and was behaving disconcertingly like a government-in-waiting, with an elected legislature, a council, executive departments and a semi-secret army of its own. Operating from a Bauhaus headquarters on George V Avenue in Jerusalem, it was a 'state within a state', the head of the British administration in Palestine said, when he appeared before the Committee of Enquiry. Another senior official told Crossman that the Agency was managing to purloin top-secret British documents the day after they were issued.[27]

Equally, the British were spying on the Agency. By the end of 1945 they had established that it was actively colluding with the terrorists. Intercepted telegrams, and their sources inside the organisation, showed that the Agency's executive had approved the railway attacks of 31 October and had responded positively to the overture made by the Irgun and the Stern Gang reported by MI6, reaching a working arrangement with both groups to 'assign tasks to them under our command'. The British found it telling that the head of the Agency, David Ben Gurion, refused to condemn the mounting violence in the mandate. In his testimony to the Committee of Enquiry Ben Gurion would only associate himself with Weizmann's disapproval of the recent attacks. He stuck to the line that any effort by the Agency to prevent terrorism would be 'rendered futile by the policy pursued by His Majesty's Government', which he blamed for 'the tragic situation created in the country'.[28]

For six months, the British high commissioner in Palestine had been asking his boss, the colonial secretary George Hall, for discretion to take action against the Agency and the Haganah, but each time his request had been rejected. His case was strengthened by the series of attacks that followed the Anglo-American Committee's departure. On 23 April 1946 the Irgun had attacked the police station at Ramat Gan, killing one policeman, but losing two of their own fighters – one killed, the other captured, badly wounded. Not to be outdone, the Stern gang attacked the Sixth Airborne Division's vehicle park in Tel Aviv two days later after dark, killing seven soldiers, two of whom were asleep in a tent. The following night the paras retaliated, going on the rampage in the two nearby towns, vandalising houses and beating up Jews they came across. The reprisals would have been worse had not some senior officers got wind of what was being plotted and confined other troops to barracks. On a visit to London in mid-May the general in command of British forces in Palestine warned that his men were approaching breaking point and that, in the event of further terrorist attacks, it might be impossible to restrain them.

The final straw came on 18 June. After two members of the Irgun were sentenced to death for their roles in an attack, the Irgun kidnapped five British officers while they were having lunch in their club in Tel Aviv. A sixth was lifted shortly afterwards in Jerusalem on George V Avenue – the same street on which the Jewish Agency was situated. The potential fate of the six hostages was clear. Unless the death sentences were commuted by the British, the Irgun said, 'We shall answer gallows with gallows.'[29]

After the high commissioner appealed, yet again, for discretionary powers, the colonial secretary George Hall interviewed the head of the Jewish Agency, David Ben Gurion, who was in London at the time. Although the Jewish leader denied any association with the Stern Gang and the Irgun, he was evasive when Hall asked him about the Agency's relationship to the Haganah. Hall's account of this conversation, in cabinet the following day, finally convinced his colleagues to grant the high commissioner the power to raid the Agency. The new chief of the imperial general staff, Bernard Montgomery, whose 'almost fanatical personality' had so impressed Willkie four years earlier, put it more strongly following his appointment a few days later. 'Now that the Jews have flung the gauntlet in our face, they must be utterly and completely defeated and their illegal organisations smashed forever.'[30]

The British launched Operation Agatha at dawn on Saturday 29 June, descending on the Jewish Agency and the homes of its executives and known members of the Haganah and its elite Palmach commando unit, early on the Sabbath. They carted away three truckloads of documents from the Agency and made nearly 3,000 arrests, which included almost half of the Palmach's strength. Simultaneous searches of Jewish settlements yielded a few hundred rifles, nearly half a million rounds of ammunition and thousands of grenades and mortar bombs. 'What we need is gas chambers,' yelled British troops involved in these sweeps when they were taunted by Jewish settlers. Jews returning to raided buildings found swastikas and graffiti like 'Death to the Jews' daubed on their walls. The Sixth Airborne Division's report admitted that the operation had 'lost us what friends amongst the Jews we still had', but it hoped the split would only be temporary. In fact it proved to be permanent.[31]

Truman's swift criticism of the raid put the onus on Attlee to justify what he had done. The operation had come at an awkward moment: Congress was due within days to debate whether it should grant the British loan, and the vote was expected to be tight. With newspapers speculating that some representatives might be swayed by Britain's conduct in Palestine, Attlee's hand was forced. Facing criticism during a late night debate on the conduct of the operation, the prime minister decided to reveal that 'We have evidence – I will produce the evidence in due course – of a very close link up between the Jewish Agency and the Haganah. We also have evidence of the close connexion between the Haganah and the Irgun.'[32]

Attlee's revelation had an appalling, unintended consequence. Worried about precisely what the British had found out, and believing that it might still be possible to destroy the evidence, the head of the Haganah ordered the Irgun's leader, Menachem Begin, to bomb the King David Hotel, which housed the headquarters of the British administration and where, he assumed, the paperwork seized on 29 June was being analysed. Begin – a future Israeli prime minister – had been planning such an operation for months. On 22 July seven Irgun members, disguised as Arab milkmen, managed to get through the hotel's security. They wheeled milk churns containing a quarter of a ton of high explosive into La Régence, the basement nightclub where Bartley Crum and his colleague had sat praising the Jews' pioneering spirit four months earlier, then shot their way out of the hotel, escaping in a getaway car parked round the corner. The explosion of a second, much smaller bomb across the street from the hotel diverted the arriving security forces, and – according to the Irgun – telephone warnings were ignored. The main bomb went off at 12.37 p.m. 'First there was a great explosion,' said one eyewitness. 'Then the south-western corner of the hotel seemed to bulge. It collapsed with a great roar and a huge column of brown-gray smoke billowed up.' Ninety-one people were killed and another fifty-three were injured. 'Bombed Hotel Property of New York Corporation', the following morning's *New York Times* also informed its readers.[33]

The head of Britain's administration in Palestine, the chief secretary, narrowly survived the blast. 'I lost nearly 100 of my best officers and old friends,' he wrote to Crossman a fortnight afterwards. 'I have been in Palestine off and on for 11 years: these people meant a lot to me, not only the British officers by any means, but also the loyal and faithful Palestinians including several Jews. My own police escort had been my inseparable companion and friend for 20 months, my own Armenian chauffeur and many other humble persons of this type were among the dead. I helped to dig out their stinking putrefying bodies and I attended about 14 funerals in 3 days.'[34]

'A large proportion of my staff are dead, missing or wounded,' the colonial secretary, George Hall, reported to his colleagues the day after the bombing. Irgun had dealt the British administration a near-fatal blow. They next turned their attentions to destroying any possibility of an Anglo-American initiative and with it, British hopes of clinging on in Palestine.[35]

FIGHT FOR PALESTINE

On 29 July 1946, a week after the bombing of the King David Hotel, a group called the American League for a Free Palestine directly challenged Truman in an open letter published in the *New York Post*. Since the president had asked Attlee to let 100,000 Jews into Palestine, it observed, a year had passed, without result. 'The million and a half Hebrews in Europe are waiting in blood-soaked ghettoes, in DP camps, on the highways and in the seaports. They are waiting for a sign from the United States, from you, Mr President, that they are not being abandoned but given the fundamental right to live in dignity and freedom.'[1]

The League, which had been set up by a man calling himself Peter Bergson, threw down the gauntlet, partly because it scented blood. By then Truman's presidency was in trouble. Unemployment was up, wages were down and demobilisation was running late. With the mid-term elections just three months away Truman's Republican opponents had boiled their message down to just two words. 'Had Enough?' their posters asked.

The League's provocative open letter played on a growing view that Truman was lacking drive. As it insinuated, since the Anglo-American Committee reported in April, the president had got nowhere with his demand that Britain accept 100,000 Jews into the mandate. Attlee had made it clear that he would only implement the Committee's recommendations if the clandestine Jewish groups operating in Palestine disarmed. Truman had then acquiesced when Attlee insisted that the questions the report had raised first be discussed and resolved by a panel of British and American experts.

The outcome, which was named after the British and American leaders of these experts, was the Morrison–Grady proposal. It envisaged that the United Nations should be the trustee of a federal state comprising Arab and Jewish provinces but it was dealt a fatal blow when it was leaked to the *New York Times* by Grady's staff, who did not like it. On 26 July that newspaper reported that the plan 'would vest strong powers in a British-controlled central government, leaving very little autonomy to the separate Arab and Zionist provinces', and a day later, that it involved a grant of $50 million to the Arabs to ensure the viability of their state. The American League's advertisement in the *New York Post* appeared two days after that.[2]

There was a further crucial reason why the American League for a Free Palestine decided to intervene at just this moment. The day after the King David Hotel bombing, Truman had issued a forthright statement, calling on 'every responsible Jewish leader' to join him 'in condemning the wanton slaying of human beings'. He also warned that the outrage 'might well retard' Jewish immigration into Palestine. The League had every reason to worry that the attack might have backfired and to want to change the subject. For it was a front for the Irgun, the terror group behind the bombing. 'Peter Bergson' was a pseudonym. The real name of the League's organiser was Hillel Kook.[3]

* * *

The nephew of the chief rabbi in Palestine, Kook had joined the Irgun in the 1930s and then come to the United States in 1940. His reason for doing so was simple. Like David Ben Gurion, he had decided that the country was key to the fulfilment of Zionist ambitions, partly because of her 5 million-strong Jewish population, partly because of the influence the US government might wield over the British as their lender of last resort. Having decided that American Zionists were failing to promote Jewish interests forcefully enough, he embarked on a series of single-issue campaigns, which were designed to win American support for Zionism by espousing issues that no one could easily oppose. He was the man behind the idea of a Jewish Army, then an Emergency Committee to save the Jews of Europe, and finally the American League for a Free Palestine, which he intended to help turn Palestine into an independent Jewish state. The aim of the League, which reflected the hardening of attitudes among Zionists in the United States and Palestine, was to generate sympathy and funds for the Irgun by comparing the Zionists' struggle against the British with the Americans' own war for independence 150 years earlier. 'As a nation born in revolution against the same brand of Britannic despotism, we know that no matter how hard and bitter the struggle, it is the Hebrew David that will beat the British Goliath,' predicted another advert paid for by the League. Kook preferred the word 'Hebrew' to 'Jew' or 'Jewish', believing that it avoided stirring anti-Semitism and resonated with Protestant Americans, who saw it as their duty to help the Israelites regain the Promised Land.[4]

Kook's genius was his ability to attract heavyweight endorsement for each of these campaigns. To put pressure on the Roosevelt administration, at the end of 1943 he had persuaded Guy Gillette to introduce a resolution calling on the US government to establish a specific agency to help Jewish refugees. Tall, white-haired and impeccably dressed, Gillette was every bit the elder statesman, and a significant catch. An isolationist with a Jewish wife, who had tried to sign up to fight for the Boers against the British in South Africa in his youth, he sat on the Senate's Foreign Relations Committee. When his proposal attracted wide support – from Truman among others – Roosevelt was obliged to establish the War Refugee Board in early 1944. After Gillette then lost his Iowa seat in the elections later that year, he accepted Kook's invitation to serve as the American League for a Free Palestine's president. It was for this reason that Truman had given him the details of his demand of Attlee in September 1945, and encouraged him to spread the news.

When late that year the Anglo-American Committee of Enquiry was established, the American League suspected a stitch-up and set up a shadow body to call for the end of the British mandate and the creation of an independent Palestinian state. Theatrically, it then mandated Gillette to go to Palestine 'to secure agreement between the Hebrew and non-Hebrew inhabitants who are kept apart artificially by the British Colonial Office'.[5]

Not surprisingly, the last thing the British wanted was Gillette in Palestine at the same time as the Committee, and in the spring of 1946 they thwarted his attempt to visit. It was only in the chaotic aftermath of the King David Hotel bombing – which the former senator blamed on 'the same hand that writes British policy in Palestine' – that he managed to slip into the country, landing on 27 July. On his arrival in Jerusalem, suitcase in hand, he went straight to survey the Irgun's handiwork, hitching a ride back to his hotel aboard a lorry used for carrying debris away from the bombsite.[6]

Gillette arrived the day after the leaked details of the Morrison–Grady plan for a federal state in Palestine hit the press. Worried that the British might exploit sympathy following the bombing to impose the plan regardless of American opinion, he wanted to do his utmost to torpedo the initiative, which offered the Jews an even smaller state than the original partition plan had mooted in 1937. Despite British opposition to his presence, a few days after his arrival he nevertheless secured a meeting with the High Commissioner who was clearly unable to resist the opportunity to give him a dressing-down. This meeting only enhanced Gillette's credibility. Afterwards the American sent a telegram to Truman. In it he declared that 'the proposal of a federal state in Palestine will have the effect of turning this nation from an independent state under temporary mandate into a province of the British Empire'.[7]

The American League could claim a victory when it emerged days later that Truman rejected the Morrison–Grady proposal, but in fact the president had already made up his mind. On 30 July, the day after the League's provocative open letter appeared in the *New York Post*, he had held a cabinet meeting at which he said that he was abandoning the initiative. Gesturing to a 4in-thick wodge of telegrams from Zionists attacking the Morrison-Grady proposal, he commented, 'Jesus Christ couldn't please them when he was here on earth, so how could anyone expect that I would have any luck?'[8]

* * *

The fortnight-long visit furnished Gillette with plenty of ammunition that he could use on his return to the US. Although the British had denied his request to meet convicted Jewish terrorists in prison, and close surveillance prevented him from meeting the leaders of the Irgun, he saw in Haifa harbour the vessels used by the British to deport arriving illegal immigrants to Cyprus. Decrying them as 'slave ships', he wrote in a press release, 'The African ships I read about as a boy were something I would not believe to be repeated in the 20th century.'[9]

On his return home Gillette flew to address the League's West Coast branch in Los Angeles, spoke on the radio in Chicago, and addressed further public meetings in Philadelphia and New York.

Gillette's visit to Los Angeles reflected Kook's success in wooing support from showbusiness. In September 1946, Kook moved to exploit these connections, when the American League premièred a new play on Broadway. Written by Ben Hecht, with music by Kurt Weill, and supported by a sponsoring committee that included Eleanor Roosevelt, Leonard Bernstein and the mayor of New York (whose electoral prospects had so worried Truman the previous autumn), *A Flag Is Born* told the story of three concentration camp survivors – an elderly couple and a young man, David, played by a promising young actor named Marlon Brando – who were trying to reach Palestine. When the couple die, and David considers suicide, three soldiers appear on the stage, representing the Irgun, the Haganah and the Stern Gang. Telling him that 'We speak . . . the language of guns', the soldiers promise to 'wrest our homeland out of British claws as the Americans once did . . . Come David, and fight for Palestine.' Hecht admitted the play was 'pure and unabashed propaganda for a race that I feel has been disenfranchised'. It ran for fourteen weeks in New York before touring a series of American cities with large Jewish populations.[10]

With no sign that a deal between Truman and Attlee would be forthcoming, the play's purpose was to raise funds to transport Jewish refugees illegally to Palestine – it raised about $400,000 in total for this cause. Some of this money went towards the purchase of a ship, dubbed the SS *Ben Hecht*, which set out for France in late December. The souvenir programme, a copy of which reached the British security service, MI5, hinted that the box office receipts bought something else. Besides a cover that compared Jewish pioneers in Palestine to American revolutionaries in 1776, it featured the emblem of the Irgun – a clenched fist brandishing a rifle, over a map of Palestine and Transjordan.[11]

As Kook intended, *A Flag Is Born* helped keep Palestine on the agenda throughout the 1946 mid-term election campaign. When the Democrats got wind that the Republican governor of New York State, Thomas Dewey, was going to announce his support for Jewish immigration to Palestine on 6 October, they panicked. Although Dewey was only repeating a call he had made three years earlier, he was Truman's most likely challenger in the 1948 presidential election and one of Truman's advisers urged the president to outbid him. On 4 October – the eve of Yom Kippur and two days before Dewey's planned statement – Truman did so, calling for the creation of a 'viable Jewish state'. Dewey upped the ante two days later, with a demand that 'hundreds of thousands' be let into Palestine. After Dewey was resoundingly returned, Truman would claim that the timing of his own declaration had nothing whatsoever to do with the poll. A few months later Bevin would reveal that the State Department had told him that there was no question that the president had been trying to outdo his rival. The British foreign secretary drew cheers in the House of Commons – and a rebuke from Truman – when he explained that 'in international relations he could not settle things if his problem were made the subject of local elections'.[12]

* * *

One reason for Bevin's tetchiness was that, by the start of 1947, it was clear that his strategy to preserve British influence in the Middle East was fast unravelling. The foreign secretary had hoped that successful talks with the Egyptians would generate goodwill in the Arab world, enabling him to close the Suez base and transfer it to the east side of the Suez Canal once he had reached an advantageous settlement in Palestine. But the talks with the Egyptian government collapsed in January following a disagreement over the future status of Sudan, which Egypt claimed but Britain wanted to continue to administer. And the idea that the Jews would tolerate a long-term British presence in Palestine was looking wildly optimistic as well.

After trying a more lenient approach in the aftermath of the King David Hotel bombing, and abandoning it when the Irgun resumed its campaign of murder in the autumn of 1946, Attlee was pressured by his chief military adviser, Montgomery, into agreeing to take 'more robust action' at a cabinet meeting in mid-January 1947. Exactly what this meant was demonstrated on 24 January when the High Commissioner confirmed a death sentence passed earlier that month, on the man wounded and captured during the Ramat Gan police attack the previous summer. Dov Gruner was supposed to be hanged for his role in the attack, in four days' time.[13]

Gruner was an extraordinary man to make an example of, for he had joined and fought for the British army during the war. The Irgun responded immediately and effectively, by kidnapping a British judge, Ralph Windham, while he was sitting in his courtroom in Tel Aviv hearing a 'rather boring' case. Facing Windham's inevitable murder if they proceeded with Gruner's hanging, the British authorities caved in. The High Commissioner granted a stay of execution giving Gruner more time to consider an appeal to the Privy Council in London – something the condemned man had so far refused to do. In private he then threatened the mayor of Tel Aviv and senior executives from the Jewish Agency that martial law would be imposed if they did not do their utmost to secure the judge's release. The Irgun released Windham unharmed the same evening.[14]

While Gruner waited in the condemned cell, in London the government flailed around for a new plan. 'We still have to find a means of holding the Middle East,' Bevin told the cabinet in February as he set out yet another proposal designed to achieve that end. But his idea – that Britain should now seek to rule a bi-national Palestine for another five years as a trustee of the United Nations – was immediately rejected by Ben Gurion. The onset of a cruel winter in Britain and a coal shortage compounded the sense of crisis. A week later, Bevin returned to Downing Street to recommend that the government refer the entire issue to the United Nations. In parliament on 18 February he announced that, as there was 'no prospect of resolving this conflict by any settlement negotiated between the parties', and the mandate gave Britain no right to impose an arbitrary settlement, the only course of action open to the government was 'to submit the problem to the judgment of the United Nations'. Britain would set out the problem, but it would not offer a solution. The United Nations constituted a Special Committee on Palestine, which would head for Jerusalem in mid-May with instructions to report back with its findings before the UN's general assembly reconvened in the autumn.[15]

* * *

With hindsight, Bevin's announcement marked the beginning of the end of Britain's rule in Palestine. But that was not what the foreign secretary intended at the time. Believing that the Jews thought he was bluffing when he had said he would refer the question to the UN, he now did as he had threatened in an attempt to draw them back to the negotiating table. As he told the cabinet, with a hint of satisfaction, on 15 February, since his announcement the Zionists had been 'running after us' and wanted to find a modus vivendi, because they wanted to avoid the uncertainty that the UN's involvement would inevitably bring. He hoped that this uncertainty would whet the Zionists' appetite for a settlement.[16]

Days later the colonial secretary made the government's tactics clearer. Britain was 'not going to the United Nations to surrender the Mandate', he explained in parliament. 'We are going to the United Nations setting out the problem and asking for their advice as to how the Mandate can be administered. If the Mandate cannot be administered in its present form we are asking how it can be amended.' The Irgun certainly understood his implication. Four days later they bombed the British Officers' Club in Jerusalem, across the road from the Jewish Agency and inside the supposedly secure zone the British army had expanded after the King David Hotel bombing. Thirteen people died, while sixteen more were injured.[17]

The location of the latest bombing showed that the British were losing the battle. Terrorism was now out of hand; so too was illegal immigration. Thanks to fundraising by organisations like Kook's American League, Jewish immigrants were now coming to Palestine in bigger, faster ships. By the end of 1946 British intelligence had identified twenty vessels that were ready to transport refugees from European ports, and a later assessment stated that nearly twenty more were probably being prepared to make the same journey.[18]

During the war the British had been able to board and take over any ship they wanted to. But in peacetime international maritime law prevailed, which meant that they could only board the ships within Palestine's territorial waters. In 1947 these stretched just 3 miles offshore – a distance that a ship capable of twenty knots could cover in just nine minutes. That left the Royal Navy, which was responsible for patrolling the coast, in the position of a goalkeeper trying to save a penalty.

After the colonial secretary said that the time had come to 'try other means' to defend the Palestinian coast, Britain's secret intelligence service, MI6, proposed a range of measures to deter immigrants from setting sail in the first place. In February Bevin approved the sabotage, in port, of ships being readied to take Jewish émigrés to Palestine, the contamination of ships' water and food supplies, and a whispering campaign 'to make the flesh of prospective sailors creep' by attributing ships attacked in this way to 'some powerful Arab underground organisation'. Five ships were attacked in this way.[19]

Despite the odds, the Royal Navy still managed to stop many other ships before they reached Palestine. One of them was the *Ben Hecht* – the ship *A Flag Is Born* had paid for. In March she was intercepted off Palestine, flying the Honduran flag and claiming rather implausibly to be bound for Chile. Her passengers were interned on Cyprus and the crew were jailed. Rather than face trial they were eventually deported, after the American League helped the mother of the ship's radio operator lobby congressmen in Washington.

Meanwhile British policy seesawed. After the British Officers' Club attack the High Commissioner imposed martial law across the country. The Irgun, convinced that Britain's aim was to demonstrate her control over Palestine in order to persuade the UN that she should be formally recognised as ruler of the country, retaliated. Following nearly thirty attacks, in which three more people died and scores more were injured, the High Commissioner performed a U-turn after just a fortnight. Although in London there was consternation at the signals that this move would send, the cabinet quickly realised that the volte-face was the right course of action. Martial law only alienated the very Jews without whom they had no chance of defeating the insurgency. The trouble, as Attlee observed, had not been the lifting of the state of emergency, but its imposition in the first place, which was 'not thought out by people on the spot'.[20]

Ironically the end of martial law led the British to take their most draconian step yet, because the civil legal process resumed. As a consequence, without warning, on 16 April, Dov Gruner was hanged in Acre prison. 'It was a sneak murder,' the American League for a Free Palestine declared, in an advertisement it published the same week, inviting readers to 'Build Dov Gruner's Memorial' by donating to its 'Palestine

Freedom Drive'. '$7,500,000 applied now in the right places will win the battle for Palestine . . . This victory will not depend on charity or upon editorial praise in the world's press. It will be won by Hebrews fighting with their blood and courage . . . and your dollars.' Protestors invaded the British consulate in New York and, at a Manhattan rally, a rabbi – who opposed the Irgun – dubbed Gruner 'another Nathan Hale'.[21]

Following the publication of another incendiary advertisement written by Ben Hecht praising the achievements of the 'terrorists of Palestine', the British protested. The permanent secretary at the Foreign Office called in the American ambassador, and apparently 'begged' the US government to stop claiming that there was nothing it could do to stop what amounted to incitement. Britain's complaint made the front page of the *New York Times*, which gave Hecht even more publicity. Although Truman did issue an appeal in June, urging US citizens to 'refrain . . . from engaging in or facilitating any activities which tend further to inflame the passions of the inhabitants of Palestine', the American League said that it would ignore his call, and the US government admitted it could do nothing. Although it had censored a promotional film produced by the Irgun, it could not stop the press advertisements and would not withdraw the charitable status of groups like the American League, which exempted them from paying tax, for fear of triggering an uproar.[22]

This inertia enabled the fundraising to continue. Indeed, in New York senior officials were actually helping the groups raise money. A woman who worked in the city's Public Solicitations Division informed a British diplomat that 'higher ups' frequently 'stretched the regulations to enable Jewish groups to have more collection days, and also reserved dates long in advance for favoured groups'. In the Bronx, Zionist fundraisers pressed residents for donations to buy weapons, chalking swastikas on the doors of those who would not give. 'The Irgun . . . received most of its financial backing from this country', a CIA officer would eventually admit, in 1948.[23]

Having already done profound damage to their reputation in the United States by executing Dov Gruner, the British alienated their remaining American sympathisers soon afterwards. On 12 July 1947 a ship named the *Exodus* set out from Marseille for Palestine. A former pleasure steamer that had once plied the Chesapeake Bay, the vessel had been bought by the Haganah, which upgraded her engine to give her the best chance of outrunning the British coastal patrols. Aboard were more than 4,500 passengers including a disproportionate number of pregnant women, mothers with young children, the old and sick. They had been selected quite deliberately by the Haganah, which knew how much outrage their treatment would generate when the British tried to repel them, which was precisely what then happened.

After MI6 saboteurs aboard a yacht shadowing the *Exodus* were denied permission by London to mine the vessel, on 17 July two British destroyers rammed the steamer while she was still in international waters. With the captain radioing a running commentary to sympathisers on the shore, British sailors boarded in order to take control of the ship, killing the American first mate and two passengers in the process; the destroyers then towed the now listing vessel into port. As there was no longer any space in the internment camp on Cyprus where the British had previously housed illegal immigrants, the British government had decided to resort to the old practice of 'refoulement', or return to origin. The passengers were disembarked by armed British soldiers at Haifa and made to board three ships waiting to take them back to France. They 'looked as though they had been through a major battle,' reported an American newspaper correspondent.[24]

By now the UN Special Committee was in Palestine. Tipped off by the Haganah and the Jewish Agency, its chairman and a colleague made it to the quayside in time to witness this episode. The sight of mothers and children being frogmarched off the vessel had a profound impact on both men, reinforcing their impression that the British had entirely lost their way.

By then the members of the commission had been in Palestine a month. When they arrived, the papers were full of an extraordinary scandal – a British soldier, Roy Farran, had been charged with the murder of a schoolboy he had found pasting up Stern gang propaganda. The British had also just sentenced three more members of the Irgun to death. When the commissioners appealed for clemency, the British told them not to interfere. The three executions took place on 29 July, just after the Commission's departure.

Irgun again retaliated in kind. Just as with Judge Windham, after the death sentences were confirmed they kidnapped two British sergeants working in military intelligence, while they were meeting a contact. Unlike Windham, however, neither man was released. Instead, on the day after the executions, the group issued a communiqué parodying British legal jargon, announcing that both had been found guilty of illegal entry into the country and illegal possession of firearms, and had been hanged. The sergeants' bodies were discovered dangling in a eucalyptus grove the next day, their 'sentences' pinned through their clothing into their flesh. The *Daily Express* put a picture of this scene on its front page beneath the headline: 'HANGED BRITONS: PICTURE THAT WILL SHOCK THE WORLD'. That prediction proved wide of the mark. While the newspaper's reporting of the murders helped cause anti-Semitic rioting in more than a dozen towns and cities in Britain that summer, in the United States it was the news of the British reprisals, rather than the appalling fate of the two men – who had spent nearly a fortnight imprisoned in an underground oubliette before being lynched – that led the coverage.

In the meantime, the three ships carrying the *Exodus*'s passengers had reached France. Only thirty-one of those aboard accepted an invitation from the French to disembark. The rest ignored a British threat that they would be shipped to Germany if they did not do so. The three ships left France on 23 August, bound for Hamburg. There, 1,000 British troops used fire hoses, truncheons and tear gas to remove the passengers from the ships, while a tannoy blasted out loud music to try to drown out their shouts of protest.

The violent scenes confirmed what most members of the UN Special Committee had already decided, that the mandate should be ended as quickly as possible, and Palestine split into separate Arab and Jewish states after a transitional period. Before the UN's general assembly could debate this proposal, however, the British government jumped the gun.

Attlee's view was that UNSCOP's proposal was unfair on the Arabs and unworkable, and his colleague Hugh Dalton was alarmed at the anti-Semitic rioting that summer. The United States' willingness to underwrite a settlement was conspicuously lacking, and it was now clear that Palestine was useless as a base. At the United Nations, on 26 September 1947 the colonial secretary announced that, if the UN pressed ahead with a proposal that did not have Arab and Jewish backing, Britain would withdraw from Palestine unilaterally the following

May, leaving 'some alternative authority' to implement the decision. The government was unwilling to be left holding the fort during what would surely be a bloody process.[25]

The partition proposal, which needed a two-thirds majority to be carried as a resolution, was debated that November at the United Nations general assembly in New York. By now the Zionists had accepted that, for the time being, this was as good an outcome as they were going to get. But a vote in favour of partition was by no means a foregone conclusion.

Once the debate was under way, and as it became clear that partition could not yet command a large enough majority to ensure the resolution passed, one man leapt into action. Bernard Baruch was the American ambassador to the UN's Atomic Energy Commission, a tall, imposing and extremely wealthy stockbroker who had effectively bought his diplomatic role by helping to bankroll successive Democratic presidential candidates since Woodrow Wilson. He was rightly regarded as a financial wizard. It was he who devised the 'cash and carry' scheme that had enabled Roosevelt to help Churchill before Lend-Lease, and who advocated the development of the synthetic rubber industry that had caused such friction between the British and the Americans in the Middle East.

Less well known was Baruch's support for the Irgun through the American League for a Free Palestine. At a time when others had started to dissociate themselves from the League because of its controversial advertisements, Baruch sought out their author, Ben Hecht. 'I am on your side,' he told the playwright. 'Think of me as one of your Jewish fighters in the tall grass with a long gun.'[26]

About 26 November, while the partition resolution debate was taking place, Baruch paid a visit to the French ambassador to the United Nations and warned him that France's failure to support the resolution would put at risk money that the United States was intending to use to finance the country's reconstruction. The French had been wobbling and the pressure worked. On 29 November France cast her vote in favour of partition. So too did France's neighbours, Belgium, Luxembourg and the Netherlands, with the result that the partition motion was narrowly carried.

Truman afterwards admitted that he had been subjected to a 'constant barrage' from 'a few of the extreme Zionist leaders' who had suggested 'that we pressure sovereign nations into favorable votes in the General Assembly'. But he denied that he had succumbed to this pressure or tried to coerce other nations before the vote. 'I have never approved of the practice of the strong imposing their will on the weak,' he claimed piously. The activity of Baruch contradicts his claim. Either the president was lying or else he did not know what his own ambassador was up to.[27]

* * *

Britain's abrupt decision to wash her hands of the problem and the mounting violence in Palestine alarmed the US government. Worried that a war might draw Soviet troops into the Middle East under United Nations auspices, on 20 March 1948 the new secretary of state George Marshall made one last appeal to the British to stay put, saying that the United States would now support ongoing British control as the UN's trustee.

Marshall's intention was to try to stop the Soviets from gaining influence in Palestine, but Bevin, still livid at how the issue had become a football in American politics, was unmoved. The Americans, he told his cabinet colleagues two days later, were 'now seeing what they should have seen before they supported Partition ... This comes from allowing US electoral needs to influence US foreign policy.' He said he now expected the Jews to carve out a state, and their neighbour, King Abdullah of Jordan, to occupy those parts of Palestine the Zionists could not hold. 'I don't think we should use British troops to check this development of events,' he told his colleagues on the day they washed their hands of the problem. 'Nature may partition Palestine.'[28]

Britain had arrived in Palestine in 1917, promising a 'new order'. Three decades later, on 14 May 1948, they left, just as they had threatened to; the first Arab–Israeli war started the next day. The Israelis declared their state, which Truman promptly recognised. Abdullah seized the land in the West Bank that he coveted; while Egypt, Syria and Iraq now tried and failed miserably to drive the Jews into the sea. When an armistice finally prevailed, nearly a year later, Israel and Jordan were the winners. The losers were the Palestinians, who were scattered to the four winds.

PART TWO

Important Concessions

1947–53

8

EGGS IN ONE BASKET

In early 1947, as Ernest Bevin realised that his Middle Eastern strategy was disintegrating around him, he started to take an interest in the prospects of another man, whose connection to the British went back more than thirty years.

Britain's relationship with King Abdullah of Jordan had begun inauspiciously. In February 1914, while passing through Cairo, Abdullah had asked if the British might supply his family, the Hashemites, with arms so that they could revolt against the Turks. But at that moment the British were still jockeying with the Germans for Turkish friendship and said no.

When Turkey then sided with Germany after the outbreak of the First World War, and her sultan called on Muslims across the British Empire to rise up against their masters, the British reconsidered Abdullah's offer. In particular, the Hashemites' status – Abdullah's father, Sharif Hussein, ruled Mecca, and he and his scions were direct descendants of Muhammad – led them to wonder whether a revolt at the axis of the Islamic world might help blunt the sultan's call to jihad. After they had made Hussein a generous but deliberately vague promise of a post-war empire that encompassed the Arabian peninsula and territory as far north as modern Syria's border with Turkey, the sharif rose up against the Ottomans in 1916. The alliance, although it had its ups and downs, had lasted ever since.

Short, regal and mischievous, Abdullah would play little part in the revolt. Portrayed by T. E. Lawrence as utterly unreliable, he was sidelined by the British in favour of his more pliant younger brother Feisal.

It was only once the war was over that the British had to start taking him seriously. When the French threw Feisal out of Syria and Abdullah moved menacingly into the eastern part of Britain's new Palestine mandate towards the territory his brother had just lost, Churchill – then responsible for Britain's new Middle Eastern mandates – hurriedly made him emir of Transjordan to defuse the danger of a conflict with the French. It was initially a temporary arrangement, but Abdullah went on to rule Transjordan as a British client for the next twenty-five years. On his behalf the British set up and paid for an Arab Legion – a 12,000-strong British-officered force – that made him the most formidable ruler in the region.

Neither a kingdom nor an army distracted Abdullah from his original quest, however. By the time Jordan gained her independence in March 1946 and French rule in the Levant was coming to an end, he was already sounding out the Jewish Agency in private about taking over Syria, and he was soon speaking openly about his ambition. 'There is neither great nor little Syria,' he told an Egyptian newspaper that summer, 'there is only a single country bounded to the west by the sea, to the north by Turkey, to the east by Iraq and to the south by the Hijaz – which constitutes Syria.' It was abundantly clear that he wanted to rule it.[1]

* * *

Whereas Eden never thought much of the 'Greater Syria' idea that Lord Moyne had championed in the war, by early 1947 Bevin no longer had the luxury of choice. As his Middle Eastern strategy disintegrated around him, so the appeal of backing King Abdullah grew. As Churchill had once observed, the new king was the only Arab ruler who had been loyal to the British throughout the war. The British continued to wield considerable influence in Jordan. Not only had they extracted ongoing military base rights as the quid pro quo for independence, but they were paying Abdullah a stipend and financing the Arab Legion. In private British officials in London began calling Abdullah 'Mr Bevin's little king'.

In Jordan, on the spot, Abdullah's most trusted British adviser was the British ambassador, Alec Kirkbride, who had fought alongside Lawrence during the Arab revolt, and whom the king had known for more than a quarter of a century. When, towards the end of 1946, Kirkbride began arguing that the new state of Jordan would need to absorb the Arab parts of Palestine in order to survive, Bevin paid attention. In January 1947, shortly before announcing that he was referring the problem of Palestine to the United Nations, the foreign secretary told his colleagues during a cabinet meeting that, since Arab Palestine would be unviable on its own, the British government 'might explore [its] fusion with other Arab States'. From then on the British government would tacitly support Abdullah's expansive ambitions. As Kirkbride put it in a communication back to London, 'Britain is putting all its eggs in one basket since all the other baskets are unwilling to accommodate our eggs.'[2]

* * *

Although these discussions supposedly took place in private, within days of Bevin's suggestion to the cabinet the Truman administration was being lobbied to oppose 'hostile' British activities by Ibn Saud's son Prince Saud. In Washington on a begging mission, Saud got relatively short shrift from the then secretary of state, James Byrnes, who said that he had seen no evidence to corroborate the prince's allegation. When, however, Byrnes resigned days later, and George Marshall succeeded him, Ibn Saud tried again. In February the king claimed he now knew that the British were planning to help Abdullah take over Syria. Marshall took a less sanguine view than his predecessor. On 14 February he decided that, in view of a 'marked recrudescence' of press and intelligence reports suggesting that something was 'definitely in the wind regarding the Greater Syria project', and rumours that the plan was inspired or encouraged by British diplomats or spies, it was time to ask the British government to clarify its position.[3]

The British response was non-committal. Although the head of the Near East department in the Foreign Office flatly denied that either British diplomats or agents were aiding or abetting Abdullah when American officials went to see him, they were clearly not convinced. In their record of the meeting they put quotation marks around his claim that his department had reminded 'every British official in the Middle East the Foreign Office could think of' of the government's equivocal position – that it was 'neither for nor against Greater Syria'. Marshall was not impressed either, and authorised his envoys in London to tell the British to rein Abdullah in because of the disruptive effect that the rumours were having in the Arab world.

Yet, even under this additional pressure, the British refused to come out against Abdullah's project. The temperature rose further when, in April, the Jordanian king signed a treaty of alliance and brotherhood with Iraq and then issued a 300-page 'white paper' which insisted that his campaign to unite Jordan, Palestine and Syria was 'guided not by private ambition but by Arab national aspiration'. Abdullah's immediate aim was simple: to influence the domestic political agenda in Syria, where elections would take place in June.[4]

* * *

What made Marshall so alarmed was that Abdullah and his British sponsors might jeopardise a vital project that was hanging in the balance: the construction of an oil pipeline from Saudi Arabia to the Mediterranean coast, known as the TAPLINE. Born from the wreckage of the US government's attempt to nationalise Aramco in 1944, and designed from the outset to needle the British to agree to talks about the oil market, it was only recently that the Americans had made real progress on the project. In March 1947, with the help of the State Department, Aramco had finally managed to dismantle the Red Line Agreement, freeing the two American shareholders in the rival Iraq Petroleum Company to invest $200 million in the 1,000-mile-long pipeline. After much wrangling, the company had agreed a route running from Saudi Arabia, through Jordan and Syria to Lebanon. It had already agreed to pay each of the Jordanian and Lebanese governments an annual royalty in exchange for the necessary way leaves. All that there remained to do was to win the Syrian government's approval.

The TAPLINE would save Aramco millions of dollars that it currently spent on tankers and Suez Canal tolls. But it was of vast strategic importance to the United States government as well. By making Saudi oil cheaper than American oil in Europe, the pipe would ensure that the Saudis would now fuel Europe's economic recovery, while the United States could conserve its domestic oil stocks in case of a war with the Soviet Union. And there were further advantages. By enabling Aramco to increase its output and so earn Ibn Saud more money, the pipe would help mend a relationship that had been damaged by Truman's pro-Zionist utterances. The revenue would consolidate Ibn Saud's position, not just as the ruler of his country, but in the countries through which the pipeline would pass – which all now had a stake in the success of the venture. And finally there was a pleasing circularity to the project. Europe's purchase of Saudi oil would generate profits for Aramco, and in turn dividends for its American owners, and tax revenues for the US government. The pipeline would thus help the United States recoup the billions that she was about to spend through the Marshall Plan, which the secretary of state unveiled at Harvard on 5 June 1947.

Marshall's great fear was that the Iraqis would try to thwart the TAPLINE project. For he could see that the commercial and political advantages it held for the United States appeared to be threats when seen from Baghdad. Not only would it demand steel – then in extremely short supply – that the Iraqis wanted in order to build a new pipeline of their own and, once completed, enable Aramco to compete with the Iraq Petroleum Company for market share in Europe, but it would also extend Saudi and American influence into a part of the world the Hashemites regarded as their backyard. And so, when the secretary of state discovered, just one week after his Harvard speech, that Abdullah had gone to Baghdad for talks, he asked his ambassador in Iraq to try to extract more information from the visiting king. When the ambassador presently reported that Abdullah had reiterated that his goal was a 'reunited Syria in federation with Iraq', Marshall seems to have decided that the time had come to wreck the Jordanian king's dream.[5]

* * *

The man who would play a central role in the American effort to ruin Abdullah's plan was a quiet young American named Kim Roosevelt, who had arrived in Cairo with his wife Polly in May 1947, on a commission to write a series of features for *Harper's Magazine*. Debonair, stocky and earnest, the 31-year-old Roosevelt was the product of a spartan New England private school and Harvard. Grandson of the swash-buckling president Theodore Roosevelt and a cousin of Franklin (who had invited him to Christmas lunch with Churchill at the White House during the prime minister's awkward visit at the end of 1941), Roosevelt was charming and presentable. He was 'courteous, soft-spoken ... well educated rather than intellectual, pleasant and unassuming as host and guest', recalled Kim Philby, who encountered him in Washington, 'the last person you would expect to be up to the neck in dirty tricks'.[6]

For Roosevelt was not a journalist but a spy. The magazine commission gave him some flimsy cover for his work for the American Central Intelligence Group – forerunner of the CIA and successor to the Office of Strategic Services, where he had got a job after graduating from university. It was as an OSS officer that in January 1944 he had first visited Cairo. There, a position in James Landis's Economic Mission provided him with cover to gather intelligence across the Middle East.

Although Roosevelt came from a family of Anglophiles, his own experience of working with the British in the war had left him jaded. Recalling 'times when British representatives on the spot were, in defiance of London's instructions, doing all in their power to knife their American opposite numbers and ... Americans on the scene whose every act was inspired by a desire to "do the British in"', he came to the conclusion that 'actually Americans and British in the Middle East get along rather badly'. Later he would succinctly explain why: 'Any power that has hoped to extend its domination over continents has learned that the domination of the Middle East is an essential step. And any power trying to resist continental expansion by another has learned in turn that the Middle East must be protected at all cost.' It was this belief that drew Roosevelt back to Cairo as soon as he was demobilised, and now motivated him to do what he could to destroy the British-backed Greater Syria plan. He decided that the best way to do so was to exploit the tensions that existed between the Iraqi and Jordanian branches of the Hashemite family, each of which wanted to be top dog in the new united state.[7]

At about the same time that George Marshall asked his ambassador in Iraq for more information, the Roosevelts decamped from Cairo to Beirut, and from there they visited Baghdad. The family name immediately opened doors to Kim and also muddied the precise role that he was playing. So when he then secured an interview with the king's uncle, the regent – 'an amiable, smooth, slight young man with a thin moustache and a superior British accent' – he was able to deliver a statement that the Americans did not like what Abdullah was doing. 'It's not exactly a reporter's job,' he wrote home to his mother, 'but no one seems to care.'[8]

After Baghdad Roosevelt then went to Amman, where he met King Abdullah. The king put his arm around his interviewer, but their meeting did not go well. 'He would not talk to me of Arab politics,' the American spy wrote later, 'probably because he had heard that I was opposed to his own "Greater Syria" ambitions, and because he suspected me of being too friendly with his old enemy, Ibn Saud.'[9]

Another interview went much better, however. While Roosevelt was in Amman he also met Abdullah's chief adviser, Alec Kirkbride. Whereas the wily king had been tight-lipped, Kirkbride fell for Roosevelt's unthreatening manner and said far more than he should have done. 'Abdullah is all right,' he explained to Roosevelt, who was twenty years his junior. 'A bit erratic of course, but a sound fellow at heart. And these Arabs need a king, you know.'[10]

Roosevelt must have realised that he was on the verge of striking gold. Days earlier in London, in response to US pressure, a British minister had again denied that the British government favoured 'Greater Syria', and stated that the attitude of local British officials like Kirkbride was one of 'strict neutrality'. Roosevelt let Kirkbride keep talking. 'This idea of separate Syrian and Lebanese republics – that's a lot of nonsense,' the veteran British official continued. 'This all used to be one country, Syria, Lebanon, Transjordan, and what we call Palestine too. It was all Syria. Wasn't till the Versailles peace conference and all that stuff came along that it was split up. One kingdom for the whole area could stand up to Soviet penetration where three or four small states can't possibly. Abdullah's the man to head it up.'[11]

'Abdullah's the man to head it up.' Roosevelt finally had what he had wanted: a quote from a British official that his government could use to rubbish British claims that they were neutral about Greater Syria, and to play Abdullah and the Iraqi regent off against each other by showing that, in private, the British favoured the Jordanian king over his Iraqi cousins.

It was not long before the time came to use it. Following the Syrian elections in July 1947, on 11 August King Abdullah called publicly for a Greater Syria conference to establish a united front against the Zionists in Palestine. In private he wrote to Syria's president, Shukri

Quwatly, pressing him to support this initiative and proposing a new Syrian constitution. Quwatly was a long-standing client of the Saudi king and passed Abdullah's message to his patron to alert him to what was going on.

Until that point Ibn Saud had been feeling more secure. Soon after the Syrian elections he had given his final approval for TAPLINE, believing that the threat of Greater Syria had passed. So he was alarmed by Abdullah's renewed pressure for the scheme and rumours that the Jordanian king was considering using his Arab Legion to achieve it.

At the same time that American diplomats were trying to reassure the Saudi king that it was inconceivable that the British would allow Abdullah to take aggressive action, Roosevelt flew into Saudi Arabia to meet the king over the course of three days in his palace in Riyadh – an ochre fortress of baked mud with crenelated towers. 'He has the incredible knack of making you feel like a member of his immediate family even though an interpreter may have to translate every word exchanged between you,' he later wrote. Meanwhile his wife Polly visited the king's harem. 'It must be nice', mused one queen, 'to have a husband all to yourself.'[12]

Ibn Saud was clearly preoccupied by Greater Syria. But his analysis was subtler than Roosevelt might have expected. It was not that Greater Syria itself was such a problem, the king said – indeed it was 'desirable and inevitable', he believed. The issue, rather, was Abdullah. 'His majesty says this scheme is not based on reason or history,' the interpreter explained. 'It is the fantasy of one man's ambition. His majesty says Abdullah is sick-mindedly greatness mad – I cannot translate it, but his majesty says there are words for it in English.'

A 'morbid megalomaniac'? Roosevelt suggested.

'That sounds good,' said Ibn Saud. 'I want that quoted.'[13]

The denouement of the crisis came in September 1947. To advance his plan for Greater Syria, Abdullah had tried to divide the Iraqi royal family by offering the regent, Abdul Ilah, the throne of Palestine and Transjordan. Then suddenly, in mid-September, the Iraqi regent publicly dissociated himself from Abdullah's plan, and announced that Iraq was neutral on whether or not Greater Syria should happen. Bland as it sounded, this statement was of enormous political significance, since it was the first time that the regent had differed publicly from Abdullah.

Ten days later, following pressure from Kirkbride, Abdullah himself let it be known that he had 'agreed to participate no further for the present in the Greater Syria controversy'.[14]

Roosevelt would later hint at his own role in changing the regent's mind. When he reviewed the episode in an article for *Harper's Magazine* that was published months later, he attributed the collapse of the Greater Syria plan to 'American representatives' who had 'correctly appraised the situation from the beginning'. Repeating what Ibn Saud had told him, he said that the idea that Abdullah was advocating had 'widespread backing among the Arabs'; but that its messenger did not: 'The idea that Abdullah should head such a state struck most Arabs as laughable,' he claimed. Just as Lawrence had done three decades earlier, he portrayed the king as charming, but untrustworthy and unserious. 'As a political figure', he wrote, 'he is a venerable joke', for whom some British officials nonetheless felt 'a sentimental attachment'. Only 'the firm position taken by the United States' had proved 'helpful in forestalling developments which might have damaged Arab, British and American interests'. While it has been long assumed that the United States and Britain stopped spying on each other during the Second World War, this episode shows that, on the American side at least, this was not the case.[15]

Roosevelt's article was published in April 1948. After his ambitions were frustrated by the Americans, Abdullah had to content himself with annexing the West Bank after Britain's withdrawal from Palestine that May. That consoled Bevin, because it made Jordan more likely to survive. But the little country represented a jagged fraction of the much grander realm that his 'little king' had once hoped to rule.

* * *

The collapse of Abdullah's grand ambition did not mean that the pipeline saga was over, however. Under pressure from Aramco, Quwatly had meanwhile given the Syrian government's approval for TAPLINE, but the deal still needed parliamentary ratification. This had still not happened on 29 November 1947, when the United States government voted in favour of the partition of Palestine at the United Nations general assembly. The American vote – and Truman's immediate recognition of Israel in May 1948 despite George Marshall's opposition – both caused

Arab outrage. In November 1947 in Damascus a 2,000-strong mob stormed the American embassy, while in Jordan, a TAPLINE encampment was attacked.

During the 1947 Syrian election Aramco and the American government had spent money in a bid to get friendly candidates elected. The company, now under significant pressure from the Saudis to improve the royalty it paid, toyed with 'aggressive action within Syria', including 'spending large sums in propitious places', to make ratification happen. To increase the pressure on the Syrians, it also started to reconsider routing the pipeline along a more expensive, southern route, to Egypt, but this tactic was frustrated when, in a rare show of unity, the Arab League's members all agreed in early 1948 that none of them should allocate any new oil concession until the Palestine situation was clarified. Aramco's efforts at bribery backfired. British diplomats reported that the rumours that money was being offered to parliamentarians were so widespread that 'those who have not been paid are out to make trouble'. In the meantime, ratification was as far away as ever.[16]

It was not only the Americans who were infuriated by the Syrians' failure to ratify the TAPLINE deal. So too were the Lebanese, who stood to gain significantly from the completion of the pipeline. It may have been the head of the Lebanese Sûreté, Farid Chehab, who, sometime in 1948 introduced a member of the CIA's Beirut station, Stephen Meade, to an ambitious and bombastic colonel in the Syrian army, Husni Zaim, who was casting around for help to overthrow his government. Having met Zaim for the first time on 30 November 1948, Meade reported back to Washington that the colonel was a '"Banana Republic" dictator type'. There was 'only one way to start the Syrian people along the road to progress and democracy', the colonel told him during one of their meetings, thwacking his desk with his riding crop and adding, 'with the whip'. When Quwatly again postponed ratification following further protests against TAPLINE, Zaim seemed just the man to break the deadlock.[17]

The head of the CIA's Damascus station, and Meade's boss, was Miles Copeland. A Falstaffian teller of tall tales with 'thick, sandy hair and . . . eyes that danced with excitement', he would admit that he had been attracted to the CIA by 'the prospect of engaging in a bit of clandestine hanky-panky with the justification that it was in the national interest'. He and Meade decided that, in order to delegitimise Quwatly's administration and justify the *coup d'état*, they should organise a sting that would suggest that the government was no longer able to protect foreign diplomats. By spreading rumours that Copeland kept secret documents at home the two men enticed Syrian intelligence officers to try to burgle the villa when it appeared to be unoccupied but when in fact they were lying in wait. When the *New York Times* reported the shoot-out that ensued after the break-in took place, it described Copeland as a 'crack shot'.[18]

Soon afterwards, Zaim dictated orders to senior army officers to seize the president and key points around Damascus, locked up the secretaries who had typed them in a cupboard, and went on to seize power, almost bloodlessly, on 30 March 1949. The Americans got what they had wanted four days later when Zaim denounced the 'anarchy and profiteering' which had prompted him to overthrow the government and then announced that he would ratify the TAPLINE deal himself. Although he himself was overthrown and murdered 136 days later, the project was unstoppable. Six years after it was conceived, the pipeline was completed in September 1950 and started pumping oil three months later.

Born out of rivalry with the British, the TAPLINE made the Middle East strategically important to the United States, and it entwined the Americans in the internal politics of its transit countries to a degree that they had never been before. It would also have another effect. By dramatically increasing how much oil Aramco could produce in Saudi Arabia, it promised Ibn Saud vast wealth. To maximise his income, he now took a step that would aggravate the relationship between Britain and the United States.

EXPLORING THE WILDER AREAS

On 25 January 1948 Ibn Saud received a telegram from the headman of a remote village in the south of his kingdom that made him 'very angry' indeed. Three days earlier an Englishman named Wilfred Thesiger had turned up, unannounced, in the mudbrick settlement, which lay 300 miles southwest of Riyadh. 'Who is this fellow?' asked the king, before ordering the headman to throw Thesiger in prison. The explorer's sudden appearance was an unwelcome reminder that the southern frontier of his kingdom was undefined, disputed and insecure. That particularly mattered now that there was thought to be oil in the vicinity.[1]

To reach the village Thesiger had had to cross 400 miles of desert. Known as the Rub al Khali, or Empty Quarter, this wilderness had an appalling reputation. Its sands drifted into dunes up to 700ft high and its few wells and meagre grazing were fought over by feuding tribes. 'Not even Allah has been there,' said people who lived on its edges. It formed a formidable barrier, if not a formal border, between Saudi Arabia and the coastal sheikhdoms on the horn and south coast of the Arabian peninsula, which were British protectorates.[2]

Cartographers of that era drew the coastal sheikhdoms' borders as dotted lines that petered out as they ventured inland towards the label 'Rub al Khali' – which was invariably expansive, to fill what otherwise would be a large blank space on the map. In 1913 the Ottoman Turks and the British had recognised their respective spheres of influence in the southern half of the Arabian peninsula, but the Blue Line Agreement – named after the colour of the pencil that was used – was never ratified and, when the war ended and the Ottoman Empire disintegrated, Ibn Saud unsurprisingly refused to recognise it. He argued that tribal loyalties were what counted. Claiming that his family had originally come from the contested area, he sent tax collectors in to stake his claim. From then on, he based his entitlement to this swathe of territory on the grounds that the tribesmen his taxmen found were ready to pay tribute to him.

Shifting desert sands and changing human loyalties had not stopped him, or, across the desert, the sheikhs of the Gulf coast and the sultan of Muscat and Oman from granting concessions to oil companies to hunt for oil within the territories they claimed as theirs. The king had granted Aramco exclusive drilling rights in 'the eastern portion of our Saudi Arab kingdom, within its frontiers', while the company's bigger, British-dominated, rivals, the Anglo-Iranian Oil Company and the Iraq Petroleum Company, had bought concessions in neighbouring Qatar, Oman and in the sheikhdoms along the Gulf coast, which all made similar reference to borders that had not yet been defined. Since by 1945 Aramco's geologists were confident that there was oil beneath the Rub al Khali, in the absence of a territorial settlement, sooner or later these competing companies' exploratory activities would bring them, and their American and British backers, into conflict. In the wake of Thesiger's appearance in his kingdom at the start of 1948, the king would take a step that brought the risk of conflict closer.[3]

*   *   *

It is not clear whether it was a complete coincidence that Wilfred Thesiger was approached to conduct a survey of the southern fringes of the Empty Quarter soon after the British heard that Aramco believed that there was oil there. But after Britain's ambassador in Jeddah reported the American belief to London in January 1945, that spring the British government decided to organise a 'summer locust reconnaissance of the area south of the Rub al Khali'. By April the Middle East Anti-Locust Unit had appointed Thesiger to undertake the expedition.[4]

'I was not really interested in locusts,' Thesiger later admitted. But he was keen to cross the Empty Quarter, and the Anti-Locust Unit, a remnant of the once-powerful Middle East Supply Centre, represented the best way to do so, because its officers – unlike European diplomats – were allowed free range by Ibn Saud. Whether or not there was an additional, surreptitious reason for this trip, the locust-hunting mission would give Thesiger the opportunity to find out more about the true loyalties of the empty desert's tribes.[5]

By then Thesiger already had a well-established reputation as a danger-seeker. Born in Abyssinia in 1910, he returned there repeatedly, after being educated at Eton and Oxford, to hunt big game and to cross a forbidden sultanate in the northeast of the country. After five years in the Sudan political service – during which time he shot seventy lions and gained vast experience of desert travel – he served on the guerrilla force that liberated Abyssinia from the Italians. He then joined the Special Operations Executive and later the Special Air Service, before Haile Selassie, whose coronation he had attended in 1930, invited him back to Addis Ababa to serve as his political adviser. It was as this job began to grate – he had a 'distaste for officialdom', said one contemporary – that the chief anti-locust officer approached him.[6]

The instructions for that first mission in October 1945 did not require Thesiger to venture into the sandy desert proper. But during this expedition he heard about a Bedu raiding party that had crossed the Empty Quarter from the Persian Gulf. A year later he returned, determined to repeat the feat that these raiders had accomplished, but in the opposite direction. Since he was 6ft 2in, and the hatred of Christians in that part of the world was fierce, his guides felt it would be wisest if he pretended to be Syrian, since he knew southern Syria from his time in the SOE.

Thesiger's crossing of the Empty Quarter over the winter of 1946–7 took place as tension over the location of the Saudi frontier was mounting. With Aramco keen to investigate the possibility of oil south of the Qatar peninsula, Ibn Saud's fearsome governor in the east of the kingdom, Ibn Jiluwi, was trying to buttress his master's claim to the disputed area by sending out tax collectors, while the king tried to make trouble for his most likely rival, Sheikh Shakhbut, the ruler of nearby Abu Dhabi, by encouraging the ruler of Dubai to attack Shakhbut's tribe. The epicentre of this conflict, the Liwa oasis, southwest of Abu Dhabi, also happened to be Thesiger's goal. But when Thesiger reached it, after a journey of 450 miles that took three weeks, his Bedu guides realised that their charge's vast footprints would give them all away. 'Then Ibn Saud's tax collectors will hear of it and they will arrest us all and take us off to Ibn Jiluwi', feared one of the tribesmen. 'God preserve us from that, I know Ibn Jiluwi. He is a tyrant, utterly without mercy.' Knowing that Thesiger's Syrian disguise would not stand up to close scrutiny, the Bedu obliged the explorer to turn east, then south, and return through the Omani hinterland to the Indian Ocean coast.[7]

On his return to London Thesiger briefed both the Foreign Office and the Iraq Petroleum Company about what he had seen, and began to undermine the Saudis' claim to the area south of Qatar. In a lecture at the Royal Geographical Society in October 1947 he glossed over the fact that it was the presence of Saudi taxmen that had forced him to turn back before completing his journey. Instead he observed that the people of the Liwa traded with Abu Dhabi, and that the only tribe that roamed the Empty Quarter was connected to the settlements of Buraimi and Ibri in what is now Oman, as well as Abu Dhabi, and not with the nearest centres of Saudi power, Riyadh and Hofuf. His knowledge was clearly valuable, and at some point soon after his talk, he was approached by Aramco, which asked if he would work for them. Thesiger would always claim that he turned down the company's offer. Within days of giving the lecture, he was on his way back to Arabia again, this time hoping to make a more westerly crossing of the Rub al Khali.

When Thesiger previously sought permission for this journey, Ibn Saud had refused to give it. This time he decided simply not to ask him. 'I should be defying the King,' he later wrote, 'but I hoped that I should be able to water at some well on the far side of the sands and then slip away unobserved.' However, rather than stick to this plan, when Thesiger crossed the sands and reached the well he had been aiming for, instead of returning at once into the desert he continued to the village of Sulaiyil, whose headman warned Ibn Saud of his appearance.[8]

Had Ibn Saud's one British adviser, the renegade civil servant St John Philby, not been present when the king received the headman's telegram, Thesiger might have ended up languishing in a Saudi jail. But Philby, who had crossed the Empty Quarter himself during the 1930s, had known of Thesiger's plan from the outset, and was willing to cover for him. Explaining that Thesiger had been working for the anti-locust mission (which was in fact no longer the case) he suggested that his compatriot had run out of water or food and had to make for the nearest well.

Ibn Saud was initially unwilling to forgive Thesiger and his Bedu guides their trespass. 'They had no right to come without permission,' he raged, 'and if we overlooked their offence, we would have others doing the same thing.' But he relented later that evening, and let Thesiger on his way once more.[9]

Thesiger again made for the Liwa. In the eleven months since his last expedition the local tribe had chased off Ibn Saud's tax inspectors, and with a truce between Dubai and Abu Dhabi in place, he was able to ride on to Abu Dhabi this time.

* * *

Brief though it was, the incident had a profound impact on the king since it gave him the impression that his British-backed rivals were stealing a march on him and he quickly moved to do something about it. At the point when Thesiger appeared in Sulaiyil, the Saudis were in the process of renegotiating their agreement with Aramco. In the original deal the king had granted the company exclusive rights for sixty years in exchange for a royalty that worked out at 22 cents a barrel. By now, however, the king thoroughly regretted these terms and Thesiger's intrusion can only have reinforced his nagging feeling that they did nothing to incentivise Aramco to work faster. By the end of the negotiation the Saudis had forced Aramco to increase the royalty it paid to 33 cents a barrel, and to make a far more important concession that would cause wide reverberations.

Concluded in April 1948, the revised agreement also required Aramco to give up large blocks of territory it did not want every three years. The company was now in a race against time to identify where else there might be oil in its concession, a hunt that would provoke the rival oil companies holding the neighbouring concessions into a similar spurt of activity. As always, the king's main motive was money. But by adding this condition, he hoped to make the oil company, its American shareholders, and ultimately the US government, which taxed Aramco's profits, his allies when finally the dispute over the frontier came to a head.

* * *

While the Saudis were finalising the new terms that they would impose on Aramco, Thesiger continued on his journey. Having arrived in Abu Dhabi, he met Sheikh Shakhbut before riding 100 miles inland in order to meet the sheikh's brother Zayid in the Buraimi oasis, a place that was to acquire an enormous strategic significance in the years that followed. Situated at the base of the 'horn' of the Arabian peninsula, and equidistant from the Gulf and Indian Ocean coasts, the oasis not only provided a natural vantage point over the Gulf sheikhdoms but also controlled the route into Oman to the southeast, which Thesiger had used to avoid the attentions of Ibn Saud's tax collectors a year earlier: whoever ruled the oasis could dominate the southeast of the Arabian peninsula.

Buraimi was not a picture-book desert pool but a collection of date palm groves that were fed by springs which rose in the surrounding area. The groves, and the traffic that stopped by, supported nine villages. Shakhbut's brother Zayid inhabited one of the six villages which belonged to Abu Dhabi; the remaining three – including Buraimi itself – were nominally under the sultan of Muscat's control. In another of the Abu Dhabi villages lived the Iraq Petroleum Company's representative, a British man named Richard Bird.

A cynic would say that IPC's main reason for buying the Abu Dhabi and Oman concessions in the first place was to deny them to its American rivals. But, having previously taken a relaxed approach to oil exploration, the company was hurrying to catch up because it was aware that Aramco had stepped up its own activity in southeast Arabia. Oddly the greatest hurdle that it faced was the man who had granted the concession in the first place, the sultan of Muscat. The sultan, whose control of the Omani hinterland was weak, did not want to put his authority to the test by offending local sensitivities, and so he was unwilling to sanction the company's exploratory activities, which required the acquiescence of the local tribes.

To bypass the sultan, in Buraimi Richard Bird was trying to negotiate access to the hinterland with the two men he had identified as its gatekeepers, a local sheikh and the man who wielded real power in the hinterland, the imam of Oman, who was the sultan's rival. Both the

sheikh and the imam were deeply suspicious of Bird's motives, probably fearing that greater British influence would end the profitable slave
trade on which the economy of the Buraimi oasis still hinged. 'It is an
extremely delicate problem this penetration of Oman,' Bird grumbled.
'No bride was ever more bashful of the advances of the other party.'
With the seduction at a crucial stage, it was a deeply unwelcome development when on 5 April 1948 Thesiger crashed in, announcing his plan
to enter this most sensitive area 'in order to obtain a specimen of the
wild goat', known locally as the *tahr*. When Bird produced the head
of exactly this animal and said that it might be bagged more locally,
Thesiger changed his tune, saying that the flora, as well as the fauna, of
inner Oman was of interest.[10]

Bird's initial instinct was to dismiss Thesiger as a poseur. The British
oilman was amused to note that, although the explorer aped the Bedu to
the extent of using his dagger point to take out his penis when he needed
to urinate, and decried 'the automobile' as an invention of the devil, he
invariably accepted the offer of a lift 'without hesitation'. But he was soon
forced into a reappraisal. The fact was that he had still to visit an area
that Thesiger had passed through a year earlier, where the explorer said
he had seen oil coming to the surface in several places. This corroborated
rumours Bird had already heard but so far been unable to verify. As he
conceded, 'Thesiger definitely knows where the oil is to be found.'[11]

When Thesiger then told Bird that the tribes who inhabited the same
area were loyal to Ibn Saud, he aroused Bird's suspicions. Realising that
such information would help Aramco and the Saudis, Bird wondered
if Thesiger might be working for them. Mischievously he asked him
whether he had agreed to work for the American company when it
approached him in London. 'It was a pure shot in the dark on my part,'
he said afterwards. With it, however, Bird hit the bullseye. Thesiger,
startled by Bird's apparent knowledge, said that he had declined the
offer – thus letting slip that one had been made in the first place. He
went on to say he knew the Americans had been into territory belonging
to Abu Dhabi. Following that conversation, Bird warned his boss that
Thesiger had been approached by their rivals, and recommended that
the IPC or the British government should hurry up and hire him.[12]

'I was averse to all oil companies, dreading the changes and disinte-
gration of society which they inevitably caused,' Thesiger would later

claim. But, by the time that he next talked about his travels, he was in the IPC's pay as 'an advance agent for exploring the wilder areas'. When he spoke at the Royal Geographical Society again in October 1948 he provided a detailed description of the Liwa, which had 'never yet been seen by a European'. Of its people, he was able to report that: 'They all owe allegiance to the Abu Fallah shaikhs of Abu Dhabi.' Of other local tribes' allegiance to Ibn Saud, whose ambassador to London was sitting in the front row of the talk, Thesiger discreetly said nothing.[13]

Again, Thesiger left almost immediately for Abu Dhabi. The pattern of his next expeditions precisely fitted the Iraq Petroleum Company's priorities. The likely true purpose of his bustard-hunting trip through the Liwa in November 1948 was to look for evidence of further American intrusion into the area. In January 1949 he ventured south into the Omani hinterland, where previously he had seen signs of oil and where the tribes displayed pro-Saudi proclivities. At some point before embarking on this trip he had received some training from the oil company about what to look out for. It was during this journey that he spotted two hills, named Salakh and Madhamar. His next article for the Royal Geographical Society's journal mentioned both in passing, but it was only in his book much later that he explicitly stated their significance. 'Both of them were dome-shaped, and I thought regretfully that their formation was of the sort which geologists associate with oil.' The sorrow was entirely disingenuous.[14]

* * *

Thesiger arrived back in Buraimi to hear news of a crisis. For several months there had been reports of growing American activity in the region. In March, IPC's Qatar subsidiary reported that Aramco had built roads and trig points in areas covered by its own concession. From Sharjah, a fortnight later, came news that an Aramco aeroplane had set out to survey territory that lay on the edge of the company's own concession in Oman. Then on 3 April 1949 – three days before Thesiger reached Buraimi – a convoy of American-made vehicles equipped for off-road driving, carrying six Americans, their Arab drivers and several guards, was spotted on the road between Dubai and Abu Dhabi. Although the Americans said that they were going to Dubai, by the time the local representative of the Iraq Petroleum Company arrived to investigate, they had vanished – behaviour that only heightened British suspicions that Aramco was prospecting for oil in an area that lay well east of territory that was indisputably Saudi. A few days later Bird reported that an American oil company official had admitted to him that his firm enjoyed State Department backing. Bird reckoned that the US government was deliberately encouraging conflict between the British and American companies, having calculated that Britain's dependence on American money meant that the British government would be reluctant to risk a clash.

The British government had stayed quiet on the question of the frontier until now, but mainly because of differences between government departments on whether they should broach the matter with the decrepit Ibn Saud, since they were unsure if his kingdom would outlast him. A formal complaint from Sheikh Shakhbut following further rumours that Aramco was surveying the area west of the Liwa finally forced Whitehall's hand. After IPC officials had flown over and located the rival company's encampment, on 21 April the British political officer in Abu Dhabi and an IPC representative set out by car across the desert to hand the party a letter telling it to withdraw, which they delivered a day later. The Aramco geologists they met at the campsite freely admitted that their maps showed that they were in Abu Dhabi territory. 'We go where our Saudi guards take us,' one of them explained.[15]

Unsurprisingly, Richard Bird suspected that this was untrue, and he speculated that the guards accompanied the party not simply to protect it, but to endow it with some useful menace. Having heard from an Arab resident of Buraimi that there had been rumours of Saudi intentions to take over the oasis *before* Aramco appeared on the edge of the Liwa and on the road between Dubai and Abu Dhabi, he reported that the local sheikhs in Buraimi believed that Ibn Saud had designs on Oman. 'So do I,' he added.[16]

In London the Foreign Office accepted Bird's argument and quickly appreciated its implications. If Ibn Saud could establish himself in Buraimi between the Gulf sheikhdoms and the sultanate of Muscat, he would be able to prevent the Iraq Petroleum Company using the oasis for exploration in either of the Abu Dhabi or Omani concessions. Bird predicted what would happen next. Once it had dislodged the British from the oasis, 'A party of Americans under Ibn Saud's auspices could enter areas which we could never penetrate ... I don't think the tribes would harm them because of their fear of Ibn Saud.'[17]

Bird raced to Muscat, hoping that the news of Aramco's intrusion might at last persuade the sultan to take action, but he was disappointed. The sultan refused to sign letters to the sheikhs of the Buraimi oasis authorising them to deal directly with Bird, probably because he did not wish to test their loyalty. When Bird returned to Buraimi and tried anyway to bribe them to accept the sultan's sovereignty, they refused. Thesiger, when invited to give his opinion, believed that it was 'extremely unlikely that the present sultan will ever establish his authority over either the insecure area east or south of Buraimi ... He is too weak and does not maintain sufficient direct contact with the tribesmen.'[18]

By now Ibn Saud's health was visibly deteriorating, and he was beginning to show signs of senile paranoia. When, in August that year in Syria, Colonel Zaim was overthrown and murdered, and his successor put a union with Iraq back on the table, the king believed the British were inciting the surrounding states to remove him. In retaliation, on 14 October 1949 he did exactly what the British had expected and made a formal claim to the base of the Qatar peninsula, the Liwa oasis and the Buraimi area – a demand rejected a month later by the British.

Contrary to what Thesiger had said in public about the loyalties of the local tribes, he told the British government privately that the facts did not favour its case. When the British government rejected the Saudi claim Thesiger was on the Gulf coast, preparing to make another foray into Oman. This time he hoped to visit the Jebel Akhdar, the mountain that screened off the hinterland from the coast. But he was nearly undone when the imam of Oman sent out a 100-strong force to try to kill him. As he reported to another IPC man in Dubai, Edward Henderson, when he finally got back to the coast, his narrow escape provided proof, if it were needed, that 'west of the mountains the sultan is without any influence at all'.[19]

Henderson had served with Thesiger in Special Operations Executive in the war and respected his old comrade, whose experience boded ill for his company's operations. 'The fact that even Thesiger has such difficulty in the Imam's territory and cannot reach certain parts demonstrates the utter fanaticism of this ruler, and the difficulty we would be in,' he concluded. The IPC would not be prospecting for oil in the Omani interior for the foreseeable future. The danger that Ibn Saud might manage to exploit the unstable situation meant that Buraimi was vulnerable.

To plug the gap, Thesiger advised supporting Sheikh Shakhbut's brother Zayid, and to encourage him to seize control of territory south-east of Buraimi. But this sounded far too bold a strategy to Britain's top official in the Gulf, who, as always, advised caution. 'It is in our interests', he suggested, 'to allow the existing situation to continue for the present in spite of its fictitious character ... it would be very dangerous to make a change.' The imam, like Ibn Saud, was growing old and was regularly reported to be dying, and there was a chance that the sultan might be able to take advantage of his rivals' deaths to impose his authority upon the tribes. In fact Ibn Saud would only die in 1953, while the imam lasted until 1954. Doing nothing, as ever, was the simplest option, and once the government had accepted its Gulf officials' ever-cautious advice, all it could do was hope and wait.[20]

GOING FIFTY–FIFTY

Although the Saudis' renegotiation of the terms of Aramco's concession had sparked a race to claim the Rub al Khali, that was nothing compared to the further change they then agreed with the company at the end of 1950, which was to have far greater implications for the British, not just in southeastern Arabia, but all over the Middle East.

Money, as ever, was the issue for the cash-strapped Ibn Saud, whose family now numbered about 1,000. Although, through the revised agreement of April 1948, the king had managed to increase his royalty by half, to 33 cents a barrel, he soon had reason to regret this deal. After Aramco – under pressure from the State Department to give independent American oil companies a slice of Middle Eastern business – had surrendered its share of the exploration rights to the neutral zone between Saudi Arabia and Kuwait, at the start of 1949 the Saudis managed to resell this lease to another US company that was willing to pay a royalty equivalent to 55 cents a barrel. The sale left Ibn Saud wishing that he had screwed Aramco for more.

Saudi disgruntlement only grew when Aramco then cut back its output. After global oil production caught up with demand in 1949, the Marshall Plan's administrators put pressure on the company to cut its prices, and demand then fell back when that year's sterling crisis led the British government to bring in measures that discriminated against American producers by discouraging oil importers buying oil priced in dollars. Assailed by both these pressures Aramco scaled back its production and postponed expansion plans. Since the concession agreement tied royalties to output, lower production meant less revenue for the

Saudis: the State Department reckoned that the combined effect of these moves by Aramco might slash Saudi Arabia's income by $25 million, or a quarter.

This calamitous drop in revenue hit Ibn Saud just at the moment when his main Iraqi rivals – whose own sterling-denominated oil sales were growing unabated – appeared to be dusting off their Greater Syria plan again and the British were dismissing his own claim to the Buraimi oasis. Convinced that this was no coincidence and that the British were trying to encircle him, the increasingly paranoid king asked Aramco if he could borrow $6 million, and then promptly re-lent the money to Syria in January 1950, hoping to kill off a union with Iraq. The first signs of another Saudi financial crisis came days later when the finance minister asked for an advance against a royalty payment he was due to receive towards the end of February. The same day that Aramco deposited the cash, one of the king's sons sent an emissary to ask when his master might expect his share, while the cashiers were still counting out the money.

To avoid friction with the Saudis, Aramco agreed to each demand. But the company's executives were outraged at the use to which Ibn Saud had put the $6 million loan, and the uncertainty surrounding the concession meant they could not shell out money indefinitely. Early in 1950 they asked the US government for help, initially over a relatively unusual matter. National Geographic was about to reissue its map of Africa and the Middle East, which currently gave Qatar the Gulf sheikhdoms and Oman boundaries that marched some way into the Rub al Khali. As the cartographer had refused to give in to the company's pressure, Aramco asked the State Department if it could ensure that 'these disputed areas be left uncolored'. The March 1950 edition of the map provides enduring proof that the State Department agreed to help. Although, following Thesiger's expeditions, it shows more details of the topography of the Empty Quarter, the dotted lines indicating the frontiers, which were present in the previous edition, have vanished.[1]

The Truman administration was reluctant to get more involved. Its diplomats in Jeddah were very sceptical of the Saudis' claim to Buraimi, not least because the king's governor Ibn Jiluwi himself privately admitted it was groundless. It saw the frontier dispute as a distraction from its main priority: to persuade the Saudis to renew the Dhahran base agreement, which had expired during 1949. But in exchange – and no doubt to put pressure on the British – Ibn Saud wanted a formal, military alliance. Washington did not wish to give this, because it knew that it would struggle to push it through Congress in the face of general suspicion of 'entangling alliances', and the likely opposition of the Israel lobby. But equally it did not want Aramco to lose its concession.

President Truman tried to assuage the Saudis and buy time by commissioning an exhaustive survey of the country's military requirements. Realising that the king was putting pressure on Aramco because he feared British designs, his administration also passed on a promise from London that the British government would use its influence to prevent the 'use of force by one Middle Eastern country against another'. But this fell far short of what Ibn Saud was after. 'The British were a people of "but",' he once declared. 'They made statements and gave you assurances but always at the end "but"'. In February 1950 the Saudis made another onerous demand of Aramco: that the company foot the bill for the protection of the nearly completed TAPLINE. Given that the pipeline ran parallel with the Iraqi frontier, the American ambassador immediately saw what the Saudis were trying to do: 'transfer to Aramco the entire cost of protecting Saudi Arabia's northern marches from the exaggerated Hashemite menace on their flanks'.[2]

Unable to give the Saudis what they wanted, the State Department decided some personal diplomacy was in order. Midway through March the assistant secretary of state responsible for the Middle East, George McGhee, set out to meet Ibn Saud in Riyadh, bearing a personal letter from Truman to the king, in which the president said he hoped strong 'ties of friendship' would continue. Though only thirty-eight years old, McGhee knew the subject and the stakes perfectly. A geologist by training, he had made such a fortune in the oil business that he could now afford to work pro bono for the State Department. His father-in-law was Everette DeGolyer, the leading oil geologist of his generation and the first man to appreciate just how vast Saudi Arabia's oil reserves might be.[3]

'My main hope', McGhee would later recollect, 'was to lay a sound basis for US-Saudi relations, in order to assist Aramco in maintaining its position as the sole developer of Saudi oil.' In preliminary talks with Ibn Saud's advisers on his arrival in Riyadh he dodged an invitation to get involved in the Rub al Khali frontier dispute and made sympathetic noises about their fears of the Hashemites. Three days later he dined with Ibn Saud, who entertained him with an account of his seizure of Riyadh with forty followers in 1902.[4]

It was only after the old king had retired to bed that the haggling with his advisers began. McGhee was adamant that his government could not enter an alliance. Instead he proposed a treaty of friendship and sugared that underwhelming offer with the offer of a loan and technical expertise under the Point Four aid programme that Truman had unveiled the year before. He wisely tied the prospect of weapons – which was what Ibn Saud really wanted – to Saudi renewal of the base agreement.

McGhee left Riyadh under the impression that he had royal agreement for his proposals, but he did not significantly ease the pressure on Aramco. For the company's tax affairs had meanwhile come under close scrutiny from the man in charge of Ibn Saud's treasury in Mecca, Abdullah Suleiman, once memorably described by a British diplomat as 'the only finance minister I ever met who drank methylated spirit'.[5]

Suleiman had been trying to understand the effect of an arcane change to Aramco's commercial relationship with its shareholders which had made the oil company significantly more profitable and thus liable to pay more tax in the United States where it was domiciled. This investigation now revealed a fact so startling that it must have had the finance minister reaching for the bottle to refill his glass: in 1949 Aramco had coughed up more to the American government in tax than it paid out in royalties to Riyadh.[6]

A recent innovation in Venezuela showed the Saudis the way forward. The South American government had enacted a law that subjected all oil company profits to a 50 per cent levy. Had Saudi Arabia applied the same 'fifty–fifty law' to Aramco in 1949, it could have wrung another $33 million from the company.

The prospect of imposing such a tax became even more appealing after an expert on US tax, hired by the Saudis, cleared up the one uncertainty that the fifty–fifty tax left. For this man was able to confirm to Suleiman that the tax hike would not harm Aramco's ability to invest in its Saudi operations since, under existing US law, the company could offset this new foreign tax bill against its domestic tax liability. So long as the Saudis taxed Aramco no more than what the company owed the

US government, it was the US taxpayer, and not they or the company, who would suffer. In May 1950 Suleiman told Bill Eddy – formerly the US minister to Jeddah and now working for Aramco – that his government intended 'to obtain a larger share in Aramco's profits'.[7]

Suleiman's alcoholism meant that Aramco's officials were never quite sure how seriously to take him, and initially they offered to defer repayments of the $6 million Syria loan, which the Saudis had been due to start making that August. When it turned out the finance minister was not bluffing they realised they had very little leverage. Even if the company wrote off every debt owed it by the Saudis, the sum was half what the Saudis stood to gain each year if they applied the Venezuelan law. In June Abdullah Suleiman presented Aramco with an ultimatum, calling on the company to contribute at least $10 million annually to a welfare fund, shoulder the cost of new infrastructure and accept deferred payment of all invoices until January the following year. Since none of these costs could be offset against US corporation tax, the aim of this demand was to make the fifty–fifty alternative appealing. In July Aramco's president told the American ambassador to Saudi Arabia that he could go no further: to make more concessions 'would not only invite additional demands by the Saudi Government but would be financially unwise'. The following month Aramco's board authorised its officers to renegotiate the 1933 agreement along fifty–fifty lines. In doing so, it was effectively volunteering American taxpayers to subsidise the lifestyle of the Saudi royal family.[8]

While this was bad news for the US taxpayer, it was good news for McGhee. Although the president had turned down his request, earlier that year, for a billion pounds in aid to help the countries of the Middle East and South Asia, for which he was responsible, in his view, Saudi Arabia's strategic importance was growing. The outbreak of the Korean War at the end of June made a war with Soviet Russia seem more likely. In that scenario, Dhahran assumed a huge importance because it was the only airbase that put US bombers within striking range of industrial southern Russia. What amounted to a disguised subsidy of the Saudis was the order of the day.

There was another reason why McGhee was happy with this outcome. He felt it would oblige the British, who were resisting similar pressure from the Iranian government to improve the royalties their

Anglo-Iranian Oil Company was paying, to come up with a matching offer. His State Department officials were by now worrying about the vulnerability of Middle Eastern states to communism and feared the consequences of the disruption that would follow if Aramco lost or abandoned the Saudi concession. But another way the Saudis might be exposed to communism was if neighbouring Iran succumbed to Soviet influence – a risk that British stubbornness increased, in Washington's opinion. 'As soon as it became clear that Aramco was going to make substantial concessions to Saudi Arabia', McGhee recalled later, 'I knew that we must warn the British so the AIOC would have an opportunity to improve their offer to Iran.'[9]

* * *

By now the biggest of the oil companies operating in the Middle East, the Anglo-Iranian Oil Company dwarfed Aramco. But when it was established thirty years earlier, the company had been the green new-comer to a market dominated by well-established rivals and needed more customers and capital. Its breakthrough came in 1914 when Winston Churchill, then first lord of the Admiralty, announced that His Majesty's Government would supply both, through a £2 million investment and a twenty-year contract to supply the Admiralty with cut-price fuel. Urged by the former first sea lord to 'do our damnedest to get control ... and to keep it for all times an absolutely British company', the British government purchased the majority of Anglo-Iranian's stock and took two seats on the board. The result defied easy description. Anglo-Iranian was, as Ernest Bevin admitted, 'really a state company', but one over which he felt he had 'no power or influence ... to do anything at all'.[10]

Churchill once described Anglo-Iranian's concession as 'a prize from fairyland far beyond our brightest hopes'. Even when the Iranians reached the same conclusion and forced a renegotiation of the deal in 1933, the outcome was, if anything, even better for the company, since it prolonged its rights for sixty years, and carved in stone the tax rates that the Iranians could levy on the company until 1963. Reopening that agreement was 'the very last thing the company desires', the company's forbidding Glaswegian chairman, Sir William Fraser, remarked in 1948, 'as no new concession could ever be as favourable ... as the one now in existence'. And so it was a deeply unwelcome development when the passage of Venezuela's fifty–fifty law dragged him back to the negotiating table the following year.[11]

For both Anglo-Iranian and the British government, the stakes the 1949 negotiation involved were huge because the war had turned the business into a massive enterprise. While Aramco produced half a million barrels of oil a day, Anglo-Iranian churned out almost half as much again. Nearly three-quarters of this output was processed at the refinery at Abadan on the Shatt-al-Arab waterway. Following enormous expansion during wartime, the plant was now the largest refinery in the world and Britain's 'most important single overseas investment'; one young Iranian described it as 'awe-inspiring'. A 'vast, smoking, spitting complex' of holding tanks, pipes and tall thin chimneys which seemed to wobble in the mirage, it had quadruple the capacity of its Aramco-owned rival down the Gulf at Ras Tanura. Reeking of sulphur and kerosene, it distilled crude oil into British power.[12]

Not only did Anglo-Iranian's Abadan refinery supply the United Kingdom with the means to fight another war, it generated a much-needed £100 million a year in foreign exchange from sales of oil in sterling and paid the British government colossal sums in tax and dividends. At a cost of about five shillings a ton, the plant turned Iranian crude oil into a commodity that sold for twenty times as much in Europe. The British government then taxed Anglo-Iranian's profits, earned a dividend as the owner of the majority stake, and taxed the dividends the company paid out to its other British shareholders. In the three years 1948–50, the British government received about £116 million.[13]

That colossal sum did not even include the tax the British government received on the profits of over fifty Anglo-Iranian subsidiaries. These the Board of Trade excused Anglo-Iranian from having to consolidate into its own annual report on the grounds – the company's directors insisted – that to do so would be 'misleading'.[14]

'Revealing' would have been more accurate a word. For the subsidiaries were involved in distribution and marketing, 'downstream' activities which, then as now, were by far the most lucrative part of an oil company's operations. What the British government was actually doing by allowing Anglo-Iranian to hive off its subsidiaries' financial results was to collude in a cover-up. The company was reinvesting most of the money it made from extracting Iranian crude oil and refining it at Abadan in subsidiary marketing businesses that made profits on which the Iranians had no claim. As the British minister of fuel and power privately admitted, the 'Persians are not getting anything like as much out of this as we'.[15]

The 'Persians' already had an inkling this was the case. Before they reopened the terms of the deal, they had hired a French law professor, Gilbert Gidel, to review the existing concession agreement and take a closer look at Anglo-Iranian's operations. Gidel not only found that the basis for the current deal was flawed and that there was a vast and growing gulf between what the British and the Iranian governments each earned from the arrangement; he also revealed the profitability of Anglo-Iranian's subsidiaries – the secret that the company, with Whitehall's connivance, had done its utmost to hide.

The Iranian finance minister used Gidel's report to argue that his country deserved a royalty of £1 per ton. But his arguments ricocheted off Anglo-Iranian's redoubtable chairman, Fraser, whose final offer, of 12/6, was less than two-thirds the finance minister's demand. Fraser argued, brazenly, that the very reason why Iran could not follow Venezuela and claim half his company's profits was because Anglo-Iranian's subsidiaries operated outside the country. The Iranians pointed out that, without their oil, the subsidiaries would have nothing to sell.

It took the Iranian ruler, the shah, to break the deadlock. After he had instructed his unhappy ministers to accept Fraser's offer, the 'Supplemental Agreement', as the company had dubbed the deal, was signed on 17 July 1949. The company's executives hoped that the shah could railroad the arrangement through the Iranian parliament, the Majlis, before it was dissolved at the end of the month.

But ratification never happened. The Supplemental Agreement was not the fifty–fifty deal the Iranians had asked for; nor did it touch their demand that they should receive a cut of the Anglo-Iranian subsidiaries' profits. When at the same time the company ineptly announced an all-time record profit, the finance minister was, understandably, unimpressed. To sabotage the deal's chances in parliament, he made Gidel's report public. Hostile deputies in the Majlis then talked out the final days of the session to stop the Agreement's ratification.

The British spent liberally to ensure the election of a sympathetic new

Majlis in early 1950. But if they believed that its pro-British majority would swiftly endorse the Supplemental Agreement, they were wrong. At the election, a new coalition calling itself the National Front, which opposed the Anglo-Iranian agreement, also won eight seats. Led by a former finance minister named Mohammad Mosaddeq, the Front blamed foreign interference for Iran's many problems, and promised fundamental change. Mosaddeq and his colleagues succeeded in forcing the Majlis to refer the Supplemental Agreement to a parliamentary committee for further scrutiny, and then managed to secure six out of the eighteen seats on the panel. Mosaddeq became its chairman.

The shah fired his prime minister and finance minister and appointed a lean, overconfident general, Ali Razmara, as the new premier. Razmara felt sure that he could push the Supplementary Agreement through the Majlis if only Anglo-Iranian made some concessions. With American encouragement, he demanded greater transparency from the company, and for the Iranians to be treated as well as Anglo-Iranian's most favoured customer, the Royal Navy.

Razmara enjoyed discreet British and American backing, and presumably expected a sympathetic response. Had he got one at this point, history might have been different. But Anglo-Iranian's managers rejected all his proposals: the last thing they wanted was for sunlight to caress the company's ledgers because then the Iranians might find out how much their marketing subsidiaries were really making. Their stance was supported by the British government, which had seen its majority pared back to single figures in that February's election, and stood to lose a lot of revenue if the concession were rewritten in the Iranians' favour. In talks with the American ambassador in London in August 1950 Bevin defended the Supplemental Agreement as 'generous', and refused to give any ground, because of the 'Iranian propensity to keep opening their mouths wider'.[16]

* * *

Worried about the consequences of continued British pig-headedness, that September the assistant secretary of state George McGhee flew to London to try to convince his British counterparts to agree to Razmara's requests, but he got nowhere. Although by then there were abundant signs that the communist-backed Tudeh Party was gaining ground in Iran, the British thought that American predictions of Iran's imminent collapse and takeover by Moscow were overblown. Even when McGhee warned them that Aramco was about to make a concession to the Saudis that was 'so large . . . that there would be no chance for Iranian ratification of the . . . Supplemental Agreement', the British would not budge. The reaction from the company was no better. 'The . . . Board, in effect, told me that I should mind my own business. They knew more about Iran than we did,' he later recalled. 'If you give the Iranians an inch they'll take a mile,' Anglo-Iranian's directors told him.[17]

So be it, thought McGhee. Having tried to save the British from themselves, he returned home and summoned senior Aramco executives and the American ambassador to Saudi Arabia to see him on 6 November. Two days earlier the Saudis had upped the ante by bringing in an income tax that targeted Aramco; McGhee told the oilmen that he favoured 'rolling with the punch'. Aramco's representatives agreed that they could afford to pay more; a fifty–fifty tax deal attracted them 'since it might involve no additional expense to the company'. When McGhee said he could not pre-empt the Treasury's response to this arrangement, it became clear that the company had already done its homework. Aramco's vice-president, James Terry Duce, told him that Treasury officials he had already approached did not seem 'particularly concerned' about the issue. That news must have delighted McGhee: he was about to get the disguised subsidy for the Saudis that he had wanted, without the rigmarole of having to gain Congressional approval first.[18]

Aramco's negotiation with the Saudi government, which coincided with the opening of the TAPLINE, took barely a month. Truman had already helped pave the way, by reaffirming that the United States was committed to preserving 'the independence and territorial integrity' of Saudi Arabia. On 10 January 1951 Duce took McGhee's assistant Richard Funkhouser through the completed deal. Barraging the young diplomat with the previous year's figures for gross profits, expenses and US tax, not forgetting royalties, rents, duties and the two new rates of Saudi tax, Duce conjured up a figure of $110 million for the Saudi share of the company's net profit. Once that share of the net profit was divided by an output of 538,000 barrels a day, it produced a very convenient result. Under the new arrangement just negotiated 'Mr Duce calculated that 1950 royalties would come to approximately 56 cents per barrel' – in other words one cent more than the Saudis had accepted from the Pacific Western Oil Company two years earlier. Whether or not Funkhouser could follow Duce's working, he got the essential point. 'It is equivalent to the highest existing formula and appears basically fair,' he judged, in a telegram summarising the deal.[19]

Funkhouser's choice of phrase was telling. For appearances were deceptive and in reality the formula was anything but fair. Like Anglo-Iranian, Aramco was massaging its profit. The figure on which the fifty–fifty calculation was founded, Aramco's gross profit, was low because the company sold oil to its four American owners at a significant discount. The owners then reaped the profit when they sold that oil on to consumers at the going rate. It was not until mid-1953 that the Saudis realised what was going on – and that they had therefore missed out on about $100 million – and pressed Aramco to change the basis for the fifty–fifty calculation. Aramco rolled over and the Saudis' royalty then leapt by almost 50 per cent, to 83 cents per barrel.

All that, in early 1951, still lay in the future. What mattered for the time being was that, with US government support, Aramco had set a generous-looking precedent: one that would have seismic consequences when the Anglo-Iranian Oil Company, backed by its main shareholder the British government, refused to follow it, until it was too late.

AN UNFORTUNATE TURN

Although the British and Americans differed over whether Iran was on the brink of collapse, the Iranian government's decision to nationalise the Anglo-Iranian Oil Company in 1951 came at a time when the country was in a parlous state. Anglo-Iranian's effective concealment of its profits meant that oil revenues represented only a small fraction of Iran's national income. The country remained an impoverished, predominantly agrarian economy. Well over half its 17 million people were illiterate peasant farmers who scraped a living on plots they rented from absentee landowners, selling any surplus locally. Their livelihoods had been badly affected by wartime occupation and inflation; widespread crop failure in 1949–50 made matters worse, quickening an exodus from the countryside to the cities, especially Teheran.

A lack of political leadership left Iran ill-equipped to cope with the challenges of rapid urbanisation. The shah, whom Wendell Willkie had encountered as a 22-year-old, was now thirty-one. But he remained an unimpressive character who, in an American analysis, could not 'make up his mind whether he should reign or rule, and consequently does neither'. Backed by the army, he was jockeying for power with the tiny clique of landowners, tribal leaders, merchants, clerics and army officers who formed the country's ruling class. Iran's parliament, the Majlis, was small enough to be controlled by the clique, whose vested interest was the perpetuation of the status quo. In the absence of effective political parties, Iranian politics resembled a carousel of familiar, ageing faces who headed up governments that lasted, on average, just six months. An MI6 officer recommended

Through the Looking Glass to anyone who was trying to get their head around the country.[1]

* * *

Mohammad Mosaddeq was one of a growing number of Iranians who were fed up with this situation. A tall, thin, bald man, whose beaky nose and jerky movements invited comparisons to a bird, he came from the very milieu he criticised. His mother was a princess of the dynasty that had ruled the country throughout the nineteenth century; his father had once served as finance minister. So, indeed had he, under the previous shah. But during this time he had established himself as an opponent of corruption and foreign influence – so much so that, during the war, the British had encouraged him to campaign against Russian attempts to acquire an oil concession in the north of the country.

That move would come back to bite the British when they became Mosaddeq's next target, but it is easy to see why they had enlisted his support. Mosaddeq was a powerful and histrionic speaker whose looks and ascetic lifestyle led one British diplomat to describe him as 'a sort of Iranian Mahatma Gandhi, but less rational'. Aged sixty-nine or seventy-nine by 1950, depending on which date of birth you choose to believe, he was beset by a chronic illness which left him frequently exhausted and prone to faint. In one celebrated incident, he collapsed halfway through a speech in the Majlis. Another deputy, a doctor, pushed through the scrum that had formed round him to check his pulse. As he did so, the apparently unconscious Mosaddeq slowly opened one eye, and winked at him. Clever, slippery and unscrupulous though he was, 'One could not help but like him,' said the US diplomat George McGhee.[2]

Anglo-Iranian's officials do not seem, initially, to have been overly worried by Mosaddeq, because they misunderstood him. Until that point in time, they had resolved all their difficulties with money. They had bribed government ministers and officials, deputies and senators in the Majlis, and perhaps the shah as well, in order to persuade him to accept the 1949 Supplemental Agreement. They even discredited their opponents by paying newspapers to run articles claiming that these people were in the company's pay.

Anglo-Iranian's mistake was to assume that these time-honoured techniques would also defeat Mosaddeq. After the Iranian took over the chairmanship of the Majlis's oil committee the company's officials drew up a list of the eighteen-strong panel's members, together with notes on their finances, political allegiances and family links. It was a preliminary to the bribery of the thirteen deputies on the committee who were not members of the National Front, but it did not succeed.[3]

The problem for the company was that Mosaddeq was not interested in money. He 'did not care about dollars, cents or numbers of barrels per day', wrote one Iranian official. 'He saw the basic issue as one of national sovereignty.' In mid-October the National Front staged a four-day debate in the Majlis to expose the oil company's techniques and blame its corrupting activities for the state of the country. Such was the success of this onslaught that once dependable supporters of the company became reticent about expressing pro-British views, fearing that by doing so they would invite accusations of corruption and treachery.[4]

As a result, when Mosaddeq then put the Supplemental Agreement to a vote in the oil committee the following month, his colleagues rejected it unanimously, despite Anglo-Iranian's efforts to bribe them. When, in the final days of December 1950, the ratification bill reached the Majlis, and the new, pro-British, finance minister produced some figures to support his argument that the Majlis should vote to approve the deal, a National Front deputy interrupted him to accuse him of being in Anglo-Iranian's pocket, since the oil company had been touting exactly the same numbers around the newspapers, saying that it would pay them to print them.

Chastened by this exchange, Razmara withdrew the bill proposing the ratification of the Supplemental Agreement the same day. In January 1951, just after Aramco had announced that it had reached a fifty–fifty deal with the Saudi government, Mosaddeq took his argument to its logical conclusion, and called for the nationalisation of the company.

* * *

Anglo-Iranian's initial response to Mosaddeq's demand was to do nothing. Its trenchant chairman Sir William Fraser stuck to the line that the company could not afford a fifty–fifty agreement, and the company's misleadingly reassuring view was that the charismatic Iranian politician's call was just a phase in the country's kaleidoscopic politics. When one of the company's most senior managers in Iran was asked in Whitehall what he made of the 'the cry for nationalisation', he replied that he 'did not attach much importance to it'.[5]

Wrong as this analysis was, the unyielding attitude that it shaped was welcome to Ernest Bevin, who was simultaneously trying to fend off calls from Egyptian nationalists to evacuate British forces from their Suez base, and was by now very ill. Reviewing the situation at the end of January, he described Mosaddeq's call as 'unrealistic', dismissed the National Front's influence as 'undue' and told his colleagues that they must stick to their existing policy. Accepting the company's and his own officials' view that the dispute could be resolved by money, he argued that they should continue to support the Iranian prime minister Ali Razmara in his efforts to push the Supplementary Agreement through parliament, since once that had happened, Anglo-Iranian would release the cash that it had promised under the 1949 deal.[6]

No sooner had Bevin given this assessment than an event in Teheran forced both Razmara and Anglo-Iranian into a rethink. Days later a leading ayatollah, Abol-Ghasem Kashani, organised a public meeting in support of nationalisation in front of the Shah Mosque – the main mosque in Teheran's bazaar. 'A shriveled little Moslem mullah', according to one newspaper, Kashani nursed an almost psychopathic hatred of the British. His father had been killed in battle with them in Iraq in 1914; as a vocal supporter of the Ottoman jihad, he had been interned by them after they invaded Iran in 1941. He had since played on his treatment to shake donations from pious fellow-countrymen which he then disbursed to build a vast network of clients, many of whom worked in the bazaar where the meeting was taking place. Kashani called them the Society of Muslim Mujahids; the American ambassador described them as 'a well-paid gang of professional hoodlums'. The ayatollah was implicated in several murders.[7]

Kashani was both an ally and a rival of Mosaddeq, since his goal was to take over the nationalisation movement – an ambition that the British and Americans would eventually successfully exploit. For the time being, however, Mosaddeq and the mullah each needed one another. While the wily politician won support from secular-minded, middle-class Iranians, it was the theatrical ayatollah who could whip up the devout. The Shah Mosque meeting at the end of January drew a crowd of about 10,000 people, who listened to a series of National Front politicians and mullahs calling for nationalisation and, by way of a finale, another ayatollah who issued a fatwa stating that the Prophet had condemned a government that had given away its people's inheritance to foreigners and so turned them into slaves.[8]

Both Razmara and the company appreciated that the fatwa represented a significant new departure. When the prime minister, who was alarmed by this barely veiled threat, now asked Anglo-Iranian if it would offer a fifty–fifty agreement, the company said that it would be willing to consider it. On 23 February the British ambassador reluctantly confirmed that the British government was also 'ready to examine an arrangement on a 50–50 basis', provided the Iranian government stood up against nationalisation.[9]

Since open acceptance of this offer would only fuel allegations that he was in the company's pocket, Razmara preferred to keep the ambassador's offer secret, so that he could appear to wring it from the British later on. Instead, fatally, he decided to argue that nationalisation would be disastrous because Iran lacked the expertise and the resources to operate its oil industry independently. It would also be illegal.

Four days after Razmara tried out this argument on the oil committee he was shot dead outside the Shah Mosque, where the fatwa had been issued a few weeks earlier. On the day after his assassination, Mosaddeq's oil committee unanimously voted in favour of nationalising Anglo-Iranian, and referred the matter back to the Majlis for a vote. Showing an uncharacteristic independent-mindedness Iran's deputies shrugged off British pressure on them to stay away so that the session was not quorate, and also voted for nationalisation on 15 March 1951. 'The situation in Persia has taken an unfortunate turn,' Britain's Joint Intelligence Committee observed the same day, from London.[10]

The British government decided that, if the current Majlis would not do as it was told, the time had come to dissolve it and elect a new one – a strategy that hinged on the complicity of the shah. But by the time that they had decided on this course of action, the American diplomat George McGhee had established that it was not viable. As soon as he received news of the Majlis's vote for nationalisation, McGhee had raced to Teheran, where he found the young shah in his palace lounging

Wendell C. Willkie and General Montgomery study a map, August 1942.

James Landis. 'Landis, in spite of everyone's best efforts, insisted in regarding the British, not the Germans, as his principal enemy,' recalled his colleague Kim Roosevelt.

Bill Eddy, bending, left, interprets for Ibn Saud and Franklin D. Roosevelt at the Bitter Lake meeting. His record of the conversation landed Roosevelt's successor, Harry Truman, in hot water.

The play *A Flag is Born*, starring Marlon Brando, raised funds for the Irgun.

Members of the United Nations' Special Committee on Palestine watch as the *Exodus*'s passengers are forced to disembark at Haifa, July 1947.

King Abdullah. The British backed Abdullah's ambitions to rule a 'Greater Syria' after their hopes of clinging on in Palestine began to crumble.

The boy king Feisal II of Iraq and his uncle, Abdul Ilah, the regent. The Americans played on rivalry between the Iraqi and Jordanian branches of the Hashemite family to destroy the Greater Syria scheme.

Wilfred Thesiger in Abu Dhabi in 1948, having crossed the desert after his arrest by the Saudis.

Aramco trains its Saudi employees to tell the time.

In January 1951,
Mohammad Mosaddeq
called for the nationalisation
of the British-owned Anglo-
Iranian Oil Company
triggering a prolonged crisis.

Flanked by Clement Attlee, Herbert Morrison fends off Tory accusations of incompetence during the Iran crisis.

Winston Churchill and Anthony Eden. 'I haven't got a log heavy enough to hold this elephant,' Eden once said of his boss.

The conspirators, from left to right: Abdel Hakim Amer, Gamal Abdel Nasser, Mohammed Neguib, and Gamal Salem.

John Foster Dulles presents Neguib with a pistol, a choice of gift that infuriated the British.

The 'Black Panther', Princess Ashraf. In exchange for a mink coat and a wad of money she agreed to try to convince her brother, the shah, to back the Anglo-American coup in 1953.

Demonstrators in Teheran after the coup. 'They scared the hell out of me,' Kim Roosevelt admitted later.

on a sofa. When he told him that he would have British and American support if he opposed nationalisation, the shah 'said he couldn't do it. He pleaded that we not ask him to do it. He couldn't even form a government.' To McGhee he looked 'a dejected, almost broken, man'. A British diplomat's verdict was harsher: 'He has no moral courage and succumbs easily to fear.' In fact, he suffered from depression.[11]

From Teheran McGhee headed again to London for further meetings with the British. Desperate to avoid nationalisation because it might give the Saudis ideas, he suggested that Anglo-Iranian could rescue the situation by making the Iranians an offer on a par with Aramco's to the Saudis. But it was crucial that it was no better, because if Anglo-Iranian now reached a more generous settlement with the Iranians that was sure to trigger renewed Saudi pressure on Aramco.

The problem was that differences between the companies' structures and in their treatment under their respective tax systems meant that what McGhee was proposing was almost impossible to achieve in practice. In particular there was no way that the British government would extend to Anglo-Iranian the same foreign tax relief that had enabled Aramco to offer the Saudis a new deal at no cost to itself, because the British regarded their company as a cash cow. 'It might be best', McGhee admitted after he had mulled over the challenge at length, 'not to attempt to clarify the complex issue of whether the 50–50 split is before or after the taxes of the country in which the company is domiciled ... let each company work out with the country concerned what the 50–50 arrangement actually means in practice.' In other words he was proposing a fudge.[12]

To pay lip service to the fifty–fifty concept, McGhee suggested that the Iranians might take back control of their resources, and enter an agreement in which Anglo-Iranian would operate production and split the resulting profits with the country. As Bevin was by now on his deathbed, the American diplomat put this idea to Bevin's unimpressive successor at the Foreign Office, Herbert Morrison. Even allowing for the fact that Morrison was new to the job, his ignorance was glaring. 'Ernie Bevin didn't know how to pronounce the names of the places either,' said one man, after Morrison got in a tangle over the word Euphrates, 'but at least he knew where they were.' The meeting went badly after Morrison decided that McGhee had probably already tested his proposal on the

Iranians during his visit to Teheran. 'McGhee's approach to some of our Middle East problems struck me as being a little light-hearted,' the new foreign secretary reported to his colleagues in the cabinet and the embassy in Washington afterwards. 'I told him to be careful.'[13]

McGhee's lunch with the chairman of Anglo-Iranian, Sir William Fraser, did not go any better. Like McGhee the Scotsman understood the technical side of the oil business perfectly, but there the similarity ended. While McGhee was young and genial, Fraser was dour and dictatorial, and when another British official said that Anglo-Iranian though 'technically highly competent ... had as much political nous as a blind rhinoceros' he undoubtedly had the company's chairman in mind.[14]

Fraser had been working in the oil business longer than McGhee had been alive and, 'a Scotsman to his fingertips' to quote one of his colleagues, he viewed everything with an eye to how his shareholders might react to it. Their returns had already been squeezed by the ailing Labour government's policy of dividend restraint and Fraser was probably looking forward to being able to be more generous if, as was expected, the Conservatives were soon back in power. When he heard McGhee's scheme, he gave it short shrift, because he could immediately see that it would eat into the profit he could distribute in dividends. 'The trouble with you, McGhee, is that you are operating on the basis of the wrong information,' he remarked. 'Fifty–fifty is a fine slogan, but it seems to me to be of dubious practicality.'[15]

McGhee must have recognised the truth in what Fraser was saying, but equally he thought that a deal was urgently needed. On his return to Washington he saw a CIA estimate that reckoned that, if the current situation persisted, Iran was 'likely in time to become a second Czechoslovakia', and so he saw the British ambassador again. Since one obstacle to nationalisation was the fact that the Iranians could not afford to compensate the company's current shareholders, he suggested that the British simply waive that right in exchange for half the profits. The ambassador, who in a previous life had taught McGhee at Oxford, took umbrage at the way in which his former student seemed to have accepted nationalisation as a fact. The British government would be opposed, he said, 'to any course which would represent straight appeasement to the pressures that had been created'. In London Herbert Morrison, who later characterised the exchange as 'not altogether smooth', continued to hold out for a solution that preserved British control over the company.[16]

* * *

Much as McGhee may have wished otherwise, the reality, by April 1951, was that the British government had no room for manoeuvre. The election the previous February had cut its majority to five, and the difficult decisions that it was forced to make that spring ahead of the Budget would spark a civil war inside the cabinet that eventually consumed the wider party. Nor was the sense of malaise that now seemed to surround the government simply metaphorical. Bevin died on 14 April, and when Attlee heard the news he was in hospital himself, recuperating after an operation on a stomach ulcer.

The last thing that the convalescing British prime minister needed at this moment was a foreign policy crisis, but it looked alarmingly like one was brewing. Since Mosaddeq's demand at the beginning of the year, the nationalists in Egypt had started talking about taking back the Suez Canal. To Attlee it was obvious that to cave in to the Iranian demand for the nationalisation of the oil company would establish a 'dangerous principle' that would not only deny the government a vital source of revenue, but would also ask for trouble in Egypt. Churchill, now leader of the opposition, could be expected to make hay out of both.[17]

News from Teheran provided Attlee and his new foreign secretary Herbert Morrison with an excuse to hold out. From the Iranian capital the British ambassador reported his belief that the National Front was 'becoming apprehensive about the possible results of their ... policy' and might yet be persuaded to come to an agreement. He also reckoned that the Iranians would welcome a strong lead from Britain and that action should be urgently taken to anticipate a likely investigation by Mosaddeq's committee of the practicability of nationalisation.[18]

This wishful assessment led the British government to make an unforced, pivotal error that, with hindsight, made the situation irretrievable. On 27 April, after Mosaddeq pushed a more detailed resolution through the oil committee setting out the framework for nationalisation, the Iranian prime minister resigned in protest. The British ambassador, who had heard that Mosaddeq realised his own proposals were unworkable, now pounced on what he saw as an opportunity to call his bluff. Hoping to install a pro-British candidate as the new premier, he encouraged another leading deputy to propose Mosaddeq for the top job. He was calculating that Mosaddeq would refuse, opening the way for Britain's man.

Mosaddeq, however, saw the trap and accepted the challenge. After the Majlis endorsed him by a large majority, he in turn saw his chance to solicit general acceptance of his plan. He said that he would only assume the premiership if the Majlis also endorsed his oil committee's resolution nationalising Anglo-Iranian. After the Majlis did so unanimously, on 29 April 1951 Mosaddeq became prime minister. In cabinet the following day Morrison decried what had happened as 'a monstrous injustice'; the minister of fuel and power was rather closer to the mark when he reflected that it was 'clear now that reports that there was no steam behind this were wrong'.[19]

Morrison now considered military action to seize Abadan and the oilfields: a plan drawn up by the military envisaged landing a force of 70,000 men. An MI6 officer suborned the commander-in-chief of the garrison in the town nearest to Abadan, Khorramshahr, so that he would offer no resistance. Simultaneously, while claiming to be going shooting in the mountains, British embassy officials began talking to the chiefs of the Bakhtiari and Qashqai tribes, in whose territory the oil wells were situated. This did not escape the notice of the CIA which speculated that the tribes might unilaterally declare their independence, creating a congenial environment that would allow 'the exploitation of Iranian oil to continue under British management'.[20]

'Sheer madness' was the new US secretary of state Dean Acheson's reaction when he learnt about the British plan and he quickly called on the British and Iranians to negotiate. His statement, released on 18 May, was a model of even-handedness. It sympathised with the Iranian decision, telling the British that Iran needed greater control over its oil resources, and warned the Iranians that a unilateral cancellation of the contract would have serious effects.[21]

Acheson's intervention was the first sign that the United States was not going to side with London in the dispute, and its tone ruffled feathers in London – it was 'as if we were two Balkan countries being lectured in 1911 by Sir Edward Grey', huffed one Tory politician. But it had the desired effect. Attlee and Morrison shelved their plan to take over southern Iran and decided instead to refer Iran's breach of contract to the International Court of Justice. And, most importantly, Morrison finally conceded in public that the government was now 'prepared to consider a settlement which would involve some form of nationalisation'.[22]

Under American pressure, the British government had made an enormous concession, which then led to naught. At a meeting in Teheran with the British and American ambassadors two days later, Mosaddeq rejected the offer of talks with the British government. When the American ambassador, already annoyed by the Iranian prime minister's repetitive, 'emotional and generally irrelevant references to the misery and poverty of his country', then asked him if he had considered how he would operate the oilfields without British help, Mosaddeq was fatalistic. 'Tant pis pour nous. Too bad for us,' he answered. 'If the industry collapses and no money comes and disorder and communism follow, it will be your fault entirely.'[23]

The result of this meeting shaped Attlee's chilly response to Truman when he received a letter from the president a few days later claiming that, since the Iranians were 'willing and even anxious to work out an arrangement', it was vital that negotiations 'be entered at once'. When British officials found out that a copy of this letter had also found its way to Mosaddeq – supposedly by accident – they were incandescent, since it confirmed their suspicions of American bias. When a delegation from the oil company, which had arrived in Teheran for talks, was then confronted with an exorbitant Iranian demand and went home empty-handed ten days later, they blamed the president.[24]

* * *

On 11 June 1951 Iranian officials took control of the company's main office in Khorramshahr, near Abadan. When the Iranians then insisted that tankers leaving Abadan should provide receipts for the oil that they were taking – a procedure that implied the oil was theirs and did not belong to the company – Anglo-Iranian's general manager, Eric Drake, refused. The loading of tankers in the port stopped. The Iranians owned no tankers of their own and, annoyed by this development, proposed a new law making sabotage of the oil industry a capital offence. Fearing for his life, Drake fled to Basra, and on 25 June Attlee insisted that the remaining tankers at the port withdraw.

Attlee and his colleagues understood the implications of this move. As Hugh Gaitskell put it, 'Our policy is to get the Persians into the position of getting themselves in a mess.' With no tankers drawing oil, Abadan's fuel tanks would rapidly fill up. Once they had done so, the company would have to cap its wells and stop paying its 80,000-strong local workforce. When that happened, the chances of rioting would leap: disorder would give the British grounds to send in troops, in order to protect British subjects. Asked in cabinet what he expected to come of this chain of events, Attlee said, 'A reasonable Government, with which we could conclude a new agreement.'[25]

Aware of what the British government was trying to do, Truman bought time by despatching Averill Harriman to meet Mosaddeq. Harriman, a former ambassador to London, enjoyed a reputation as a trouble-shooter and, despite becoming exasperated by the Iranian prime minister's erratic behaviour, produced the verdict the president desired. 'It is my impression that an atmosphere exists in Teheran today in which the British can make a satisfactory settlement,' he concluded after a fortnight in the capital. 'I doubt whether as favorable a situation will present itself again.'[26]

Harriman's optimism left the British with no choice but to send out a junior minister, Richard Stokes, to investigate the opening that Harriman had supposedly identified. When Stokes met Mosaddeq, the Iranian prime minister told him that his government had 'divorced the company'. 'It was a curious arrangement for a man to divorce his wife and then attempt to starve her to the point where she is obliged to kill him,' was the British minister's disconcerting reply. Stokes would only offer a deal that left Anglo-Iranian substantially in control of oil operations, and after almost three weeks in the country he too left Teheran empty-handed. He realised that the window for a negotiated settlement had already closed. 'Fifty–fifty won't do in Persia', he reported after his return, 'because they've had a worse basis for so long.'[27]

The matter was still unresolved when Attlee called an election that September. In what turned out to be his final cabinet meeting, he and his colleagues reviewed the situation one last time. Having heard the news of the election, Mosaddeq had just announced that he would expel the

British technicians working at Abadan on 4 October, the date of parliament's dissolution. The deliberate timing of this move left Morrison splenetic. 'The Persians tear up the contract without consultation with us. Push our people around. Steal their personal property. Pinch British asset,' he railed to his colleagues. Now they 'propose to push British personnel out'. The foreign secretary still favoured the use of force, but Attlee did not. Although he was well aware that such a move would be very popular, he knew that he lacked Truman's support to take it and, thinking it anyway unlikely to succeed, preferred to refer the matter to the Security Council. He was backed by his colleague Hugh Dalton. 'We can't flout the United States, on whose aid we depend so much,' was the former chancellor's matter-of-fact observation.[28]

After the British ambassador to the UN broached the issue on 1 October 1951, his Iranian counterpart asked for time, to enable Mosaddeq to come to New York to speak. 'The British give me the impression of singing the last act of "The Twilight of the Gods" in a burning theater,' observed America's ambassador to the United Nations, after he had heard his ally speak. An MI6 officer was blunter still. 'In the last crucial days there was nobody at the helm.'[29]

A change of government now looked almost certain. The Conservatives were some way ahead in the polls, while Attlee looked 'tired and rather disillusioned', American diplomats reported from London. Their impression was that the Labour Party seemed 'willing to give up office at the present time ... but with the hope that they will come back ... in the not too distant future following the failure of the Conservatives to solve the present world-wide problems which they would inherit from Mr Attlee's Government.'[30]

Mohammad Mosaddeq was not so sure. He had come to New York to represent his country at the United Nations, and George McGhee was keen to keep him there, hoping that it might be possible to broker a rapid solution with the new British government. When he met McGhee on 28 October, after it was clear that the Conservatives had narrowly won, he admitted to being 'somewhat disquieted' by the outcome, because he feared that Churchill would turn out to be 'more intransigent' than Attlee. Although McGhee tried to convince him otherwise, he was entirely right to be.[31]

SECOND FIDDLE

When Dean Acheson met the new British foreign secretary, Anthony Eden, for the first time, on the margins of a meeting in Paris in November 1951, he hoped to make a breakthrough on the long-running Anglo-Iranian dispute. Having attributed the Labour government's inflexibility to electoral pressures, tiredness and infighting, he anticipated that the new Conservative government would be strong enough to be more generous to Teheran. He was to be disappointed.

In reality, the new British government was in no stronger a position than its limping predecessor had been. Campaigning on a manifesto that promised a 'Britain Strong and Free', Winston Churchill had won the previous month's election, but far less decisively than he would have liked. Labour had in fact polled more votes: it was only a collapse in the Liberals' vote and the vagaries of the UK's electoral system that had given him a narrow majority, of seventeen.

A month short of his seventy-seventh birthday, Churchill was well aware that many people – foremost among them his impatient understudy Eden – thought that he was too old for the job. On the stump he had tried hard to counter the perception, on one occasion tucking in to an enormous fry-up followed by a large whisky and soda and a huge cigar – all at half past seven in the morning. That feat impressed Harold Macmillan, the up-and-coming Tory politician who was with him on that occasion. But Macmillan would, however, later skewer his boss as 'admired, but on the whole disliked'.[1]

By the time that Churchill re-entered 10 Downing Street, he faced a further Middle Eastern crisis. Days after Mosaddeq decreed that the

British staff in Abadan must leave within a week, the Egyptian government had presented its parliament with a bill abrogating the 1936 treaty with Britain – the agreement that gave Britain the right to station troops along the Suez Canal. The day after the abrogation bill passed into law, the Egyptian government publicly rejected an Anglo-American proposal for a Middle East Command, which would have internationalised the Suez base and provided the basis for an ongoing British presence. That same day Egyptians rioted in Ismailia, the city where the British military headquarters was situated. 'This is the example we must follow in our struggle with the British,' an Egyptian newspaper declared as the British were forced out of Abadan. 'It is only the weak whom they oppress. Their prestige in the Middle East is finished.'[2]

Churchill had no doubt whatsoever that Britain's unceremonious expulsion from Abadan had emboldened the Egyptians to take action, since he described the developing Suez crisis as the 'bastard child of the Iranian situation'. Well aware that he owed his narrow victory in part to his repeated accusations that Labour had failed to defend the Empire, he was in no mood to make concessions to Egypt or Iran.[3]

Nor, at that point, was Eden. When the foreign secretary met Acheson in Paris that November, he had just come off the telephone from the prime minister. With Churchill's warning 'not to yield an inch' ringing in his ears, he told the secretary of state that his proposal – which accepted nationalisation as a fait accompli – was 'totally unacceptable'. Mosaddeq – still then waiting in New York – should be made to go home empty-handed, he continued, since if the grandstanding Iranian prime minister fell as a result, 'there was a real possibility that a more amenable Government might follow'. Acheson disagreed, feeling that his counterpart had failed to appreciate that it was impossible to turn back the clock. 'You must learn to live in the world as it is,' he told Eden's adviser Evelyn Shuckburgh, tartly, afterwards.[4]

Eden showed no sign of wanting to take Acheson's advice. To his next encounter with Acheson three days later, he brought two senior officials, from the Treasury and the Ministry of Fuel and Power. After the oil expert had dismantled the American proposal, showing rightly why it was commercially unviable, the Treasury mandarin observed that there would be 'catastrophic' consequences if it became more widely known that the British were even considering negotiating on the basis suggested by Acheson. The secretary of state's face betrayed his feelings. 'He seemed irritated by our experts', a British diplomat recorded, 'when they explained the damage that might be done to our interests all over the world if we gave the Persians a premium for having seized our installations.'[5]

Only after Acheson had spent six days in Paris did the penny finally drop. Neither Churchill nor Eden had any intention of accepting a settlement that suggested that Mosaddeq had profited by his actions while Britain was humiliated. Nor were they willing to lift the highly effective boycott of Iranian oil that was now bringing the country to its knees. The secretary of state's argument that the blockade left the country on the brink of a collapse from which Moscow could only benefit did not register with Eden or his advisers. 'If your appraisal of the Iranian situation is correct, then the choice before you is whether Iran goes Commie or Britain goes bankrupt,' a member of the British delegation had told him. 'I hope you would agree that the former is the lesser evil.' Acheson's disappointment was obvious. 'The only thing which is added to the Labor party attitude is a certain truculent braggadocio. They have not been returned to office to complete the dissolution of the empire,' he concluded.[6]

That nod to Churchill's defiant statement at the Mansion House in 1942 was apt, for the prime minister referred constantly to the war. The fact that there were 'more than 50,000 British graves in Egypt' was as powerful an argument as any for an ongoing British presence there, in his view. His magic formula for dealing with the crisis facing Britain was unchanged from a decade earlier. 'It is of utmost importance to get America in,' he wrote days after his return to power, on 10 November – the exact same day that Acheson described him and his colleagues as 'depressingly out of touch with the world of 1951'.[7]

While Churchill, oblivious to Acheson's opinion of him, waited for the Truman administration to come round to his way of thinking, his strategy was simple. Do nothing 'sharp or sudden', he instructed Eden. There was 'no need to hurry either in Egypt or Persia', he reiterated in Cabinet a few days later, 'Time is now on our side.' His hope was that a mounting sense of crisis in both Iran and Egypt would force the United States to back him, creating pressure on the rulers of both countries to appoint new governments that would deal with him. It was a strategy that was deeply flawed.[8]

* * *

By the end of 1951 the chances that the Iranians would accept any outcome that stopped short of nationalising Anglo-Iranian were nil, as Acheson had already grasped, and in Egypt the list of politicians willing to risk their reputations by negotiating with the British was short. In the decade since the then British ambassador, the bullying Miles Lampson, had parked his tanks outside the Abdin Palace, relations between the British and their unwilling Egyptian hosts had not improved. Egypt's unstable situation had not helped. Following the war's end, boom had given way to bust and mass unemployment, which a series of coalition governments all failed to solve. Egypt's defeat by Israel in the 1948 war reinforced the sense of national crisis, while the ongoing presence of tens of thousands of British troops on the canal continually tweaked Egyptian insecurities. The major beneficiary of the mounting discontent at the country's predicament was the Muslim Brotherhood, the half-million-strong Islamist and anti-imperialist movement born two decades earlier in Ismailia, the city where the divide between the Egyptians and the British was glaring.

Had the British left Egypt in 1949 as Ernest Bevin had originally intended, they would have avoided becoming such an easy scapegoat for the country's woes. But as they had not, they became the targets of an insurgency organised by the Muslim Brotherhood that, by the end of 1951, had been going on for over eighteen months. Its foot soldiers were the fedayeen, commandos who would coat themselves in grease and then roll in sand for camouflage. Trained by former German army officers, they were joined by moonlighting Egyptian auxiliary policemen who were sent to Ismailia to keep the peace after the 16 October riots. Benefitting from the auxiliaries' inside knowledge, the fedayeen's attacks increased in frequency and accuracy.

The nature of Britain's Suez base, which was in fact a series of sep-arate encampments covering an area of 750 square miles, left it and troops travelling between its different installations extremely vulnerable to fedayeen attacks. Barbed wire, arc lamps, dogs and anti-personnel mines did not prevent several break-ins each week. Since the British controlled the oil refinery at Suez, the Labour government's response to these attacks had been to cut off the supply of fuel oil periodically, on which Egyptian bakeries, sewage works and light industry across the Nile delta depended. Churchill enthusiastically continued this policy, hoping it would bring matters to a head. 'Touch 'em up on the black oil,' he urged on 12 November, 'Let the temperature rise.'[9]

And rise it did. Five days later two British army officers were murdered when they came under fire from a police station while out shopping with their families in Ismailia. The British government responded by evacuating military families from the city and, under pressure from the generals to take tougher action, imposed stiffer oil sanctions which cut off the supply one day each week. Churchill's justification for this policy was that the troops involved in checking vehicle traffic needed some respite, but Acheson correctly saw it as deliberately provocative. When he saw Eden on the margins of a foreign ministers' conference the same day, he told the foreign secretary that the British approach would achieve nothing and that he was wholly wrong to endorse it.

Meanwhile the attacks continued. There was night-time sniping, cable cutting and ambushes. British soldiers were sandbagged in the streets and murdered. Their mutilated bodies were usually found floating in the Sweet Water Canal which linked the Nile to the Canal Zone. The British retaliated. In the six weeks following the 16 October riots, their soldiers killed 117 Egyptian civilians and wounded another 400. They caused outrage when on 5 December they made nearly 300 Egyptians homeless when they bulldozed their houses to widen a particularly ambush-prone road.

The British had given no warning of this operation to the Egyptian government, which now recalled its ambassador to London in protest. The American ambassador reported that Egyptian anger had reached 'such white heat that a real explosion seems inevitable'. Ominously, he warned that, 'There are no longer elements of the press, officialdom or even the public to whom we can look for rationality on this question.'[10]

By the end of 1951 the situation in the Canal Zone bore striking similarities to Palestine five years earlier. More and more British troops were embroiled in an insurgency which was unwinnable now that they had lost the support of the majority of local people. The two British generals in Egypt asked London for powers enabling them to detain, try and punish fedayeen they captured, but Eden quickly dismissed their request for what amounted to a local martial law. Setting aside the fact that executions would be as counter-productive as they had been in Palestine, the Egyptians were bound to retaliate by cutting off food and water supplies on which British forces in the Canal Zone depended. To work, the generals' proposal required the government either to supply the Suez base itself, or else to sanction the takeover of Egypt. Since neither option was remotely feasible, Eden instead suggested giving the commanders on the ground the power to detain suspects indefinitely instead. Although he admitted that this measure was of 'dubious legality', Churchill was unfussed. 'Pig it,' the prime minister suggested, when the issue came before the cabinet. 'Don't be too scrupulous about the law.'[11]

A few days later, after dinner in the British ambassador's residence in Paris, Eden raised the question of what to do about the Egyptians when the prime minister was present. The whisky had been flowing and a witness recalled how Churchill rose from his chair and advanced towards Eden with clenched fists. 'Tell them that if we have any more of their cheek we will set the Jews on them and drive them into the gutter, from which they should never have emerged,' he growled at the foreign secretary.[12]

The morning after, Eden asked his office to draft instructions for the British ambassador to Cairo, telling him to approach King Farouq and suggest he replace his government with one willing to negotiate with him. Recalling how the Anglo-Egyptian relationship had worked in wartime, he also told his envoy to 'lecture King in Miles Lampson way'. Whether or not Eden really wanted the ambassador to do this is moot. The fact that this message was shown to the US ambassador before it went tends to suggest that the foreign secretary hoped to scare the Americans into doing his dirty work for him. Whatever, possibly after being tipped off by the Americans, Farouq did not throw out his government but instead appointed two well-known Anglophiles to advise him. One of them was the ambassador his government had just pulled out of London. Heartened by this encouraging gesture, Eden argued that it was time to try to help the king.[13]

* * *

In early January Churchill and Eden went to Washington in search of Truman and Acheson's support to resolve their Middle Eastern woes. Before Truman met Churchill he read an acute and devastating assessment of the prime minister by his ambassador in London, and knew what to expect. Churchill, said the ambassador, was 'definitely aging and is no longer able to retain his full clarity and energy for extended periods. Also he is increasingly living in the past and talking in terms of conditions no longer existing. These developments in his personality mean that he is more difficult to deal with.'[14]

Churchill, Truman, Eden and Acheson dined together on 5 January 1952. 'Did you feel', the prime minister asked Acheson afterwards, 'that around that table this evening was gathered the governments of the world – not to dominate it, mind you – but to save it?' How Acheson responded is not recorded. Eden, and his advisers, on the other hand, were horrified by Truman's treatment of their boss. When Churchill raised his hope that the Americans might commit troops to Suez and stand shoulder to shoulder against Mosaddeq, Truman delegated the matter to Acheson and Eden to discuss. The president 'was quite abrupt . . . with poor old Winston,' one of the British team wrote afterwards. 'It was impossible not to be conscious that we are playing second fiddle.'[15]

The talks went nowhere. Churchill again appealed to the Americans to send troops to the Canal Zone to help, telling Congress it had become 'an international rather than a national responsibility'. But Truman and Acheson were determined to keep their distance. 'We would be like two people locked in loving embrace in a rowboat which was about to go over Niagara Falls,' the secretary of state said. He 'thought we should break the embrace and take to the oars'.[16]

With that analogy Acheson got a laugh out of Churchill, but nothing more. He wanted the British to recognise Farouq as king of Sudan, believing that this would break the deadlock over the Middle East Command talks. But Eden refused. The foreign secretary had an unmatched command of the finer points of the 1936 treaty because he had originally negotiated it. Since the treaty had deliberately left the awkward question of Sudan's future unresolved, he argued that to do as Acheson suggested would implicitly concede that Britain accepted Egypt's abrogation of the agreement, a concession he did not want to make.

Eden arrived back in London ahead of Churchill, and candidly briefed his colleagues. 'He had been forcibly struck – indeed horrified – at the way we are treated by the Americans today,' Harold Macmillan wrote afterwards. 'They are polite, listen to what we have to say, but make their own decisions. Till we can recover our financial and economic independence, this is bound to continue.'[17]

* * *

While the British and American governments struggled to find common ground, the Egyptian crisis deepened. In Ismailia on 19 January 1952 a bomb hidden in a barrow of oranges exploded, killing two British soldiers and wounding six others. The murders sparked open celebration of the streets of the city, with fedayeen firing their weapons in the air. A battle for a bridge over the Sweet Water Canal ensued, during which an American nun in a nearby convent was killed.

The British military authorities knew that auxiliary policemen were moonlighting as fedayeen: the orange barrow bomb convinced them that the time had come to disarm them. Having got the go-ahead from London, on 25 January they launched Operation Eagle. After surrounding the Ismailia auxiliaries' headquarters before dawn, the British force called on the policemen to surrender, using a loudspeaker.

The British had deliberately timed the attack for a Friday – the Muslim day of rest – and expected a walkover. But, over the telephone from Cairo, the minister of the interior ordered the auxiliaries to resist. After the British sent their tank crashing through the main gate of the Egyptians' compound, a fierce battle erupted. During nearly four hours' fighting fifty Egyptian policemen and ten British soldiers were killed. For Britain's commander-in-chief in the Middle East it was a sobering encounter. 'Whereas we once thought that all Egyptians are cowards and would pack up when confronted by force,' he admitted, 'that is certainly not the position today.'[18]

The Egyptians responded with a devastating day of arson the following day. After a rumour spread that the interior minister had made his no-surrender phone call from his bathtub while smoking a cigar, Cairo's auxiliaries took to the streets. Around lunchtime, when their protest was winding down, news arrived that a series of fires had broken out in the European part of the city. When the auxiliaries arrived they found organised gangs torching British and other foreign-owned properties and businesses and joined in. So too, later in the day, did members of the

Muslim Brotherhood. Two totems of the British presence, Shepheard's Hotel and the Turf Club, were gutted by fire; the mob beat several of the Turf's escaping members to death, throwing their bodies back into the building to be consumed by the flames. Nor did the local branches of Barclays, WH Smith, Thomas Cook, BOAC and the British Council escape the rioters' attentions. On 'Black Saturday', as that day became known, nine Britons and twenty-six other westerners were killed, and over 700 buildings were ruined.[19]

The British thought that Farouq had encouraged the riots, or at least made no effort to suppress them, never envisaging damage on the scale that then occurred. What was known for certain was that unfounded rumours that British army units were moving westwards from the Canal towards Cairo had made the king take action. Fearing the reoccupation of his country by British troops, on the day after Black Saturday the king dismissed his government.[20]

The new prime minister, Ali Maher, was notoriously anti-British, but Eden nonetheless saw an opening, since a new government meant elections. Believing that Maher would want to go to the country able to show that there had been progress over the treaty, the foreign secretary argued that there was an opportunity to reach a quick settlement. When, however, he suggested in cabinet that the British government should show that it was willing to withdraw its troops within a year, Churchill exploded. In opposition the Tories had hammered the Labour government hard on exactly this issue, and what Eden was now proposing was 'worse than Abadan', he said. In the aftermath of the Black Saturday riots, he feared Eden's offer could easily be interpreted as appeasement. For Churchill, like many Tories, Egypt had acquired a talismanic importance as the key setting for the lonely British stand against Hitler during the war, and while Eden was undoubtedly being realistic, the prime minister knew that most of his party remained behind him. A few weeks later Harold Macmillan would privately compare the cabinet to 'the directors of a rapidly deteriorating concern. They dare not tell the shareholders the facts, for fear of destroying the credit of the company so completely as to destroy all hopes of recovery.'[21]

* * *

Like Eden, Acheson was also searching for a breakthrough in Egypt. Whereas the British liked to portray themselves, to borrow Churchill's old phrase, as a rock in an uncertain world, the secretary of state's fear was that in Egypt, their continued presence produced anger and instability. Soon after 'Black Saturday' he sent the CIA officer Kim Roosevelt back to Cairo, to see if King Farouq could be persuaded to implement far-reaching reforms and establish a new government that could negotiate a speedy British departure.

At Acheson's behest, Roosevelt had just spent several months chairing a committee tasked with defining a new American approach to the Middle East. 'Our principle', he and his colleagues had concluded, 'should be to encourage the emergence of competent leaders, relatively well-disposed toward the West, through programs designed for this purpose, including, where possible, a conscious, though perhaps covert, effort to cultivate and aid such potential leaders, even when they are not in power.' This represented a sea change. Where once the Americans had invested all their hopes in democracy to transform the region, they would now actively hunt for competence. That shift heralded a more pragmatic American approach, which represented a challenge to King Farouq, who embodied neither value.[22]

Although the king willingly connived in the removal of the prime minister Ali Maher, the man the Americans had once thought 'could probably be developed into a very useful, progressive and influential young monarch' no longer looked like the potential saviour of the country. Having divorced his first wife after she had failed to bear him a male heir, a year earlier Farouq had married his second, Narriman. She came to their wedding in a gown embroidered with 20,000 diamonds to become queen of a country whose inhabitants, at birth, could expect to live to the grand old age of thirty-six. The newly-weds did not endear themselves to ordinary Egyptian Muslims by going on honeymoon during Ramadan and when, after a conspicuously short pregnancy, Narriman gave birth to a son, it became obvious that the couple must have consummated their marriage some time before exchanging their vows. Other rumours swirled around the king: that, after a nightmare, he had shot all the lions in Cairo zoo, that he had once let some porters compete for a handful of gold coins he had dropped in a bucket of liquid that turned out to be sulphuric acid, that he had forced a female peasant on his estate to have sex with an ape.

The list was long and lurid. Whether these stories were true was impossible to say. What mattered was that they spread because they sounded all too plausible, and reinforced the perception that the king believed he was above the law.[23]

Other officers in the CIA's Near East Division referred to Roosevelt's mission as 'Operation Fat Fucker', and it is hard to imagine that there was much surprise when the king rejected Roosevelt's advice. But the spy was no longer depending on Farouq and, in keeping with the new policy that he had helped devise, arrived in the Egyptian capital with some more competent leaders in mind. A few months earlier he had been put in touch with the Free Officers, a group of middle-ranking army officers who were disenchanted by their country's downward spiral. Having met three representatives of the movement secretly on Cyprus, Roosevelt offered them his country's backing and appears to have been instrumental in ensuring that six of them were among fifty Egyptian officers who were then invited to the United States for training. Egypt's chief of air-force intelligence, Ali Sabri, who was a sympathiser, spent six months on an intelligence course in Colorado.[24]

Early in 1952 the Free Officers decided to test the water by putting up a popular general for the presidency of the Officers' Club, against Farouq's own candidate, who was normally elected unopposed. Mohammed Neguib was affable, courteous and not terribly bright. He won.

While Eden later admitted, 'The coup happened so quickly that no one was aware as late as the morning before,' the Americans well knew what was brewing. On 13 July, by which time King Farouq was on his fourth prime minister that year, the assistant air attaché in the US embassy in Cairo was told that the Free Officers were on the point of making a move against the government. A week later, after the king had tried and failed to sack Neguib, the US ambassador said that his embassy would not 'interfere in the domestic politics of another country' – a tacit declaration that his country would not stop the rebels if they decided to act.[25]

The Free Officers did so in the early hours of 23 July 1952 when 300 officers, and 3,000 of their men, occupied army headquarters, the radio station and a number of other key buildings in Cairo, including police stations and ministries. At breakfast time an army officer named Anwar Sadat came on the radio to tell the country that Neguib was now commander-in-chief, and that the army was 'now in the hands of men in whose ability, integrity and patriotism you can have complete confidence'.[26]

Later the same day the Free Officers recalled the man the king had only just sacked to serve as prime minister once more. The choice of Ali Maher reflected their own political inexperience, but the effect of choosing such a well-known figure provided some reassurance to the country's establishment and the king, who had unsuccessfully appealed to both the Americans and the British to reverse the coup. Although the British feared that the Free Officers were a front for some more extreme organisation, on the day after the coup a senior British diplomat, John Hamilton, went to see Neguib to tell him that his government viewed the takeover as an internal matter and would only intervene if foreign lives were threatened. To Neguib, who had been born and brought up in British-run Khartoum, the experience was oddly familiar. 'Y'know Hamilton,' he reminisced, as he copied out what the British diplomat was telling him, 'this reminds me of taking dictation at Gordon College.'[27]

It appears that the Free Officers had not considered what to do about the king, who was in Alexandria. After reports reached them that he had asked the British to intervene, they briefly considered court-martialling and shooting him, before Ali Maher intervened. Maher went to the port city on the 26th to tell Farouq he had to abdicate. 'Sir, it is too late to do anything else,' he said, when the king bridled at the prospect. 'You have only two choices ... do you go by air or by sea?'[28]

'In a few years there will be only five Kings in the world,' Farouq had long predicted. 'The King of England and the four Kings in a pack of cards.' Helped on his way by the CIA's clandestine support of the Free Officers, he sailed for Italy and exile that evening.[29]

* * *

The British had long prided themselves as the kingmakers in Egypt, while the Americans were mere spectators. But the coup had swept away the king and, in the following weeks, the British were forced to acknowledge that they had effectively been usurped: an abrupt role reversal had taken place. A request from the Free Officers that Britain not interfere in the coup reached them via the US embassy. And while a timely tip enabled an enterprising American diplomat, William Lakeland, to make friends with one of the Free Officers' ringleaders, a reserved young army officer named Gamal Abdel Nasser, who turned out to like hotdogs and Esther Williams films, a British spy complained that he had been kept waiting by the new Egyptian chief of intelligence because the American military and air attachés were already in seeing him.[30]

By the end of August 1952 British diplomats suspected that the American ambassador, Jefferson Caffery, was encouraging the junta to keep them at arm's length. The British ambassador admitted that, because his 'crystal' was 'not in working order', he had no idea what would happen next. The ambassador's and his colleagues' sense of being passengers only grew when, a week later and without warning them, Acheson issued a statement welcoming the 'encouraging developments' in Egypt and wishing the new government 'every success'. The new regime interpreted this as a green light to arrest sixty people, many of whom had been close to the British. Ali Maher resigned in protest at the interference the following day and Neguib succeeded him as prime minister, supposedly at the American ambassador's instigation. 'Caffery could not be worse,' raged Eden, in London. 'The British are showing a few signs of being a little unhappy that they have practically no relations with the Egyptian military and our relations are so cordial,' the American ambassador purred, a few days later.[31]

In London on 27 September, Macmillan summed up the situation. 'Perhaps the most noticeable, and painful difference between our position now and when we were last in office ... is our relationship to the US. Then we were on an equal footing – a respected ally ...Now we are treated by the Americans with a mixture of patronising pity and contempt.'[32]

PLOTTING MOSADDEQ'S DOWNFALL

Although the Free Officers' July 1952 coup put paid to British influence in Egypt, it also gave the British elsewhere an idea. Four days after the revolution in Cairo, a British diplomat named Sam Falle met a well-known opponent of Iran's Prime Minister Mosaddeq in Teheran. On his return to his embassy, Falle reported that his contact, Seyyid Zia Tabatabai, had recommended that the British support a military *coup d'état*. And, since the British had just failed again to oust Mosaddeq by parliamentary means, Falle was inclined to agree with him.

The following day Falle met the man most likely to be able to make this happen, Zia's enormously influential sidekick, Asadollah Rashidian. Like Zia, the Rashidians had been allies of the British since the 1920s, a family of fixers who had grown even more rich and powerful when the British made them their sole purchasing agents following the 1941 invasion and occupation of the country. By the war's end the family knew everyone: the shah and his twin sister (with whom they had some sort of financial connection), his chief of protocol, the court and Anglophile members of the Majlis. They also wielded enormous influence deep in Teheran's society – inside the government, within the army and police, with clerics like Ayatollah Kashani, the newspapers and – crucially, as it turned out – with the bosses of the thuggish underclass which toiled in the meat and fruit and vegetable markets of south Teheran – men with names like Mohammad the Simpleton, Mehdi the Butcher and Shaban the Brainless. By mid-1952 the family was on a retainer from MI6 of £10,000 a month.

The name of the general whom Asadollah Rashidian now recommended to replace Mosaddeq was all too familiar to Falle and his colleagues. As a commander of a provincial garrison during the war, Fazlollah Zahedi had been responsible for the deaths of a number of British officials. When intelligence then suggested he was conspiring in a German attempt to take over the country, the British had abducted him and exiled him to Palestine. His kidnapper recalled 'a dapper figure in a tight-fitting grey uniform and highly polished boots', in whose bedroom he had discovered 'a collection of automatic weapons of German manufacture, a good deal of silk underwear, some opium [and] an illustrated register of the prostitutes of Isfahan'. Since then Zahedi had served as Mosaddeq's minister of the interior and was now a member of the Senate. At first sight then, he was an insalubrious and unlikely candidate. And that, as Falle quickly realised, was what made him so ideal: his career path would make it hard for any claim that he was a British stooge to stick.[1]

The British had been hunting for someone to replace Mosaddeq for over a year. Originally they had hoped that Zia himself might be that man, until they realised that the Seyyid was too openly pro-British to have any chance of selling any oil deal to a sceptical Iranian public. They then transferred their allegiances to Zia's rival, Ahmad Qavam, but he too had failed spectacularly that summer. Made prime minister when Mosaddeq theatrically resigned after an altercation with the shah, Qavam had ordered troops onto the streets to break up the demonstrations that followed his appointment. After seventy-nine protestors were killed, he was forced to resign and the shah had no choice but to recall Mosaddeq, who saw his triumph capped a day later when, at the Hague, the International Court of Justice ruled in his favour, declaring that it had no jurisdiction in the case that the British government had referred to it back in 1951.[2]

*　*　*

It was against this backdrop that Sam Falle met Zia and then Rashidian. Falle's boss, the chargé d'affaires George Middleton, thought Rashidian's suggestion that they might back General Zahedi was worth wrapping into a letter he was writing to Eden describing the unstable situation in the country. By now the British-orchestrated boycott of Iranian oil was clearly working. A few days earlier Mosaddeq had offered to negotiate if Britain would give him financial assistance, before abruptly withdrawing his offer, amid reports that his overture had triggered rioting around the country. Describing his impression that Mosaddeq's 'megalomania is now verging on mental instability', Middleton reported that 'it now looks as though the only thing to stop Persia falling into communist hands is a coup d'état'. Although there was 'no outstanding candidate' from the military to replace Mosaddeq, he thought Zahedi 'might be adequate'.[3]

Though hardly a glowing endorsement, Middleton's suggestion had a significant effect on Eden nonetheless. On 29 July the foreign secretary told the cabinet that Mosaddeq 'must be nearly mad' to have withdrawn his offer, and that all hopes of a settlement had vanished. Accepting Middleton's contention that the communist-backed Tudeh Party was the most likely beneficiary of Iran's growing turmoil, he told his colleagues that he had asked the American ambassador in London if they couldn't 'find someone else to back . . . a military man, as in Egypt?' His impression was that the ambassador was 'not averse' to that idea.[4]

Eden became all the more determined to find a 'local Neguib' to solve his problem in Iran when Acheson came up with a new set of proposals designed to break the deadlock before Truman's presidency finished at the end of the year. At the end of July the secretary of state proposed to give Mosaddeq $10 million to tide him over, the establishment of an international arbitration to determine the amount of compensation Iran should pay Anglo-Iranian's shareholders, and that the British should further improve Iran's financial position by buying the oil trapped in Iran by the boycott at a discount.[5]

Since this would undo all the pressure that the oil boycott had heaped on Mosaddeq, Eden instinctively opposed it. But, given the uncompromising American mood since the Egyptian coup, he realised that Acheson would probably release the money anyway. Having heard promising news from Teheran that Zahedi – whom Falle had just met – believed that he could count on the support of several disaffected members of Mosaddeq's National Front, he told the cabinet that, while Zahedi's plans developed, he planned to string Acheson along by showing a willingness to discuss the terms of the arbitration, 'though mainly as a delaying tactic' designed to put off the moment when the secretary paid out the money.[6]

Acheson, however, immediately saw through Eden's conceit. 'The only resemblance I could see between the aide-memoire we had given the British government and Mr Eden's reply,' he wrote, 'was that they were both written on paper and with a typewriter.'[7]

* * *

By the second half of August Mosaddeq was aware that there was plotting against him but he does not appear to have known precisely by whom, because he then took a step that played straight into Zahedi's hands. On 23 August he took the rash decision to press 136 military officers into an early retirement. Their unexpected new status did give them one right – to join the Retired Officers' Association, the president of which was none other than Zahedi. 'I saw General Zahedi today,' Falle reported a fortnight later, 'and found him full of the joys of Spring.'[8]

Zahedi's role did not remain secret for long. In late September the general met Ayatollah Kashani, the rabble-rousing mullah who had played a vital role in destroying Ahmad Qavam's premiership earlier that year, and whose support Zahedi clearly needed if his own attempt to topple Mosaddeq were to succeed. News of their meeting soon leaked. On 4 October the *Wall Street Journal* reported that Zahedi was trying to persuade Kashani and others to support him against Mosaddeq. Describing the general as 'a sort of prospective Iranian "strong man" in the style of Egypt's Naguib', the paper said, 'He has tried to conduct these overtures with careful secrecy – but it's known Mossadegh is already aware of them.'[9]

The revelation that his rivals were conspiring to remove him only increased the pressure on Mosaddeq. Already desperately short of money, early in August he had had to absorb the news that Kashani had just been elected president of the Majlis. The American ambassador happened to be with him at the time. 'Mosaddeq was obviously shocked,' he reported to Washington. 'For a moment he seemed to forget my presence and did not seek to hide his distress and agitation. He fell back on his bed and closed his eyes. I thought he might lose consciousness.' Then, towards the end of the month he received a joint message from Truman and Churchill which offered him the prospect of $10 million and an end to the oil sanctions if he would agree to put the question of compensation to the International Court of Justice. The powers, which he had tried so hard to divide, now appeared to be ganging up against him.[10]

On 13 October, Mosaddeq took action against his opponents, arresting a senior general, as well as Asadollah Rashidian, his brothers and their father. Zahedi and several other opponents enjoyed parliamentary immunity, however, and took sanctuary in the Majlis. The prime minister could only accuse them of complicity in a plot to overthrow him. Three days later, as he had long threatened he would, he finally severed diplomatic relations with Britain. Middleton, Falle and their colleagues were given ten days to leave.

The closure of Britain's embassy in Teheran meant that the British would now be dependent on the Americans for their plan to remove Mosaddeq to succeed, but there was no sign at this point that the Americans were interested. Although the American ambassador reported in September, following a meeting with an unnamed man who was most likely Zahedi, that 'hints of a coup d'état or resort to tactics of violence are becoming more open', he refused to get involved, and had extracted a commitment from his British counterparts that neither of their embassies should encourage or support a coup – a promise that the British had promptly broken. By October 1952 the CIA took a more sanguine view of Mosaddeq's prospects. It now reckoned that the Iranian leader would survive 'at least for the next six months', and would probably see out 1953, providing he could stave off Kashani. That helped explain why Acheson, right up to the end of Truman's presidency, remained committed to the diplomatic track, complaining that there was 'not enough cheese' in Britain's offer. 'We are both very fed up of being lectured by Acheson,' Eden's adviser Evelyn Shuckburgh wrote in his diary.[11]

* * *

Winston Churchill hoped that Truman's successor would view the situation differently. On 4 November 1952 Dwight D. Eisenhower won the presidential election. 'Ike' was a familiar and hugely popular figure in Britain: he had commanded the D-Day landings and, in extremely trying circumstances, had managed to ensure good relations between his own forces and Montgomery's. Eden, on the other hand, was under no illusions that the new president would make their lives any easier. Although, like Churchill, he admired Eisenhower, he recognised that the Republicans distrusted the British even more than the Democrats did, none more perhaps than the man whom Ike had chosen as his secretary of state, John Foster Dulles. It was an appointment, one British diplomat noted with uncanny foresight that November, that 'will make great difficulties for us in the immediate future'.[12]

It would be fair to say the British had never taken to the dour new secretary of state. He was 'the woolliest type of useless pontificating American ... Heaven help us!' Eden's chief wartime adviser Alec Cadogan exclaimed, when he first met him a decade earlier. Eden himself was nauseated by Dulles' bad breath and his tendency to talk down to him. 'Dull, Duller, Dulles,' intoned Churchill. Even Ike admitted that his pick could seem 'a bit sticky at first', and – this would be crucial – had 'a curious lack of understanding as to how his words and manner may affect another personality'. He clearly knew how the appointment would go down in London because his tone was 'almost apologetic' when he confirmed to Eden that Dulles would be his secretary of state.[13]

Dulles, however, seemed born for the role: certainly he had coveted it all his adult life. His grandfather – to whom his name Foster was a tribute – had been secretary of state; so too had his uncle, Robert Lansing. The family connection explains why, in 1919 as a thirty-year-old, he had joined the American delegation at the Paris peace conference. As it was for Roosevelt, Paris was a formative experience: in Dulles' case it left him with a very low opinion of the British. Disillusioned, he departed for the blue-chip law firm Sullivan and Cromwell, but he did not give up thinking about foreign policy. When it became clear, midway through the Second World War, that the Roosevelt administration had begun considering the post-war era, he accepted the chairmanship of an independent commission examining the 'bases for a just and durable peace'. No doubt Dulles was promoting the commission's proposal for a post-war world government when Cadogan encountered him. That was utopian, but three years later Dulles was on hand to witness the birth of the United Nations in San Francisco.[14]

Although Dulles had worked for Truman, he was a Republican by instinct. Around the time that Macmillan was likening Churchill's cabinet to the board of a bankrupt company, Dulles went to see Eisenhower, then running NATO, at his headquarters outside Paris and urged him to run as the Republicans' candidate for president. Alarmed by the Soviet threat, he put to Ike a 'policy of boldness' that advocated pushing back aggressively against communism, and threatening to use nuclear weapons as a first resort in a way that was designed both to deter Russian expansionism and also save money.

Ike, who was also being courted by the Democrats, would accept the Republican nomination and put Dulles' idea at the heart of his campaign. He quickly became reliant on Dulles. As Macmillan observed later, 'he couldn't do without him'. What Dulles thought therefore mattered. He believed, as he had always done, that American leadership was key to the security of the world. The British, on the other hand, were something of a menace, 'a rapidly declining power' whose 'clumsy and inept' behaviour encouraged nationalists like Mosaddeq, causing tensions that the communists could then exploit. According to one of his assistants, the new secretary of state felt that 'you simply could not count on the British to carry on in any responsible way' and 'he had no admiration for them'. He thought Eden was a dandy.[15]

* * *

Once again oblivious to this thinking, Churchill travelled to New York in January 1953 to bid farewell to Truman and, more importantly, to meet Eisenhower for the first time in several years. His aim, he told the cabinet before departing, was to 'do all we can to get the United States involved'. He believed that he could rekindle the close wartime relationship he felt he had enjoyed with Roosevelt.[16]

'I admired and liked him,' Eisenhower wrote of Churchill in his 1948 memoir of the war. He also acknowledged that Churchill 'knew this perfectly well and never hesitated to use that knowledge in his effort to swing me to his own line of thought in any argument'. Forearmed with this knowledge, the president-elect met Churchill three times in early January. Churchill started out by describing the enjoyable sensation of sitting 'on some rather Olympian platform' with Roosevelt during the war and 'directing world affairs from that point of vantage'. He clearly hoped that it might be possible to establish a relationship with Ike that worked along exactly the same lines. Together, he suggested, the two allies could tackle the two most pressing foreign policy problems, Egypt and Iran. With Britain and America jointly sharing the burden, he ventured, 'other nations should recognize the wisdom of our suggestions and follow them'.[17]

Like others, Ike was struck by Churchill's decline. Although the prime minister was 'as charming and as interesting as ever', he recorded in his diary, he was 'quite definitely showing the effects of the passing years'. Most striking was the fact that he seemed to have 'developed an almost childlike faith' that any problem could be solved by an Anglo-American partnership.[18]

Ike thought that Churchill was making a strategic error that stemmed from wishful thinking. In line with Dulles he believed that the 'two strongest Western powers must not appear before the world as a combination of forces to compel adherence to the status quo'. Moreover, he clearly also thought that the assumption on which Churchill was basing his suggestion that the two powers work arm-in-arm was flawed. From personal experience he knew that the wartime alliance had been far rockier than the prime minister was either able to remember or willing to admit. And so his reaction to Churchill's hope of a special partnership was withering: 'any hope of establishing such a relationship is completely fatuous'. He wished the prime minister would retire.

These were Eisenhower's thoughts, not what he said, and so Churchill pressed on oblivious. In a further meeting on 7 January he made a proposal. He was planning to go on to Washington to see Truman, and from there to visit Jamaica for some winter sun. Building on his idea of a special Anglo-American relationship he suggested that he might return from the Caribbean to Washington a fortnight after Eisenhower's inauguration for a summit. Ike dodged a direct answer, saying that he would defer to Dulles' advice.

The same day after dinner Dulles paid Churchill an unexpected visit at his hotel and poured cold water on the prime minister's idea, which he described as 'most unfortunate'. The American people feared Churchill's ability to 'cast a spell' on their leaders, he explained; it would be wise to wait a while before holding any summit. After Dulles had left,

Churchill launched an angry attack on 'the Republican Party in general and Dulles in particular'. He told his private secretary that he wanted to have 'no more to do with Dulles, whose "great slab of a face" he disliked and distrusted'. Piqued by his failure to get Ike to agree with him, he would later call the president 'weak and stupid'.[19]

With no signs of support either from Truman in Washington or Eisenhower in New York, Churchill and Eden realised that they had no choice but to offer to negotiate with both Neguib in Egypt and Mosaddeq in Iran. 'I ended today extremely gloomy about British prospects everywhere,' admitted Eden's aide Shuckburgh on the same day that Churchill received the bad news from Dulles. Shuckburgh saw the very international framework that the new secretary of state had helped to create conspiring against Britain. 'International law and the temper of international opinion is all set against the things which made us a great nation, i.e. our activities outside our own territory,' he feared. 'Bit by bit we shall be driven back into our island where we shall starve.'[20]

Britain's hopes of ousting Mosaddeq now looked extremely remote. It took a change of heart on the part of the Americans to revive them.

THE MAN IN THE ARENA

In February 1953, a fortnight or so after Eisenhower's inauguration, a British delegation led by MI6's chief, Sir John Sinclair, travelled to Washington to meet the new director of the CIA in a bid to convince him to launch a coup against Mosaddeq. Allen Dulles, Foster's younger brother, listened as Sinclair went into the details of 'Operation Boot', as MI6 had dubbed the plan to overthrow the Iranian prime minister.

Twinkly, charming and tactile – he was nicknamed 'the shark' by his long-suffering wife – Allen Dulles might have passed himself off as a college professor were it not for the three telephones – black, white and red – that stood ready on a sideboard behind his desk. He also knew the territory Sinclair was talking about. After serving in the Office of Strategic Services in the war he had re-joined his old law firm Sullivan and Cromwell, where Foster was a partner. In 1949, on behalf of a consortium of engineering firms, he went to Teheran to meet the shah and negotiate a development deal that would have been worth $650 million had it not then been rejected by the Majlis during the furore over the Supplemental Agreement in December 1950. Unlike his older brother, Dulles was not a rich man, and the failure of a project that would have paid him a fortune hurt. He too was keen to see the back of Mosaddeq and would ultimately earmark $1 million for his removal.

Besides Allen Dulles' personal vendetta, there was another reason why the new administration was suddenly willing to take action: Mosaddeq was now directly threatening its interests in a way he had not done before. Until that point Aramco had profited nicely from the Iranian crisis, dramatically increasing its output to fill the gap caused by the British-led boycott of Iranian oil. But then, a few days earlier, the Iranian prime minister had threatened to sell Iranian oil at a 50 per cent discount – a move that would have calamitous implications for Aramco and the Saudis if he followed through with it.

Had Mosaddeq made the threat any earlier, it would have been easy to dismiss. Until the previous December the combination of the British-orchestrated boycott and, more important, a lack of tankers, meant that Iran could not have exported its oil anyway. But in the final days of Truman's presidency Acheson had abandoned the boycott, and falling maritime charter rates would soon make more tankers available. 'It is rapidly becoming apparent', wrote Foster Dulles around the time that the British delegation was in Washington, 'that the future tanker situation . . . will be such in the very near future that Mosaddeq may be able to carry out his threat.' After Sinclair and his colleagues had returned to London the CIA reported that the Iranian prime minister was on the point of announcing the failure of negotiations with the British and intended to ask the Majlis for permission to sell the country's oil at whatever price he could get.[1]

More turmoil in Iran days after Sinclair's meeting with Allen Dulles also provided further grounds for intervention. In mid-February the Bakhtiari – the tribe into which the shah had married – attacked an Iranian army column in the heart of the oilfields, killing forty-two Iranian soldiers. Mosaddeq blamed the British and the shah, and threatened to resign, before changing his mind and arresting Zahedi, who had been all too obviously getting ready to succeed him.

Alarmed by the turn of events, the shah offered to leave the country for a holiday, a prospect that appalled Ayatollah Kashani – not because he liked the shah, but because his absence would give Mosaddeq an opportunity to consolidate his position further. After Kashani had tried and failed to use members of the Majlis to convince the shah not to depart, he ordered Shaban the Brainless to organise a mob to close the bazaar and spread the rumour that the shah had resigned following pressure from Mosaddeq. Swelled by angry bazaaris, the mob then marched on and surrounded the shah's palace to stop the shah from leaving. Mosaddeq, fearing for his life, fled his own home in his pyjamas.

This raw demonstration of Kashani's power alarmed the CIA because the Agency had long argued that if the ayatollah seized power the most likely beneficiary would ultimately be the communist Tudeh Party, which would quickly attract those repelled by Kashani's style of politics. The day after the demonstration in Teheran it argued that, even if the ayatollah did not replace Mosaddeq, the rivalry between the two men was still likely to create a chaotic situation in which a communist takeover became 'more and more of a possibility'.[2]

Three days later, on 4 March, Allen Dulles talked through what had happened and its implications in a meeting of the National Security Council. 'If Iran succumbed to the Communists,' he said, 'there was little doubt that in short order the other areas of the Middle East, with some 60 per cent of the world's oil reserves, would fall into Communist control.' When his brother Foster then said that he expected Mosaddeq to last just one or two years more, Eisenhower was alarmed. 'If I had $500 billion to spend in secret,' the president exclaimed, 'I would get $100 billion of it to Iran right now.' But had he had it at that moment, he would undoubtedly have used it to prop up Mosaddeq.[3]

Eisenhower's attitude to Mosaddeq would change in the course of the next week. On 8 March the CIA produced a further report on the stand-off between Mosaddeq and Kashani, who had meanwhile organised a boycott of parliament by his supporters to prevent it being quorate. Whoever won, the Agency suggested, the implications for the United States were serious. If Mosaddeq failed to recoup the prestige that he had lost and Kashani took over, Eisenhower's administration would have an even more hostile government to cope with. On the other hand, the present deadlock was likely to make Mosaddeq increasingly authoritarian. If he succeeded Iran would take 'one step further along its present revolutionary road', because the communist Tudeh Party was now openly supporting him, having calculated that its interests were best advanced by doing so. The report came as McCarthyite hysteria in Washington was approaching its zenith. Anyone reading it in the capital at that moment would have appreciated its implication: if the communists were backing Mosaddeq, then Eisenhower's administration absolutely could not be seen to be doing so as well.[4]

If Mosaddeq's reputation in the US was tarnished by his association with Tudeh, it was the Iranian prime minister's erratic threats about oil that ultimately doomed him. Late on 10 March Dulles received a telegram from his ambassador in Teheran reporting that Mosaddeq had told him that his negotiation with the British was over. The ambassador advised him not to deal with the Iranian prime minister any further. The next day, at the next National Security Council, Eisenhower observed that 'he had very real doubts whether, even if we tried unilaterally, we could make a successful deal with Mosaddeq. He felt that it might not be worth the paper it was written on, and the example might have grave effects on United States oil concessions in other parts of the world.'[5]

Days later the State Department authorised the CIA to 'consider operations which would contribute to the fall of the Mosaddeq government' and the CIA's director of operations, Frank Wisner, then contacted MI6 in London. He wanted to discuss the detail of a plot.[6]

* * *

By the time that Wisner's message reached MI6 headquarters in March 1953, two points concerning the plot were already clear: it had a leader and a figurehead. In February in Washington, Sinclair had proposed Kim Roosevelt to lead the operation. Roosevelt, seemingly unaware that the British had long been in touch with the general, had suggested that they replace Mosaddeq with Zahedi.

Roosevelt, however, preferred a more fluid approach to the detailed operation Sinclair had set out, and in April tasked Donald Wilber, an archaeologist who had been roped into the OSS in Iran and now acted as a consultant to the CIA, with drawing up a more flexible plan. The challenge, in Wilber's words, was that 'the Persian is not a joiner nor does he find it natural to work with others toward a mutually desired goal'. It was not until mid-May that he put his effort to MI6's Norman Darbyshire in Cyprus, to where the members of the British secret service's Iran station had decamped when they were kicked out of Iran. A fluent Farsi speaker, Darbyshire had joined MI6 from Special Operations Executive. Though not the easiest of men to get on with, he was very highly regarded by his peers, not least because he had spent eight of the last ten years in Iran. He was in contact with the Rashidian family by radio and occasionally met Asadollah in Geneva.[7]

Up to this point both sets of spies had been unwilling to disclose their assets to the other. Darbyshire now shared the identities of the Rashidians with Wilber, but Wilber kept back the names of the two men who ran a network disseminating anti-communist propaganda and were the CIA's most important agents, Ali Jalali and Faruq Keyvani, though Darbyshire would later claim that he guessed who they were. Agreeing that what mattered in Iranian politics was now the shah, the Majlis and the mob, he and Wilber came up with a 'quasi-legal' takeover which entailed a propaganda blitz, large-scale bribery of the Majlis and a march on the parliament that would scare its deputies into passing a vote of no-confidence against Mosaddeq, paving the way for the appointment of Zahedi, who would by then be touting decrees showing that he enjoyed the shah's support.[8]

The combined planning was straightforward. Wilber noted, apparently surprised, that there was 'no friction or marked difference of opinion during the discussions'; Darbyshire, clearly envious of the CIA's superior resources, was under instruction to let Wilber set the pace. As Wilber later commented, 'The British were very pleased at having obtained the active cooperation of the Agency and were determined to do nothing which might jeopardize US participation.'[9]

From Cyprus Wilber flew via Cairo to Beirut where he met Roosevelt, the CIA head of station in Teheran Roger Goiran, and George Carroll, an expert in paramilitary warfare, all of whom were to play key roles in the events that followed. Operation Ajax, as they had renamed the plan – seemingly in tribute to the powers of the abrasive cleaner – was finalised in a room in the Hotel St Georges overlooking the Mediterranean, with the radio on full blast as a defence against eavesdroppers. Wilber and Roosevelt then went back to London where they ran their proposal past Darbyshire and several of his colleagues at the secret intelligence service's headquarters beside St James's Park tube. Damp-stained and down-at-heel, the building was only notable to its American visitors for a sign bearing the red-lettered legend, 'Curb Your Guests' – the exact opposite of what MI6 was doing in this case. 'The British, from burning desire more than judgment, were all for the operation,' Roosevelt recalled later.[10]

All that remained was to secure political sign-off for Ajax, which the MI6 officers warned might 'take some time'. Their relationship with the Foreign Office was, as Roosevelt later realised, 'neither close nor cordial', and the plan might have encountered serious resistance had the prime minister not temporarily been in charge of British foreign policy while Eden recovered after major surgery on his bile duct. 'Churchill enjoyed dramatic operations and had no high regard for timid diplomatists. It was he who gave the authority for Operation Boot to proceed,' an MI6 officer recalled.[11]

Roosevelt went back to Washington where, on 25 June, he met Foster Dulles, his brother Allen and the US ambassador to Teheran Loy Henderson, as well as other officials with a stake. There, approval came easily because McCarthy's toxic influence meant that the opponents of the coup held their breath. 'That's that then,' said Foster Dulles, wrapping up the meeting, 'let's get going.'[12]

To put pressure on Mosaddeq the US government leaked a private letter from Eisenhower, which told the Iranian prime minister that no more aid would be forthcoming. Henderson, who had left Teheran at the end of May, took an extended holiday. At the same time Roosevelt flew back to Beirut under a pseudonym. Driving a car loaded with low denomination banknotes out of the Mediterranean city, through Damascus and Baghdad, he crossed into Iran on 19 July and laid up in the CIA head of station's country house in the hills outside Teheran. All he could now do was wait, while the CIA-funded propaganda began to do its work.

The propaganda hammered three themes. Mosaddeq favoured Tudeh. Mosaddeq was an enemy of Islam. Mosaddeq was running down the army to allow Tudeh and Moscow to take over. In trying to associate the prime minister with Tudeh, the spies were following a time-honoured method, which Roosevelt had summed up a decade earlier. 'It is not easy to hate for his principles a man whose principles differ very little from your own,' he had written in an article on English Civil War propaganda. 'Let him be regarded, however, as a member of a party, and his individual beliefs are swallowed up by the larger body, which contains in fact 100 shades of opinion, but which can, by judicious simplification, be represented by the most extreme.'[13]

* * *

When they planned Operation Ajax, Wilber and Darbyshire had made three important assumptions: that the shah would do as they wanted provided he was put under enough pressure; that Zahedi would take action if he knew the shah supported him; and that the army would rally to the shah rather than Mosaddeq when it was forced to choose between them. Everything, in other words, depended on a man who was known for being utterly unreliable.

That was why the plan did not demand great heroics from the shah, but simply envisaged that he would sign two decrees – *firmans* – one appointing Zahedi as chief of staff, the other calling on all ranks of the army to support the chief, that would enable the removal of Mosaddeq to take place. But the shah was not overly keen on Zahedi, whom he regarded as an 'adventurer lacking judgment and balance' and told the Americans that 'it would be unwise for him openly to oppose Mosaddeq until the myth of his greatness has been exploded'. When he refused to sign the *firmans*, Operation Ajax began to unravel.[14]

To prod the shah into action, Darbyshire and Wilber were relying on his feisty twin sister. Nicknamed the Black Panther, Princess Ashraf was as forceful as her brother was feeble. Recalling an encounter with Stalin, she described her relief on finding that, far from being large and terrifying, the Soviet leader was 'soft and fat, but above all he was small'. Her natural habitat was Paris: it was there that Darbyshire tried and failed to find her before finally tracking her down on the French Riviera on 16 July. Aware that she liked gambling and expensive clothes, the British spy offered her a mink coat and a wad of cash if she would help him. 'Her eyes lit up and her resistance crumbled,' he would recall later.[15]

When, however, Ashraf arrived in Teheran her twin refused to see her. Although he relented four days later, the encounter was stormy and the princess failed to persuade her brother to sign the *firmans*. She was at least able to give him a letter telling him to expect another visitor, General Norman Schwarzkopf. Schwarzkopf had headed up a wartime US military mission to Iran and was confident that he could persuade the shah to cooperate. When they met on 1 August the shah insisted that they conduct the meeting sitting on a table placed in the middle of the ballroom, as he believed his palace was bugged. Schwarzkopf, too, got nowhere.

There was nothing for it but for Roosevelt to go to see the shah himself. Having let him know via an agent inside the palace to expect an American authorised to speak for Eisenhower and Churchill, late on 1 August, Roosevelt had himself driven into the palace, hidden under a blanket. He had last met the shah while working on his commission for *Harper's Magazine*, six years earlier. 'Good evening, Mr Roosevelt,' said the shah when he appeared. 'I cannot say that I expected to see you but this is a pleasure.'[16]

Convinced that the Americans still supported Mosaddeq, the shah wanted proof that Eisenhower was behind him. Asadollah Rashidian, whom he was also seeing regularly, had already managed to arrange for the BBC Persian service to tweak its usual nightly greeting, 'It is now midnight in London', to include the word 'exactly' so that the shah would know that Rashidian was speaking for the British government. By chance Eisenhower referred to his concerns about the deteriorating situation in Iran in a speech in Seattle on 4 August, and Roosevelt claimed that these comments too amounted to a covert signal that the president was behind the operation. But the shah still wanted more time to make up his mind.

Mosaddeq inadvertently sped up this process. Wanting to outmanoeuvre Kashani's boycott of the Majlis, but knowing that the shah would not agree to the dissolution of parliament, he encouraged deputies to resign, and when that met resistance from those members of parliament who were in the CIA's pay, announced that he would put the dissolution of parliament to the country in a referendum. Confronted by separate ballot boxes for Yes and No votes, opponents of the measure wisely stayed away. Mosaddeq won overwhelmingly, but the ruse backfired on him, playing into the CIA's line that he was trying to turn the country over to Tudeh and the Soviets.

Unsure whether he could rely on a vote of the Majlis to endorse Zahedi, Roosevelt decided that the shah now needed to sign off a *firman* that explicitly sacked Mosaddeq, and another naming Zahedi as prime minister. This the shah refused to do. It was only when Rashidian met him and told him that Roosevelt would leave the country 'in complete disgust' unless he quickly took action that the shah finally changed his mind.

Overwhelmed with relief, Roosevelt and his colleagues in the CIA station celebrated with a drinking binge; he did not get to bed until five o'clock the following morning. But the party was premature: before the *firmans* could be drawn up the shah abruptly departed to the Caspian Sea resort of Ramsar. Once Rashidian had prepared the two documents on the evening of 12 August the commander of the imperial guard, Nematollah Nasiri, took them to the shah.

By now the military preparations had come together, after a very unpromising start. Since Zahedi had taken sanctuary in the Majlis in May, it was not until he left the parliament for a safe house on 21 July that the CIA head of station Roger Goiran was able to meet him. The encounter left Goiran unimpressed. Zahedi 'appeared lacking in drive, energy and concrete plans', while his best contact in the military, a colonel named Hassan Akhavi, was 'full of desire to do something, but had no idea how to go about it'.[17]

Having realised that Zahedi could not count on the support of any of the five brigades garrisoned in Teheran, Goiran summoned George Carroll, the paramilitary expert who had been at the meeting at the St Georges Hotel, to try to salvage the operation. On 5 August Carroll made a breakthrough when he met a contact of Akhavi's, Colonel Zand Karimi. Karimi had contacts throughout the units stationed in the capital; within four days Akhavi had a list of forty officers which he was able to show the shah. Once Nasiri returned from Ramsar with the signed *firmans* on the thirteenth, the coup was set for the night of the fifteenth – a Saturday and the first day of the working week.

The delay was necessary because Karimi needed Friday 14 August to tip off these forty officers about what was going to happen. It seems that one of them alerted Mosaddeq, who knew that a coup was imminent by the end of that afternoon. As a consequence, when Nasiri tried to arrest Mosaddeq at his home at one o'clock in the morning of the sixteenth, he was arrested himself. Zahedi was reportedly so nervous that he could not button his own uniform. A CIA officer, 'Rocky' Stone, did it up for him, while Mrs Stone held Zahedi's wife's hand. Once it became obvious that forces loyal to Mosaddeq had pre-empted the coup, the plotters' fragile morale disintegrated completely. Zahedi went into hiding while the shah fled by plane to Baghdad and ultimately Rome. 'Let the plane go,' Mosaddeq said, when he was asked if it should be intercepted and shot down. In Rome the shah checked into the Excelsior. Beside him at the counter was Allen Dulles, who had arranged the shah's accommodation. 'After you, your Majesty,' he said.[18]

From Roosevelt and his colleagues' perspective, by the small hours of the sixteenth there were already disconcerting signs that the plot had not gone to plan. For one thing, the city's telephones were still working. But it was not until one of their agents inside the Iranian army arrived at the embassy seeking sanctuary that it became clear that the coup had failed. 'Rocky' Stone remembered the reaction: 'The safe house exploded with expletives and pointed fingers assigning the blame. Before the place became violent, Roosevelt raised his hand, calmed the group and quietly announced that he accepted the blame for the failure – to the appreciative applause of all.'[19]

* * *

Roosevelt must have realised that his CIA career was on the line, but he was not the quitting type. Four decades earlier, his grandfather, Theodore, whom he venerated, had made a famous speech at the Sorbonne. 'It is not the critic who counts; not the man who points out how the strong man stumbles, or where the doer of deeds could have done them better,' the former president had said.

> The credit belongs to the man who is actually in the arena, whose face is marred by dust and sweat and blood; who strives valiantly; who errs, who comes short again and again, because there is no effort without error and shortcoming; but who does actually strive to do the deeds; who knows great enthusiasms, the great devotions; who spends himself in a worthy cause; who at the best knows in the end the triumph of high achievement, and who at the worst, if he fails, at least fails while daring greatly, so that his place shall never be with those cold and timid souls who neither know victory nor defeat.[20]

Soon after eight o'clock that Sunday morning Roosevelt drove north out of the city to meet Zahedi, who was in hiding with his son Ardeshir. Like him, neither man had entirely given up; they believed that their task was now to convince Teheran that it was Mosaddeq who had staged the coup, after getting wind of the *firmans* that dismissed him and appointed the general. Roosevelt agreed and his colleagues in the CIA station went about spreading the rumour, starting with a message to Associated Press and then arranging for Ardeshir to meet the *New*

York Times correspondent, Kennett Love, so that he could show him the original *firman*. Independently and shrewdly, the CIA agents Jalali and Keyvani had reached the same conclusion and published a broadsheet that morning alleging that the purpose of the coup had been to force out the shah.

Mosaddeq now made another error that played into Roosevelt's and Zahedi's hands. At noon he issued a statement announcing the dissolution of the Majlis; that afternoon his foreign minister published an article savagely attacking the shah in the newspaper that he owned. That evening the foreign minister announced that the shah had fled to Baghdad and demanded his abdication, at a public meeting outside the Majlis, which was broadcast on the radio. The combined effect of Mosaddeq's announcement and his minister's article and statement was to reinforce the impression Zahedi wanted to give – that Mosaddeq had tried to overthrow the shah after being dismissed by him. To give it further momentum, the CIA had hundreds of copies of the *firmans* made and distributed, both to the newspapers and in the streets.

Despite this, the two most senior diplomats in the US embassy in Teheran had 'given up hope'. Their mood infected that of the under-secretary of state, Walter Bedell Smith, in Washington, who warned a British diplomat the next day that the 'latest developments' made a 'new look at policy towards Persia' necessary. 'He thought it would be necessary to cultivate good relations with Mosaddeq,' the British man reported, alarmed, to London. 'Perhaps American technicians might be sent. Whatever his faults Mosaddeq has no love for the Russians and timely aid might enable him to keep Communism in check.'[21]

The Foreign Office viewed this as 'an ignominious climb-down' which would only encourage Mosaddeq 'to blackmail the United States further'. So too did MI6. When Bedell Smith then sent a message to Roosevelt telling him to halt the operation, Darbyshire, in Cyprus, and in charge of all communications between Washington, London and Teheran, did not immediately pass it on. 'While ... the apparent faith shown by the SIS station in Nicosia was altogether admirable,' the CIA consultant Don Wilber noted afterwards, 'it should be remembered that they had nothing to lose.'[22]

Unaware of Bedell Smith's order thanks to Darbyshire, Roosevelt carried on. His priority was to dramatise how the Tudeh would exploit the vacuum left by the departure of the shah. To do so, he had asked Jalali and Keyvani to muster a mob of agents provocateurs for a large demonstration in the city centre. When they refused, he offered them $50,000; when they still refused, he threatened to kill them. Jalali and Keyvani had a change of heart. By lunchtime on 17 August their rent-a-mob, swelled by genuine Tudeh supporters, had pulled down two statues of Reza Shah. Thanks to their efforts, by that point senior clerics had also started to receive letters, written in red ink and purporting to come from the Tudeh, warning them that they would soon be hanging from the lampposts. When, that evening, Roosevelt held a long council of war with Zahedi and his son and the Rashidians, they agreed that they would take action two days later. The Rashidians would mobilise their followers from the city bazaar. The nineteenth would be the day of reckoning.

Meanwhile the disturbances inspired by Jalali and Keyvani continued. On the eighteenth their thugs attacked and looted shops on two main streets, all the time acting as if they supported the Tudeh. They 'scared the hell out of me', Roosevelt would admit later. That evening Ambassador Henderson, who had just returned after ten weeks' absence, saw Mosaddeq and, on Roosevelt's advice, warned him that he would be obliged to advise Americans to leave Iran if the security forces could not protect them. Mosaddeq, his honour challenged, called his chief of police and told him to put down the disturbances. He also ordered his own followers not to protest.[23]

What that meant was that, on the morning of 19 August, when many newspapers ran photostat copies of the *firman* appointing Zahedi, Mosaddeq's supporters were not on the streets. His opponents, on the other hand, were out in force. Paid with money from Kashani, which came from the CIA via the Rashidians, they were market porters and day labourers, members of the city's athletic clubs and ruffians who made a living from extortion, were always in trouble and reliant on the Rashidians to bail them out. Two groups, armed with identical wooden staves, moved in parallel northwards up the slope Teheran is built on, out of the slums in the south of the city into the smarter, higher neighbourhoods where they would be encouraged to attack the offices of the main, Tudeh-supporting newspapers. The athletes gave the demonstration a carnival-like flavour. An eyewitness reported that the crowds included 'tumblers turning handsprings, weightlifters twirling iron bars and wrestlers flexing their biceps'. By a quarter past ten that morning they controlled the city's main squares and had been joined by soldiers from the local garrisons and Bakhtiari tribesmen bussed in from the south. Tanks sent in to break up the demonstration turned out to be crewed by men loyal to the shah. They were surrounded, and surrendered without putting up any resistance.

Shouting 'Long Live the Shah', 'Death to the Tudeh', and later 'Death to Mosaddeq', the gathering crowd freed Nasiri and other officers arrested on the night of the abortive coup from the cells in police head-quarters, and then seized control of the telegraph office, and attacked the army's headquarters and the ministry of foreign affairs. Radio Teheran fell into the protestors' hands at about two that afternoon. 200 people were reported to have been killed in a fierce battle for Mosaddeq's home. Mosaddeq himself escaped but gave himself up a day later. By then his possessions had been sold on the street to passers-by.[24]

When it became clear that the royalists were in control of the radio station, Roosevelt went to find Zahedi, who made a broadcast to announce that he was now prime minister and that his forces were in control of the city. The previous day Roosevelt had received the order from headquarters telling him to call time on the operation. He now belatedly acknowledged the message, adding that he was pleased to report that Zahedi had been safely installed and that the shah would be flying home shortly. He ended, 'Love and kisses from all the team.' Roosevelt stayed in the city long enough to meet the shah, who arrived back on the 22nd. 'I owe my throne to God, my people, my army,' the shah said, 'and to you!' and toasted him with vodka.[25]

After being spirited out of the country by the American naval attaché, Roosevelt reached London on 25 August. MI6's chief Sinclair was delighted to see him, particularly when Roosevelt then explained why so little information had got back to London. 'If they had simply reported what they were doing, London and Washington would have thought they were crazy and told them to stop immediately,' he said. 'If they had reported the reasons why they felt justified in taking such action they would have had no time to take action; accordingly they followed the third course which was to act, and report practically nothing.' Sinclair asked him to repeat this to everyone he was about to meet.[26]

In the next twenty-four hours, Sinclair took Roosevelt on a whirlwind tour of Whitehall, from which he clearly hoped that MI6 would profit. Roosevelt's final interview was with the prime minister, who had been poleaxed by a stroke several weeks earlier and was recuperating. The American spy would milk the symbolism of this encounter, describing how he had recounted the story of the coup to a bedridden, dozy Churchill, who seemed barely aware of what the CIA was. 'Had I been but a few years younger, I would have loved nothing better than to have served under your command in this great venture,' the prime minister apparently told him. It was a metaphor for the role reversal that was well under way.[27]

*　*　*

Mosaddeq might have hung on had he not threatened to flood the market with cheap oil, for the coup would not have happened without American support. But it would never have succeeded had Mosaddeq been as popular as he had been a year earlier, before the oil sanctions began to bite, and had the British not played a part as well, by mobilising the Rashidians to support the operation and then preventing the State Department from calling time on it when it appeared to have failed. As a consequence the former prime minister was put on trial later that year and, having been convicted, spent the remainder of his life under house arrest.

For Britain, the price of American involvement in the removal of Mosaddeq was the loss of her monopoly. Following protracted negotiations in 1954, Anglo-Iranian was joined by five American companies in a new consortium which left the British company with a 40 per cent stake. To avoid upsetting the arrangement in Saudi Arabia, the consortium split the profits with the Iranians fifty–fifty. Eden's desire that 'Persia must not obtain better terms than other Middle Eastern countries ... nor must she be seen to benefit by her wrongful action' could just about be said to have been satisfied. But the victory was pyrrhic, and the Anglo-American conspiracy that had achieved it was the exception rather than the rule.[28]

Some time after Roosevelt returned to Washington he briefed the president, emphasising his own role in rescuing the operation. 'It seemed more like a dime novel than an historical fact,' Eisenhower wrote in his diary, impressed by Roosevelt's courage. 'The things we did were "covert." If knowledge of them became public, we would not only be embarrassed in that region, but our chances to do anything of like nature in the future would almost totally disappear.' But news of the CIA's involvement soon leaked out and, as Ike predicted, it has poisoned US-Iran relations ever since.[29]

PART THREE

Descent to Suez

1953–58

15

THE GIFT OF A GUN

In the spring of 1953 Foster Dulles became the first US secretary of state to visit the Middle East – a move that signalled a new era of more active American involvement in the region. On 11 May he arrived in Cairo and met the man the CIA had helped to power the previous year, Egypt's prime minister, Mohammed Neguib.

Talks between the Egyptian and British governments over the Suez base had started late the previous month, and Dulles was under the impression that they were on the verge of delivering an agreement that would fix dates for the withdrawal of British forces and, further in the future, for the handover of the base to Egypt. The secretary – who, as ever, had the fight against communism foremost in his mind – was keen to start discussing the regional defensive pact that would give the British government the political cover that it needed before it announced that it was abandoning its biggest foreign base. The Middle East Defence Organization he envisaged, in which the United States and Britain would play major roles, would organise the states of the region to confront the Soviet threat. But Neguib had bad news.

Not only had the talks with the British broken down, the prime minister explained, but the Egyptian people, who had been let down by the British on so many previous occasions, would never accept a defence organisation of the type that Dulles sought, because it would involve the British. 'Free us from the British occupation first,' Neguib told the secretary of state, 'and then we can negotiate in good faith.' The prime minister, as Dulles knew, was 'merely a front', but a day later the man who really ran the country, Gamal Abdel Nasser, made exactly the same point. The pact that Dulles advocated was seen by the Egyptian people as 'a perpetuation of occupation', Nasser explained quietly. 'British influence must entirely disappear.'[1]

Two days eye to eye with the leaders of the new regime in Cairo brought home to Dulles the ferocity of their hatred of the British, and made him appreciate – in a way that no telegram from the embassy had previously done – how close the situation was to boiling point. The fedayeen's attacks on the British base had already resumed following the collapse of the talks, the British were hinting that they might have to reoccupy Cairo and Alexandria, the Egyptians were moving troops to oppose any British attempt to do so, and Neguib had warned him that further Black Saturday-type outrages could not be ruled out. It seemed entirely possible that a new Middle Eastern war might suddenly break out.

Before Dulles flew on to his next meeting with Ibn Saud at Dhahran, he telegraphed his impressions home to Washington. 'Observers here are convinced, and I share their view, that the possibility of open hostilities in the near future is real', because the Egyptians 'would rather go down as martyrs than concede' to the British in the talks. 'It is almost impossible to overemphasize the intensity of this feeling,' he reported. 'It may be pathological but it is a fact.' In these circumstances, he accepted, his Middle East Defence Organization did 'not have a chance'.[2]

By the time Dulles arrived back in Washington at the end of the month he had an alternative in mind. Although the Egyptians were too preoccupied by the British to be useful in the fight against communism, the leaders of Turkey, Syria, Iraq and Pakistan, whom he met later in his tour, had an awareness of the Soviet threat that reassured him. On his return home, in an attempt to calm the situation in Egypt, Dulles said publicly that the Middle East Defence Organization was 'a future rather than an immediate possibility'. He told the National Security Council that a different and less formal approach, involving the 'Northern Tier' of states which were all 'feeling the hot breath of the Soviet Union on their necks', was more likely to succeed. Iran's role in this chain of defence helps explain why he was so keen to see Mosaddeq removed.[3]

Dulles' abandonment of the Middle East Defence Organization did not, however, mean that the secretary of state had washed his hands of the long-running Anglo-Egyptian dispute over the Suez base. Although

Suez would not serve as the nucleus for the new 'Northern Tier' arrangement, Dulles believed that he could not afford to leave the problem unresolved. As it had become a cause célèbre across the Arab world, he felt certain that, if it were allowed to fester, the Soviet Union was certain to exploit it. Until recently United States policy had been to leave the defence of the Middle East to Britain. But the secretary had found 'an intense distrust and dislike for the British' on his trip and, convinced that the British troops still based in the area had become 'more a factor of instability ... than stability', he now believed the time had come for the United States to take charge of the situation and to ease the British out.[4]

* * *

In British eyes Dulles' visit to Egypt had been defined by an extraordinary gaffe. Although the secretary of state knew that the regime was directing the attacks by the fedayeen, at the beginning of his 11 May meeting with Neguib he had presented the Egyptian prime minister with a pistol as a gift from Ike. The moment, which the Americans sheepishly said was 'intended to be in private', was captured by a photographer and the image of Neguib holding the weapon reproduced around the world. Afterwards, Churchill – in charge of the Foreign Office during Eden's convalescence – hauled in the American ambassador. It was 'slightly irritating', he told him, 'that Dulles in his globe-trotting progress should be taking pains at every point to sympathise with those who were trying to kick out or do down the British'.[5]

Dulles ignored Churchill's complaint. With Ike's approval the secretary of state drafted a new proposal for his ambassador in Cairo to give to Neguib, so that Neguib could send it back to Washington, aware that it would elicit a favourable response. On 15 July 1953 Eisenhower replied, offering economic aid and help to strengthen the country's armed forces if Egypt could reach a deal with Britain over the base. In hinting at what would follow if the Egyptians played ball, the president's gift of the pistol to Neguib was quite deliberate.[6]

The prospect of new weaponry was a significant incentive, given Neguib's complaint that the Egyptian army was 'fit only for funeral celebrations', but Nasser, who had just formally become deputy prime minister, was by now keen to achieve a breakthrough to divert attention from his troubles elsewhere. The Revolutionary Command Council, which he and his colleagues had established in the wake of the previous year's coup, had proved an ineffective talking shop, which had failed to make headway on any of the domestic reforms that they had promised. The Free Officers were uncomfortably aware that the most important of these, land reform, was not feasible, because there were simply too many Egyptians to divide the large estates between.

Meanwhile the Egyptian economy continued to stagnate, and falling cotton prices were contributing to an angry public mood, which the Muslim Brotherhood was successfully exploiting. As Nasser's colleague Anwar Sadat explained, the regime sanctioned the fedayeen's attacks on the canal base because: 'If our people do not fight you, they will fight us, and we prefer that they should fight you.' Worried that the situation was getting out of hand, Nasser made himself deputy prime minister and minister of the interior in June. A deal that would speed Britain's peaceful departure from Suez, and thus deny the Brotherhood its central grievance, held great appeal.[7]

When the British and the Egyptians restarted discussions late in August they had three questions to answer. The most important concerned the circumstances in which Britain and her allies might reoccupy the base, and the duration of the deal. Yet it was not over these two, but the third question that their discussion then quickly foundered: whether the British technicians maintaining the base before its handover would wear uniforms. The British believed wrongly that the Egyptians had already conceded that they could; Nasser was adamant that they had not. When the British refused to budge, in late September he 'lost his temper and stalked out'.[8]

Trivial though it seemed to be, the uniforms question encapsulated the greater but vaporous issues of national pride and sovereignty that lay at the heart of the dispute. Uniforms, as the politicians on both sides instantly appreciated, were the emblem that the man in the street would grasp and care about. While there were uniformed British servicemen on the base Nasser could not claim to have ended the British occupation, but equally Churchill could deny allegations that he had sold out, by arguing that nothing much had changed. There was also, in the British prime minister's mind, a more important point. Lacking any faith that the Egyptians would respect the terms of the deal once it was done, he had always been adamant that the wearing of uniforms by British personnel on the base represented a vital safeguard: any attempt by the Egyptians to molest them could be interpreted as an act of war.

Having previously been assured by the British in Cairo that the question of uniforms 'need not become a major issue', the Americans were not impressed when it caused the collapse of the talks. In their ambassador to Cairo's eyes, the focus on a 'question of haberdashery' – rather than the far more important strategic issue of the future availability of the base – proved his own view that 'the British had bungled these negotiations from the start'. Once Eden had returned to the Foreign Office after six months' absence, in October, Dulles confronted him about the situation and later warned his counterpart that he would soon have to give Nasser the military aid the president had promised him that summer. Since Dulles' implication was that the British would soon be facing fedayeen armed with US weaponry, the British leaked this threat to the *New York Times* on the basis that it would alarm Jewish readers of the paper.[9]

Despite Dulles' unsubtle approach, Eden, who thought Churchill's insistence on the subject was ridiculous, agreed with his American counterpart that the British should withdraw from the base as quickly as they could. But when Churchill asked him, 'What security have we got that the Egyptians, now breaking your treaty of 1936, will keep any agreement that you will make with them?' he had no answer. Desperate to take Churchill's job, but realising that the prime minister's tough line was supported by many in the parliamentary party, Eden hardened his own views over the winter of 1953–4. This was the period when the influence of the Suez Group – the forty or so Tory MPs who vehemently opposed Britain's withdrawal from the canal base – was at its height. A fight between the ailing prime minister and his skittish foreign secretary to hold the party's steering wheel ensured that government policy on Egypt veered between pragmatism and inflexibility throughout this time.[10]

* * *

It was the CIA officer Kim Roosevelt who, fresh from his triumph in Teheran, managed to break the deadlock in Cairo in January 1954. Convinced that Nasser was 'the one man I have met who has impressed me with the feeling that he possesses the capabilities to lead the Near East – not only Egypt but through Egypt her Arab friends and neighbors – out of the barren wilderness', the CIA officer had muscled in on the relationship with the Egyptian leader soon after Dulles' visit the previous May. On 24 January Roosevelt arrived in Cairo; Nasser made a significant concession the following day, by indicating that he would allow the British to reoccupy the Suez base in the event that Turkey – a NATO member – were attacked. Six weeks later, and having ousted Neguib as prime minister, Nasser made a further overture to the British via Roosevelt, to say that he was eager to reach a quick agreement if the British made a concession over the vexed question of uniforms.

Seizing the opportunity, Eden argued that the base should be turned over to civilian contractors and that the government should instead focus on trying to extend the lifespan of the deal. Grudgingly, Churchill went along with it. Dulles recalled that the prime minister 'merely grimaced to show his distaste for the proposal', when he had mentioned it approvingly. But Eden now had the support of the chairman of the Conservatives' Foreign Affairs Committee. A bluff Tory squire who was respected across the party, Charles Mott-Radclyffe visited the base that spring and reported that, in the absence of a friendly local population, it was a 'useless white elephant'. The 80,000 troops who lived on it were guarding neither the base nor the canal: they were 'merely guarding each other'. Meanwhile the United States' detonation of a hydrogen bomb over Bikini Atoll in March gave Churchill the fig leaf he needed, because it supplied a compelling military argument for not concentrating a large number of troops in one place. On 22 June the prime minister finally conceded that 'our position in Egypt is not militarily advantageous'. It was only now that he gave up trying to sabotage a deal.[11]

Until that point Dulles had conspicuously refused to offer what Eden wanted: a joint approach that would make it clear to Nasser that there was a united Anglo-American front. 'The whole point is to be "ganging up" – and to be seen to be "ganging up",' said Eden – which was precisely why Dulles was averse to the idea. It would be the happiest day in his life, the secretary of state told the president, 'when we don't have to modify our policies to keep up a façade of unity'. The secretary of state kept up the pressure on his British counterpart by negotiating military aid deals with Iraq that April and Pakistan the following month, as if to remind Eden that he would not let the lack of progress in Egypt impede him from establishing direct alliances with countries that Britain regarded as her allies in the region.[12]

Dulles did, however, need British support for a similar defensive alliance in southeastern Asia. In exchange for this, at an Anglo-American summit in Washington at the end of June 1954, he made it clear to Churchill and Eden that he would use the economic aid that Eisenhower had promised Neguib the previous year to ensure the Egyptians kept their side of the deal, once it was done. On their return to London, Eden said that the Americans had been 'unusually helpful'. But Ike was unable to resist a dig at Churchill in a letter to the prime minister three weeks later. 'Colonialism is on the way out as a relationship among peoples,' he wrote. 'The sole question is one of time and method.'[13]

The Washington summit nevertheless cleared the way for a rapid deal with Nasser. After Churchill had squared the parliamentary party, at the end of July Antony Head, the secretary of state for war, and Evelyn Shuckburgh, Eden's adviser, flew to Cairo. At a dinner in the shadow of the pyramids on 26 July, the two men put a proposal to Nasser and his colleagues. The British would withdraw their forces within twenty months, and civilian contractors would maintain the base for seven years, during which time the British could return in the event of an attack on Egypt, Turkey or any country belonging to the Arab League's security pact – a provision that the H-Bomb made pointless, but which was politically necessary to salvage British pride. After half an hour's discussion, the Egyptians agreed. On 6 August Nasser expressed his hope to Eden that the agreement would 'really inaugurate a new and happier chapter in the relations between our two countries'. It was to be brief.[14]

* * *

Eisenhower's gift of the pistol to Neguib and his subsequent promise that the United States would strengthen Egypt's army had opened the way for a deal, but trouble followed when it soon became clear that the presidential pledge was undeliverable. United States law – specifically the Mutual Security Act – required the Egyptians to enter a security pact with the US and to accept the presence of American military advisers in order to receive military aid. But these were conditions that Nasser, having only just got rid of the British, could not possibly accept.

Even before the Anglo-Egyptian agreement was signed that October, setting a departure date for British forces on 20 June 1956, Egypt's foreign minister warned the American ambassador that the Revolutionary Command Council no longer wanted US arms. The ambassador tried to see the positive side, arguing that the Egyptian decision relieved Washington of an awkward commitment, because military aid to Egypt – at a time when the country was still officially at war with Israel – would undoubtedly encounter fierce opposition from a coalition of isolationists and pro-Israelis in Congress, but it was undoubtedly a setback.

It had been clear from the outset that the Egyptians wanted new weaponry, and the CIA were desperate to avoid accusations of bad faith. Since Eisenhower had also promised economic aid, Kim Roosevelt came up with a plan to hide $5 million for weapons purchases within a larger grant of $40 million for infrastructure investment. He also proposed that Miles Copeland – the man who had lured the Syrians into a gunfight, who was now the Agency's direct liaison with the Egyptian leader – should hand Nasser a further $3 million in cash to buy new uniforms and transport. An American delegation, which went to Cairo in November to deliver the good news to Nasser and his sidekick, the commander-in-chief of the Egyptian army, Abdel Hakim Amer, received a rather chilly reception, however. Amer's wish list, which included bombers, tanks and artillery, showed that he had wild expectations the Americans were never going to satisfy, while Nasser, according to Copeland, explained 'for the thousandth time' that he could not accept any aid that appeared to come from Washington DC. He was also very worried that, were anyone to find out about the suitcases of money that Copeland had given him, he would be accused of being in the Americans' pay. He eventually blew the money on the construction of a monument on an island on the Nile. If we believe Copeland, it was soon christened 'Roosevelt's erection'.[15]

Unable to supply Nasser with arms, the CIA instead supported the establishment of a powerful new radio station, Voice of the Arabs, that enabled Nasser to broadcast propaganda across the Middle East, interspersed with popular music from singers like Umm Kulthum. 'How can you listen to "The Voice of the Arabs" when you see what they say is not true?' a puzzled British journalist asked a Palestinian. 'Because what they broadcast is what we like to hear,' came the reply. In time the folly of the CIA's move became clear. 'We shall continue to preach hate,' Sadat said later when he was challenged about the nature of the station's broadcasts. 'What of?' he was asked. 'The West,' he said. 'We shall continue until you reform your policies and give the Arabs what they want.'[16]

As 1954 came to an end, Foster Dulles had managed, through brokering the Anglo-Egyptian agreement, to remove one source of tension that the Soviets might exploit. But by making the promise of weaponry with conditions that Nasser could not accept, he had managed to introduce another. Egypt wanted modern weaponry, and Dulles knew that if the United States did not supply it, there was now a danger that the Russians would. To add to the secretary of state's problems, Eden now tried to regain the initiative in the Middle East.

BAGHDAD PACT

As Dulles slotted in the pieces of his Northern Tier plan, the British looked on with mounting alarm. Following the signature of the Turco-Pakistan Pact on 2 April 1954, and the US government's announcements that it would supply military aid to Iraq and Pakistan weeks later, they realised that they had no time to lose if they were to maintain any semblance of influence in the region. Otherwise, as one Foreign Office minister admitted, 'the Iraqis and others may get the idea that we are leaving it to the Americans to make the running in that part of the world'.[1]

Following the withdrawal from Palestine in 1948, and with the departure of British forces from Suez now scheduled for June 1956, Jordan and Iraq were the two remaining countries where the British retained a presence in the northern Middle East. When Eden reviewed the implications of Dulles' Northern Tier strategy he argued that Britain should build up her position in each country to resist American encroachment.

The problem was that in both countries the British military presence was unpopular and hung on the elites' support. A 1930 treaty sanctioned Britain's base rights at Shaiba and Habbaniyah in Iraq. But it was due to expire soon after the British quit the Suez base, and an attempt to renew it just before the British left Palestine had ended with rioting in Baghdad that left bodies floating in the Tigris. The British had had more luck in Jordan. But the Anglo-Jordanian Treaty of 1948 committed them to come to Jordan's aid in the event that she was attacked. As tensions mounted along the country's disputed frontier with Israel on the West Bank the Jordanians had asked for help. While this had enabled the

British to deploy more troops to Jordan surreptitiously, it threatened to drag them into a war that they did not want to fight. If Iraq and Jordan were going to fulfil the roles that Eden envisaged, then Britain needed a new basis for her position in Iraq and an Arab–Israeli peace agreement that reduced the danger that she might end up fighting the Israelis on the Jordanians' behalf.

By August 1954 MI6 knew that Nasser was also interested in a peace deal and that December Eden and Dulles agreed to try to pursue a peace initiative between Egypt and Israel, which they codenamed Alpha. While Eden's motive for doing so was to remove a threat to his new strategy in the region, Dulles' interest was both anti-Soviet and domestic. He wanted to resolve an issue that the Russians would try to exploit, and that gave the pro-Israeli lobby an unwonted leverage in US politics largely to the benefit of his Democratic Party opponents. Simultaneously, the recent return of the great survivor in Iraqi politics, Nuri Said, to power in Baghdad offered the British an opportunity to reinforce their own position in Iraq.[2]

Nuri saw adhesion to Dulles' Northern Tier as a way to regain ground against Nasser who, since his agreement with the British over the Suez base, was well on his way to acquiring hero status in the Arab world. After the signature of the Turco-Pakistan Pact in April 1954, Nuri confided to the British government his own hope of concluding a treaty with the Pakistanis into which he would then draw Syria and Lebanon, and so 'leave the Egyptians out in the cold'. His return to the premiership that summer put him in a position to pursue that goal.[3]

For Nuri, the beauty of joining the Northern Tier in order to advance his old pan-Arab ambitions was that it would be difficult for Nasser to block him without risking his own relationship with the United States. When he met Nasser in September 1954 the Egyptian leader told him that he would not oppose Iraq's accession to the Turco-Pakistan Pact, but would not join in because of the likely opposition of the Muslim Brotherhood. So in November Nuri went to Istanbul, to see if he could do a deal with Turkey's leader Adnan Menderes, who felt exposed by Britain's decision to abandon the Suez base. Although the two men agreed nothing on that occasion, in January 1955 Menderes paid a return visit to Baghdad. While he was there, he persuaded Nuri to sign off a communiqué in which both men declared their willingness to sign a bilateral defence deal that would be open to other states to join as well.

Eden now saw an opportunity. Having long opposed the Northern Tier, which he felt was 'ostentatiously provocative' towards the Soviets, he now realised that if Britain associated herself with the Turco-Iraqi move, he might steal a march on Dulles, who could not do the same without annoying the Israelis. Two days after the pact was initialled, he sent a message to Nuri welcoming his move and hinting that Britain would like to join in. Like Nuri, Eden believed that Nasser would not oppose this move. In mid-December the Foreign Office had received a report from Cairo detailing off-the-record comments made by the Egyptian leader during an interview with the Arab News Agency, a Cairo-based newswire that appears to have been a front for MI6. In it Nasser said that while he was not enthusiastic about Nuri's plans, 'if Iraq insisted on going ahead, Egypt would raise no objection'. Although she would not support Iraq's move in the Arab League, the Egyptian press would not attack Iraq. And so Eden welcomed the news from Baghdad.[4]

Nasser, on the other hand, reacted furiously, despite everything he had previously said. In an attempt to stop the agreement being signed, the government-controlled Egyptian press mounted an immediate and violent attack on Nuri. Seizing on the fact that he had allied himself with Turkey, a country that had normal relations with Tel Aviv, Voice of the Arabs declared him 'the ally of the ally of Israel' in broadcasts beamed across the Middle East. Nasser called an urgent meeting of the Arab League in Cairo. Nuri, however, claimed illness and refused to attend. In his absence the summit descended into farce when the representatives of several other states all said that they were not willing to begin discussions, and Nasser was then forced to shelve a resolution committing the League's membership not to join the pact when Syria and Lebanon refused to support it. Although the Egyptians were subsequently able to prevent the Syrians following in Nuri's footsteps by leaking a secret recording of the Syrian foreign minister at the conference, which led to the collapse of Syria's government, in the meantime Nasser made the impulsive, unwise step of threatening to withdraw Egypt from the Arab League's security pact if Iraq went ahead and signed the treaty.

Offered the chance to leave Nasser looking isolated if he carried out his threat, or thoroughly stupid if he did not, Nuri did not hesitate. When he persisted with his agreement, Nasser had to eat his words. Thereafter the Egyptian prime minister would blame his self-inflicted humiliation on Nuri. A British spy, who got to know Nasser quite well, described his hatred of Iraq as 'almost pathological'; in a conversation a year later he noted moments when Nasser 'could hardly bring himself to pronounce' Nuri's name.[5]

The first estimates of Nasser had described a man whose wide-swinging handshake conveyed confidence and energy, and whose quiet, frank and often humorous conversation suggested a shrewdness that intrigued western diplomats. The events of early 1955 revealed another, previously unseen, side to the Egyptian prime minister – a man who was acutely status-conscious and easily offended. In the interval between the announcement and the signature of the Turco-Iraqi deal, Nasser admitted that his country had an 'inferiority complex', but he might as well have been describing himself. A village postman's son, he never forgot how the wealthy local landowners had talked down to his father. A Saudi prince believed that this boyhood experience was key to understanding the Egyptian leader. It was, he said, 'at least partially responsible for his behaviour and aggressiveness in seeking Egyptian hegemony over a wide area'.[6]

* * *

It was in these unpromising circumstances that Eden met Nasser for dinner at the British embassy in Cairo on 20 February 1955. The British foreign secretary had agreed with Dulles that he would stop in Egypt on his way to a summit in Bangkok in order to broach the subject of the Alpha peace plan. But the encounter got off to a poor start when Eden, in his dinner jacket, asked Nasser, in his army uniform, if it was the first time he had ever entered the building. Nasser admitted that it was. It was interesting, the Egyptian prime minister continued, to see the place from where his country had once been governed. 'Not governed, perhaps,' Eden ventured, 'advised, rather.'[7]

Although the two men do seem to have discussed the peace initiative briefly, the deal that Nuri had just struck with Turkey's Menderes dominated their conversation. Nasser said that he agreed with the strategic idea behind the pact but he did not like it because it smacked of 'foreign domination'. At the recent Arab League meeting, he continued, the Iraqi foreign minister had told him that he personally opposed the deal, but that his government had been forced to proceed with it following British pressure. Eden, who was in an ebullient mood, having just heard that he would soon be prime minister as Churchill was on the point of resignation, did nothing to dispel the impression that his diplomats had been heavily involved in the negotiation of the Turco-Iraqi agreement. He invited Nasser to suspend judgement on the deal until he knew its terms: 'It might then not turn out to be so objectionable as they now imagined.' The Egyptians, he suggested, 'should not treat this pact as a crime'.

'No,' replied Nasser, laughing. 'But it is one.'[8]

It was, in all, an uncharacteristically high-handed and ham-fisted performance by Eden, an unflattering preview of what was to come once he had crossed the threshold into Number 10. Although he reported breezily to London that the meeting had gone well, he managed only to needle the Egyptian prime minister's insecurity. 'What elegance!' Nasser reportedly exclaimed afterwards, of his British hosts' attire compared to his own. 'It was made to look as if we were beggars and they were princes!'[9]

Worse was to come for Nasser. Four days after the signature of the Turco-Iraqi pact, on 28 February Israeli forces attacked Gaza, killing thirty-eight. The attack was a premeditated reprisal for Egypt's execution of several Israeli agents provocateurs earlier in the month, but it had the effect of exposing Egypt's military weakness just as Nasser was reeling from the setback in Baghdad.

Although Eden guessed that Nasser's objection to the Turco-Iraqi pact was down to 'jealousy ... and a frustrated desire to lead the Arab world', he was in no mood to give Nasser any quarter. On his way back to London from the Bangkok summit, he stopped off in Baghdad where Nuri now showed him a draft Anglo-Iraqi agreement, which terminated the 1930 treaty, and replaced it with a framework for full military cooperation. On 15 March this proposal was discussed in cabinet. 'This is the moment to go forward,' declared Eden, describing the new arrangement as securing 'solid advantages for us, though dressed up for Iraqi consumption'.[10]

Dulles had discussed these matters with Eden on the margins of the Bangkok summit. It appears he only belatedly realised what his British counterpart was trying to achieve. On his return to Washington he told his advisers of his worry that Eden's determination to help Nuri draw Syria, Jordan and Lebanon into his pact would not only 'further isolate and embitter Nasser', but also damage American relations with the Israelis, who would fear that they were being encircled. Fearing that 'the UK had grabbed the ball on the northern-tier policy and was running away with it in a direction which would have ... unfortunate consequences', he asked British diplomats to communicate his alarm to Eden in London.[11]

The foreign secretary, however, was unwilling to back down. It would be 'most unwise to try to help Nasser at the cost of weakening our support for the Turco-Iraqi Pact', he replied to Washington. 'Our declared object is to make the pact the foundation for an effective defence system for the Middle East. If this is to be achieved, Syrian, Lebanese and Jordanian accession will eventually be necessary.' Eleven days later, on 4 April 1955, Britain joined what had become known as the Baghdad Pact. Having waited for what seemed like an eternity, Eden became prime minister the day after.[12]

* * *

American assertiveness had led Britain to join the Baghdad Pact, and the threat that this posed to Nasser reminded the Egyptian prime minister of his lack of modern weaponry. The talks with the United States government about military aid had foundered over the accompanying conditions and the British were reluctant to release arms Egypt had already purchased, because they did not want to tip the military balance with Israel. Meanwhile the Israelis had taken delivery of new tanks, artillery, radar and jet fighters from the French. The growing disparity infuriated Nasser. One day in Cairo, while he was talking to Miles Copeland of the CIA, the city was buzzed by Israeli jets. 'I have to sit here and take this,' he cursed, 'and your government won't give me arms.' When Copeland told him that the State Department was stopping the Pentagon from supplying him with weapons, Nasser decided that it might help break the deadlock in Washington if he conducted a semi-public courtship with Moscow.[13]

Nasser had been trying for two years to draw the Russians into this game, without success because the Russians had guessed what he was up to. But then in May 1955, a month after the signature of the Baghdad Pact, the Soviet ambassador obliged, offering him Russian weapons in exchange for Egyptian cotton and rice. Having pocketed this offer, the Egyptian leader went to see the new US ambassador, Hank Byroade. 'This is the last time I shall ask for arms from the US,' he told him theatrically. 'If I do not get them from you I know where I can and will ask the Soviets for them.'[14]

Nasser's aide Hassan Tuhami set out the strategy: the aim was to preserve Egyptian freedom by encouraging the Great Powers to fight over her. But in fact the idea that Nasser could choose between America and Russia was an illusion. For one thing, he could not now easily accept American arms without damaging his anti-imperialist credentials; for another, the Americans were starting to show signs of impatience, because of his unwillingness to start talking about peace. At the 9 June meeting Byroade accused him of 'spreading disruption throughout the Middle East'. Nasser had tried to answer Nuri's diplomatic coup by cobbling together an alliance with the Syrians and the Saudis, but the ambassador now told him in no uncertain terms that, if he believed that this arrangement put him in a stronger bargaining position, he was 'basically wrong'.[15]

As a consequence, when the Soviet ambassador suggested to Nasser that Dmitri Shepilov, the editor of *Pravda*, might visit Cairo for discussions about arms, Nasser agreed. Shepilov met the Egyptian leader on the eve of the fourth anniversary of the Free Officers' coup and offered him 200 tanks, 100 fighter aircraft and jet bombers, which Egypt could repay in cotton over thirty years. With this offer in the bag, Nasser now played hard to get with the Americans. Byroade had left open the possibility that Egypt could still buy American-made weaponry. In mid-August Nasser told him that the Egyptians could only do so if they were allowed to pay in their own currency, knowing that this would be unacceptable but aiming to put the Americans in the position of having to reject his offer. Earlier the same day Byroade had learned the details of Shepilov's offer.

Like the Soviets, Foster Dulles suspected he was being played, and he initially told his younger brother that he did not know 'how seriously we should take the Russian proposals about Egypt'. But, whether they were serious or not, if the news that they had been made to Nasser got out, it was likely that Israel's recently re-elected prime minister David Ben Gurion would take unilateral action, given that he was a well-known believer in the use of force. Dulles would then face irresistible pressure from the Israeli lobby in Washington to support Tel Aviv, which would destroy his ability to pose as an honest broker in any peace talks. And so he brought forward his speech announcing the details of the peace plan by a fortnight, to 26 August.[16]

The speech came too late. On 22 August, four days before Dulles spoke, Israeli troops invaded the Gaza strip. Three days later, and despite Byroade's last-ditch efforts, the Egyptians retaliated with a series of fedayeen raids that reached the suburbs of Tel Aviv and killed eleven Israelis. Israel responded with an offensive in Gaza, killing thirty-six Egyptians. Dulles' Alpha peace initiative was dead before it had got started.

* * *

Israel's invasion of the Gaza strip put Nasser under further pressure but it also enabled him to justify the arms deal with the Russians. On 19 September the CIA reported that the Egyptians looked 'likely' to accept the Russian offer, which was 'said to be almost embarrassing in size'. Two days later Byroade confirmed that there had been a deal. The Russians were supplying 'Stalin' tanks, Nasser admitted a little while later. 'We shall have to change their name,' he said.[17]

The news reached the United States as the world's foreign ministers were congregating in New York for the opening of the UN general assembly, and so Dulles was able to confront the Soviet foreign minister, Vyacheslav Molotov, directly. When Molotov tried to pass it off as a commercial sale without political implications, Dulles was unconvinced. In London Harold Macmillan, whom Eden had made foreign secretary, agreed. 'This is a most alarming and perilous success for the Russians,' he wrote in his diary, 'and we must stop it somehow.'[18]

Dulles did not think Macmillan's hope was realistic. For starters the Russian offer, in the words of one member of the Joint Chiefs of Staff, came 'very cheap'. Believing that Nasser would be ousted by the army if he went back on the deal, and aware that Byroade had had an argument with the Egyptian leader the previous week, he decided to send Kim Roosevelt – long Nasser's main advocate in Washington – to Cairo to try to limit the damage.[19]

Roosevelt and Copeland met Nasser for three and a half hours at his home on 26 September, during which time Nasser agreed to issue a statement that his intentions were peaceful and that he was willing to discuss with Dulles ways to calm Arab–Israeli tensions. The subsequent drafting session was disrupted by news that the new British ambassador was coming to see the Egyptian leader. Since Dulles had not told Macmillan that Roosevelt was visiting, the two Americans decided they should go and hide upstairs. Before they did so they advised Nasser to tell his British visitor that the weapons came from Czechoslovakia rather than directly from the Soviet Union, to make the deal sound marginally less incendiary. Copeland joked that it would have been entertaining to have seen the British ambassador's reaction had they gone downstairs to interrupt, 'Excuse me, Gamal, but we're out of soda.'[20]

After the meeting the spies reported their conversation to Washington, appealing for confirmation from Dulles that a 'statement of the kind suggested would do at least *some* good'. They admitted that they were 'still somewhat uneasy' that Nasser was merely taking their word for the trouble that his decision would cause in the United States, rather than acting as a result of a change of heart. They were adamant, however, that Nasser remained 'our best, if not our only, hope here'.[21]

* * *

Dulles was not so sure. A day earlier he had had the first of a series of extremely significant conversations with the British foreign secretary, Harold Macmillan, who had come to New York for the UN's general assembly. It was the first time that the two men had met, and they seem instantly to have hit it off, slipping into an easy conspiracy, which was sealed a few weeks later when Dulles excitedly told Macmillan that together they must start a 'counter-reformation' in which they would 'disprove slanders against the old western civilisations, shew that "colonialism" was a false charge; prove the immense benefit that the British Empire had been and was; and lead the young nations to our side'.[22]

In New York, a sense of outrage united the two men. While Macmillan was furious that Soviet technicians would be working from airfields built by the British, it was Nasser's ingratitude that rankled with Dulles. They 'got more and more worked up' according to Macmillan's adviser, Shuckburgh, who was also present.[23]

Thinking aloud, Macmillan wondered whether 'we could make life impossible for Nasser and ultimately bring about his fall by various pressures'. Dulles was thinking along similar lines. A few days later he would ask Macmillan 'if we had enough troops to re-occupy Egypt'.[24]

'Not in Suez,' Macmillan admitted. 'But it could be done from Cyprus, no doubt.' The lesson he drew from the conversation was that Dulles was not averse to the idea of military action.

Both men appreciated the stakes. Dulles' own reputation was on the line, for he had unwisely lauded Nasser as a Middle Eastern George Washington during his visit to Cairo two years earlier. 'In the United States we will not be able to put a good face on the matter,' he declared. 'It will be regarded as a major defeat.' Accordingly, he told Roosevelt in Cairo that he did not think the proposed statement would help at all, and that Nasser 'should not be encouraged to believe it would'. For his part Macmillan knew that, when the news of Nasser's purchase became public, the Suez Group would crow that they had been right all along.[25]

When Macmillan suggested abandoning the Suez base agreement and the troop withdrawal, Dulles was clearly interested. But the US secretary of state did not want to take 'any threatening or drastic step' while they waited to see what Nasser actually bought. It was 'not a very attractive policy', he admitted, saying that he only offered it 'for lack of a better alternative'. It was also very difficult to criticise Nasser when the west had also welcomed Khrushchev, and the possibility of détente.[26]

Returning overnight by air to London, Macmillan briefed his colleagues on the crisis in the cabinet meeting on 4 October. The arms the Russians were offering were obsolescent, he explained, but the decision to offer them indicated that Moscow had now decided 'to fish actively in Middle Eastern waters', and had probably made an offer to the Saudis as well.[27]

Ignoring the role that his pursuit of an alliance with Nuri had played in the affair, Eden blamed the Americans for the debacle. 'Mr Dulles started all this, and if he has got himself into trouble, it is not for us to help him out,' he told his colleagues. After Macmillan had summarised the situation at the 4 October cabinet meeting, Eden called for a drastic review of Middle Eastern policy, and then launched into an unprecedented attack on the Americans, describing them as having 'almost always been wrong on the Middle East', ignorant and erratic. The minutes of the meeting set out the logical, but ominous conclusion he drew from this: 'We should not therefore, allow ourselves to be restricted overmuch by reluctance to act without full American concurrence and support.'[28]

The following year would see him practise what he preached, starting, days later, in the southeast Arabian backwater of Buraimi.

17

OVERREACH

By the beginning of October 1955, the dispute over the ownership of Buraimi, the oasis that lay on the edge of the Empty Quarter of southern Arabia, was about to rumble into its seventh year, having recently looked set to be decided in the Saudis' favour. Following the explorer Wilfred Thesiger's repeated intrusions into territory Ibn Saud regarded as his, in mid-October 1949 the ageing king had laid claim to the area southwest of Buraimi. Although the British had rejected that claim, in their role as protectors of the rulers of Qatar and Abu Dhabi, in August 1952 the Saudi king despatched an official named Turki bin Ataishan to occupy Buraimi itself. The strategic position of the oasis meant that this move put the entirety of southeastern Arabia in play.

The British, who were at that moment reeling from their relegation following the Free Officers' coup in Egypt, had handled bin Ataishan's arrival in Buraimi clumsily. Their decision to send jets to buzz the oasis and to encourage the sultan of Oman to send a force to eject the Saudi party led Ibn Saud to threaten to refer the dispute to the UN's Security Council. Uncertain whether they would be able to count on American support if the king did make such a move, the British acquiesced to a standstill agreement that left the sultan of Oman in the lurch. As Churchill put it somewhat apologetically in a conversation with the sheikh of Bahrain the following year, 'We try never to desert our friends – unless we have to.'[1]

On Ibn Saud's death in November 1953, the king's son, Saud, succeeded to the throne, providing the opportunity that British diplomats had long argued their government should wait for. After much haggling, in July 1954 they agreed with the Saudis to put the Buraimi dispute to international arbitration. The two sides would put their respective cases to a five-man tribunal, comprising British and Saudi nominees and three others from neutral countries. In the meantime detachments of British and Saudi forces were supposedly to keep the peace at the oasis.

In the meantime, however, the stakes had grown considerably, following the discovery of oil in the vicinity of Abu Dhabi and, as a consequence, both sides ignored the standstill agreement. The British encouraged the sultan of Oman to spend money shoring up the support of key tribes in the area, and in late 1954 the Saudis made an unsuccessful effort to overthrow Sheikh Shakhbut of Abu Dhabi by paying his cousins to oust him. The detachment they sent to Buraimi included an intelligence officer, Abdullah Quraishi, who was in direct contact with King Saud's foreign policy adviser, Yusuf Yassin, and bought off the most influential sheikhs in the oasis. In August 1955 Quraishi approached Shakhbut's brother Zayid, who lived on the oasis, and offered him the stupendous sum of 400 million rupees – or £30 million – to switch sides.

The arbitration was scheduled to take place in Geneva in September, and while the Saudis nominated Yassin to sit on the tribunal, the British rather naively proposed an utterly decent, recently retired diplomat, Sir Reader Bullard. These two men were joined on the panel by Charles de Visscher, a former judge of the International Court, who would also serve as its chairman, a former foreign minister of Cuba, and a Pakistani educationalist, Mahmud Hassan, who delayed the start of the proceedings by stopping to undertake the pilgrimage in Mecca.

Aware that the Saudis had tried to bribe Zayid and suspecting – correctly – that they had successfully suborned Mahmud Hassan during his stop in Mecca, the British hoped to win the arbitration by exposing Saudi malfeasance. Accordingly they briefed the former Nuremberg prosecutor Sir Hartley Shawcross to represent the sheikh of Abu Dhabi and the sultan of Oman. While waiting for Hassan to arrive, Shawcross told the remaining four members of the tribunal that he would be making serious allegations about the Saudis when Hassan turned up and the proceedings finally got going. When they did, on the eleventh, the British silk accused Saudi Arabia of trying to buy the loyalty of the sheikhs on the oasis by large-scale bribery. But his arguments, the testimony of his witnesses, who included Sheikh Zayid, and the implausibility of Quraishi's account all failed to sway Visscher and the other neutral members of the panel. On 15 September, after the tribunal had adjourned for its deliberations, Bullard warned the British that, behind closed doors, Yassin and Hassan were dominating their colleagues by insisting they had a far greater understanding of Islamic law and Arab culture. What the British labelled bribery, they said, was simply Arab generosity. As matters stood, the veteran diplomat advised, the arbitration was on the verge of delivering a finding that, a British official later wrote, 'would have been disastrous for us'.[2]

Just in time, British intelligence made a breakthrough the following day, establishing – probably by intercepting and decrypting Pakistani diplomatic telegrams – that the tribunal's Pakistani member, Hassan, had twice taken money from the Saudis which he had not declared. The British delegation in Geneva put the evidence to Bullard, who immediately told Visscher he was stepping down. Unable to refer to his real reason, because of the risk of compromising its source, Bullard could only blame Yassin's behaviour and, more vaguely, 'other distasteful matters' which had come to his notice. Visscher suspended the arbitration on the sixteenth.

Deciding that they needed to give Visscher the full story, but unwilling to give away how they had found it out, the British sent an MI6 officer, posing as an oil company executive, to meet Hassan. Visscher resigned when, shortly afterwards, he was presented with the transcript of the ensuing conversation, which the spy had taped, during which Hassan admitted he had taken a £600 'loan' from the Saudis. On 4 October – the same day that Eden demanded a rethink of Middle Eastern policy in cabinet – the government announced that it supported Bullard's decision to resign from the tribunal, after 'confirmation was secured of Her Majesty's Government's suspicion that attempts had been made by the Saudis to tamper with the impartiality of the Tribunal behind the President's back' – a form of words designed to send the clearest signal to Riyadh and Hassan.[3]

* * *

Clandestine British action had derailed the arbitration, but not killed it off altogether, because the agreement that had established it provided for the replacement of any members who resigned. The Foreign Office summarised the options for Macmillan. The British government could either continue with the process once the tribunal was reconstituted, or renege on the arbitration agreement by abandoning the tribunal. While continuing might avoid or postpone an international row, the new panel would be just as susceptible to Saudi pressure as its predecessor, British participation would look like acquiescence to bribery and when, almost inevitably, the arbitration went against the British, the local loss of faith in the value of British protection would be profound. Macmillan's officials recommended confronting the problem head-on. The government, they argued, 'must ... announce that the Agreement has been terminated by Saudi action, re-occupy the area and be prepared to defend it diplomatically and militarily'.[4]

The British knew that the Saudis had only managed to occupy Buraimi in 1952 thanks to Aramco's support. They had agreed to a standstill because they were not confident that they would enjoy American support were Ibn Saud to carry out his threat to refer the matter to the Security Council. Their willingness now to confront the United States' main ally in the region was an extraordinary sign of how far their thinking had moved on.

The collapse of the arbitration coincided with the discovery of the Soviet arms sale to Nasser, and it was not until 20 October that the cabinet formally discussed its options, after considering a Foreign Office report on Middle East Oil that warned that the region was slipping out of Britain's grasp 'because of the indigenous forces of nationalism, and because our enemies are making a greater effort than we'. Against this alarming backdrop, Macmillan favoured informing the Americans that they were going to break off the arbitration, and then overpowering the Saudi police contingent without warning, to reduce the likelihood of casualties. But Eden clearly did not trust Washington not to tip off the Saudis. He preferred that 'the disputed area should be reoccupied first, and an explanation given afterwards'. The cabinet agreed with him and, once the chiefs of staff had come up with a plan, approved 'Operation Bonaparte' two days later. 'Let's hope it comes off,' the foreign secretary wrote in his diary.[5]

Before dawn on 26 October two parties of the Trucial Oman Levies – a British-led Arab force – drove from the camp into the neutral zone, surprising the Saudi police as they were washing before their dawn prayers. Following a fierce gun battle with tribesmen loyal to the sheikhs bought by the Saudis, and a tug of war between the leader of the Saudi detachment and a British officer over a despatch box, the British took control of the oasis. The box turned out to contain a quarter of a million pounds-worth of rupees and a mass of incriminating paperwork which showed that Quraishi had been lying under oath in Geneva, and that Yassin knew what he was doing. The British felt it vindicated their decision to abandon the tribunal.

The Saudis again threatened to go to the Security Council, but never did. Better still, so far as the British were concerned, was the muted American response to what became known as the 'Buraimi incident'. When Macmillan broke the news to Dulles in person later the same day, on the sidelines of a NATO meeting in Paris, he claimed that he had not provided any advanced warning so that his counterpart could deny any complicity. Dulles does not appear to have taken issue with this unconvincing explanation. The secretary of state 'did not like the news', recorded Macmillan's adviser, Evelyn Shuckburgh. 'But he was not unpleasant about it.'[6]

* * *

With the revelation that the Saudis had offered Zayid £30 million and the discovery that they had nearly swung the arbitration by giving Mahmud Hassan a tiny fraction of that sum, the Buraimi arbitration brought into sharp relief an issue that the British increasingly regarded as the root cause of their difficulties in the Middle East – the scale of Saudi bribery.

While the Iraqi prime minister Nuri Said was exaggerating when he claimed that the Saudis spent £100 million a year on bribery and subversion, the number was certainly large. Although the Saudi kingdom's finances were opaque, its oil revenues had rocketed since the fifty–fifty negotiations of 1950, reaching a figure of about £100 million in 1955. By borrowing aggressively, the Saudis could spend even more. Where the money went was far from clear. The expenditure set out in a rare budget, published in August 1955, only accounted for half the country's income, and of this it allocated sums under vague headings like 'tribal subsidies' and 'charitable grants' that could be going anywhere. All that could be said for certain was that, at a time when Britain's Middle East budget amounted to a puny £15 million (or $42 million), the Saudis – to quote the CIA – had 'almost limitless funds to spend'.[7]

The problem dominated the first meeting of the council of the Baghdad Pact, which took place in the Iraqi capital in November. On his arrival, Macmillan was immediately buttonholed by Nuri who was alarmed by the situation developing in Syria. Earlier that year the Egyptians and the Saudis had helped their long-standing client Shukri Quwatly win the presidential election. Quwatly now seemed to be repaying his sponsors by threatening to cut off the oil pipeline from Iraq if the Iraq Petroleum Company did not pay Syria a higher transit fee. Nuri told Macmillan he was convinced that Syria was 'almost wholly' in the Saudis' pay.[8]

The other country that the delegates agreed the Saudis were energetically targeting was Jordan. Following the assassination of King Abdullah in Jerusalem in 1951, Abdullah's son Talal had succeeded to the throne but he suffered from some sort of mental illness and abdicated within two years in favour of his seventeen-year-old son, Hussein. While Talal spent the rest of his life in a sanatorium, his glamorous wife, Queen Zein, remained a force to be reckoned with in Jordan's politics. The Saudis, having established that she was, like them, extremely hostile to the ambitions of the Iraqi branch of the family, were now subsidising her extravagant lifestyle. The Iraqis felt that 'far too much ... royal money was being spent on shopping'.[9]

Macmillan returned to London via Beirut, where he heard a similar story from the Lebanese president, who complained that his prime minister had just taken £10,000 from the Saudis, and begged the British foreign secretary not to push the question of Baghdad Pact membership too hard. Back in London, he briefed the cabinet and wrote up his impressions for Eden, warning him that 'if we do not get Jordan into the Baghdad Pact now, she will drift out of our control', because the country, like her neighbours, was being 'rapidly undermined and corrupted by Saudi money'. He was confident that Hussein would accept the invitation, were it accompanied by a threat that, if he didn't, Britain would stop paying the £12 million a year subsidy that financed his Arab Legion, leaving his country defenceless against an Israeli invasion. More fundamentally, Macmillan continued, action was needed to prevent the Saudis' oil royalties from undermining the Arab states and opening the way for communism. If Eisenhower was unwilling or unable to take action to stop American money being spent on subversion, Britain should tackle the oil companies directly. 'Alternatively, it may be a question of Anglo/US action to upset King Saud and remove this canker.'[10]

Eden had previously feared that bringing Jordan into the pact increased the risk that Britain could be dragged into a war with Israel. Swayed by Macmillan's argument that the threat to Jordan now outweighed that danger, he changed his mind. On 30 November Macmillan approved Shuckburgh's idea that the new chief of the imperial general staff, Sir Gerald Templer, go to Amman to convince King Hussein to sign up to the pact, by offering a sweetener of £25,000 a year if necessary to do so. Templer set out for Jordan six days later, shortly before a message arrived from Dulles asking London to 'wait a little' before trying to secure Jordanian membership of the pact. 'It is a great gamble,' Shuckburgh admitted, 'for the Egyptians are as thick as flies in Amman, trying to stop the King from joining the pact, and we have got to overcome them now or never.'[11]

Having once told Lord Mountbatten, 'Dickie, you're so crooked that if you swallowed a nail you'd shit a corkscrew', Templer was certainly a bold choice of envoy. Described as 'a man who lives on his nerves and "gets there" by quickness of thought, intelligence and sheer guts', Britain's top general was an Irishman who had made his name waging a successful counter-insurgency against the communists in Malaya. His rasping voice, tendency to peer over the top of his spectacles and use of his swagger stick 'like a matador's sword' disconcerted his subordinates. 'He looked a dangerous sort of general,' recalled one of them, remembering, 'His interrogation of me started with a jab in the navel from the cane, a move I found unendearing.'[12]

Templer's mission failed miserably. Although King Hussein was keen to accede to the pact, the British general wanted to be sure that the king had the backing of his government, and this was not forthcoming. Jordan, once dominated by three tribes, had been transformed by King Abdullah's annexation of the West Bank and the influx of refugees during the 1948 war. Palestinians, who blamed the British for their plight, now made up a majority of the population, a fact the Egyptians exploited. 'We can do what we like in Jordan because of our stand against Israel,' Nasser boasted.[13]

By the time of Templer's visit, Hussein had been forced to appoint a government that reflected the divide in Jordanian society. Following a well-timed visit by Nasser's sidekick Abdel Hakim Amer, the four Palestinian members of the cabinet insisted on referring the matter to Cairo before taking a decision. On 11 December Macmillan summarised the telegrams he was receiving from Templer. 'He is striving hard to get Jordan into the Baghdad Pact, but it's touch and go. The ministers are mostly timid or bribed by the Saudis. The Prime Minister he describes as jelly.' When all four Palestinian ministers suddenly resigned, the prime minister had no choice but to tender his resignation. Templer left empty handed a day later.[14]

Templer was in Amman for barely a week, but the shockwaves resulting from his visit reverberated for another month. King Hussein appointed a man from the most southerly of the three tribes, Hazza al-Majali, as his next prime minister. Majali's job was to try to bring Jordan into the pact. By then, however, Nasser's CIA-supplied radio station, Voice of the Arabs, was in full cry. Its ceaseless attacks on the Baghdad Pact cut through and on 17 December riots broke out across the West Bank, as well as in Amman and two other towns on the east side of the Jordan. Lacking adequate police, Majali sent in the Arab Legion to quell the protests. At least fifteen people died; the Saudis, seeking to aggravate the situation, claimed the figure was much higher. Whatever the death toll, the use of British-led forces to restore order played straight into the hands of Egyptian propagandists. After just five days in office Majali, too, was forced to resign.

Hussein appointed a successor and dissolved parliament, hoping to turn a general election into a referendum on Baghdad Pact membership. In the circumstances this was an enormous gamble, and a high court judgement that the king's dissolution decree was illegal gave him the opportunity to backpedal. But the news that he had cancelled the elections triggered further rioting and when a mob broke into one ministry, the government again called on the Legion, which this time used tear-gas, rather than live rounds, to break up the crowd. Only the appointment of yet another prime minister, who declared that he would not pursue membership of the pact, bought an uneasy calm. But

Jordanian politics had changed for ever. 'Your Majesty,' a Palestinian delegation from the West Bank town of Nablus told Hussein, 'among the Arabs there is a saying that the people follow the religion of the king. Today things have changed. Now we say that the King must follow the religion of the people.'[15]

The British suspicion that the Saudis had orchestrated the riots was given further weight days later when intelligence reached London that a 3,000-strong Saudi force was moving towards the Jordanian border. By now Eden's once-huge popularity had evaporated. Criticised on all sides for lacking leadership, the prime minister reshuffled his government, shifting Macmillan to the Treasury and replacing him with the junior Foreign Office minister Selwyn Lloyd. At the same time he decided to send two Parachute Regiment battalions to Cyprus and deploy RAF units based at Habbaniyah in Iraq to Amman. Lloyd warned the Saudis that British troops would be sent in to support Jordan if they attacked. 'We have lost the first round,' Macmillan admitted the next day. 'However the game is not over yet; and we have got to win.' The stakes, he said, were very high, 'no less than the economic survival of Britain. For if we lose out in the Middle East, we lose the oil. If we lose the oil, we cannot live.'[16]

The fact that the Saudis were ferried to the Jordanian border in lorries provided by Aramco added piquancy to Anglo-American talks on the Middle East at the end of January 1956. Requested by Eden after the Tories' house journal, the *Spectator*, had reported 'a terrifying lack of authority at the top', they took place amid growing tensions between the two allies over Middle Eastern policy. An openly pro-Arab Mansion House speech by Eden the previous November had riled the Israelis and vexed Dulles, who must have regarded the consequences of Britain's failure to heed his advice not to push the Jordanians on the Baghdad Pact as entirely predictable. On the other hand, Dulles' manifest reluctance to put pressure on Aramco infuriated the British. Believing that the Americans could try harder, in January the government briefed the press that when Eden arrived in Washington he would be raising the Saudis' subversive activities, which depended on 'money derived from the American oil company, Aramco'. A further article in the *Sunday Times* the following week directly accused the Saudis of using Aramco royalties to foment anti-British riots in Amman.[17]

Preliminary talks between the two sides' officials had revealed a gulf between them over what to do about Saudi Arabia. The British, aware that there was interest inside the CIA for the dismemberment of Saudi Arabia, hinted at regime change, while the Americans wanted their ally to go back to arbitration, not least because they feared an argument might derail the smooth extension of the Dhahran base agreement which expired later that year. But by the time Eden arrived in Washington on 30 January 1956, he found that the atmosphere had markedly improved. Eisenhower had sent an old friend, Robert Anderson, to the Middle East to speak to the Egyptians and the Israelis about peace, but Anderson had made little headway. Dulles was absorbing the fact that Nasser's latest suggestion – that he would be willing to discuss peace with the Israelis in six months' time – would push any talks into the presidential election campaign. The secretary of state was now clearly considering the option of moving against Nasser and dealing with the Syrians at the same time. And when Eisenhower, who was recovering from a stroke, joined Eden and Dulles to discuss Buraimi, he was far more sympathetic towards the British view of the Saudis than either Dulles, or his State Department advisers, had ever been. 'Some way must be found of breaking the deadlock and getting past the evil counsellors who surrounded the King,' Ike mused, appreciating that the British would not return to arbitration under the same conditions. Eden could live with the American desire for direct talks with the Saudis. He left Washington on 3 February elated: 'This is the best meeting in Washington we have ever had.'[18]

The talks brought out a useful piece of information which suggested a way forward to the British. It concerned the exact way that the Saudis were raising their money. Contrary to British impressions that the king was leaning on Aramco to advance him ever greater sums against future royalties, the Americans explained that the Saudis were in fact borrowing from American banks on the security of 'tax anticipation warrants' that authorised the banks to collect directly from Aramco money that the company owed to the Saudis in tax. This ingenious method spared the bankers from having to deal with the Saudis, but it relied on their ongoing faith in the survival of the Saudi monarchy and state, which the British now decided to try to undermine.[19]

Four days after Eden told the cabinet, on his arrival back in London, that he had agreed with Eisenhower that they should try to divert Saudi spending into 'roads, hospitals, etc.', a well-known British journalist wrote on exactly this theme. The *Daily Express*'s chief foreign reporter, Sefton Delmer, had worked for the Special Operations Executive during the war running black and grey propaganda designed to undermine German morale. Writing from Beirut following a visit to Saudi Arabia, Delmer reported anger at the failure of the king to build the roads, schools and hospitals he had promised, and mounting criticism of Saud's Syrian and Palestinian advisers, who were lining their own pockets with money given them to fund subversion in Jordan and Iraq. Leading the critics was the king's own brother Faisal, who Delmer claimed had recently been urged, during a visit to Cairo, to oust his sibling. Firm action by Saud, he ended, 'would avert the danger of two lots of rebellion: that which the Saudis with their money, are trying to spread in Jordan and Iraq; and that other revolt which they are going to cause at home in Saudi Arabia by not using their money properly.'[20]

* * *

The British counter-offensive came too late to save their key official in the region, the commander of the Arab Legion, Glubb Pasha. A veteran of the First World War, Sir John Glubb enjoyed hero-like status in Britain but he had never hit it off with King Hussein. Taking it upon himself to act as a khaki-clad godfather to the king, four years earlier he had taken the then sixteen-year-old for a day out in Battersea Park, where he was amazed to discover that the teenage prince 'did not want to go on the merry-go-rounds or the scenic railway'. Their relationship had been tense since.[21]

The real problem, so far as Hussein was concerned, was not that Glubb was a patronising old fart – it was that he was too powerful: not without reason was the pasha known as the 'uncrowned king of Jordan'. Glubb's power came from controlling the money: he received the £12 million subsidy that the British paid to maintain the Arab Legion, and he spent it how he wanted. In old Transjordan, his recruitment of jobless youths from Bedu families had made him very popular; west of the Jordan, however, the picture was very different. His scrupulously defensive posture in the face of Israeli border raids was controversial, and the opposition argued that, until he was thrown out, the country was not truly free. Hussein was alive to these concerns and asked Glubb to Arabise the Legion completely and when Glubb prevaricated, he grew increasingly annoyed.[22]

Glubb's position was therefore vulnerable even before Templer's visit, but the Arab Legion's involvement in suppressing the riots that had followed it rendered it unsustainable. The pasha was, quite simply, too big a target for Voice of the Arabs, which spread the untrue, but all too plausible rumour that he was about to launch a coup. On 1 March, a day after he had submitted Hussein a list of Arab officers he suspected of nationalist sympathies and wanted sacked, the king fired him instead. 'Were things slack today at the office?' his wife enquired when he arrived home early from work. 'My dear,' said Glubb, 'the king has dismissed me. We leave Jordan at seven o'clock tomorrow morning – and we shall never come back.'[23]

While Glubb was sanguine, putting his removal down to a 'young King wanting to run his own show', Selwyn Lloyd, who was in Cairo at the time on a tour of the region, and Eden both leapt to the conclusion that it was Nasser who had masterminded the coup, timing it to cause maximum humiliation, when in fact the Egyptian leader was as surprised as they were. By 3 March – the day that the papers reported the news – Eden had become 'violently anti-Nasser', comparing him with Mussolini, his adviser Evelyn Shuckburgh recorded.[24]

When Lloyd went on to Bahrain and he and the political resident were yelled at by an angry mob, the opposition Labour Party scented blood and called for a debate on the government's Middle East policy. To allay King Hussein's anxieties, behind the scenes Eden had been trying to arrange for Iraqis to replace the British officers seconded to the Legion. But when the debate took place on 7 March it was too early to say whether this decidedly optimistic plan would work. When the prime minister wound up the debate for the government, he was forced to admit that he was not in a position to say what the government's policy on Jordan was, almost a week after Glubb had been fired. With nothing of substance to offer he resorted to personal abuse instead, accusing the leader of the opposition, Hugh Gaitskell, of serving as a mouthpiece for Moscow.

Shuckburgh had a grandstand view of the proceedings from the officials' box beside the Speaker's chair. Eden seemed to have 'completely disintegrated', he wrote immediately afterwards, describing his old boss as appearing 'petulant, irrelevant, provocative, at the same time as being weak'. Even Eden's loyal wife Clarissa described her husband's performance as 'a shambles'. What really wounded the prime minister, however, was the universal drubbing he received in the press the following day.[25]

The debate showed that, barely eleven months into his premiership, Eden was utterly beleaguered, and for the prime minister it was a turning point. Whereas the reality was that the threat of Saudi bribery had driven Macmillan to push for the enlargement of the Baghdad Pact, creating pressures in Jordan that had forced the king to sack Glubb, Eden was convinced that Nasser had masterminded the pasha's removal. He now feared that the Egyptian leader would be his nemesis as well. 'It is him or us, don't forget that,' he told Shuckburgh a few days later.[26]

Yet Eden had every reason to feel confident that it was a vendetta he would win. For, from the other side of the Atlantic, came the signs of a dramatic shift in American thinking as well. 'Today', Shuckburgh recorded in his diary on the day after the debate, 'both we and the Americans really gave up hope of Nasser and began to look around for means of destroying him.'[27]

18

DITCHING NASSER

On 6 March 1956, the eve of Eden's disastrous performance in the House of Commons, President Eisenhower's Middle East envoy, Robert Anderson, wired home from Cairo with some bad news. A day earlier, after a meeting with Nasser, the Egyptian prime minister had kept Kim Roosevelt behind. 'What was Mr Anderson talking about?' he asked the CIA officer, having been unable to understand Anderson's Texan drawl.

'I think he believes that you've agreed to meet with Ben Gurion to resolve all your differences,' Roosevelt explained.

'I could never do that. I'd be assassinated,' said Nasser. 'Go stop him. Don't let him send that cable!' he urged. In a further meeting with Anderson that day he had set out his position more clearly. His fear of being murdered meant that not only would he not meet with Ben Gurion, he also would not say that he supported a peace deal with Israel himself.[1]

That mattered, because the Americans had assumed that Nasser would. Their ongoing effort to build up his prestige, in the face of mounting British opposition, was based on the belief that the Arab world would not accept a peace deal with Israel unless the offer came from Nasser personally. On 6 March it became clear that either there had been a misunderstanding or, as Anderson believed, the Egyptian prime minister had finally decided to admit that he had no intention of doing what the Americans wanted, because he feared a backlash in the Arab world if he did. 'I doubt the fruitfulness of any additional conversations,' the American concluded.[2]

Eisenhower agreed that the Alpha peace plan was dead. 'We have reached the point', he wrote two days later, 'where it looks as if Egypt, under Nasser, is going to make no move whatsoever to meet the Israelites in an effort to settle outstanding differences.' Dulles, who was in Karachi with Lloyd at a conference at the time, set out the implication. 'Unless Nasser did something soon, we would have to "ditch" him,' Britain's foreign secretary reported his American counterpart as saying.[3]

This telegram was of crucial importance, because Eden read 'ditch' to mean that the administration was contemplating the overthrow of Nasser, which was what he wanted himself. In it, therefore, lay the origin of the Suez crisis.

* * *

The prime minister and an inner circle of officials had been considering a coup since receiving intelligence late the previous year that Nasser had also promised to collectivise the Egyptian economy in exchange for the Soviet weaponry he received. Their discussions acquired new impetus in March after the British ambassador in Cairo reported further secret intelligence that Nasser was planning to go to war with Israel, probably once the last British troops had left the Suez base in June. That was an alarming possibility because Britain, together with the United States and France, was committed by the 1950 Tripartite Declaration to guaranteeing the de facto borders between Israel and her neighbours established by the armistice in 1949. If Egypt invaded, Britain would be obliged to defend Israel against her erstwhile Arab allies. Having to take sides with Israel was a prospect that Eden himself described as 'appalling' because it would destroy Britain's remaining alliances in the Arab world – a calculation that was remarkable given what would happen later in the year.[4]

Since Lloyd was making his way home from Karachi, it was his junior minister, Anthony Nutting, who drafted the memorandum setting out a plan to isolate Nasser internationally and to undermine him at home. To isolate the Egyptian leader, Nutting proposed additional support for Britain's Baghdad Pact allies, drawing the Hashemite monarchies of Iraq and Jordan closer together, seeking 'a rearrangement of affairs' in Syria, and detaching Saudi Arabia from Egypt. To make life difficult for Nasser at home the British would encourage the Sudanese to make trouble over the Nile waters, renege on their offer of finance towards the costs of the construction of the Aswan Dam and encourage his opponents to oust him.

When Eden read Nutting's effort he was unimpressed. Tracking the author down to the Savoy, he rang up the hotel and summoned his minister to the phone. 'It's me,' he said, after Nutting had picked up the receiver. 'What's all this poppycock you've sent me? I don't agree with a single word of it.' When Nutting said that he had followed his brief, Eden was not satisfied. 'But what's all this nonsense about isolating Nasser or "neutralising" him, as you call it? I want him murdered, can't you understand?'[5]

On 21 March Lloyd, now back from Karachi, told the Cabinet that a new policy towards Nasser was needed. In Cairo, he explained, he had offered the Egyptian leader a deal: if Egypt dialled down its anti-British propaganda, Britain would not push for the enlargement of the Baghdad Pact. Since then, he continued, a further onslaught by Voice of the Arabs against Britain's position in her South Arabian colony at Aden and the Gulf States showed that Nasser had rejected his overture. 'We must therefore go for him, recognising that he will be a formidable opponent,' the foreign secretary argued, before running through the elements of Nutting's plan, which included 'seeking an alternative regime'. Everyone round the table must have known what this entailed. For after Eden had cagily admitted that the options had been discussed by a 'smaller group', another minister, Lord Salisbury, said that he supported the new policy: 'Write him off – and see him off,' he declared, adding that it was 'a pity we didn't decide earlier to take this line'.[6]

* * *

Meanwhile in Washington Dulles was simultaneously drafting his own plan, which – now that the Alpha initiative was dead – he labelled Omega. Much of it mirrored British thinking, but in one fundamental respect it was completely different. Contrary to what Eden assumed, by 'ditching' Nasser, Dulles did not mean his overthrow. Rather, what he had in mind was the transfer of American support to the leader of another Arab state, if Nasser's conduct did not quickly improve. Nasser would be left to kick his heels.

That idea appears to have been Eisenhower's. Impressed by Anderson's account of how Nasser intended to lead the Arab world by championing opposition to Israel, and then by more intelligence from Eden, which alleged that the Egyptian prime minister was planning to oust the Hashemite, Libyan and eventually Saudi monarchies, the president suggested to the State Department that 'we begin to build up some other individual' to disrupt Nasser's plans. 'My own choice of rival', Ike said, 'is King Saud.'[7]

This was becoming something of a theme. Like Franklin D. Roosevelt before him, Ike hoped that the Saudi king might become the 'spiritual leader' of the Arab world, a man who might one day achieve peace with Israel and thereby resolve America's great Middle Eastern problem – that her two best allies in the region hated one another. The problem was that this vision put the United States on a collision course with their British counterparts, a fact that became apparent when two of their spies arrived in London for talks with MI6.

James Eichelberger and Bill Eveland each had significant Middle Eastern experience. Eichelberger had served in Cairo as the CIA's first head of station after the Free Officers' coup. His first encounter with Eveland came when Eveland, then working for the Operations Control Board, which managed covert operations for the National Security Council, arrived in Cairo late in 1954 on the ill-fated mission to establish what the new regime wanted by way of arms. In contrast to most of his peers who came from the East Coast, Eveland came from the mining town of Spokane in Washington State, and he was acutely conscious of, and determined to conceal, his humble origins. As he stepped off the plane in Cairo wearing a three-piece suit and homburg hat, Eichelberger had gawped. 'Jeezus,' he whistled. 'He's in fancy dress.'[8]

Eveland may have attracted ridicule from his colleagues but, as a fluent Arabic speaker, he was better qualified than they were. When, a year later, Syrian politics was once again in turmoil, he was the man whom Kim Roosevelt sent to Syria to bolster the CIA officers who were trying to stop the country's disconcerting drift into the arms of the Russians. Since regime change in Syria was common to both Nutting's and Dulles' plans, Eveland was the obvious man to join Eichelberger on the mission to London.

The two men came at the invitation of Selwyn Lloyd, who had admitted at the cabinet meeting on 21 March that the British government could not oust Nasser alone and would need Foster Dulles' and Ike's support to do so. Believing that, just as with Mosaddeq four years earlier, the way to go about this was to convince Allen Dulles first, the foreign secretary now sought to inveigle the Americans again by suggesting that the CIA and MI6 might come up with a joint appreciation of the available intelligence.

On 31 March Eveland and Eichelberger arrived at MI6's damp-stained Westminster headquarters to meet George Young, MI6's director of Middle East operations. 'A big man, tough-looking', in Eveland's recollection, the red-haired Scot was one of the 'robber barons' who ran the secret service. Recruited into MI6 after the war, he had made his name as a buccaneering head of station in Vienna before witnessing the Black Saturday riots in Cairo in January 1952. 'When the British Council premises go up in flames the odour of roasting pansy is incense in the nostrils of Allah,' he commented laconically later. There was, he claimed, 'no gladder sound to the Arab ear than the crunch of glass'.[9]

Young set out his service's view of the situation. Syria, Saudi Arabia and Egypt all threatened Britain's survival, but since Nasser could not be tackled immediately, the priority was Syria. As the overthrow of President Quwatly and his government would undoubtedly trigger a hostile Saudi reaction because Quwatly was a client of Riyadh, lasting change in Syria also required the overthrow of King Saud and his replacement by a Hashemite king. Finally, the British would deal with Nasser, who Young claimed was now inextricably entangled with the Russians.

Eveland and Eichelberger did not know what to make of Young's presentation. Back at the Connaught Hotel in Mayfair (for Eveland spared no expense when the American taxpayer was footing the bill), they agreed that what they had just heard was 'sheer lunacy', designed, they suspected, to provoke them into giving away details of how they were planning to oust the government of Syria.[10]

'The professional skill of espionage is the exploitation of human weakness,' Young once said. If so, Eveland was a rather better spy than he. Noticing that the British spy's vulnerability was his desire to prove others wrong, the American now claimed that his own recent experience in Syria meant that he knew the score better than Young did.[11]

Unable to resist his instinct to correct Eveland, Young divulged the British plan. Incidents on the Turkish border, Iraqi incitement of the Syrian desert tribes, and subversive activities by the Lebanon-based Syrian People's Party, he explained, would create chaos inside Syria, giving the Iraqis an excuse to intervene. The following day Eveland extracted the final vital detail from Young by commenting on how much his scheme seemed to depend on the Iraqis. The idea, he continued, that they might be able to overthrow Nasser as well, was wishful thinking.

Again unable to resist the bait, Young shook his head and told Eveland that he had forgotten about the 'snipcocks' – his disparaging term for the Israelis – who were going to launch special operations against Egyptian military targets and attack Gaza and other areas along the border. That evening, with Young looking menacingly over their shoulders, Eveland and Eichelberger sent an urgent telegram to Washington, to warn Allen Dulles that 'our plans for an area peace settlement were now in real trouble'.[12]

Allen Dulles had been due to travel to London with Kim Roosevelt for further discussions. Aware that if he did so he might seem to be endorsing the British strategy, he cancelled his trip, claiming a bad attack of gout. Roosevelt went to London on his own. To mollify the British he accepted the need for a change of government in Syria, but he rejected their plans to remove King Saud and Nasser. Unlike in Teheran in 1953, he rather caustically observed, there was no other man to whom the Egyptians would gravitate. Lloyd got the message that the CIA was 'obviously more dubious than the British . . . that the operation could be carried out'. His attempt to convince the Americans to back the British plan had failed.[13]

* * *

Not convinced that Roosevelt's performance would stop MI6 from carrying on singlehandedly, Eichelberger and Eveland took matters into their own hands. Eichelberger sent a message to Nasser in Cairo, warning him that the British were 'determined to "do a Mosaddeq"' on him. Eveland, in the meantime, returned to Beirut. On 3 May, over drinks in the bar of the Hotel St Georges with the *New York Times* correspondent, he learned of an article in that day's *Daily Telegraph*, reporting that the Syrians had concluded a large arms deal with the Czechs some six weeks earlier. Recalling his CIA colleagues' view that the *Telegraph*'s reporter was probably a deep cover agent for MI6, Eveland suspected that the article was a deliberate plant, designed to pave the way for imminent military action in the country, a possibility he felt his bosses in Washington were not treating seriously enough.[14]

Eveland knew Allen Dulles read the *New York Times* every morning as he was driven into work; its Beirut correspondent was therefore well worth cultivating. He had also just returned from a trip through Syria and he was able to tell the journalist categorically that he had seen no evidence at all of the 200 tanks and armoured cars the British newspaper said the Syrians had just purchased. 'Syrian Deal Doubted', the next day's *New York Times* reported.

Concerned that Britain's plans were 'not . . . wholly realistic or likely to achieve the desired results', Allen Dulles recalled Eveland to Washington in late May. There the spy voiced his concern that the British might be 'stampeding us into an ill-conceived operation that Syria's conservatives couldn't sustain'. Dulles ordered his officials to tell Britain and Iraq that the United States opposed any covert action in Syria, while Eveland returned to Syria to assess how best to carry out a coup.[15]

Eveland's job boiled down to choosing which of two potential candidates the United States could back – Syria's former dictator Adib Shishakli or the former foreign minister, Michael Ilyan. On his way back from his reconnaissance of northern Syria, the American intelligence officer had spotted Shishakli, who was supposed to be living in exile in Spain, in a town in the Bekaa Valley in eastern Lebanon. A hard-drinking opportunist who had bounced between various foreign cities since his expulsion from Syria in 1954, Shishakli was now working for the Iraqis and the Syrian Popular Party, which favoured a union between Syria and Iraq. That made Eveland wonder, rightly, whether the British might be involved with him as well. Ilyan was also a good friend of the Iraqi regent, Abdul Ilah, but Eveland saw him regularly enough to feel he was the safer bet. The former foreign minister, a Christian from Aleppo, was predicting that the current government would not last long; he expected its successor to be dominated by the right, and to include two men that he would nominate. Eveland, reassured, told Washington that it was best to wait.

As Ilyan predicted the government collapsed, but the right-wingers were not able to form a government on their own. Syria's leftward journey continued when a new coalition government then awarded two key ministries – foreign affairs and economics – to the national-socialist Baath Party which, having been forced underground during the Shishakli years, was now increasingly popular. When the two Baathist ministers called for union with Egypt and invited the Soviet foreign minister to visit, the Americans were forced to revisit the idea of a coup. Kim Roosevelt and his cousin, Archie, who also worked for the CIA, both hurried out to Damascus to meet Ilyan and see what help he needed. Eveland remembered Ilyan's delight when he heard the Roosevelts were coming. 'He'd always admired FDR, he said, and to meet his sons would be an occasion of great historical moment.' Deciding that the truth would be a disappointment, 'I let this comment pass,' Eveland recalled.[16]

Kim and Archie Roosevelt arrived in Beirut on 1 July and drove over the mountains to Damascus, a journey they had first made when Kim was pretending to be a journalist in 1947, and that he had repeated, in a car loaded with banknotes, on his way to Teheran in 1953. First they met the army chief of staff, and supposedly the real power in Syrian politics, but found him disappointing. The meeting with Ilyan went much better. Asked what he needed to stop the communists taking over the country, Ilyan said that he needed the support of a few senior military officers, the Damascus and Aleppo radio stations and enough money to buy the newspapers that were currently in Egyptian or Saudi pay. Eveland recalled that what the Roosevelts wanted to know most of all was whether this could be accomplished with American support alone. 'Without question,' Ilyan responded. But when a few days later the chief of staff was suddenly dismissed, Ilyan suspected that he had been rumbled and fled Damascus for the relative safety of Beirut.[17]

The broader purpose of the Roosevelts' Middle Eastern mission was to start the process of isolating Nasser. From Damascus the two cousins went on to Amman where, on 16 July, they met King Hussein of Jordan. A month earlier the king had driven his silver gull-wing Mercedes to Beirut to take part in a car race in the mountains. At a time when there were rumours that the Egyptians and the Saudis were plotting to depose him, he had used the opportunity to meet Eveland and ask for weapons. The Roosevelts now came to see the king, going a step further by finalising a monthly payment of about $15,000 which the CIA head of station would leave behind, in a white envelope and without comment, when he met the king at the end of each month. Unusually, the Roosevelts' arrival in Amman was reported in the *New York Times*. Whether or not this was deliberate, it must have sent the clearest message to London that the United States was now supporting Hussein. That support denied Britain another excuse to take unilateral action in Syria.[18]

* * *

'Our efforts should be directed toward separating the Saudi Arabians from the Egyptians and . . . in making the former see that their best interests lie with us, not with the Egyptians and the Russians,' Eisenhower had written that March. Courting no further publicity, the Roosevelts flew from Amman on to meet King Saud in Riyadh and carry out this stage of Ike's plan.[19]

A taller, fleshier version of his father, Saud otherwise bore little resemblance to Ibn Saud. Cursed with poor eyesight, he hid his pale watery eyes behind dark glasses, a habit that contributed to what one British politician called an 'effete and generally rather sloblike appearance', which his lifestyle reinforced. 'A notorious consumer of Cointreau', he had dismissed his father's wise advice to live simply and traditionally like his people and built himself a concrete and steel palace that owed more to Las Vegas than to Mecca. A 'garishly-lit funfair' in the words of one British visitor, it was decorated with hundreds of multicoloured neon lights. Its centrepiece was a grand reception room that could accommodate 200 people sitting on gilt chairs, which was illuminated by four large light fittings styled as palm trees, made of green and golden glass. 'They are hideous', the same visitor remarked, 'but for some strange reason do not seem out of place.' It was in this kitsch setting, midway through July 1956, that the Roosevelts met Saud to warn him that the Egyptians, in league with his half-brother Faisal, were trying to destroy him.[20]

The Roosevelts' job was made easier by the fact that it had become impossible for Saud, however poor his sight, to ignore what was going on. In May 1955 his supporters had broken up a conspiracy to overthrow him plotted by officers who were mostly Egyptian-trained. Despite this, following a deal brokered by Faisal, the Egyptians had sent military advisers to train the Saudi army later in the year. The American ambassador felt sure that the Egyptian aim was 'to Egyptianise the army under the guise of the Egypto-Saudi Pact and having got the Army completely under their thumb, to throw Saud out whenever they want to'.[21]

The effects of growing Egyptian influence in Saudi Arabia were all too clear. When Nasser visited Jeddah earlier that year, he had been greeted by the locals with shouts of 'Nasser, you saviour of Islam', and 'There is no God but Allah and Nasser is beloved by God.' This enthusiasm unsettled Saud, who feared that he had 'become a follower of Nasser, as far as Arab politics were concerned, when he was once a leader'. And then in June, during a visit to Aramco's headquarters at Dhahran, the king was confronted by a demonstration by Saudi workers, who the CIA believed were being encouraged by Egyptian propaganda. Affronted, Saud decreed days later that anyone inciting or organising strikes at the company would face two years in prison.[22]

Whatever the Roosevelts did say to him, it worked. Saud resisted Nasser's pressure to recognise communist China, as Egypt had already done that May. Within weeks he would expel the Egyptian military mission from his country. And he stopped trying to undermine the Hashemite monarchies of Iraq and Jordan soon afterwards, having realised that such activity was counterproductive. 'If one [king] goes, the second will go, and after him how long will I last?' he asked rhetorically, in 1957.[23]

* * *

By the time that the Roosevelts returned to Washington, the final element of the plan to isolate Nasser was about to fall into place. Dulles and Lloyd had regretted the offer they had made the previous Christmas to help finance the construction of a new Aswan dam from the outset. Not only was it domestically unpopular but it had also led the Egyptians to ask Moscow for most of the rest of the money, making it highly likely that the Russians would be awarded the contract to construct the dam – the very outcome the Anglo-American offer had been intended to forestall in the first place. And yet, despite this, the British, in particular, were reluctant to withdraw the offer, fearing that to do so might court reprisals.[24]

By mid-July it was clear that the matter was about to come to a head, whether the British liked it or not. On 16 July came the unwelcome news from the United States that, in four days' time, the Senate Appropriations Committee intended to pass an amendment to the following year's Foreign Aid bill that would effectively give it the ability to veto the American part of the Aswan loan. On the seventeenth, the Republican leader in the Senate went to see Dulles, warning him that he would 'proceed at his peril' if the administration pressed ahead with the offer. Dulles, who had no desire to cede control of foreign policy to the Senate, ad-libbed. 'We have just about made up our minds to tell the Egyptians we will not do it.'[25]

Dulles saw another advantage in suddenly dropping the loan: to do so would checkmate the Russians. Either they would have to follow suit, undoing their efforts to build their influence in Egypt, or they would have to pick up the entire tab, a move the United States could then exploit with propaganda in the Eastern Bloc. Over the telephone Dulles tried out the line he was thinking of on his younger brother: 'You don't get bread because you are being squeezed to build a dam.' On the morning of the nineteenth, having put this argument to Eisenhower and gained the president's approval, he summoned the British ambassador to tell him the decision. When the ambassador, seemingly failing to appreciate that he had been informed of a fait accompli, replied that his government 'would prefer to play it very much longer and not give a definite refusal', Dulles replied that he would have liked to as well, but 'Congressional circumstances' prevented it. Just after four o'clock that afternoon the secretary of state called in the Egyptian ambassador to tell him the bad news. 'I wish he hadn't done it quite so abruptly,' Eden reputedly remarked when he heard what had happened.[26]

The Egyptian diplomat 'had handled himself surprisingly well', Dulles told his brother afterwards. So too did Nasser. In Cairo on 21 July, the day after the British government followed suit and said that it would not help fund the project, the *Sunday Times* correspondent rang up the Egyptian prime minister to find out whether a rumour that he was very upset was true. It was 'terrible news', the reporter suggested.[27]

'Not terrible,' replied Nasser, who said he had foreseen it, and chuckled as he spoke. 'Things are never as bad as they seem.' He gave away no hint of what he would do next.

A SORT OF JENKINS' EAR

For all his bravado over the telephone, Nasser knew that the loss of the Anglo-American loan was a disaster. His promises to the Egyptian people hinged on Aswan – whether it was for the electricity and irrigation that the new dam would provide, or the vast tract of land that could be reclaimed and farmed once the Nile had been tamed. Now the project lay in ruins: not only had the Americans and the British pulled their funding, so too had the Russians, who dodged the trap that Dulles had tried to set for them. And the reason that the American secretary of state gave publicly for his change of mind – that Egypt would struggle to repay the loan – was a humiliating reminder of Egypt's third world status. Nasser needed to create a distraction, fast. It was a measure of how desperate he was that he decided to nationalise the Suez Canal Company, even though he believed that move was highly likely to provoke military retaliation.

The Suez Canal Company had been set up in 1858 to build and then manage the canal on a concession that would have expired in 1968, had Nasser not intervened. Despite its directors' tendency to play up the complexity of its operations, it was a utility, levying a fee on every passage, in exchange for providing each ship with a pilot to guide it. Although registered in Egypt, it was foreign-owned. In 1875, the bourgeois French who had initially bought shares were joined by the British government, which had relieved the cash-strapped Egyptian ruler, Ismail Pasha, of his stake. That investment reflected British recognition that the canal had become 'a link in our chain of Imperial defence' and 'our backdoor to the East', as Eden himself put it in a speech in 1929. 'None of us should be content', he continued, 'to leave the protection of a vital artery, the jugular vein of the British Empire, to the good will of the people of Egypt.'[1]

The Egyptian press had mooted the idea of nationalising the canal after Mosaddeq's takeover of the Anglo-Iranian Oil Company in 1951, but Britain's ongoing presence on the canal deterred successive Egyptian governments from pursuing it. By mid-June 1956 the company, though only a fraction of the size of Anglo-Iranian, was vulnerable, however. Days after the last British soldiers departed Egypt on 13 June, it reported record income of $97 million.[2]

Rounded up, that was $100 million – the figure that Nasser then flourished when, in a speech in Alexandria on 26 July 1956, he announced that he would pay for the dam with the profits from the canal, which he was nationalising. 'Today, in the name of the people, I am taking over the company,' he announced. 'Tonight our Egyptian company will be run by Egyptians. Egyptians!' He then promised to compensate the company's shareholders at the previous day's closing price and claimed that the $100 million a year that would accrue to Egypt meant that the country now needed no foreign financial help at all.[3]

The reality was rather different. What Nasser did not mention in his speech was that $100 million represented the Company's gross profit. Whittled down by ground rent, significant expenses and a contribution towards future improvements, the net figure, the sum the company paid out to its shareholders, was just $30 million. That was all that Egypt would actually earn a year by taking over the canal.

So convincing was Nasser that afternoon, however, that very few people appreciated the discrepancy immediately. 'However one may condemn such action on the part of a Government,' a British correspondent in Egypt commented, 'it is a very bold and imaginative move which is bound to increase his popularity and status among the Arab nations still higher.' Half right, the journalist predicted that his country would do nothing about it, and Nasser 'will get away with it'.[4]

* * *

In London Anthony Eden only heard the news at the end of a dinner he had thrown in Number 10 for Iraq's young king Feisal II, his uncle

Abdul Ilah and Prime Minister Nuri Said, at the end of a state visit by the king. 'Hit him,' Nuri advised Eden. 'Hit him hard and hit him now.' Otherwise, he continued, it would be too late. 'If he is left alone, he will finish all of us.'[5]

By now Eden's debilitating illness had returned and the prime minister was riding a pharmaceutical rollercoaster of uppers and downers prescribed to fight his pain and the side effects of one another, effects that include insomnia, anxiety, overconfidence and paranoia. At this distance, exactly how they affected his judgement is impossible to say, but it seems fair to assume that they would have done nothing to allay his conviction that Nasser was trying to destroy him. Eden also knew that the closure of the canal would be catastrophic for the British economy, because two-thirds of Britain's oil came through it.[6]

As fear and fact collided in Eden's imagination, he jumped to the conclusion that he had to deal with Nasser before Nasser strangled Britain. Ivone Kirkpatrick, the fiery permanent secretary at the Foreign Office, rationalised the prime minister's instinct for the benefit of the British ambassador to Washington. 'If we sit back whilst Nasser consolidates his position and gradually acquires control of the oil-bearing countries, he can and is, according to our information, resolved to wreck us,' he wrote. If Nasser were able to deny Britain sterling-priced Middle East oil for 'a year or two', Britain would exhaust its gold reserves buying oil in dollars. Once the gold was gone, there was no prospect of the country's sterling creditors ever being able to turn their credit into dollars. The sterling area would collapse, and with it Britain's purchasing power abroad and her ability to pay for her defence. 'And a country which cannot provide for its defence', Kirkpatrick ended, 'is finished.'[7]

Eden brought the banquet to a close and summoned the chiefs of staff, the French ambassador and the American chargé d'affaires to Downing Street. There they were joined by the other four cabinet ministers who had been at the dinner, for a meeting that went on deep into the night. Given that one of Eden's advisers had once observed that wine at lunchtime made the prime minister 'too elated', these were less than perfect circumstances for a clear-headed assessment of why Nasser had done what he had, and how best, therefore, to react. The American chargé alluded to the post-prandial atmosphere in the report that he sent home at five o'clock in the morning on the 27th. The British took 'an extremely grave view of the situation, and very strong feelings were expressed, especially by Eden, to the effect that Nasser must not be allowed to get away with it'.[8]

In that respect, the chiefs of staff brought unwelcome news. Since the departure of the last British troops from Suez six weeks earlier the nearest forces were now on Cyprus. But they were equipped for fighting the long-running insurgency on the island, not an amphibious operation – a fact that Nasser had carefully established using his own spies before announcing his takeover of the canal. Although the First Sea Lord, Mountbatten, dangled the idea of a landing by Royal Marine Commandos to seize Port Said, he admitted that it would be difficult to sustain them there. A full-scale military operation would take at least six weeks to organise. It would therefore not be possible to follow Nuri's rather prescient advice.

When the cabinet met at eleven o'clock that morning Eden made it clear that it might take military action to dislodge Nasser, and they should prepare on the assumption that it would. In that event, he told his colleagues, he believed that 'as on previous occasions the United States would follow our lead if we took it'. The objective of the military plan, he declared, should be the 'elimination of Nasser'.[9]

The military plan, Operation Musketeer, would ultimately go through three iterations, and, as is so often the way, ended up roughly where it started. After a bombing campaign had given Anglo-French forces air superiority, there would be a second phase, of intense propaganda activity, and finally a landing at Port Said, from where an Anglo-French force could advance southwards to take control of the canal.

After the meeting Eden wrote to Eisenhower to tell him that they could 'not afford to allow Nasser to seize control of the Canal in this way' and that he was prepared to use force if necessary to stop British influence throughout the Middle East from being 'irretrievably undermined'. To convince Ike to take action, he said that the immediate threat was to the oil supplies of Western Europe, in which case Britain and other countries might need eastern hemisphere oil. The unsaid implication was that such a demand would lead to unpopular fuel shortages in the United States in the run-up to the presidential election on 6 November, just as there had been on the East Coast in 1943.[10]

Eden asked Eisenhower to send Dulles for urgent talks in London. But

Dulles was in South America and the president, influenced by a meeting with Allen Dulles and the under-secretary of state Herbert Hoover, who regarded Nasser's action as desperate rather than malevolent, in the first instance sent Robert Murphy, a diplomat who had worked closely with Macmillan in North Africa during the war.

Murphy arrived in London on 29 July for talks with Lloyd and the French foreign minister Christian Pineau to find that both men were arguing that preparations for war should start immediately because it might be necessary to take action soon. That encounter was unsettling, but it was conversations with Macmillan and Eden on the 30th that really rattled the US envoy. If the British people had to go down fighting, Macmillan had told him, they would 'rather do so on this issue than perhaps become another Netherlands'. Murphy cabled Dulles at two o'clock the following morning to report his conversations. Both men had told him that they were determined to remove Nasser and that a British expeditionary force would be ready for this purpose in six weeks. 'If we were with them from beginning chances of World War III would be far less than if we delayed.'[11]

Eisenhower was annoyed, rather than frightened by Macmillan's histrionics. Fortified by a CIA estimate that Nasser was unlikely to disrupt the canal's operations in the short run, whereas a British invasion certainly would, he dashed off a letter to the prime minister for Dulles to deliver by hand. In it he warned his British counterpart of the 'unwisdom even of contemplating the use of military force at this moment', and insisted that a conference of the most affected nations took place first.[12]

Dulles took Ike's letter with him to London but promptly undermined its uncompromising message. The president had dictated it in a hurry, he told Eden and Lloyd on 1 August, and he, Dulles, had not had time to polish it. Since the British view was that Dulles, and not Ike, was in charge of US foreign policy, Eden and Lloyd discounted the letter and treated Dulles' remarks as the American position.

And yet, as always, determining Dulles' view was no easy task. While the verbose secretary of state agreed that Nasser should not 'get away with it' and said that a way had to be found to make the Egyptian leader 'disgorge' what he had just seized, he also repeated the president's warning. Military action 'without at least the moral support of the United States' would be 'a great disaster', he said. Moreover the British risked becoming mired in a guerrilla war that Russia would send volunteers to exacerbate. It was as if Dulles was saying no to military action, while simultaneously nodding his head.[13]

Just as Eden had read his own desire into Dulles' use of the word 'ditch' a few months earlier, he and Lloyd now both inferred from the secretary of state's repeated and deliberate use of the word 'disgorge' that Dulles was open to coercion and Lloyd quoted it when he briefed the cabinet that evening. Dulles wished 'to help and support', he told his colleagues. 'We have got to make Nasser "disgorge".' Precisely what Dulles meant by the word is unclear. What is certain is that he wanted to delay.[14]

It was, however, on the basis of his interpretation of the meaning of 'disgorge' that Eden agreed to the secretary's proposal, made over lunch on 1 August, that there should be a conference of interested states, providing it took place quickly and did not signal acquiescence to what Nasser had done. But he was determined not to be caught out in the way he had been after Glubb's dismissal and wanted to announce the measure when the House of Commons debated the crisis the next day.

Dulles would not let Eden do this, however. He guessed that, if the prime minister did announce the conference in parliament, and then faced questions about what he would do if it failed, he would probably say that Britain would resort to force. And so he played for time. While Eden wrote his speech the following morning, Dulles strung out the concurrent discussion with Lloyd and Pineau so that nothing could be finalised before the prime minister went into the chamber that afternoon. 'Trouble about Foster, he is not straight,' Eden grumbled, when he realised what was going on.[15]

Only once Eden had finished speaking did Dulles iron out his differences with Lloyd and Pineau so that the communiqué, announcing that the conference would open in London on the sixteenth, could go out that evening. Dulles left for Washington, satisfied with what he had achieved. 'I think we have introduced a valuable stopgap into a dangerous situation and while the danger is still there we have perhaps made it more remote and more manageable,' he wrote to Eisenhower on his way to catch the plane.[16]

Compared to March, the verdict of the following day's papers on Eden's speech was positive. They reported how Eden had entered the chamber to cheers, before going on to dissect Nasser's arithmetic and contrast the reassuring statements about the company's position that Nasser had made with his subsequent action. 'These undertakings are now torn up,' the prime minister had told the House. 'One can have no confidence – no confidence – in the word of a man who does that.' Having cast doubts on Nasser's honesty and his ability to run the canal in the future if all of its revenues were needed to pay for the construction of the Aswan dam, he argued that only an international authority could be trusted with the waterway. 'It is upon this we must insist. It is for this that we are working in negotiation at this moment with other Powers deeply concerned,' he concluded. 'Nothing less than this can be acceptable to us.'[17]

There was a weakness to Eden's argument however and it was this: Nasser had so far done nothing unlawful. Since his 26 July speech Nasser had been careful to allow the canal's operations to continue uninterrupted. Calculating that the more time that passed, the harder it would be for Britain and France to take military action, he let ships of all flags pass through the waterway unhindered, even though many were refusing to pay the Egyptian government any money. And so, whereas the newspapers reported that Mr Butlin had banned any Egyptians from taking part in his annual cross-Channel swim, and that a former Chindit 'armed . . . with a piece of string' had pulled the live radio mast off the roof of Egypt's London embassy, opinion polls showed that a majority of British people opposed military action against Nasser, even if he refused to accept foreign oversight of the canal. Within days the opposition Labour party, whose leader Gaitskell had gone further than Eden in the debate by describing Nasser's behaviour as reminiscent of Hitler's and Mussolini's, performed a screeching U-turn in order to align itself with the public mood, leaving the prime minister isolated.[18]

'We need a popular "casus belli" – a sort of Jenkins' Ear', wrote Macmillan on 9 August. Despite the fact that Nasser claimed he had found the Company's gold reserves, Eden hoped that financial pressures would soon create one. While Nasser's cautious policy was wise, it also meant that his revenues were about a third of what they should have been, and Eden reckoned that was unsustainable. Either Nasser continued to do nothing, and exposed himself to the taunts of the British radio propaganda that his new asset was worthless, or he could refuse passage to non-paying ships, which would give a pretext for action. The grounds for British optimism surely grew when Abdel Hakim Amer, the chief of Egypt's army, told the British journalist and MI6 agent, John Slade-Baker, on the 22nd, 'Don't worry. You will win!'[19]

While Eden waited for Nasser to feel the pinch, Dulles pinned his hopes on the diplomatic process, which, just as he intended, trudged on through August and September. The London conference opened on 16 August and finished a week later. 'Oh these delays,' groaned Eden after finding out that a delegation of its representatives bearing a proposal for international control of the canal would not start for Cairo before the 31st. 'Every day's postponement is to Nasser's gain and our loss.'[20]

It was not until the end of the first week of September, after Nasser had rejected the proposal, that it was clear that the conference had failed. No matter, for Eisenhower brightly announced that he was determined 'not to give up' the search for a peaceful solution, 'even if we run into other obstacles', and by that time Dulles had come up with another time-wasting scheme to defer a British threat to put a resolution condemning Egypt to the Security Council. This was a temporary association of canal users, which would supply pilots and take transit fees for the duration of the dispute. It was dubbed SCUA after it was pointed out that the original acronym, CASCU, sounded too like the Portuguese word for testicle and the French for 'a pain in the arse'.[21]

'A pain in the arse' was certainly how Eden hoped Nasser would see it. For the British prime minister, the sole attraction of Dulles' latest proposal was that it might finally bring matters to a head. By now he was deeply frustrated with Washington. The Americans took the view that British military action against Nasser was likely to cause uproar throughout the Arab world, and he replied hotly to Eisenhower's suggestion that British sabre-rattling was only strengthening Nasser's domestic position, with a letter in which he likened Nasser's behaviour to Hitler's. It concluded: 'I can assure you that we are conscious of the burdens and perils attending military intervention. But if our assessment is correct and if the only alternative is to allow Nasser's plans quietly to develop until this country and all Western Europe are held to ransom by Egypt acting at Russia's behest it seems to us that our duty is plain. We have many times led Europe in the fight for freedom. It would be an ignoble end to our long history if we tamely accepted to perish by degrees.'[22]

The end of Eden's letter struck Ike as rather Churchillian in style, and Dulles feared that the British were preparing to expend blood, sweat and tears. While Ike told Eden that he was 'making Nasser a much more important figure than he is', Dulles reassured the British ambassador that the president had not ruled out the use of force. 'Between us', the ambassador reported to London, 'we could get Nasser down and the US administration were quite determined this should happen.' In response to British pressure – since parliament was due to reconvene on the twelfth – he also agreed to let Eden announce the formation of the canal users' association. This announcement would include the all-important detail that SCUA would collect transit fees, which Eden reckoned would tip Nasser over the edge. Despite Lloyd's misgivings, Eden decided to go with Dulles' plan. Macmillan was supportive, telling his colleagues in cabinet, 'This is a manoeuvre to put us in good posture to use force.'[23]

When Eden announced the canal users' association on 12 September, however, his Labour opponents saw straight through it. 'Deliberate provocation!' shouted one left-wing MP; his colleagues called on the prime minister to resign. Eden ploughed on and issued a threat. If the Egyptian government did not cooperate, or tried to interfere, with SCUA's activities, then the government and the others involved in the new scheme would be free to take steps 'either through the United Nations or by other means, for the assertion of their rights'. The government decided to put support for Eden's statement to a vote of confidence the following day.[24]

Eden's threat caused uproar on the Labour benches and consternation in Washington. There a spokesman for the State Department initially refused to say whether the US government would take part in the initiative and suggested that Dulles had not seen an advance copy of Eden's speech, when in fact he had.

After Dulles heard that there were rumours circulating in London that he was the author of the plan, he decided to hold a press conference the following morning in order to distance himself from Eden. Unsurprisingly, when he met the press he was asked what he would do if Egypt resisted the plan. First he said that the United States would reroute shipping round the Cape. Later he confirmed, 'We do not intend to shoot our way through.' In other words, SCUA had no teeth.[25]

Reports of Dulles' unhelpful comments reached London less than halfway through the eight-hour confidence debate in parliament, giving Gaitskell time to incorporate them into his closing speech that evening. Using Dulles' 'do not intend to shoot our way through' repeatedly, he invited Eden to use the same phrase when he wound up the debate. Eden ducked the challenge and, when pressed, would only say that he was 'in complete agreement with the United States Government about what to do' – an evasion that provoked shouts of 'Answer!' Such was the pressure on the prime minister that, in the closing moments of his speech he conceded that, if the Egyptians would not cooperate, and unless there was an emergency, then the government would take the matter to the Security Council, a pledge that drew roars of triumph from the Labour benches opposite, since it seemed to avert the possibility of war.[26]

Before the British government resorted to the UN, however, it had one more tactic up its sleeve. As the last European pilots left the canal, where they had been working under duress since the Egyptian takeover, the British planned to test their Egyptian replacements to breaking point by organising fifty ships to gather at the approaches to the canal and demand passage simultaneously. Operation Pile-Up, as the British optimistically called it, began on 14 September.

The Egyptian pilots proved perfectly able to manage the canal, however, and on 15 September Nasser announced that the British effort had failed. When he met the British journalist and spy John Slade-Baker two days later, he was in ebullient mood. Asked if he would stop a British ship passing through the canal under the auspices of SCUA, he replied that he would not but predicted that eventually there would be an accident that blocked the canal, which would be SCUA's fault. If the British then invaded, he went on, he was ready to fight a wide-ranging guerrilla war. Not only were resistance cells ready throughout the delta, he disclosed, but Egypt had also made plans across the region 'to destroy whatever can be destroyed and to do the maximum amount of damage to British interests in the quickest time possible'. Slade-Baker passed this information straight to the British ambassador in Cairo.[27]

By the second half of September, the British government was in disarray. Its attempts to goad Nasser into taking action had all failed, denying it the grounds to go to war. But the prospect of imminent conflict meant that it was haemorrhaging money from its reserves as foreign investors pulled their money out of Britain. Support within the cabinet, the parliamentary party and the country for military action was now fading, and Eden's repeated efforts to convince Eisenhower that Nasser now represented an existential threat seemed to have had no impact at all.

Towards the end of September Eden confided his fears to Churchill, who had avoided making any public pronouncements about Suez. 'I am not very happy at the way things are developing here,' he wrote to his predecessor. 'Foster assures me that the US is as determined to deal with Nasser as we are – but I fear he has a mental caveat about November 6th.'

Eden desperately needed a breakthrough – one that would simultaneously provide him with a casus belli and ensure American acquiescence. Three weeks before polling day in the United States, he got it.

THE SUEZ MISCALCULATION

Sunday 14 October 1956 was 'a glorious autumn day, radiant with sunshine and crisp as a biscuit', the Foreign Office minister, Anthony Nutting, later remembered. He had come to the prime minister's country residence, Chequers, in the countryside northwest of London, to bring Eden Selwyn Lloyd's overnight report from the United Nations. The news was mixed. Although the Security Council had unanimously approved the first part of a two-part Anglo-French resolution concerning the future operation of the canal, the Russians had then spiked SCUA by vetoing the second part, which would have given the users' association the right to collect the fees owed by its members and forced the Egyptians to cooperate with it. The question now was what to do next.[1]

Nutting was not the only visitor to call on Eden that day. Albert Gazier, caretaker at the Quai d'Orsay while Pineau was in New York, and Maurice Challe, of the French general staff, had also come to Chequers. Itching to attack Nasser, the French were increasingly disgruntled by Eden's insistence that, for the sake of his own party's unity, they must exhaust all the diplomatic options first. Now they reckoned that they had come up with a way to force the British to take action – a method that relied on Britain's knowledge of France's conspiratorial relationship with Israel, which dated back to the time, a decade earlier, when the French had supplied arms and money to the Irgun and the Stern Gang, in order to speed up the end of Britain's mandate in Palestine.[2]

Gazier opened the conversation by saying that they had come to pass on Israeli concerns about the tensions on the frontier with Jordan, which he rightly guessed Eden would share. Since Glubb's exit the Jordanian Army's new chief of staff, Ali Abu Nuwar, had allowed the Egyptians to use his country as a base for fedayeen attacks. The killing of seven Israeli soldiers in Jerusalem in September had triggered an escalating tit-for-tat that led Hussein to request military assistance from the Iraqis, and then also from the British after a massive Israeli attack on 10 October left over 100 people dead. When Eden readily agreed to intercede with the Iraqis to try to stop them deploying troops to Jordan, giving grounds for the Israelis to aggravate the situation further, the Frenchman abruptly changed the subject. What if Israel attacked Egypt, he asked.

Britain was obliged under the Tripartite Agreement to defend the current borders, said Eden, automatically – an answer that left Gazier incredulous. Surely Eden would not step in to protect Nasser, he retorted. Eden admitted that was unlikely, then turned to Nutting. 'Didn't your agreement say something about our not being obliged to send troops if Egypt was attacked by Israel?' he asked, since it was Nutting who had signed the 1954 evacuation agreement with Nasser. Nutting said it did, but added that the deal did not override the commitment Britain had made in the Tripartite Declaration. Eden looked momentarily dismayed, before Gazier offered an extraordinary piece of information: Nasser had recently said that the Tripartite Agreement did not apply to Egypt. 'So that lets us off the hook,' exclaimed Eden. 'We have no obligation, it seems, to stop the Israelis attacking the Egyptians.'[3]

The French were not simply planning to stand back. Gazier asked Eden's private secretary to stop taking notes and turned to Challe, who outlined the plan that they were thinking of. They would encourage the Israelis to attack Egypt, at which point Britain and France would order both sides to draw back from the canal, and send in troops 'to separate the combatants' and take charge of the waterway. Eden said he would think about it and that he would give the French a reply by Tuesday. The two Frenchmen were amazed that he had not had the same idea already.[4]

In fact, the British had considered using the Israelis to deal with the Egyptians but until now they had discounted the idea. A well-watered Churchill had raised the possibility of getting Israel to do Britain's dirty work in Egypt after dinner at the British embassy in Paris at the end of 1951. But such a move went against Eden's instincts. When Macmillan again made the case for allying with Israel to remove Nasser in August 1956, on the grounds that the Israelis would seek to profit from the situation whatever Britain did, Eden refused to circulate his paper and the Foreign Office warned against such a scheme. Since the Egyptians were sure to portray Anglo-French action as 'an imperialist plot hatched with Israel', it argued, the government should do everything it could 'to keep Israel right out of the dispute'. On each occasion the chief counter-argument had been the damage that such an alliance would do to Britain's allies in the Arab world, especially Nuri Said in Iraq. But Nuri himself, during his July visit to London, suggested encouraging the Israelis to attack Egypt, and between then and the beginning of October British reservations melted away.[5]

During that time, the stakes had grown so dramatically that a plan like Maurice Challe's no longer seemed unthinkable. Three months' diplomatic effort had just failed and yet the Americans were as opposed to military action as ever. British efforts to prod Nasser to do something that would give grounds for war had come to naught. And the latest intelligence suggested that the Egyptian leader was trying to overthrow the kings of Libya and Iraq, two countries where Britain had military bases, and that he was stockpiling Soviet weaponry in Syria.

Most alarmingly, Jordan now appeared to be on the brink. Elections would take place there in a week's time. To Eden it seemed inevitable that the nationalists would triumph and that the country would become an Egyptian satellite. Certainly Nasser had played his hand there brilliantly so far. By provoking incidents along the Israeli frontier he had pitted his greatest enemy and his main Arab rival against one another, as well as distracting the British, who, by virtue of the Anglo-Jordanian treaty, faced having to come to the aid of a country they could no longer really count on as an ally.

After being told by his chiefs of staff that they could fight Nasser or the Israelis, but not both simultaneously, Eden toyed with denouncing the Jordanian treaty unilaterally, but realised that to do so would be a gift to Egyptian propagandists looking to undermine confidence in Britain. Redirecting Israel at Nasser, on the other hand, as the French envisaged, would spring him from the trap: once Israel was fighting Egypt, the danger that Britain would have to fight a war in Jordan disappeared and Eden could focus all his energies on eliminating Nasser.[6]

Finally, the French plan elegantly resolved the problem that Eden had been grappling with for months – the question of how the United States would react to British military action – by bypassing it altogether. If the Israelis, rather than the British, attacked Nasser in the final moments of the American presidential election campaign, would Eisenhower dare object, given the power of the Jewish lobby, which Dulles so frequently mentioned? Macmillan, who had just visited Washington, thought not. While he was there, Dulles had recalled a favour he had done the British before their own election a year earlier, and asked if they 'could not do something in return and hold things off until after November 6th?'[7]

'I know Ike,' pronounced Macmillan after his return to London. 'Ike will lie doggo.'[8]

* * *

The French plan offered a pretext for intervention in a manner that the Americans would have difficulty opposing. Out of a mixture of desperation and opportunism, Eden seized it with both hands. Having bidden farewell to the French, he telephoned Lloyd in New York and told him to come home immediately.

Flying overnight, Lloyd arrived back on the morning of 16 October to find Eden, Nutting and several others midway through a discussion of the French proposal. Lloyd did not like it, but then, as one official put it, he was 'very coy about agreeing to anything'. Over lunch Eden battered him into submission. That afternoon the two men flew to Paris where they met Pineau, and the French prime minister, Guy Mollet. If Israel attacked Egypt, would the British intervene, asked Mollet. Eden said they would.[9]

Back in London, Lloyd and Eden briefed the cabinet on 18 October. After they had explained how they hoped to resuscitate talks with the Egyptians, Lloyd turned to the unstable situation in Jordan. The latest news was that the Jordanians, under Egyptian pressure, had now withdrawn their invitation to the Iraqis to send troops. Eden set out the dilemma. Faced with the possibility that 'Jordan may go over to Egypt this weekend', they could either do nothing, or they could advise Iraq to send in troops regardless, even though that created the grave risk of an Israeli attack. 'This is the main reason why we went to Paris,' Eden claimed. 'We tried to secure in Paris that if Israel moves, she will not move against Jordan but against Egypt.' If Israel did so, he continued, 'We have made it plain to Israel through the French that ... we should not feel obligated to Egypt.'[10]

As expected, the nationalists won the Jordanian elections on 21 October. The following day Lloyd returned to Paris for further discussions with the French and the Israelis without Eden, who now wanted to keep his hands clean. Lloyd, having told his colleagues in the Foreign Office that he was off sick with a cold, reached a villa in the well-to-do suburb of Sèvres at four o'clock that afternoon. There he found Pineau, as well as the hawkish Israeli prime minister, David Ben Gurion, and General Moshe Dayan, who had lost an eye fighting with the British against the French in 1941. They had the look of people who had already been talking for some time.

* * *

Lloyd had never expected to be foreign secretary. 'I think there must be some mistake,' he reputedly told Churchill when the great man first made him a minister, at the Foreign Office, in 1951. 'I do not speak any foreign language. Except in war, I have never visited any foreign country. I do not like foreigners,' he continued.[11]

'Young man,' Churchill had said, 'these all seem to me to be positive advantages.'

The Sèvres meeting did not go well. Ben Gurion thought Lloyd was aloof; Lloyd thought Ben Gurion was arrogant. They quickly disagreed. Ben Gurion wanted all three nations to attack simultaneously, while Lloyd, to keep up the charade that Britain and France were only breaking up the fight, insisted that the two European powers should only come in two days later, by which time Ben Gurion feared that Tel Aviv would have been reduced to rubble. Since only the RAF had the heavy bombers to put Egypt's runways out of action, but early use of these would admit collusion, the meeting ended in deadlock.

Lloyd returned to London that night, telling Nutting when he arrived in the Foreign Office the next morning that it did not look as if the French plan would come off. As Eden obliquely reported to Cabinet the same morning, it 'now seems that Israel won't attack'. He raised the possibility that the French might 'act alone – or even with Israel' and ask for access to British bases on Cyprus.[12]

Eden and Lloyd underestimated the ingenuity of the French. At the same time as they were discussing the matter in London, in Sèvres Pineau offered to base French fighters in Israel to guard the Israeli coast. Ben Gurion, thus reassured, agreed to launch an attack on a scale that would give London and Paris grounds to intervene thirty-six hours later. Pineau flew to London that evening. After dinner with Lloyd and talks with Eden, the British agreed to send an envoy back to Sèvres to have another go.

That job fell to the Joint Intelligence Committee chairman Patrick Dean, who was brought into the conspiracy by Eden very early the next morning and instructed to go to Sèvres. There he was to tell the others that the British would only participate if the Israelis invaded Egypt and there was a threat to the canal. By the time that Dean arrived at the villa, Pineau had returned from London to report that Eden had been much warmer than Lloyd, and that the prime minister was signed up to the outline plan. Ben Gurion had also been squared by the French prime minister's offer of air defence. Still deeply suspicious of the British, he suggested – before Dean arrived – that Pineau's plan be typed up so that representatives of all three nations could sign it.

When, on his arrival, Dean was confronted with the 'Sèvres Protocol', which had been cooked up by French and Israeli officials working in the villa's kitchen, he felt he had no choice but to sign. After he arrived back in London that night and told Eden what he had done, the prime minister was horrified and sent him back to Paris the next day to try to retrieve the French and Israeli copies. It proved a fruitless errand. After being locked in a room at the Quai d'Orsay for several hours, he left empty-handed.

On 25 October, while Dean was trying to recover the errant copies of the Protocol in Paris, Eden briefed the cabinet. 'Bright-eyed and full of life', according to one man in the room, he explained that it 'now appeared' that the Israelis were getting ready to attack Egypt. He then asked his colleagues to consider whether Anglo-French intervention would be necessary if war broke out in the area. Given that the French were strongly in favour of intervention and might take action alone, or 'in conjunction with Israel' if Britain did not intervene, he said that his own preference would be for Britain and France to issue an ultimatum to both sides calling on each to withdraw 10 miles from the canal. 'Israel might well comply with such a demand,' he suggested. 'If Egypt also complied, Colonel Nasser's prestige would be fatally undermined. If she failed to comply, there would be ample justification for Anglo-French military action against Egypt in order to safeguard the Canal.'[13]

'We must face the risk that we should be accused of collusion with Israel,' Eden said. 'But this charge was liable to be brought against us in any event.'

'Doubts were expressed,' the minutes of that meeting state, though they do not say by whom. The doubters were concerned about the offence to the Americans that British action would cause, that the 10-mile demand implicitly favoured the Israelis, that Britain would be breaking the Tripartite Declaration and that Anglo-French police action lacked a United Nations mandate. Despite this, the cabinet still approved the plan.[14]

At about this time, unnamed British officials sidled up to Ali Maher, the former Egyptian prime minister, who was then in Beirut. Would he be prepared to form a government, they asked, if Nasser's suddenly collapsed? Yes he would, he said.[15]

* * *

Straight after the Jordanian elections King Hussein had said that he was determined to fight Israel, and on 24 October came the news that Egypt, Jordan and Syria had agreed to a military alliance by which their forces would come under Egyptian command. By the 26th Dulles knew that the Israelis were mobilising, though to what end was far from clear. Since the British embassy had gone oddly quiet, he passed the news on to Winthrop Aldrich, the ambassador in London, asking his envoy if he could find any evidence to support his suspicion that the French, and possibly the British, were complicit in whatever the Israelis were up to.

Aldrich told Dulles he was seeing Lloyd for dinner on the evening of the 28th and would be able to probe for information then. In the meantime, the CIA's Watch Committee concluded that the scale of Israeli preparations, and Britain's known commitment to defend Jordan, meant that the most likely target of an Israeli attack, which it expected 'in the very near future', was in fact Egypt. Later the same day it issued a further report that noted that eighteen French air transport aircraft had just arrived on Cyprus, meaning that the British and French together could now lift as many as 3,000 men.[16]

Facing Aldrich's questions over dinner, Lloyd took refuge in semantics. He too was concerned about the Israeli mobilisation, he said, and although British reports also indicated that the Israelis were moving troops south rather than east, he was 'inclined to believe' that Jordan was the real target, which of course justified Britain's own despatch of ships from Malta the previous morning. He was 'unwilling to believe' that the Israelis would attack Egypt and said that his conversations with the French gave him 'no reason to believe' that the French were encouraging the Israelis to do so. Unwisely Aldrich believed him.[17]

The following lunchtime the American ambassador reported to Washington that, although Lloyd had told him 'he would like to see something happen to Nasser, his concern over the consequences of Israeli initiative carried sufficient conviction for me to conclude that any UK complicity in such a move is unlikely. Similarly, I thought his doubts that the French would find it in their interests to stimulate Israeli ventures at this time are genuine.' Two hours after Aldrich sent this message, Israeli paratroopers dropped near the Mitla Pass, 45 miles east of the town of Suez, at the southern entrance to the canal. The war had begun.[18]

* * *

Unlike Aldrich, Dulles saw through Lloyd's evasive comments. Soon after the Israeli parachute drop had taken place, but before news of the invasion had reached the outside world, he sent another cable, this time to his ambassador in Paris. The previous evening he had finally managed to talk to the top French and British diplomats in Washington. 'Their ignorance' of the movement of French warships to the eastern Mediterranean, he told Eisenhower over the phone, was 'almost a sign of guilty conscience'.[19]

'I just cannot believe Britain would be dragged into this,' Eisenhower responded, when Dulles gave him the numbers proving the Anglo-French build-up on Cyprus.[20]

By the time the Israelis invaded, Dulles had decided that the British were going to be involved, however. 'Bits of evidence are accumulating', he told the US ambassador to Paris, that the French, perhaps with British knowledge, were working closely with the Israelis to provoke a war with Egypt in which France and Britain would then intervene.[21]

Dulles went on to warn his man in Paris of what would happen next, in much clearer terms than he had ever used when talking to the British. 'As you know, it is the profound conviction of the President and myself that if the French and the British allow themselves to be drawn into a general Arab war they will have started something they cannot finish', which would result in growing anti-western sentiment from which the Russians would then profit, and weaken the economies of both countries and the remainder of Western Europe. Given that they had started the war, it was 'unlikely' that the United States would come to their aid. Interestingly Dulles appreciated that the United States' two supposed allies might be banking on the calculation that 'Jewish influence here is such as to assure US sympathy with such operations as are outlined'. If so, he finished, that was 'a miscalculation'.

* * *

The next morning in London, the government's Joint Intelligence Committee informed the chiefs of staff that the United States would take 'a strictly neutral attitude towards the Operations'. But by ten o'clock it was already clear that its assessment could not be more wrong. When Eden's cabinet met that morning Lloyd reported that he had been already told by the American ambassador that the United States government would shortly be asking the Security Council to consider a resolution condemning Israel as an aggressor. Lloyd said that he had argued that such a move would be open to criticism, given that Israel was acting in self-defence, but Aldrich was unsurprisingly unmoved. When later that day he learned that Eden and Mollet had issued their ultimatum calling on both sides to pull back 10 miles from the canal, he told the Foreign Office that there would be 'hell to pay'.[22]

If the publicly available evidence, the intelligence and instinct had left Dulles fairly certain that the British and the French were colluding with the Israelis, the implicit bias of the Anglo-French ultimatum removed any residual doubt. Since Eden and Mollet issued it at a moment when the centre of the battle was still about 100 miles further *to the east*, they were effectively sanctioning an Israeli advance further into Egypt.

When Shuckburgh, who had left the Foreign Office several months earlier due to stress, heard the demand reported on the radio he was 'staggered'. Knowing that, at a stroke, it would destroy Britain's credibility in the Arab world – the very asset Eden had so long striven to maintain – he concluded, 'We think A.E. has gone off his head.' That was a judgement shared elsewhere. 'Nasser found the whole situation made no sense at all,' recalled one of his advisers. 'It was in fact, quite mad.'[23]

Eisenhower now wrote to Eden a schoolmasterly letter showing no hint of warmth. 'I should like to ask your help in clearing up my understanding as to exactly what is happening between us and our European allies – especially between us, the French and yourselves,' it began, ominously. The Americans, the president continued, knew that the French had provided far more equipment than they had let on, and that communication traffic between Paris and Tel Aviv had then leapt, suggesting that France and Israel were working together. When they had approached the British ambassador to the UN, Pierson Dixon, the previous evening, 'We were astonished to find that he was completely unsympathetic, stating frankly that his government would not agree to any action whatsoever to be taken against Israel.' Dixon had argued that the Tripartite Declaration, which committed Britain to defend the current borders, was completely outdated. Whether or not that was the case, Ike suggested, when such an agreement was renounced by one of its signatories, it was 'only fair that the other signatories should be notified'.[24]

Eisenhower's and Dulles' fury at the Anglo-French ultimatum drove them to force the issue in the Security Council. But their draft resolution, which called for a ceasefire and the Israelis' withdrawal, and urged all members to avoid the threat or use of force, was vetoed by France and Britain. The Yugoslav member of the Security Council pushed for a new resolution, calling an emergency session of the general assembly. This option had been established to anticipate exactly the blockage that had just occurred in the Security Council. Although Britain and France could vote against it, they could not veto this resolution. That meant that their conduct would now be subject to the scrutiny of the general assembly in two days' time.

* * *

'Britain at War', declared the *Daily Mail* of 1 November, the day on which the general assembly would meet. Overnight, and again that morning, British bombers attacked nine Egyptian airfields, though they aborted a raid on their main target, the West Cairo airbase, after discovering that it lay near the route that American citizens were using to escape towards Alexandria. When, however, Eden refused to say whether the country was at war in the House of Commons that morning, the violence of the reaction from the Labour benches was such that the Speaker had to suspend the sitting for half an hour to allow tempers to cool down.

The time difference meant that Egypt's ambassador to the United Nations was able to quote from Gaitskell's response to Eden in his own speech that evening in the general assembly debate in New York. After Dixon had attempted to defend the British government's position, Dulles spoke. The resolution which he went on to propose called for an immediate ceasefire, a halt to the movement of military forces and arms into the area, and the withdrawal of all forces behind the 1949 armistice lines. It was carried by sixty-four votes to five. Only Australia and New Zealand voted with Britain, France and Israel. Six other countries abstained. One of them was Canada, whose prime minister, Lester Pearson, had been his country's representative on the UN's special commission on Palestine in 1947. He suggested creating and sending in an emergency UN force to keep the peace.

News of the late-night vote in New York reached London by dawn on 2 November. In the House of Commons Gaitskell asked Eden if he would abide by the general assembly's resolution. Eden played for time by saying that he wanted to read it first and would answer the next day.

By now the Egyptians were retreating and the Israelis were close to the canal. British bombers had knocked out Cairo radio, enabling 'Voice of Britain' to squat on its frequency and bombard the Egyptians with bloodcurdling propaganda. In two cabinet meetings that afternoon Eden, in whose view the military situation was 'very satisfactory', argued that the British and French governments should use the speed of the Israeli advance to justify a landing as soon as possible, by troops who would then hand over to the United Nations force. To shouts of 'murderer' from the Labour benches, this was the policy he announced to the House of Commons the next day.[25]

Eden's insistence on quick action required the use of paratroops because the main Anglo-French invasion force was still en route by sea. This, however, created a quandary. The situation that Eden was now trying to exploit had only come about because the Egyptians had withdrawn to the canal to avoid being trapped on its east bank by the Israeli advance. This meant that in the Port Said area – the very spot where the paras would be landing – there were large numbers of Egyptian troops who, aerial reconnaissance showed, were ready for a fight. The British could drop in parachutists rapidly, knowing that this lightly armed force would meet fierce opposition, or they could bomb the Egyptians' new positions to make a landing easier, a move that would take time and make a mockery of Eden's claim on television that evening that: 'All my life I've been a man of peace.' Nevertheless, the defence minister, Antony Head, headed out to the British headquarters on Cyprus to see what could be done.[26]

Head returned to London on 4 November with news that gave the cabinet grounds to hope that British troops might land unopposed. The Egyptians seemed to be withdrawing from Port Said, he reported; he felt that the 'world will accept a fait accompli, if neatly done'. In back-channel messages to London the CIA were implying the same thing.

With an anti-war protest going on in the streets outside, that evening the Cabinet considered the options: to drop the paras straight away, to wait twenty-four hours to try to get UN endorsement for the operation, or to abandon it altogether. The minutes show that opinion was divided. Eden favoured action. Lloyd feared that the UN would impose oil sanctions if they went ahead. Salisbury, once hawkish, now thought that there was no chance that Egypt and Israel would accept their peacekeeping role and that therefore their job was done. News that the Israeli government had not, in fact, accepted the terms of the ceasefire helped simplify the decision. In the end Eden went round the table and found there was a majority for immediate action: the parachute drop would go ahead. Lord Home seems to have summed up the mood around the cabinet table. '[We] can get away with this, if it can be done without heavy casualties.'[27]

668 British paras went in just after seven in the morning, local time. One man was killed in the drop, another was wounded, and

twelve more were wounded in the fight to secure the airfield where they landed. From there they faced a 5km advance to reach Port Said. Although by now the main, seaborne, force was lying offshore, the Egyptians' resistance had been stiff enough to deter any last-minute change to the plan. The main landings would take place the following dawn. Meanwhile elite French troops had landed south of Port Said. Their task was to take the bridges on the causeway linking the port to the mainland, isolating the town. It was they who succeeded in forcing the Egyptian commander into asking for a ceasefire, by cutting the fresh water supply into the port.

The news of this development reached London during another parliamentary debate on the situation. Lloyd, at the despatch box, had been parrying a series of awkward questions since the revelation that the British had been dropping leaflets in the delta threatening bombing raids if the Egyptians resisted. Eden stood up to intervene, reporting that he had just received a Flash message from the front. 'Governor and Military Commander, Port Said now discussing surrender terms with Brigadier Butler. Cease-fire ordered,' he read, triggering roars of approval from the government benches. On his return to Downing Street, the prime minister summoned his chiefs of staff and hugged the air marshal. 'Oh my dear Chiefs, how grateful I am to you! You have been magnificent! It's all worked out perfectly.' But the sense of triumph was to be brief.[28]

Earlier that day, knowing that the parachute drop had gone ahead, Eden had written to Eisenhower justifying his actions, and what he still planned to do. It was an odd letter – at once confident, self-righteous, confessional and complacent, which invited the president, if not to 'approve ... at least understand the terrible decisions we have had to make'.[29]

'I know that Foster thought we could have played this longer,' Eden conceded, 'but I am convinced that, if we had allowed things to drift, everything would have gone from bad to worse. Nasser would have become a kind of Moslem Mussolini and our friends in Iraq, Jordan, Saudi Arabia and even Iran would gradually have been brought down. His efforts would have spread westwards, and Libya and North Africa would have been brought under his control.' Although Eden stated his willingness to hand over to an international force as soon as he could, the implication of 'would have' was obvious. He was determined to remove Nasser first.

Eisenhower's initial reaction to the letter was sanguine. Not only was Eden facing almost unanimous condemnation from the United Nations, but the Syrians had also sabotaged the IPC pipeline and Nasser had blocked the Suez Canal. It would only be a matter of time before the prime minister had to cave in when, because of his own actions, he was faced with the very oil shortage he had once feared that Nasser would engineer. But after the president had drafted a surprisingly warm response urging Eden to do no more than carry out the landings and looking forward to renewed cooperation once the current crisis had passed, a message arrived from the Soviet premier Nikolai Bulganin in Moscow. Seeking to shift attention from his own country's simultaneous and bloody suppression of the Hungarian uprising, he suggested that the two nuclear-armed superpowers should take action to restore peace in the Middle East. Soon afterwards came news that the Port Said ceasefire had broken down.

Eisenhower instantly rejected Bulganin's letter for what it was – a diversionary tactic that was also designed to drive a wedge between the United States and her estranged European allies. But the Russian had also written to Eden, making a none-too-subtle hint that Britain might face a Soviet ballistic missile attack, and Ike worried that, after Budapest, the Soviets were 'scared and furious, and there is nothing more dangerous than a dictatorship in this state of mind'. Fearing that the Russians might use the ongoing fighting at Port Said as a pretext to intervene, he decided not to send his letter to Eden.[30]

Bulganin's letter reached London at about two in the morning of 6 November, and at eight-thirty Eden rang up Dixon, the British ambassador to the UN. Dixon told him he had just been in an emergency session called by the Russians. He thought that Russia's aim was to 'get themselves into a position where they could say that they had tried the UN and having failed, now had their hands free for some independent action'. That must have sounded rather familiar to Eden. Although he did not think the Russians would attack Britain, he feared that the message might be 'cover for a military move' – most easily into Syria, in the worst case against the British force in Egypt.[31]

Far more significant, Dixon went on to warn that the Americans were drafting their own resolution calling for economic sanctions on Britain and France. From there the end came quickly. A few days earlier Lloyd had suggested that one way to counter oil sanctions, were they imposed, would be 'to occupy Kuwait and Qatar' – the two oil producers which were not members of the UN – but this madcap scheme was not followed up. In cabinet on the morning of 6 November Macmillan – who seemed to have turned overnight from tawny hawk to snow-white dove – ran through the financial position, which was deteriorating fast as currency traders sold off their sterling holdings. For reasons that are still mysterious he exaggerated the loss by a factor of three, claiming that £100 million had drained from the country's reserves in the first week of November when in fact the real number was nearer £30 million. But his colleagues were not to know that, and accepted his bleak message that, if the reserves continued to run down at that rate, the coffers would be empty soon after Christmas. The country's finances were not robust enough to withstand international isolation: as Macmillan later ruefully admitted, the Suez crisis had not changed Britain's parlous economic situation, but it had revealed it. That evening, Eden announced that Britain had ordered her forces to cease fire at midnight. Defence Minister Antony Head was among those disappointed. It was 'like going through all the preliminaries', the former brigadier said, 'without having an orgasm!'[32]

* * *

Ike won the 6 November election. When, days later, he received a message from Macmillan, asking for 'a fig leaf to cover our nakedness', he could afford to be magnanimous. The president had known Macmillan since their days together in North Africa in the war and rang up his ambassador to London. 'Could you get them informally and say of course we are interested and sympathetic and, as soon as things happen that we anticipate, we can furnish "a lot of fig leaves"?' Once Eden had left on an extended holiday, and Lloyd told the House of Commons on 3 December that British troops would be withdrawn 'without delay', that help was rapidly forthcoming. Britain was now allowed to draw on the IMF, and the US government waived the interest repayments it was entitled to on Britain's 1946 loan. American oil arrived to make up for the shortfall caused by the sabotage of the IPC's pipeline in Syria and the blockage of the Suez Canal.[33]

Macmillan, who would succeed Eden as prime minister, blamed everything on his predecessor, despite having driven him to disaster. He told Dulles that 'he, personally, was very unhappy with the way in which this matter was handled and the timing, but that Eden had taken this entirely to himself and he ... had had no real choice except to back Eden'. He was more honest to his colleagues in cabinet. 'I advocated firm, but quick, action against Egypt,' he said, as he argued that they had no choice but to accept the unpalatable demands that Ike was making of them. 'We have failed in that. What else can we do now?'[34]

FAILED COUPS

The Anglo-American plot to overthrow the Syrian government was another casualty of Suez; resuscitating it was to consume significant American energy over the following twelve months.

The British and Americans had planned to launch their coup on 25 October 1956 but, when they heard that the Syrian president Shukri Quwatly would visit Moscow at the end of the month, they first put back the date so that it would take place during his absence and then, after a further change of heart, postponed it again so that he would be back in Damascus, pushing it beyond the date of Israel's invasion of the Sinai. Although by then the formidable head of Syrian intelligence, Abdul Hamid Sarraj, also knew what was being planned, it was this delay that killed the coup attempt.

The plotter whom the CIA had thrown its weight behind, the former Syrian foreign minister Michael Ilyan, was livid when he heard of the Israeli invasion of Egypt. 'How could you have asked us to overthrow our government at the exact moment when Israel started a war with an Arab state?' he asked his American contact, the intelligence officer Bill Eveland, who was asking much the same question himself. Eveland's uncertainty about British motives for supporting the coup was shared at the top. When, the same day in Washington, Foster and Allen Dulles discussed whether the coup should go ahead, Allen Dulles told his brother that he was 'suspicious of our cousins and if they want a thing ... we should look at it hard'. Although both men felt that it would be 'good to have an anti-communist government in Syria', they agreed with their operatives on the ground that it would be 'a mistake to try to pull it off'.[1]

Although Eisenhower's administration resisted further British pressure to launch the coup during November, the situation in Syria concerned them. Following the failed coup the national-socialist Baathists had successfully demanded a purge of their right-wing opponents, strengthening its own grip upon the government. They were encouraged by the Syrian communists, whose influence seemed to be growing. American diplomats wondered whether Quwatly might have struck some sort of military deal while he was in Moscow, and during the Suez crisis the US president ordered high-altitude reconnaissance of Syria to see whether the Soviet Union was moving aircraft into the country. Although this showed nothing untoward, the British ordered their own aerial reconnaissance, and Lloyd told a NATO meeting in December that the Soviets appeared to be stockpiling tanks and artillery in Syria. Ike declared on 12 December that he had 'no intention of standing idly by to see the southern flank of NATO completely collapse through Communist penetration and success in the Mid East'.

In a speech to Congress less than a month later, on 5 January 1957, Eisenhower asked for the authority to divert $200 million from the Mutual Security Act budget to spend more freely on economic and military aid in the Middle East. More controversially, he also requested carte blanche to commit armed forces to defend any country facing 'overt armed aggression from any nation controlled by International Communism'. Even though this represented a significant expansion of the presidential powers, Congress approved both measures, and the 'Eisenhower Doctrine' became law on 9 March. A few weeks later the United States also joined the military committee of the Baghdad Pact. This set the scene for a further American attempt to overthrow the government in Syria.[2]

* * *

The man who most urgently needed money from Ike's $200 million pot was Syria's southern neighbour, King Hussein of Jordan. Soon after the Suez crisis had ended, his nationalist prime minister, Suleiman Nabulsi, had announced that he intended to abrogate the country's 1948 treaty with Britain and forgo the subsidy of £12 million that came with it. It was as if Nabulsi had just 'shot Santa Claus', the British ambassador joked. The new British prime minister Harold Macmillan, who had decided that his country's presence in Jordan was an expensive and ineffective liability, made no effort to stand in his way, letting Nasser rush in to exploit the gap.

Inviting Saud, King Hussein and the Syrian prime minister to Cairo, the Egyptian leader brokered a deal to fill the hole in Jordan's budget. On 19 January 1957 the four men signed the 'Arab Solidarity Agreement', which pledged Jordan $40 million a year for the next ten years – the sum the country stood to lose by abandoning the treaty – in a ratio that ensured that Egypt and Syria would pay Jordan more than Saud.[3]

Two days before the British ambassador began the talks that called time on the treaty, Hussein made a barely disguised appeal for American help. On 2 February the king warned Nabulsi in public about the dangers that communism posed to Arab nationalism, a lecture his prime minister correctly interpreted as a vote of no confidence. The British ambassador later wrote that by mid-March Nabulsi was thought to be in direct contact with the Soviet government, which, possibly by blackmail, was 'able to establish a considerable influence over him'.[4]

At the end of March the American ambassador warned his own government that he had 'no doubt' that Nabulsi was 'intent on destroying Jordan as presently constituted and throwing out the King in favor of a still undefined federation with Syria and Egypt'. His telegram remains partly redacted, but it implies that intelligence on a Syrian plot would soon be presented to Hussein, probably by Kim Roosevelt, who spent a significant period of time in Jordan during March. Whatever it was, the American ambassador expected the information to give the king the appetite to replace Nabulsi. 'Probabilities of sort of "coup de palais" in near future growing,' he added, a prediction that showed either uncanny foresight or, more likely, inside knowledge.[5]

According to the CIA officer Miles Copeland, Nasser would claim later that Kim Roosevelt gave both Nabulsi and the head of the army, Ali Abu Nuwar, disinformation that convinced them that they could successfully launch a coup against the king. What is certain is that a month-long crisis began on 3 April when Nabulsi announced, apparently without forewarning Hussein, that Jordan would open diplomatic relations with Moscow. Four days later he presented the king with a list of court officials he wanted removed. Aware of Nabulsi's popularity,

Hussein had no choice but to agree. The following day Jordanian army armoured cars, stationed just north of Amman at Zarqa, drove into the capital and surrounded Queen Zein's palace and took up key points around the city. When summoned by the king, Nuwar claimed that it was a routine security operation and agreed to withdraw the vehicles the next day. The British ambassador saw it as 'a half-baked attempt' to put pressure on Hussein.[6]

Hussein no longer trusted Nuwar, who had started aping Nasser's wide-swinging handshake since returning from a trip to Cairo the previous year. But he also knew that Nuwar commanded limited support from the highly conservative Bedu units of the army, which remained loyal to him. By the time that Nabulsi called for further heads to roll on the tenth, Hussein was confident that the army and the police were behind him, and most probably the Americans as well. So he sent a message back to the prime minister with a demand for his, and his government's resignations. Nabulsi calculated that he could frustrate Hussein's attempts to form a new government and accepted the challenge. The following day the sacked ministers held a press conference at the hotel where all the foreign press were staying. Kim Philby, by now a foreign correspondent for the *Economist* and *Observer*, was present. He reported that Nabulsi's ministers were 'jubilant' and expected to be 'back in power in less than 48 hours'.[7]

That was not what happened, however. Just over forty-eight hours later, on the evening of the thirteenth, Bedu soldiers based at a camp near Zerqa heard a rumour that the king had been murdered. Disobeying an order to go off on a night exercise in the desert – which they suspected was a ruse to get them out the way – they made for Zerqa and started fighting with the other unit based there, which comprised men from towns like Salt, where Nuwar hailed from. When news of this disturbance reached Hussein in Amman he summoned Nuwar, who admitted that the situation was out of his control and reluctantly agreed to accompany the king to Zerqa. On the road they encountered the Bedu, whom Hussein managed to calm down, but not before they had accused Nuwar of being a traitor to his face. Nuwar, shaking uncontrollably, begged to be allowed to return to Amman. Hussein agreed. 'You are weak and I never attack a weak man. I will not allow you to be killed,' he told him. It seems very possible that

Hussein provoked the rumour and thus the incident precisely in order to frame Nuwar, a suspicion reinforced by the extremely convenient discovery of two copies of a flag for the would-be Jordanian republic in Nuwar's office. As the British ambassador put it, Nuwar 'proved himself still an amateur conspirator, while the king was moving towards professional status'.[8]

The crisis was not over yet. When an Israeli invasion had seemed likely late in 1956, both Syria and Saudi Arabia had sent troops to Jordan, where they had stayed. The day after Hussein had ousted his top general came news that 3,000 Syrian troops had started to move southwards towards Amman. Hussein sent troops north to block them, and appealed to Syria's president to withdraw them. At this moment Saud came to Hussein's aid, offering immediate payment of his £5 million share of that year's subsidy, and placing the two brigades of his own troops, then in the Jordan valley, under Jordanian command. The Syrians withdrew but Hussein only drew a line under the crisis when on 25 April he decided to end the country's brief experiment with democracy and pick a government of trusted supporters who would rule in future by decree. The Americans showed their approval by allocating Jordan $20 million of the Eisenhower Doctrine money. 'The young king was certainly showing spunk,' Eisenhower was reported to have said. 'Let's invite him over one of these days.'[9]

* * *

The events in Jordan sharpened the Eisenhower administration's appetite for regime change in Damascus, to where Nuwar rather incriminatingly fled following his removal by King Hussein. In Syria the right had been tainted by its involvement or association with the previous year's attempted coup. The left profited, and by the spring of 1957 the country was ruled by just four men: the left-wing landowning defence minister Khalid al Azm, the national-socialist Baath Party leader Akram al Hawrani, Khalid Bakdash, the bull-like, moustachioed Kurd who controlled the Syrian Communist Party and Abdul Hamid Sarraj, the head of Syrian intelligence, whose reputation had soared after he unravelled the 1956 plot. 'Not an ant moves but Sarraj knows about it,' it was said. Sarraj's loyalties were moot. A portrait of Nasser hung in his office, one visitor noted; Syria's president Quwatly's likeness was nowhere to be seen.[10]

In April 1957, while Kim Roosevelt was in Jordan, his cousin Archie tried again to mount a coup in Syria, again using Michael Ilyan and the Iraqi military attaché in Beirut, who had been deeply involved in the previous year's plotting. Its timing suggests that it was perhaps conceived as a pincer movement to coincide with King Hussein's move against Nabulsi and Nuwar; whatever, it went nowhere.

Presented with 'irrefutable evidence' that both the Egyptians and Syrians were carrying out covert operations against Jordan and that the Egyptians were trying to murder Hussein, the CIA director Allen Dulles knew that he could not afford to let the matter lie. 'We have to start new planning' for a coup in Syria, he told his brother on 7 May. The situation, he insisted, was 'not hopeless'.[11]

Intelligence that the Russians were building air defence installations on Syria's border and hoped to use the country as a base to mount air attacks on Turkey and Iraq increased the pressure to act. So too did a report that the Russians had given Sarraj $50 million to meddle in the Lebanese elections which took place in July that year. Then Quwatly called the United States an 'overt foe'.[12]

All this was capped when, on 6 August, the Syrian defence minister Khalid al Azm signed an agreement on economic and technical aid with the Soviet Union during a visit to Moscow. Under the deal, the terms of which were initially obscure, the Russians agreed to provide infrastructure know-how, and to make the Damascus government a soft loan of half a billion dollars, repayable over twelve years at a rate of 2.5 per cent – at a time when western countries would only lend at 7 per cent for a maximum of three years. 'Syrian leaders seem more inclined to accept Soviet influence blindly than in any other country in the area,' Eveland's colleagues at the Operations Control Board in Washington observed, adding that there was evidence that the Soviets were 'making Syria the focal point for arms distribution and other activities, in place of Egypt'.[13]

The OCB managed covert operations for the National Security Council and, as its interest hinted, a further coup attempt was already being planned. Within two days, Washington had approved an operation led by 'Rocky' Stone, the man who had helped a nervous Fazlollah Zahedi button up his uniform on the day of the Teheran coup. Having tried and failed twice with Ilyan, for variety this time the CIA aimed to return the former dictator, Adib Shishakli to power. But Stone's conversations with dissident young Syrian army officers quickly got back to Sarraj, who managed to inveigle the CIA into sending one of the plot's ringleaders to Damascus, where he was identified. On 12 August Syria's sullen head of intelligence announced that he had uncovered a plot in which American diplomats were involved, and expelled Stone and two of his colleagues the next day. Five days later the government purged the army of its remaining right-wing officers, sacking the pro-western chief of staff and replacing him with Afif al-Bizri, who, earlier in his career, had played a part in an unsuccessful Nazi-backed coup attempt against the Hashemites in Baghdad in 1941. The British and American press instantly labelled Bizri a communist. On the day after Stone and his colleagues were declared personae non gratae, the Foreign Office decided that Syria could 'now be regarded as a Soviet satellite'.[14]

Reviewing these events, Dulles detected 'a dangerous and classic pattern'. First the Soviets offered aid. Then they used this aid to promote sympathisers like Bizri to positions of power. Finally the country would fall under communist control and become a Soviet satellite directed from Moscow. This marshalled the previous months' events into more order than was really the case, and Dulles conceded that his ambassador to Syria took a less formulaic view. 'We do not yet know how far along this pattern Syria has yet gone,' the secretary admitted, but he was certain that 'what has already happened is a sign of danger'.[15]

Carried along by his secretary of state's zeal, Eisenhower convened a meeting a day later to consider 'fairly drastic action' that would address the situation. At this it was decided to encourage Turkey's and Syria's Arab neighbours to take charge of a new effort to change the government in Damascus; the US would supply arms to them if war then broke out. That evening Dulles sent a message to Selwyn Lloyd in London. With 'little hope of correction from within', he wrote, the time had come to 'think in terms of the external ... We must perhaps be prepared to take some serious risks to avoid even greater risks and dangers later on.' But this appeal received an unexpected reception in London.[16]

Compared to Eden, Macmillan was an altogether calmer man, and under his more cautious leadership, in the nine months since Suez, a strange role reversal had taken place. During the Suez crisis, Britain's then ambassador to Washington had observed how: 'We press for immediate action while the Americans are inclined to move with greater phlegm and deliberations. This is the opposite of what our natural temperaments are supposed to be.' By now the natural order had reasserted itself. While Dulles was itching to concert action, Macmillan was hesitant. It was like 'Suez in reverse', he wrote in his diary. 'If it were not serious (and really unsatisfactory) it would be rather comic.'[17]

The reason for Macmillan's caution became clear in the first Cabinet meeting after the summer break: it was the security of Britain's oil supply. The IPC pipeline, which the Syrians had sabotaged during the Suez crisis but which was now functioning again, carried 25 million tons of oil across Syria every year; TAPLINE carried another 12 million tons. Worried about the consequences of yet another disruption that would lead to petrol rationing, the prime minister admitted that he didn't want Britain or America to take any action that would provoke Syria to cut the pipelines, 'unless it precipitates a lasting solution. If US were willing to do a Suez, we would support it. But [we] don't want them merely to make faces at them.' Macmillan's dilemma was how far to get involved. As he put it in his diary, the choice was whether to: 'Stand on the side lines and cheer? Or take a leading role?'[18]

Meanwhile Dulles had sent another veteran of the Mosaddeq coup, the former ambassador to Teheran Loy Henderson, on a mission to the Middle East to meet American diplomats and CIA officials face to face and canvass support from the Turkish, Lebanese, Iraqi and Jordanian governments. 'The situation is serious, extremely so,' Henderson confirmed on his return, before giving a fuller report to Eisenhower and Dulles at the White House. Three problems confronted the three men: one was that Syria's neighbours were split on what to do; the second, which would make this problem even worse, was that Israel might take unilateral action, at which point the Arab countries would inevitably side with Syria; and finally there was the question of how the Soviet leader Nikita Khrushchev would react, given that he was already making threatening noises.

Washington did not have long to wait. On 10 September the usually taciturn Soviet foreign minister, Andrei Gromyko, revealed that Turkey was massing troops along its southern frontier and warned that a local conflict might turn into a world war. Allen Dulles described Gromyko's intervention as 'perhaps the bitterest attack ever made by a Soviet official on the United States', and that evening his elder brother tried to reduce the tension slightly by saying that he did not think American troops would be needed in the area.[19]

On 13 September an Anglo-American Working Group, which had been set up in Washington a week earlier to consider the options, produced a preliminary report. Agreeing with Dulles that only outside force could rapidly change the situation, it set out a plan to encourage unrest inside Syria, border incidents and false flag operations in neighbouring countries that would give Syria's neighbours grounds to intervene, as well as sabotage, harassment and the assassination of Sarraj, Bizri and Bakdash. When this 'Preferred Plan' was signed off on the eighteenth, both sides agreed that it would be better if the Arab states could be persuaded to act, with Turkey – the region's old imperial power – only intervening in the last resort.

Yet again, the plan came to naught. The Turks were champing at the bit along the Syrian frontier. The Syrians successfully elicited Arab sympathy by pointing to the Turkish threat. The Iraqis – who were also concerned about neo-Ottoman expansionism – dragged their feet, and then King Saud, Nasser and Khrushchev all intervened. On 25 September King Saud visited Damascus and tried to mediate. He was prompted, said one intelligence report, by fears that the success of an American-driven coup in Damascus might finally bring about the Fertile Crescent scheme that he, and his father before him, had always feared. Then, in a *coup de théâtre*, Nasser landed 1,200 Egyptian troops at Latakia on the Syrian coast, to help the Syrians repel a Turkish attack. Finally, on the following day, Khrushchev warned Europe's socialist parties that they were in serious danger of being dragged into a war over Syria. Dulles saw Khrushchev as 'crude and impulsive rather than calculating and careful' and believed he was 'an extremely dangerous man to be at the head of the state'. As a consequence he was unwilling to run the risk of sanctioning Turkish military action. Macmillan took the same view. 'We are compelled at present towards containment policy towards Syria, for lack, at present, of better.'[20]

Throughout the crisis, the Americans maintained a limited diplomatic presence in Damascus and on 16 October, the United States chargé d'affaires reviewed the situation in a telegram that has a rather modern ring. With US policy towards Syria having failed, 'what alternatives do we have?' he mused. 'Force is ruled out. Clandestine activities would not succeed. A hard line from West alone would only drive Syria closer to the Soviet Bloc. Unhappily there is no satisfactory alternative as far as I can see, to leaving the handling of the problem to King Saud and other moderate Arabs.' He concluded: 'The best we can hope for from Syria for a long time would be genuine neutrality.'[21]

THE YEAR OF REVOLUTIONS

Eight weeks after the Americans admitted to themselves that they had failed in Syria, an offer of help arrived from an unexpected quarter. On 11 December 1957, the American ambassador to Cairo reported that an Egyptian journalist had told him that Nasser was convinced by information, given him by the US, that the new Syrian chief of staff, Afif al-Bizri, was indeed a communist and felt that 'something must be done about it'. Nasser, the ambassador continued, 'asks of us only that we keep [our] hands off Syria for a maximum period of three months and particularly that we do nothing which could have unintentional effect of making heroes out of Bizri, Bakdash and Khalid al Azm'.[1]

The journalist was a known confidant of Nasser, and since what he said tallied with American reports from Damascus that the Egyptians were supporting the Baath against the communists, the American ambassador decided that the overture was probably genuine and gave it a guarded welcome. 'It is possible', he reported to Washington, 'that Egypt, though largely responsible for present chaos in Syria, may now be prepared to exert serious effort to pull situation out of fire.' Dulles responded the following day to say that he would welcome any action designed to impede communist penetration in Syria. Since all American efforts to intervene decisively in the country's politics had failed, there was, as Nasser had probably calculated, nothing else that he could say.

Exactly what Nasser was planning became clear the following month when, on 12 January 1958, a delegation of fourteen Syrian military officers, led by Bizri himself, came to see him in Cairo. Fed up with the swirling chaos enveloping their country, they begged him for a political

The shah and his wife during their brief exile in Rome, August 1953.

Glubb Pasha. His dismissal was a major blow for British prestige and convinced Eden it was time to try to oust Nasser.

The three men MI6 was plotting to oust in March 1956: Shukri Quwatly, Saud and Nasser.

Drinkers in a south London pub watch Eden's broadcast, 10 August 1956.

Burning oil tanks at Port Said, 5 November 1956.

King Hussein of Jordan. Probably with US help, the king organised
a counter-coup against his domestic enemies in 1957.

The US Marines arrive off the coast of Beirut to preserve Lebanese independence, July 1958.

Abdel-Karim Qasim overthrew the Hashemite monarchy in Iraq. Fear for his own life, rather than his work ethic, subsequently led him to sleep in his Ministry of Defence office.

Crown Prince Faisal of Saudi Arabia. Faisal supported Nasser until Nasser backed the coup in next-door Yemen in 1962.

British soldiers watch an airstrike during their fruitless campaign against the Yemeni National Liberation Front in the Radfan, 1964.

The Yemeni imam Muhammad al-Badr commanded the loyalty of many of the country's tribesmen and enjoyed covert support from Britain.

A soldier of the Northumberland Fusiliers breaks up a demonstration in Aden.

The CIA officer Kim Roosevelt. Once the foremost American supporter of Nasser, he admitted that American interests were incompatible with Nasser's after leaving the Agency.

union between Egypt and Syria on whatever terms he wanted; the rumour was that they had said they would seek an alliance with Russia if he could not agree.[2]

According to the CIA Nasser said afterwards that he had been surprised by Bizri's proposal, but this is difficult to believe. All eyes had been on Syria for months, and Nasser's own ambassador to Damascus had long encouraged Baathist calls for a union with Egypt, a campaign that had grown louder as the Baathists' fears of both Russian and American interference in their country grew. What is sure is that Nasser set the Syrian delegation two conditions – that Syria would be ruled from Cairo and her parliament and political parties dissolved, and that the army would now come under Egyptian command and play no further role in national politics. By 20 January he and Bizri had reached an agreement; the Syrian general, on his return to Damascus, summed up the choice for the remaining doubters in the government. 'There are two roads open to you,' he told them. 'One leads to Mezze [the political prison outside Damascus]; the other to Cairo.' Bizri himself took what turned out to be a dead end. Within eight weeks he had been sacked by Nasser.[3]

On 1 February the United Arab Republic came into being. The Syrian pound slumped as investors shifted their money into other currencies, and land and share prices also fell. At the celebration in Cairo, Syria's president Shukri Quwatly struck a cautious note. 'You have acquired a nation of politicians,' he is supposed to have told Nasser. 'Fifty per cent believe themselves to be national leaders, twenty-five per cent to be prophets, and at least ten per cent to be gods.'[4]

Photographs taken that day suggest that Nasser was far more enthusiastic than Quwatly about the birth of the new union, which marked the zenith of his power. Elsewhere, the birth of the UAR also caused mixed emotions. While there was general jubilation in the Arab street, where people hoped it was a harbinger of long-dreamt-of Arab unity, the news caused consternation in the chanceries and palaces of the rulers of Syria's immediate neighbours, Lebanon, Jordan and Iraq, as they digested the implications of having Nasser as a next-door neighbour. The Lebanese foreign minister feared that Nasser's supporters in his own country would now mount a bid to join the Union, King Hussein of Jordan realised the appeal that it would have on his country's large Palestinian population, and Iraq's crown prince Abdul Ilah wondered what Nasser might do now that he controlled the Iraq Petroleum Company's pipeline. The tumultuous events of 1958 would show that all three men were right to be extremely worried.

* * *

At King Hussein's invitation, on 11 February King Feisal of Iraq and his advisers arrived in Amman by plane for talks. Born six months apart, the two kings got on very well with one another, but their families, as the British ambassador to Amman put it diplomatically, 'were on less good terms'. In fact they had fallen out spectacularly the previous year, and the root cause of the ill feeling was money. As the British ambassador observed, while Feisal's suits were made for him on Savile Row, Hussein made do with a tailor on the Salt Road in Amman. The Jordanians disliked their 'rich but stingy cousins'.[5]

It was Iraqi money that King Hussein so desperately needed. The Egyptians and the Syrians had, to no one's great surprise, never honoured the £7 million-a-year promise they had made in the previous year's Arab Solidarity Pact, and then in January King Saud told Hussein that he could no longer afford to keep up his payments of £5 million either. Facing the simultaneous challenge of the UAR and a £12 million-sized hole in his finances, Hussein now suggested a federation with a rotating monarchy to his richer cousin. When Feisal refused to consider this, Hussein offered to stand down in Feisal's favour. Having reached a deal by which each man would remain king of his own country, three days later the two kings announced the creation of the Arab Union, which would have Feisal as its king. 'Any union is better than none,' admitted Jordan's ambassador to Baghdad. But on the West Bank, Hussein's Palestinian subjects disagreed. According to a State Department report, most of them were 'Convinced They Are In The Wrong Union'.[6]

King Saud had received an invitation to join the Hashemites' Arab Union, which he declined. Although, like the Iraqis, he worried that Nasser might be able to turn his pipeline on and off, he thought that he had come up with a better idea. By mid-February he was indiscreetly telling all and sundry to 'expect wonderful news from Syria shortly'.

On 3 March one of his officials more specifically told the American ambassador to Riyadh that 'a successful military revolution' was about to take place in Damascus.[7]

The Americans, having been burnt by the Syrians themselves the previous year, urged caution, which Saud ignored. On 5 March, Nasser, on his first visit to Damascus, announced that Sarraj – Syria's intelligence chief – had recently been approached by an envoy from Saud, who had paid him nearly £2 million to launch a counter-coup against the union with Egypt, and promised him £2 million more if he assassinated Nasser during his Syrian visit as well. At a press conference soon afterwards, Sarraj distributed copies of the three cheques he had been given, which had been drawn on the Arab Bank in Riyadh. Pictures of the cheques were reproduced in the Egyptian press the following day. According to Kim Philby, who visited Riyadh soon afterwards, the bank's manager admitted that the money had been deposited by one of Saud's officials. It looked like the Saudis had fallen for a sting.[8]

In Washington, the CIA director Allen Dulles despaired. 'We had tried to warn Saud, vainly, that he was falling into a trap.' The plot was a significant setback for Washington, since it damned the Americans by association, and led Saud's pro-Egyptian half-brother Faisal to seize most of the king's remaining powers and embark on a course of studious neutrality. By 1959 it was reported that Saud did 'little more than distributing charity, signing death warrants, State papers, etc.'[9]

* * *

If Saud was the first casualty of the United Arab Republic, the Americans and the British feared that the Lebanese president Camille Chamoun might be the next. In office since 1952, Chamoun had taken an openly pro-American stance which, while welcome in Washington, had made him lots of enemies at home where it went against the commitment to non-alignment that had underpinned the country's politics since independence in 1943. Now nearing the end of his six-year term of office and buoyed by the way in which a tidal wave of CIA money had helped him win the previous year's parliamentary election, he wanted to stand for the presidency again – an ambition that was not as simple to achieve as it sounded.

As it stood, the Lebanese constitution barred the president from two consecutive terms of office: Chamoun would first need to seek parliament's approval to amend its text before the legislature broke up in May if he was to put himself forward that summer. In theory, given that he enjoyed a substantial parliamentary majority, it should have been easy. But, in the eight months since the parliamentary elections, anti-western feeling had grown. By March 1958, Chamoun was unpopular and vulnerable. Moreover, the fact that the constitution was now seen by many Muslim Lebanese as flawed (because it institutionalised Christian dominance in a country where the majority of the population was now Muslim) made tinkering with it in such a transparently self-serving fashion, while failing to address its deeper shortcomings, potentially incendiary. Chamoun's outraged opponents said that he was risking a civil war.

The US government realised that Chamoun had become a liability, and wanted him to retire. On 5 March the American ambassador met the president to discuss who might succeed him. Chamoun 'went through [the] process of elimination, ticking off one by one potential candidates' before reaching the conclusion that the 'only politician who could lead [the] country and evaluate its present foreign policies was himself', the ambassador reported back to Washington. The following month Chamoun changed his mind, and started to think that the army chief of staff, Fuad Chehab, might be acceptable. By May he was back to thinking that only he would do.[10]

Before Chamoun could announce that he was standing, however, the country erupted in civil war. Following the murder of a Christian, pro-Nasser journalist on 8 May, Chamoun's opponents – who included leading Sunnis, the Druze warlord Kamal Jumblatt, and Christian leaders – called for the president's resignation and a general strike. In Tripoli, during three days of violent clashes, protestors also set fire to the United States Information Service Library. On the twelfth the violence spread to Beirut itself, and the next day Jumblatt attacked the presidential palace southeast of the capital, although Chamoun was not there at the time. After Fuad Chehab refused to take action against the rebels, fearing that his army would split if he did, Chamoun warned both the American and British governments that he might have to ask for military help.

Chamoun's warning left the Americans, in particular, with a

dilemma. As Dulles put it, to send in troops risked creating 'a wave of anti-Western feeling in the Arab world' which might lead to the removal of the remaining pro-western governments, the sabotage of the pipelines running through Syria, and so another major oil crisis for the west. To do nothing, however, would show that the United States was not willing to stand by her allies, a failure Moscow would certainly exploit.[11]

In London, Macmillan and his colleagues considered the situation the same day. After Lloyd warned that 'unless we arrest this drift, Lebanon will be absorbed into the United Arab Republic', the cabinet agreed that it would join with the United States to tell Chamoun that, if he asked for help, then he would get it. Chronicling the cabinet meeting in his diary that night, Macmillan feared that, after Lebanon, Iraq 'will be next to go'. That comment seemed eerily prescient when, exactly eight weeks later, the Hashemites and their hangers-on were bloodily overthrown.[12]

* * *

Iraq's inequality had long worried the British, who encouraged the king and his advisers to spread their oil wealth more widely. And so in 1950 Nuri Said had set up an Iraq Development Board. Anticipating its effects, four years later the country's interior minister predicted to a visitor that 'in five or six years the face of the country will have been changed and there will be no more talk of communism. Come back and see us again and you will see.' But Nuri's fondness for *grands projets* over less obtrusive schemes encouraged the Board to squander its funds on vanity projects, when repairing existing infrastructure would have been more cost effective and housing was a far more urgent priority.

Nuri's grip over the Board, and its failure to make an impact, were symptoms of a much deeper malaise. By December 1956, an MI6 officer, Michael Ionides, reported hearing 'bitter complaints from the younger men, up to 30 or 40, that Nuri has never brought the next generation along, has kept everything to himself, never built up the structure of Government and Parliament, never even tried to make elections work as other emergent countries have done'. There was, they grumbled, 'no outlet for discussion', 'no means for the younger people to take part'. When the MI6 agent John Slade-Baker visited the following year he heard exactly the same story from an Iraqi contact, who said that discontent had now spread into the army. Intellectuals, meanwhile, were calling for 'al islah al jathri' – reform from the root. 'It is not a question of pruning the twigs and cutting out a certain amount of dead wood,' this man explained, when Slade-Baker queried what exactly that phrase meant. 'The tree must be destroyed to the very roots.'[13]

In 1957, shortly before Nuri became prime minister again, for the eighth, and as it turned out, final time, Sam Falle – who had helped organise the overthrow of Mosaddeq in Iran – was posted to Iraq. Nuri was now just shy of seventy, and the British government was uncomfortably aware that there was no one to step into his shoes once he was gone. Before setting out for Baghdad he remembered being asked a question by his boss in London. 'What we want to know, Sam, is "After Nuri, what?"'[14]

Having travelled the length of the country soon after his arrival, Falle could report that the signs were not reassuring. Some Baghdad contacts he inherited from his predecessor told him, over dinner, that their country's independence was a sham because successive governments simply took orders from the British. 'Their criticism of the Iraqi regime, particularly the Crown Prince and Nuri as Said, was blistering,' he recalled. Their strength of feeling was all the more astonishing given that it was the first time they had met him and Nuri was not even in government at the time. The situation outside Baghdad was every bit as bad, but in a different way. Downstream at Kut, Falle discovered peasants working in feudal conditions and 'hardly able to scrape a living'. On his return to the embassy he summarised the main problems facing the country as 'predatory landlords and inefficient farming'.[15]

From Cairo, Voice of the Arabs fanned smouldering resentment. By the time that Nuri became prime minister, on 3 March 1958, there was mounting disquiet about the country's situation. 'The ruling classes here are getting more and more worried at the gap between the Government and the people and at the extent to which Nasser has captured their imagination,' said Ionides three days later.[16]

The British ambassador, Michael Wright, was not oblivious to what was going on, but discounted it. He lived a cloistered existence in a residence hidden behind high walls and, after nearly four years in post, he relied too heavily on Nuri for information. When Nuri reassured him that his security forces had already uncovered four plots that year and that the army was loyal to the monarchy, Wright was inclined to believe him: after all, Nuri was the consummate survivor and people had been predicting the collapse of the Iraqi state for years and it had never happened. And so when Falle raised his fear that a revolution seemed likely, Wright took little notice. He told the new boy not to attach too much significance to the views of a 'discontented middle class'. He also warned him not to mix with the opposition in case it prejudiced his own relationship with Nuri. 'The Embassy feel that so long as Nuri is back in the chair all is going well and that nothing more is required', claimed one of Nuri's rivals. The ambassador's view reassured Selwyn Lloyd in London. During one cabinet meeting the foreign secretary acknowledged that the Iraqi government was going through 'a serious crise de nerfs', but said that it was nothing that 'dollops of short-term aid' could not resolve. But this time Wright turned out to be wrong.[17]

In fact it was probably too late for money, in whatever quantity, to save the situation. In response to repeated provocation by Nuri, who travelled to London in June and called, in an interview, for Anglo-American help to bring down the Syrian government, Nasser was doing his utmost to destroy the Hashemites' Arab Union. In Jordan a young officer cadet, Ahmad Yusif al-Hiyari, was arrested on suspicion of plotting to kill Hussein and his uncle. Under interrogation he revealed that the UAR was planning to stage simultaneous coups in Jordan and Iraq in mid-July.

The Americans meanwhile were also uncovering evidence that a conspiracy was afoot. In May the FBI sent the CIA the tape of a telephone conversation between the Jordanian and Egyptian military attachés in Washington, which suggested that the Jordanian was the leader of a plot against King Hussein. When, at the end of June, the CIA intercepted a radio message from Syria to the Jordanian conspirators telling them to launch the coup, it tipped off the king, who ordered the arrest of some forty Jordanian army officers.

Realising the potential significance of al-Hiyari's confession, Hussein called his cousin Feisal in Baghdad and asked him to send a trusted envoy to Amman so that he could brief him on the threat. On 10 July the commander-in-chief of the Iraqi army, General Arif, came to see him. When Hussein warned him about what he knew, Arif was dismissive. 'Your Majesty,' he responded, 'I appreciate all your trouble, but I assure you the Iraqi Army is built on tradition . . . It has not had the problems – nor the changes – your army has had, sir, in the past few years. I feel that it is rather we who should be concerned about Jordan, Your Majesty. This coup applies to your country, and it is you we are worried about. I beseech you to take care.'[18]

It was, ironically, Hussein who then ensured his cousin's fate. Worried when the arrested plotters refused to talk, he asked Feisal to send troops to Jordan to strengthen his own army in the event that Syria invaded. In response, Nuri Said decided to task one of his favourite soldiers, Abdel-Karim Qasim, with taking an Iraqi brigade to Mafraq near the Syrian frontier.

As Qasim's force was based at Baqubah, east of Baghdad, it would have to pass through the capital on its way to Mafraq. Despite General Arif's claims that the army was loyal, it was revealing that its standing orders mandated that troops passing through the capital did not carry live ammunition with them. On this occasion, however, that directive was ignored. After Qasim's force had crossed the Tigris during the night of 13–14 July, it dispersed in order to take over the radio station, the railway and major government buildings, and to assault the royal palace. When Feisal and Abdul Ilah emerged from the building to try to reach an agreement with their attackers, they were both shot dead. The rebels then stormed the palace, killing the remainder of the royal family. Abdul Ilah's decapitated body was tied by its feet to a car and dragged through the streets. A day later, Nuri, who escaped his own home disguised as a woman, was found and murdered.

As the imagined power behind the throne, the British were also targeted. Driving to the embassy on the morning of the coup Falle found himself surrounded by a baying mob which started hammering on the roof of his car. 'This did not look good,' he said, but his luck held when an Iraqi corporal in a jeep appeared, dispersed the crowd and told him to go home immediately. One of Falle's colleagues was also stopped and asked his nationality. 'Scottish,' he answered. 'Lucky for you,' came the reply. 'We are killing all the English today!' The embassy was attacked and the comptroller, a distinguished-looking former army officer whom the rioters had probably mistaken for Wright, was murdered. The closeness of this shave was lost on Wright's Marie-Antoinetteish wife. 'Oh, I still love my Iraqis,' she was quoted saying afterwards.[19]

* * *

The news – and, worse, the photographs – from Baghdad caused palpitations in Beirut and Amman. After Chamoun had made a formal request to the United States for help, Macmillan convened his cabinet early in the evening to discuss what they might do. Although he clearly felt Chamoun's appeal presented a golden 'opportunity to check Nasser and clean up the situation in the Middle East generally', his colleagues were more cautious. While none of them was willing to do nothing, since that would only reinforce the impression that Britain was irrelevant, they feared that an American landing in Lebanon would make it more likely that they would have to intervene in Jordan, and that they would have to pick up the pieces when American interest proved short-lived. To use Macmillan's words, he did not 'want to be left sitting in this tuppenny ha'penny place'.[20]

To try to force the United States to recognise that intervening in Lebanon carried regional consequences, Macmillan sent a telegram to Eisenhower asking him what forces he would be willing to commit to a British operation to support Hussein. But when the two men spoke over the telephone later that evening, Eisenhower dodged that issue, because he and his advisers rightly wondered whether Macmillan's real motive was to use Jordan as a base from which to launch a counter-revolution in Iraq.

Instead, Macmillan learned from the president that American forces would shortly be landing in Lebanon alone. 'You are doing a Suez on me,' the prime minister responded, at which Eisenhower just laughed. The clear American determination to take unilateral and unassisted action was, as the home secretary, Rab Butler, remarked when the cabinet reconvened afterwards, 'Quite a blow to our prestige.'[21]

The Americans landed at Beirut the following day. 'We were just in time to watch as amphibious tanks eerily surfaced through the waves and stood on the shore rotating their gun turrets,' recalled a British journalist, who had seen the US Sixth Fleet materialise on the horizon and had run down to the beach to watch. 'They were followed by fearsome-looking marines ... who leapt into the surf from landing craft. They were loaded with machine-guns, mortars and flame-throwers, and muttered "excuse me Ma'am" as they advanced past sunbathers in bikinis, while Lebanese beach boys tried to sell them Cokes and ice creams.'[22]

When the same day Hussein asked Macmillan for help, should it 'prove necessary to preserve the integrity and independence of Jordan', the British realised that they were now on the hook, just as they feared they would be. A further plea from the king reached Macmillan in parliament the following evening just after he had wound up a debate on the events of the previous two days. Once again he convened the cabinet, this time in his office in parliament behind the Speaker's chair. In a meeting that lasted deep into the night, Macmillan set out the military risks entailed in sending a lightly armed force of paratroops who might face serious Jordanian opposition and whose resupply would depend on Israeli agreement. 'Determined not to repeat Anthony's mistake', he then asked each of his colleagues for his view. Shortly before three o'clock in the morning of 17 July, the cabinet decided to send in the paras in a show of support for King Hussein. Two battalions of the Parachute Regiment, with light artillery and six fighter jets, left Cyprus for Amman soon afterwards. Hussein was given 'intelligence' of a plot timed to take place later that morning, to give the British grounds for intervention.[23]

As Macmillan recounted, the operation nearly resulted in a 'terrible disaster' that would have caused the fall of the government. Although the Foreign Office had assured him that the Israelis would not prevent the British airborne force from crossing their airspace, when the RAF tried to do so early on 17 July, the Israelis ordered them to land. The leading aircraft, carrying the paras, decided to ignore the command and safely reached the Jordanian frontier, but its escort turned back to avoid the risk of being shot down. To the horror of the British commanders on Cyprus, Macmillan ordered the operation to stop, while they waited for a response from the Israelis.

In the meantime Macmillan stewed. 'What was I to say in the House? I must announce the facts at least at 3.30. But what were the facts? No one seemed to know,' he wrote afterwards, recalling how he had spent the morning trying to hide his 'sickening anxiety'. It was only that afternoon, while he was briefing Gaitskell on the reasons for the overnight intervention, that an aide put a most welcome piece of paper in his hand. 'The Israeli Govt has agreed,' was all it said.[24]

Despite this positive reply, Israel's stance towards overflights was to change repeatedly in the next few days. Inside the country her coalition government was split on whether it was better to help King Hussein survive, or to connive with Jordan's other neighbours in the break-up of the barely feasible state. As this tug of war continued, the government gave and withdrew permission for overflights several times. The uncertainty only increased Macmillan's determination to withdraw the British force as fast as possible, especially after he was obliged, against his better judgement, to commit more troops in August to secure the paratroopers an alternative line of communication, between Amman and the port of Aqaba, Jordan's only outlet to the sea.

Although the Americans helped break the impasse with Tel Aviv by operating the airbridge themselves, their continued refusal to send troops to join the British contingent in Amman reinforced Macmillan's desire for a swift exit. So too did the election of Lebanon's army chief of staff, Fuad Chehab, as Chamoun's successor as president, on 31 July. With every sign that the Americans had stabilised the situation in Lebanon, on 12 August Macmillan told his colleagues that his hope was to hand over to the United Nations. A United Nations general assembly resolution, which called on all Arab states to respect each other's territorial integrity and was sponsored by the Arab League, passed unanimously on 21 August. It provided the necessary cover that would give the British grounds to leave.

Before Macmillan was willing to beat the retreat, there was one thing left to do. King Hussein had been counting on Iraq to fill the gap in his finances. The murder of his cousins and their advisers not only left him grieving, but also confronted with yet another financial crisis. Until the matter of Jordan's future funding was resolved, Macmillan knew that the kingdom would not be stable. By the end of August, however, the matter had been fixed. The United States agreed to give Jordan $50 million to tide the kingdom over until the following April, enabling Hussein to recruit two extra Bedu brigades that would decisively tip the balance in the army in his favour.

* * *

Macmillan had emerged unscathed from a crisis that, as he was all too aware, could easily have destroyed his reputation. For the British, 1958 marked the end of an era. The collapse of the Hashemite regime in Iraq, so long forecast and yet so long delayed, removed the last strong British ally in the northern Middle East and dealt a severe blow to British influence in that part of the region. There was, moreover, nothing that the British could do about it. Britain had lost Palestine, then Egypt, and now Jordan and Iraq. From now on, her primary interests lay to the south, along the shores of the Arabian peninsula. The British were back where they had started.

PART FOUR

Clinging On
1957–67

23

REBELS ON THE JEBEL

Britain's imperial interest in the Middle East began, just as it would eventually end, in southeastern Arabia. In 1798, following Napoleon's invasion of Egypt, the British secured a promise from the sultan of Muscat that he would support them, rather than the French. Then, following a series of naval campaigns that aimed to secure the sea approaches to India, in 1820 they forced a truce upon the sheikhs of the Gulf coast that obliged them to give up piracy. The British would call the Gulf sheikdoms the Trucial States.

A little later, the British persuaded the Trucial sheikhs to abandon the slave trade that represented their other major line of business, then, in the face of Turkish expansionism, to cede control of their foreign relations in exchange for British recognition and protection. A network of British political agents and officers arrived to manage the relationship, and soon found themselves dealing with the sheikhs' knottier problems. 'He decides fishing disputes, negotiates blood-money, examines boundaries, manumits slaves,' wrote the outgoing political agent in Dubai, of his own role, in 1964. 'He presides over the Shaikhs' Council. He exempts, pardons, appeases, exacts, condemns, ordains. Over a large but undefined field he in effect rules.' The British took on a similar role in Muscat and Oman, where in 1920 they brokered the Treaty of Sib between the sultan and his rival the imam, which, for a time, brought peace to southeastern Arabia.[1]

If it took the French threat to India to draw the British into the Gulf, it was the German *Drang nach Osten* that led them to take the step that would make them determined to cling on there. In 1899, following rumours that the Berlin–Baghdad railway might terminate in Kuwait, the British government offered the ruler of the benighted territory, Mubarak al Sabah, £1,000 if he would sign away his rights to enter any negotiation with, or lease any land to, another foreign power. After the outbreak of war in 1914, it then offered him the mantle of British protection. 'We don't want Koweit, but we don't want anyone else to have it,' a British official admitted. This dog-in-the-manger calculation obtained right up until the moment when oil was discovered in the country, at a shallow depth and near the coast – a combination that was, as the American ambassador to Riyadh put it, 'an oil-man's dream'.[2]

Mubarak's grandson turned a silver wheel to fill the first tanker-load of crude oil in June 1946. When Mosaddeq nationalised his country's oil industry five years later, Anglo-Iranian – which owned half the Kuwait Oil Company – switched its focus to the emirate. By 1957 Kuwait was producing half of Britain's oil. In British eyes, it had become the most important country in the Middle East. Just as important, the ruler of Kuwait, whose income was estimated at £1.25 million a week, had become the single biggest investor in the City of London.

One of the British government's two greatest fears was that the ruler of Kuwait might switch his reserves from sterling into dollars; the other was the threat posed to its advantageous position in the Gulf by Nasser. By 1957 the British were uncomfortably aware that Egypt was encouraging growing domestic opposition to the reactionary rulers of Kuwait and Bahrain – opposition that, in their role as the protectors of both men, they might ultimately be called on to help crush. Until this point the rulers of the poorer sheikhdoms down the Gulf were by and large unchallenged. But then, in July 1957, just as Britain's foreign secretary Selwyn Lloyd was weighing up whether masterly inactivity or the gentle encouragement of reform was more likely to prolong Britain's decidedly anachronistic position in the Gulf, a revolt broke out, in inland Oman.[3]

* * *

Immediately after the Buraimi incident in 1955, the sultan of Muscat had embarked on a car journey to stake his claim to inner Oman, but the effect of his royal progress was short-lived. Although his forces took Nizwa – the capital of his inland rival, the imam – without firing a shot, the imam simply retired to his village and his ambitious younger brother Talib fled to Saudi Arabia, where he received help from King Saud and Nasser to recruit and train a 500-strong army of disaffected Omanis. In June 1957 Talib and his guerrillas landed from dhows along the coast east and west of Muscat and established themselves in their home villages inland. Meanwhile the imam returned to Nizwa and raised his standard over the drum tower of the fortress that commanded the town.

As Britain depended more and more heavily on Kuwaiti oil, Oman had acquired a new strategic significance because it commanded the entrance to the Gulf. After the sultan requested British help, Macmillan discussed the matter in the cabinet on 18 July. He and his colleagues were acutely aware that failure to defend any one of the states might lead their sheikhs to look to the United States for protection. As the defence minister Duncan Sandys observed during that cabinet meeting, 'All these rulers are looking to see whether we shall support them or let them down.'[4]

Convinced that Aramco's and the State Department's sympathies would lie with the rebels if they declared independence, Macmillan was determined to nip the rebellion in the bud. The best way to do so, he argued, was by a direct attack on the imam's fortress at Nizwa, even though such action would probably elicit a 'howl from the Saudis, Egypt and perhaps the United States'. His colleagues agreed with him. That day they sanctioned an air strike on the forts that were now in rebel hands; worried about international criticism, Lloyd insisted that 'rockets not bombs' should be used. On 24 and 25 July British jets attacked but the rockets exploded harmlessly on the great drum tower at Nizwa. When the sultan's forces followed up the aerial attack the rebels drove them off.[5]

To further complicate the situation, the Americans were angry at what the British had done. Although Macmillan had sent a message to Eisenhower on the day after the cabinet meeting (a Friday) to forewarn him of the rocket attack, the president only received the message the following Monday. By then British journalists were claiming that the rebels had Aramco's support and were using American-made weapons supplied by the Saudis – allegations that Lloyd, who felt that Washington was being 'suspiciously quiet', then had to dodge when he was summoned to the House of Commons to make a statement the same day. When Dulles saw the coverage in the British press he assumed, probably correctly, that the allegations were officially inspired and mounted a counter-attack. After a State Department spokesman dismissed the allegation about Aramco as 'hogwash' and said that there was 'no evidence' that American weapons were involved, Ike sent a tersely worded reply to Macmillan, which, while not quite denying the rumours, encouraged the prime minister to quash them. Dulles, simultaneously, warned the British that the fundamental problem was the still unresolved dispute over Buraimi.[6]

Macmillan and Lloyd then managed to dig themselves into a deeper hole. After the foreign secretary had promised Dulles that 'there was no question of using British troops there', a day later the British government had an abrupt change of heart. However, at a further meeting with Dulles on 31 July neither Macmillan nor Lloyd could bring himself to admit that British troops were being sent into action. Dulles was justifiably annoyed when he found out about it by other means soon afterwards, and refused to do more than abstain when the Arab League raised Britain's conduct at the UN.[7]

To end the uprising the British had to send in a company of infantry and a troop of armoured cars. Despite temperatures that reached 110 degrees in the shade, by mid-August this force had brought Nizwa into the sultan's hands. But once again, the imam and his brother Talib got away.

Macmillan wrote in his diary that the military operation had been 'brilliantly conducted', but from the diplomatic and political standpoint, the handling of the episode left much to be desired. Not only had the Americans proved hostile, so too had the British press. Its journalists were furious that they had been denied access to the frontline in Oman, and had spent the campaign cooped up in Bahrain where they were spoon-fed disinformation by the British political resident.[8]

In a series of editorials, *The Times* blasted the British government's handling of the uprising, arguing that its unwarranted faith in the effectiveness of air power had led to a situation in which it was then obliged to put troops on the ground, a deployment that Nasser's Voice of the Arabs mercilessly exploited. A pair of articles at the end of the campaign concluded that the sultan needed to do more for his people, and that Britain was jeopardising her interests in the developed sheikhdoms of the Gulf by propping up such a reactionary man. 'The basic lesson of the Oman adventure', the second article concluded, 'is surely that it should not happen again.'[9]

* * *

The problem was that further military action looked all but inevitable. From Nizwa, the imam and his brother Talib had escaped north to the Jebel Akhdar, the green mountain that divided the coastal plains of Muscat from the hinterland of Oman, where they were joined by the Jebel's self-styled 'Ruller' (so said his business cards) Suleiman bin Himyar, who believed that the two brothers might advance his own separatist ambitions.[10]

Part natural fastness, part lost world, the Jebel was protected on all sides by 45-degree flanks, pierced in a few places by sheer-sided wadis that ran off a 6,oooft-high plateau, which was in turn surrounded by higher peaks. The temperate climate and running water all year round created, by Omani standards, a veritable Elysium on the plateau: fruit and cereal crops grew abundantly there. Last conquered by the Persians in the thirteenth century, the Jebel retained a mysterious reputation. 'An Arab from the mountain', Thesiger recounted, 'once told me that in the winter the rain sometimes turns into a soft white powder like salt.'[11]

Since the British had withdrawn almost all their troops following the United States' unwillingness to support them enthusiastically at the UN, the sultan's forces had to deal with the situation alone. Initially they made a futile attempt to blockade the Jebel. But, as they lacked the numbers to do so on their own, they relied on local tribesmen whose sympathies were really with the rebels. As a result, the cordon was utterly ineffective and a stream of volunteers and weaponry continued to find their way up the mountain.

By the end of 1957 the sultan's forces were outnumbered and had been pushed onto the defensive. Pinned down in their bases at night by sniper fire, they spent their days trying to de-mine the road between Muscat and the Fahud, the location of the dome-shaped hills that Thesiger had spotted eight years earlier, where the oil company was now hunting for oil. By early 1958, according to one of the British officers who led the sultan's force, the American-made mines had become such a menace that: 'Our entire effort, physical and intellectual, was absorbed by this nuisance.' On bad days they were losing two or three trucks each day. The British resorted to laying sandbags on the floors of all their vehicles to try to absorb the blast.[12]

* * *

The under-secretary for war, Julian Amery, witnessed the British officers' frustrations when he paid a flying visit to Muscat in January 1958 and decided that the answer was to beef up the sultan's army. The man he turned to was his old wartime colleague, David Smiley. The two men had known each other since the war when they had both parachuted into Albania together for Special Operations Executive. Smiley, who earned a bar to his earlier MC for blowing up 'Albania's third largest bridge' during that escapade, was lucky to survive a later mission in the Far East, when the thermite briefcase he was using to carry top secret papers prematurely self-combusted, burning him severely. Since then he had worked with MI6 trying to subvert the communist regime that then took over Albania after the war, before commanding his old cavalry regiment, the Blues, and serving as military attaché at the British embassy in Stockholm. It was just when he was coming to the end of that posting in early 1958 that he received a call from Amery.[13]

Smiley recalled the conversation vividly. Would he like to go to Muscat to command the sultan's army, his old friend asked. When he queried whether he was the right man for the job – given that he spoke not a word of Arabic and had never worked in the Middle East – Amery reassured him. Smiley recalled him saying that 'I had probably got more active experience of guerrilla warfare than almost any officer in the Army and would therefore be well suited for commanding troops who were engaged in guerrilla war.' Unable to resist the offer, he flew to the Middle East that April.[14]

After staying five nights with the British political resident, Bernard Burrows, he went on to Muscat to take up his job at the headquarters of the sultan's Armed Forces, the Beit al Falaj, a whitewashed, crenelated fort that flew the sultan's scarlet flag. Although Burrows' residence looked like 'a ghastly abortion of the architecture of Harlow and Crawley' in the opinion of one visitor, it did at least have the merit of effective air-conditioning. By contrast the Beit al Falaj felt like a furnace. To quote an old Persian proverb, as one of Smiley's colleagues did to him, 'The sinner who goes to Muscat has a foretaste of what is coming to him in the other world.'[15]

After a few days at his new headquarters, Smiley returned to Muscat to meet his new employer, the sultan. Dressed in a black cloak edged with gold, and a turban of purple, green and gold, he wore a jewelled, curved dagger in the middle of his belt; his grey beard smelt faintly of frankincense. Described by Macmillan as 'a good old boy' because of his willingness to stand up to the Saudis, Said bin Taimur had inherited the throne as a 22-year-old after his father abdicated, leaving the country in a financial crisis. 'Now Said in jail, I free,' his father was reputed to have said as he set out for exile.[16]

Now forty-eight years old, Sultan Said bin Taimur was a short, round despot, a man who had had his favourite slave's tongue cut out to ensure his discretion. Averse to trousers and sunglasses, both of which he banned, he also resisted western pressure to improve his subjects' lot. 'At present many children die in infancy and so the population does not increase,' he told Smiley (infant mortality ran at about 70 per cent). 'If we build clinics many more will survive – but for what? To starve?' He was even more suspicious of schooling. 'That is why you lost India,' he told one of his British advisers. 'Because you educated the people.' And he flatly rejected the idea that some of his Arab officers might be trained for higher command, up to – Smiley ventured – the rank of lieutenant colonel. 'You must know, Colonel Smiley,' he replied in faultless English, 'that all revolutions in the Arab world are led by colonels. That is why I employ you. I am having no Arab colonels in my army.'[17]

Bernard Burrows, the political resident, admitted that Britain was partly responsible for the sultan's woes. Not only had the British damaged his prestige when they stopped him from trying to take back Buraimi singlehandedly in 1952, but they had then encouraged him to overextend himself by permitting the Iraq Petroleum Company to hunt for oil in the interior. The British plan – that the discovery of oil would bring the sultan revenue which he could then spend on security and development, making his benighted subjects happier – had one small but significant flaw. The dome-shaped hills of the Fahud, which Thesiger had first spotted on his travels a decade earlier, had not yet yielded any oil. The sultan was left trying to police the hinterland on a shoestring.

By the time Smiley arrived in-country in April, it was already too hot for serious military campaigning. And so he decided to spend the period before he was due to take summer leave making a 700-mile circuit of the Jebel Akhdar where the rebels were now based. No sooner had his convoy entered the main pass through the mountains than the leading scout car struck a mine, losing a wheel which landed dangerously close to Smiley's Land Rover. 'After spending a large part of my military career laying mines and teaching others to lay them on enemy roads, it was galling now to find myself at the receiving end,' he commented later. Measures, such as fining or burning villages where mines were found, or forcing 'mascots' – local people – to sit on the bonnet of the lead vehicle, a tactic the British had used in Palestine between the wars, were now deemed indefensible. More effective would have been to stop the Americans from supplying their mines to Riyadh in the first place. 'I know we tried,' said Smiley, 'but the Americans were brutally unsympathetic. Their reply was that they supplied the mines to Saudi Arabia under their military Aid Programme, and it was not their concern how the Saudis chose to employ them.'[18]

Smiley visited Nizwa and the oil prospectors' camp before retracing his steps and cutting northwest past the Jebel's southern flank to visit Buraimi, where the contrast in fortunes between the people living in the sultan's and Sheikh Shakhbut's villages was noticeable. He then returned to the north side of the mountain, from where he drove to Sohar on the coast.

In Sohar he heard news of an important development. A truck from Saudi Arabia, carrying a cargo of machine-guns, mortars and ammunition, as well as forty volunteers, had managed to get across the border. Assuming it must be bound for the Jebel, Smiley decided to give chase. But the patrol he led up one of the wadis on the north side of the mountain came to grief. 'We had made about five miles up the gulley when there was an explosion behind me, and I heard the cries and groans of wounded men.'[19] The Land Rover immediately behind Smiley's had hit a mine and its four occupants were now lying among the wreckage of their vehicle, 'badly charred and covered in blood'. There was nothing for it but to call off the pursuit.

As Smiley made his way back down the mountain, towards the coast and the white, hot Beit al Falaj, he realised that there was only one way to regain the upper hand. 'I decided that our first objective must be to secure ourselves a foothold, somehow, on that plateau, from which we could harry the rebels.' If the Persians had managed it 800 years earlier, he reasoned, then 'so could we'. But to do so, he knew he required more, and better troops, and that he would have to go to London to persuade the government to send them.[20]

Smiley's return to Britain was delayed by the July coup in Iraq and it was not until about 11 August that he reappeared in Whitehall. There he found that the Foreign Office was very wary of a repetition of the previous year's trouble in the United Nations. As he recalled, 'The very suggestion that regular British troops might again be committed to action in Oman made their well-groomed hair stand on end.'[21]

Smiley received a warmer welcome at the War Office, where he met Amery and the secretary of state for war, Christopher Soames. His warning – that 'within six months there will be a major uprising and the entire country will turn against us' – chimed with a telegram which had just arrived from Air Vice Marshal Maurice Heath, commander-in-chief of British Forces on the Arabian peninsula. Heath also felt that the current campaign against the rebels on the Jebel was ineffective. He requested permission to mount an operation to capture the mountain. As a consequence, Soames called Heath home from Aden, and Oman joined Jordan as one of two items on the agenda for the Cabinet Defence Committee meeting on 19 August, when the most likely opponent of military action, the foreign secretary Selwyn Lloyd, happened to be absent.[22]

After Heath had outlined a plan for a swift operation in which troops would parachute, or be helicoptered, onto the Jebel after a week-long aerial bombardment that would be over before the press could reach the scene, the prime minister and his colleagues agreed that secret preparations for a ground operation should begin. But Macmillan, too, worried about the likely international reaction. Unless the sultan turned over a new leaf, Britain would gain nothing to offset the political damage that her resort to force would cause. As the earliest the operation could take place was at the end of November, he said that he would defer the decision on whether or not to go ahead until late September.

Predictably, Lloyd shared Macmillan's doubts. Present when the Defence Committee met again in September, he warned that it would be unwise to launch Heath's operation in November since it would coincide with the United Nations general assembly. He preferred to spend the money earmarked for the operation on development and an attempt to reach a political settlement instead. He returned to the offensive when the committee met again on 3 October, arguing that, since it would be impossible to conceal the preparation for the attack, which 'the Americans (in particular)' were likely to leak to the press, the British government would come under intense pressure in the United Nations to abandon its plan. If the government persisted regardless, the operation would buy time at best. At worst it would cause a backlash in Kuwait and Bahrain, the two states in the Gulf that, by virtue of their oil reserves, now really mattered. Lloyd's salvo was decisive, and that day the Committee agreed to cancel the operation. But the underlying problem remained. In Oman, the rebellion was gaining momentum and the sultan's forces were incapable, alone, of crushing it.[23]

Refusing to be beaten, the War Office then came up with an alternative suggestion to allay the diplomats' fear that Britain would yet again be hauled before the UN. A squadron of the Special Air Service, then fighting communist terrorists in Malaya, would be flown secretly to Oman, where they would climb the mountain and find and 'kill the rebel leaders'. In the last week of October the commanding officer of 22 SAS flew in to Muscat to conduct a recce. Tony Deane-Drummond had parachuted into Arnhem in the war and evaded capture afterwards by standing in a cupboard for a fortnight in a house full of Germans until he was finally able to escape. He struck Smiley as 'the kind of man to whom difficulties and obstacles were a challenge rather than a deterrent'.[24]

There were good reasons why Deane-Drummond was keen to get involved. A month earlier he had heard that the SAS would soon be recalled to the UK where, because it was seen as good only for jungle warfare, it risked being disbanded in the hunt for defence budget cuts. He seized the chance to show his men could operate elsewhere. Smiley backed him up: 'There is a sporting chance that they might succeed in killing Talib.' On 13 November the Defence Committee sanctioned 'a special operation'. Taking advantage of rumours that the rebels had had enough, the British were by now talking secretly to their leaders, unknown to the sultan. If the talks had not achieved anything by 15 December, the SAS would go in. Once the rebel leaders were dead, the logic ran, the sultan would be in a better position to impose a settlement.[25]

The eighty men of D Squadron, 22 SAS, arrived in Oman on 18 November and split into two groups, of two troops each. One group began a reconnaissance of the southern flank of the Jebel a week later, moving by night and watching by day. One patrol lost a man almost immediately when, used to the jungle backdrop, he stood up against the skyline and was shot by a sniper. The other had more luck. Having identified an extensive cave complex on the top of the plateau, they called in airstrikes by RAF jets on 1 December, which killed a man who turned out to be a cousin of Talib.

The other group tried to exploit a breakthrough that one of Smiley's own officers had made earlier in the month, when he discovered that the ancient path cut by the Persians up the north side of the mountain was unguarded. It was only when the SAS took this path to the top that they realised why this was so. Between the peak that the path led to and the main plateau there was a rough and narrow mile-long ridge commanded at its far end by two conical peaks. These the men immediately dubbed 'Sabrina' after the model who had attracted significant publicity when she insured her chest 'against deflation' at Lloyds of London the previous year. The SAS scaled the peaks by rope, and fought a close-quarter battle in the darkness with the rebels, who shouted 'Come on Johnnie!' at them, before they withdrew back along the saddle to their base.[26]

After the initial death, the SAS sustained no further casualties, but they were fighting constantly and by mid-December it was obvious to them and other British officers on the ground that they needed reinforcement. Deane-Drummond, by then back in Malaya, heard about the strain his men were under and appealed to the War Office to allow a second SAS squadron to join the first. Since the first squadron had attracted no publicity whatsoever – the Foreign Office's only fear – on 19 December the Defence Committee waved through the request, on the condition that all the troops were out by April, when the Middle East was due to be discussed at the UN. Deane-Drummond reached Muscat on New Year's Day; A Squadron, SAS, joined him eleven days later. By then he had come up with a plan to assault the Jebel soon after the full moon on 24 January 1959.

What intelligence there was suggested that Talib was most concerned that the British might attack either by the Persian route up the mountain, or by the wadi that ran up from Tanuf, a village on the south side of the Jebel. Deane-Drummond aimed to nourish these suspicions with displays of military activity in both areas, while the real attack would be made up a rock buttress that rose out of Wadi Kamah, a valley further to the east and nearer to the villages on the plateau where Talib, his brother the imam and Suleiman bin Himyar were most likely to be staying. Once on the top, the SAS would be relieved by Smiley's forces and resupplied by airdrop, enabling them to press on with their objective of despatching Talib. To help convince Talib to reinforce his pickets at Sabrina and at the head of Wadi Tanuf, the British also gathered together the local donkey drovers and, swearing them to secrecy and on pain of death asked them about conditions for watering the animals in Wadi Tanuf, knowing that the query would soon reach Talib's ears.

After being delayed by bad weather, the assault began late on 26 January. It took the SAS nine and a half hours to reach the plateau, meeting almost no opposition along the way, although two men would die after a stray bullet exploded an Energa grenade attached to one trooper's rucksack. The tribesmen, meanwhile, mistook the airdrop as a parachute landing, and surrendered. The SAS advanced to the first village, Saiq, where tribesmen offered to show them where Suleiman bin Himyar had been staying. A fire was still burning in the cave when Smiley arrived. While there was no sign of the sheikh, nor of Talib or his brother, there were nearly 1,000 letters, which set out in detail the rebels' network across the sultanate.

Malcolm Dennison, Smiley's shrewd, MI6-trained intelligence officer, tracked the three outlaws to a house in the Sharqiyah, the hills immediately south of Muscat, about a fortnight later. But premature action by another of Smiley's colleagues, who fancied receiving the credit for capturing them, gave the game away, and all three escaped by dhow to Saudi Arabia.

The Jebel Akhdar operation avoided the publicity that had vexed earlier British operations and it bought the sultan a few more years. But, measured by the exacting standards that the SAS had set itself, it was, strictly speaking, a failure. The SAS did not succeed in killing either Suleiman or the imam, who were pictured in Alexandria later that year, shaking hands with Nasser. Although, following their escape, the rebellion lost impetus, the mine-laying campaign, directed by Talib from afar, continued unabated. The ultimate solution to the crisis would be political, as Lloyd had acknowledged when he considered Britain's options midway through 1957. It required the British to establish better relations with Saudis, which happened, and the sultan to grasp the advantages of development, which did not. As a consequence, the British were to play a leading role in his overthrow in 1970. It was the British, and not Arab, colonels who did for him in the end.

IRAQ AND KUWAIT

Assessing Britain's options in the Gulf in June 1957, the foreign secretary Selwyn Lloyd admitted that the country's dominant position in the sheikhdoms, and the security of her oil supplies from Kuwait, depended to a great extent on Iraq. As long as Iraq remained friendly, she would prefer to see the sheikhdoms of the Gulf come under British protection and not Saudi influence. 'Collapse in Iraq', he went on to imagine, 'would of course at once create an extremely dangerous situation.' When, a year later, Abdel-Karim Qasim ousted the Hashemites, the British government was forced to confront it.[1]

Iraq had always maintained what the British ambassador called 'a shadowy claim' to Kuwait. In the months before the July 1958 coup in Baghdad the Hashemites had put heavy pressure on their neighbour to join their ill-starred Arab Union, and after Abdel-Karim Qasim seized power, many Kuwaitis expected him to invade as soon as he had consolidated his position. But Qasim never managed to do so. He quickly fell out with his conspirator, Abdul Salam Arif, who wanted Iraq to join the United Arab Republic. That September, he ousted Arif, but he grew increasingly dependent on the Iraqi Communist Party.[2]

The British and the Americans reacted differently to this development. While the Americans, encouraged by Nasser, started to consider how they might remove Qasim, the British were more sanguine. Although they readily acknowledged that Qasim's was 'not ... a very savoury government', once they had decided that he posed no immediate danger to Kuwait and was not in Nasser's pocket, they were content to wait and see.[3]

The effect of these conflicting analyses of the situation would pit the British and the Americans against each other in Iraq for most of the next year. In the autumn of 1958 the British received intelligence of a plot to overthrow Qasim. Having told the Americans that they felt they should tip off the dictator, it seems they went ahead and did so. The Americans – who certainly knew about the plot and may actually have been encouraging it – were annoyed by Britain's course of action. Although the new British ambassador, Humphrey Trevelyan, would later claim that it would have been 'stupid of us to get mixed up in any local plots, whether by encouraging them or by warning Qasim about them', that was not a denial, and it appears that he went on to warn the Iraqi prime minister of another plot to kill him soon afterwards. Britain's strange determination to protect Qasim bemused the Americans. Ike's vice-president Richard Nixon hit the nail on the head when he wondered aloud whether the British 'considered Nasser a greater danger than the Communists to the Near East'. The short answer was they did.[4]

In early March 1959 a revolt did break out in Mosul. Half-heartedly supported by Nasser, it was supposed to be one of several simultaneous uprisings across the country which would have challenged Qasim severely, had the others ever happened. But they did not, and Kurdish forces loyal to the Iraqi dictator were able to subdue the rebellion in the restive northern city four days later, by which time as many as 3,000 people were dead. The revolt, and Iraq's subsequent signing of an economic agreement with Moscow and withdrawal from the Baghdad Pact all nourished fears about the direction the country was heading in.

In late June an Egyptian newspaper reported the discovery of another plot, this time implicating Qasim's own aide-de-camp. Although the Iraqis denied the story, Qasim was unable to conceal the signs of growing paranoia. He had started going out, late at night or early in the morning, to see things for himself. The Ministry of Defence became 'the only place he dared to live', according to Trevelyan, but a visitor to the building reported that, even there, Qasim's relations with his henchmen were obviously tense. Then, at a press conference early in July he lost his rag and shouted at a questioner. When, later the same day, at a reception for a militia which he had created but recently disarmed, the militia men asked for their weapons back, he retorted, 'I have not come here to listen to you, but to talk to you.'[5]

In July 1959 Qasim launched a crackdown on the communists, sanctioning a massacre in Kirkuk. The Americans were delighted at this turn of events, but the British were unnerved, believing that Qasim was isolating himself. Those concerns grew when, a few weeks later, Qasim suddenly ordered the executions of those convicted in the show trials that had been held after the fall of the *ancien régime*. Qasim had resisted pressure from the communists to carry out the death sentences ever since, and the issue had acquired something of a barometer-like status among western analysts and expats: the stay of executions had been a welcome sign of strength.

One of those hanged was a good friend of the British, the country's former interior minister, Said Qazzaz. Just two days earlier his wife had received a reassurance from Qasim that her husband would not be executed. Trevelyan, who described Qazzaz as 'a man of superb courage' because of how he had handled himself during his trial, was horrified: the executions caused him to advocate a complete change of policy towards Qasim. 'We should not now deliberately take action designed to help him remain in the saddle,' he wrote to London five days later. 'The situation is too uncertain for that, and he is far too uncertain a character for us to be sure that his retention of power will be a certain benefit to . . . ourselves.'[6]

While foreign diplomats were still struggling to interpret Qasim's abrupt change of heart, on 7 October 1959 a group of Baathists including a young activist named Saddam Hussein tried and failed to assassinate the Iraqi prime minister in the main street in Baghdad, firing eighty bullets at his car, three of which hit him in the arm and the shoulder. 'The Baathists had been criminally careless,' recalled Trevelyan. As a result of the circular firing squad that they had organised, 'A bullet from one side of the car had killed one of the gang on the other side. In his pocket-book was a note with the names of the conspirators.' And so, while Saddam got away, several of his accomplices were arrested and sentenced to death.[7]

This time, however, Qasim commuted the death sentences. Trevelyan suspected that the reason why was because some communists were also awaiting execution. With Moscow calling for clemency, Qasim could not be seen to be hanging Baathists but not communists. On the other hand, to hang both groups of condemned men might cause an irredeemable breach with the communists whose support – he now realised – he still needed. Qasim celebrated his discharge from hospital two months later by giving a six-hour speech in which he blamed the Baathists for the attempt on his life.

It had long been said that Qasim lived 'in a little pink cloud 3ft off the ground', and Trevelyan and his oriental counsellor, Sam Falle, had nursed doubts about his sanity since they first met him, mainly because he had strange eyes. 'We're off to see the Wizard, the wonderful Wizard of Oz!' the British ambassador would sing en route to meetings with him. But Qasim's behaviour after the attempt on his life grew still more disconcerting. He had the bloodstained shirt he had been wearing on that day displayed in a glass-fronted bookcase – 'next to the cuckoo clock', Trevelyan noted – in the room in the Ministry of Defence where he saw visitors. He talked about building a monument that encased his colander-like car inside a dome made out of bulletproof glass. 'I am above trends and inclinations,' he proclaimed – always a bad sign. Falle's conclusion at the end of 1959 was that the Iraqi dictator 'genuinely believes that he is divinely-protected'. The British were not alone in being alarmed by Qasim's increasingly unpredictable behaviour. So too was the Kuwaiti emir.[8]

* * *

While Kuwait's oil boom had made the emir one of the richest men in the world, ordinary Kuwaitis had to cope with its downsides. The mass of migrant workers that the oil industry demanded caused overcrowding, inflation and disease. Meanwhile the ruling family's unwillingness to share the proceeds of the boom, and its unconcealed fondness for 'Cadillacs and concubines', made it deeply unpopular. In a bid to defuse mounting political pressure, soon after Egypt and Syria joined to form the United Arab Republic, in February 1958 the emir revived a system of councillors which he had abandoned four years earlier. But he refused to allow direct elections, creating a 500-strong electorate instead.

Not surprisingly, the emir's nod in the direction of democracy was not enough. A British salesman who went to a cinema in Kuwait City the following month noted that the audience sat through a cowboy film impassively. But when the western was then followed by an Egyptian newsreel showing Nasser's latest exploits, 'the place became a pandemonium of cheering, shouting, etc.'. In February 1959 a meeting of the country's youth clubs, held to celebrate the first anniversary of the UAR, turned into a rally in support of the Egyptian leader and then got out of hand. 'We will make the Princes slaves, and the slaves Princes!' the young men chanted. 'Kuwait oil belongs to the Arabs and not to the Ruling Family!' After the police broke up the meeting, and the authorities banned four of the clubs, a British man who worked for the Kuwait Oil Company observed that the reaction had been 'pretty drastic'. He thought that the authorities might get away with such action once or twice more, but not indefinitely. There was 'bound to be an explosion sooner or later'.[9]

The possibility that Qasim might invade his country joined the emir's growing list of worries. In May 1959, he took the unprecedented step of inviting the British political resident to come to see him. At the meeting that followed, the emir expressed his hope that Britain and Kuwait might jointly work out how they would confront such a threat. No planning ever happened; it seems the ruler simply wanted reassurance that the British were behind him. But in London the War Office had been pondering the same possibility. In response to its request, the Joint Intelligence Committee predicted that the Iraqis could mobilise a force comprising two brigades and no more than seventy tanks. Crucially – because of the implications for British planning of the defence of Kuwait – the JIC also warned that, although the British government might expect 'no less than four days' warning' of the assembly of the force in the Basra area, there could be 'little or no warning of an actual invasion' because Basra was so close to Kuwait. This challenge created what Macmillan called 'the usual dilemma. Shall we go in now? If so, it is "aggression". Shall we wait? If so, we may be too late.'[10]

That choice presented itself abruptly once again midway through 1961. Following Kuwaiti pressure, on 19 June 1961 the British and Kuwaitis exchanged notes, cancelling the 1899 treaty and Kuwait's status as a British protectorate. Anticipating the possible Iraqi reaction, the notes agreed that Britain would provide military assistance if the emir requested it.

Qasim welcomed the end of British rule but, ominously, did not mention Kuwaiti independence. Then six days later in a speech he declared that Kuwait was an integral part of Iraq, and designated the emir its *qamaikam* – the local governor, subordinate to the governor of Basra province. In Baghdad, Trevelyan was now faced with a vital and very unenviable task: trying to work out whether Qasim would actually attack.

* * *

Britain's plan to defend Kuwait against an Iraqi invasion was codenamed Operation Vantage and was shaped by Kuwait's political constraints and Britain's limited military resources, since the Americans were only willing to be discreetly involved. The hostile political climate in Kuwait was such that the emir would not ask for British help before he absolutely had to. The demands on Britain's military meant that they could not keep forces on standby in the vicinity. Vantage therefore relied on the JIC's assessment that the British would have four days' warning of Iraqi intentions, and that the emir would react promptly enough that British forces could then be landed in sufficient numbers in time to deter the Iraqis from crossing the Kuwaiti border, which lay just 40 miles from Basra.

A few years earlier the British would have used high-altitude surveillance to corroborate the sources MI6 had inside the Iraqi army. But, since Khrushchev had threatened retaliation following the U-2 incident, the British government was reluctant to sanction photographic reconnaissance of Iraq, at least while Qasim's intentions were still unclear. A lot therefore depended on the human factor, and especially on Trevelyan.

Trevelyan would have been all too aware that the career of his predecessor in Baghdad, Wright, had never recovered from his failure to predict the bloody removal of the Hashemites. His own previous posting, to Egypt, had been cut short by the Suez crisis, and he must have wondered whether his time in Baghdad was about to be abbreviated too. To cover himself, the day after Qasim's speech he warned London that, while there was a chance that he and his staff might see Iraqi troops moving from the north of the country towards Basra, if the Iraqis deployed forces already based south of Baghdad, it was unlikely he would be able to give London any warning. Precisely for this reason, MI6 had once considered sending Wilfred Thesiger back to the marshlands of southern Iraq (where he had spent a chunk of the early 1950s) to win over the tribes by providing them with anti-malarial medicine, and turn them into scouts who could warn of any Iraqi troop movement southwards. But this idea was never followed up.

Clearly there was debate within the embassy about the likelihood of an attack. While the MI6 station took the view that Qasim's announcement was propaganda, because neither the air force nor the main tank force had been mobilised (although railway transport was available to take it south), the military attaché disagreed. He thought that the Iraqis' most likely move would be 'a quick dash from Basra', involving a much smaller force than the JIC predicted, which would enable them to retain an element of surprise.[11]

In a memoir Trevelyan later claimed that the military attaché then made a breakthrough at a drinks party. Sidling up to a senior Iraqi railway official, who had had too much to drink, he asked him, 'Why did you allow your rolling stock to be used for moving tanks?'

'Yes, I am very angry,' the unwitting official answered. 'They arranged it through my subordinates without telling me.'[12]

It is a funny anecdote, and it is quite possible that the conversation took place. But it seems likely that more definite information came from a different source. The declassified archives contain references in files dating from early 1962 to the fact that the military attaché had a good source, a staff officer, inside Iraq's first tank regiment. Besides recounting the party anecdote, Trevelyan also later admitted that 'we began to get reliable information that the first tank regiment was moving to Basra'. Early on 29 June, Trevelyan told London that he now believed Qasim was indeed planning to attack with a light force that could enter Kuwait by 1 July. Crucially, this was much faster than the JIC envisaged. Home reported this fact to the cabinet that morning. In a message to Washington, he admitted that the evidence was 'still somewhat tenuous but pointing unmistakeably at preparations by Qasim to reinforce his troops near Basra with a tank regiment'.[13]

Trevelyan's telegram caused a flap. The soonest that the British could land troops in Kuwait would be towards the end of 1 July, by which time the Iraqis might already be in Kuwait City. As the emir of Kuwait had still not asked for help, Home sent him the same information that day, in an attempt to chivvy him along. When there was still no answer from Kuwait he sent another message early on Friday 30th. By the time that the cabinet met midway through the morning, he had had a positive response. That afternoon, Macmillan decided to send in 500 Royal Marines Commandos by helicopter from HMS *Bulwark*.

By Monday morning, 3 July, the Iraqi attack had still not materialised. When Macmillan addressed the cabinet that morning he reminded his colleagues, a touch defensively, that when they had taken the decision to send in troops there were 'indications that the Iraqis could have moved'. As further justification for the move he added that it was believed that the Iraqis had been planning a coup on 12 July. The job was done, he said, but 'how we extricate ourselves is another matter'.[14]

Once it became clear that Qasim was not going to attack, Macmillan soon faced international pressure to withdraw the force he had sent in, not least from the Americans who believed that the British had walked into a trap set by Qasim to show that Kuwait was not really independent at all. They also wondered whether the intelligence London had shared with them had any basis.

Britain was by no means the only country alarmed by Qasim's increasing volatility, however, and help ultimately came from the Arab League, which quickly admitted Kuwait to its ranks, and then sent a force that allowed the British to disentangle themselves. Macmillan realised he had had a lucky escape. 'Our policy is a pretty short-run affair,' he admitted to the cabinet secretary, Sir Norman Brook, a few weeks later. 'What we are doing is to get the oil out of these territories for as long as the inhabitants remain fairly primitive ... We ought not to be looking at Kuwait as a long-term commitment.'[15]

It soon became clear that the threat to Kuwait was likely to recur. At the end of 1961 there were again reports that Qasim was planning to invade. Once again the British heard rumours at a party – this time that Iraqi paratroopers were being deployed south. Once again, the rumours came to nothing. The Turkish military attaché assured the British that Qasim's comments were a smokescreen, designed to divert people's attention away from the parlous state of Iraq, which had once been a net exporter of wheat, but following a bodged land reform and drought was now in the humiliating position of having to buy in both grain and rice.

By now Qasim was also fighting a Kurdish rebellion in the north of the country. A Kurd himself, such was his lack of trust in his own kinsmen that he removed Kurdish officers and NCOs from the forces fighting the insurgency, but not before there had been desertions to the rebel side.

Qasim accused the Iraq Petroleum Company of supporting the Kurdish insurgency to justify taking a harder line against it. After talks between his government and the company collapsed, in December 1961 Qasim issued Public Law 80, under which the Iraqi government clawed back rights over certain territory from the company, most importantly in the south of the country.

Qasim's aggressive move against the company furnished critics of American policy in Iraq with ammunition on the grounds that two American oil majors owned nearly a quarter of the IPC. By now John F. Kennedy was president and, while experts in the State Department argued that Qasim was best left alone, Kennedy's national security adviser, McGeorge Bundy, and his deputy, Robert Komer, took a different view. They convinced him to put pressure on the State Department to consider regime change.

The CIA had been working on this goal fitfully since 1960, the year that it set up the 'Iraqi Health Alteration Committee'. This disturbingly named outfit apparently came up with the idea of sending Qasim a handkerchief 'treated with some kind of material for the purpose of harassing that person who received it'. Certainly, Qasim did not receive it; what is not clear is whether it was ever sent.[16]

At the same time the CIA considered trying to help the regime's opponents inside Iraq and exiles who had left the country to oust Qasim. In February 1960 the former CIA officers Miles Copeland and James Eichelberger, who had by now set themselves up as consultants in Beirut, stuck their oar in. In a letter, possibly written to the CIA's head of station in Lebanon, they argued that 'nobody of any significance in Iraq thinks there is any chance whatever of stopping the Communists through the internal mobilisation of non-Communist elements'. Their sources said that the only real chance of removing Qasim would be through external intervention. As old allies of Nasser, they suggested that the Egyptian leader, and the Baathist exiles he was giving sanctuary to, were more likely to be successful. One of these was the 26-year-old Saddam Hussein.[17]

With much of his army tied up fighting the insurgency in the north of the country, Qasim was vulnerable. On 8 February 1963 Baathist officers launched a coup in Baghdad. Trevelyan recalled how the following day Iraqi television interrupted an episode of the cartoon *Felix the Cat* to show footage of Qasim, sitting in a chair in his office in the palace surrounded by rebel officers. William Lakeland – the man who some years earlier had made friends with Nasser – was now working at the US embassy in Baghdad. He also saw the footage. Years later he recalled how the rebels had turned Qasim's head 'so we could see where the bullet had gone through his temple, just so nobody would doubt the fact that he was dead'. This brief intermission was then followed by an English programme on gardening.[18]

'While it's still early, Iraqi revolution seems to have succeeded. It is almost certainly a net gain for our side,' Komer told President Kennedy in Washington, as the details of what had happened started to become clear. A leading Baathist would later claim that Lakeland was in touch with the conspirators, and it is widely believed that the CIA and Egyptian intelligence then supplied the new government with lists of the names of Iraqi communists. Certainly, Qasim's murder was followed by a purge in which several thousand people were murdered. Iraq's new interior minister was candid. 'We came to power on a CIA train' he admitted later.[19]

PANDORA'S BOX

Britain could only send troops at short notice to Kuwait because of her long-standing presence in the opposite corner of the Arabian peninsula, at Aden. There, between two fists of black volcanic rock, lay the best deep-water harbour in the region: it had been seized by the British in 1839. Though oven-hot and utterly unprepossessing, the port gained added strategic importance following the opening of the Suez Canal. It then profited enormously from the crises that beset Britain elsewhere in the Middle East during the 1950s. Having learned from the Iranian oil crisis, Anglo-Iranian decided to build a new refinery on the western promontory to process the crude oil it was drilling in Kuwait: in 1954 Queen Elizabeth II visited and laid the plant's foundation stone.

Aden's strategic location at the pinch-point between Arabia and the Horn of Africa made it the obvious new base for Britain's Middle East Command after the withdrawal from Suez in 1956. In the next three years, the number of British troops stationed in the colony quadrupled. Duty-free shopping sucked in passing tourists. By 1962, what had once been a village of 200 mud houses was now the second or third busiest port in the world, surveyed by a statue of Queen Victoria and a clock tower modelled on Big Ben. Aden was not simply key to Britain's Middle East strategy. In the words of Duncan Sandys that November, it was 'a vital stepping stone' on the way to Britain's far eastern base, at Singapore. The colony was now integral to Britain's self-portrayal as a global power. And, once the United States was embroiled in Vietnam, even the Americans were keen for the British to hang onto it.[1]

In the years following their seizure of the port the British tried to create a buffer zone by offering protection to the sultans who ruled the hinterland to the immediate north and, when they had accepted, grouping them into eastern and western protectorates. But try as they might, they could not insulate the port from Nasser's fiery rhetoric. Aden, and its new refinery in particular, relied on tens of thousands of migrant workers who came from the protectorates and Yemen further north. Poorly housed and denied any democratic rights, by 1956 the Yemeni immigrants had formed themselves into an effective trade union which Voice of the Arabs harangued with propaganda.

British officials on the spot initially played down the nationalist movement that was developing in tandem with the trade union, describing its leaders as 'moral perverts, people with a chip on their shoulders ... failures, misfits, etc.'. But such was its influence that by 1958 the British governor of Aden was arguing that the best way to maintain any British presence in the area would be to dilute the nationalists' power by merging the colony and the friendlier protectorates into a new state with which Britain could then sign a treaty preserving her base rights. In London, however, Macmillan initially vetoed this idea. Convinced that the inhabitants of this new country would only 'sell their freedom to Egypt' on independence, he was backed up by Lloyd, who believed that Aden was 'Nasser's next target'.[2]

* * *

In fact, Nasser's priority was Yemen, next door. Backward, and going backwards, the rugged highlands of the Yemen were like Oman's Jebel Akhdar, but on a national scale. Never successfully colonised, they had been ruled since the ninth century by an imam from the Zaidi, Shiite tribes concentrated in the north and east of the country. Although the Zaidis were a desperately poor, barely educated minority, the imam lorded it over the more prosperous Sunni, Shafii majority who lived in the towns further south by virtue of the fact that he was generally accepted by both sects as the successor of Muhammad and thus infallible. In the case of the current incumbent this involved an athletic leap of faith. For the sixty-fifth imam, Ahmad, was a corpulent, pop-eyed and sex-mad tyrant who had once 'summoned his household to observe and celebrate his achievement of an erection' following a successful course of hormone drugs. But, as Nasser appreciated, the view that defying the imam was akin to disobeying Allah himself was not universal. Proof of this came in the form of the three bullets lodged inside the Yemeni leader, an unwelcome souvenir of an attempt on his life in 1961 that left him in near-constant pain.[3]

By then Nasser had been trying to dispose of Ahmad for nearly four years. In 1958 he had met the imam's son Badr in Damascus and offered to help him overthrow his father. Badr, who was jockeying with his uncle, Hassan, to succeed to the imamate, agreed but could not carry out the coup. Ahmad, in the meantime, realised that he was vulnerable and joined the United Arab Republic in a bid to cosy up to Nasser; but when Syria seceded from the UAR in 1961, he could not resist attacking Nasser. 'Why do you pollute the atmosphere with abuse?' he asked the Egyptian leader, who responded by ending their union.[4]

Syria's secession was a huge blow to Nasser's prestige, and Nasser did not forget Ahmad's slight. He redoubled his efforts to destabilise Yemen during 1962. Again he called on Badr to remove his ailing father, but Badr refused, saying that the old man had become suspicious of, and was monitoring, his activities. A separate coup attempt in the spring, a strike and student demonstrations all failed to bring the imam down. When, against all expectations, Ahmad died peacefully in his bed on 19 September, his brother Hassan was in exile. And so Badr was elected the sixty-sixth imam at the age of thirty-five.

Badr knew of several plots to kill him but was reluctant to take action: his renowned love of cheap South African brandy did not endear him to the more devout among his subjects and he preferred not to make any extra enemies. A week after his election, on 26 September, one of his own bodyguards tried to shoot him. There was 'a click and a scuffle', recalled Badr, who owed his survival to the fact that the man's gun had jammed. Tipped off about a further plot by the Egyptian military attaché, he invited a seemingly trustworthy brigadier, Abdullah Sallal, to bring his forces into Sanaa to protect the royal palace. Sallal turned against him, however, and that night Badr found himself under attack from point-blank range. Initially he grabbed a machine gun and shot back, before thinking better of it and fleeing for the mountains. On the radio the next day he heard that a republic had been established and that he lay dead beneath the rubble of his palace. Other members of the *ancien régime* were not so lucky. Caught and shot without a trial, their bodies were 'left in the open to be eaten by stray dogs and birds', it emerged later.[5]

Although the coup had his fingerprints all over it, its timing was highly inconvenient for Nasser. At that moment he was trying to sideline his incompetent but popular rival, the head of Egypt's armed forces Abdel Hakim Amer. But Amer, realising what was about to happen, resigned before Nasser could shunt him and then vanished, six days before the coup took place in Yemen. Amid a general feeling that 'something must be done' to help the new regime in Sanaa, but disagreement as to precisely what, Nasser saw the coup as a test of his leadership. Reflexively he despatched an aircraft carrying a number of Yemeni exiles, gold, guns, a radio transmitter and a squadron of aircraft, protected by a company of commandos, to help the Yemenis. He also asked Moscow for Antonov transport aircraft which could operate in Yemen's primitive conditions, so that he could send more troops and supplies.

The Russians rapidly agreed to Nasser's request and on 1 October 1962 the Soviet Union followed Egypt in recognising the new Yemeni Arab Republic. Within a few days the first of many Egyptian reinforcements started arriving. 'I sent a company to Yemen and had to reinforce it with 70,000 soldiers,' Nasser would complain in 1967. He would eventually call Yemen his 'Vietnam'.[6]

* * *

In a White House caught up in the Cuban Missile Crisis and Vietnam, Yemen was never a priority. 'I don't even know where it is,' John F. Kennedy confessed, when he and Macmillan first discussed the country in November. But the news from Sanaa was nonetheless unwelcome in Washington, because the president was trying to mend fences with Nasser following a National Intelligence Estimate that described the outlook for 'conservative and western aligned regimes' in the Middle East as 'bleak'. After Syria's secession from the UAR, the administration tried to lure Nasser away from the Russians with the promise of aid. The hope, as Kennedy's envoy Chester Bowles put it, was that Nasser might now 'forsake the microphone for the bulldozer' – in other words, focus his energies on developing his own country.[7]

A familiar problem now presented itself to Kennedy's administration. While the Egyptian leader had thrown his weight behind the new republican regime in Sanaa, the royalists' de facto leader, Badr's uncle Hassan, had been to see the British, King Hussein of Jordan and King Saud, who all looked very likely to lend him their support. Although the Americans were minded to recognise the new government, their allies would probably not. 'If we come down on UK/Jordan/Saudi side, there goes our new relationship with Nasser,' commented the deputy national security adviser, Bob Komer; 'if we come down on other side, we open Pandora's box.' The Americans' greatest fear was that Saud and Hussein's willingness to support the royalists would only give ammunition to their many opponents at home.[8]

On Komer's advice the administration put off recognition in the hope that the problem might resolve itself. Perhaps Nasser and the republicans would gain ground fast enough that the Saudis would realise that resistance was futile, the deputy national security adviser suggested. 'Let's wait till it becomes clear to Saud and Hussein that they're losing, so they won't blame it on US recognition.'

King Saud's brother, Crown Prince Faisal, was in the United States at the time of the coup and he did not share Komer's analysis at all. Faisal was worried that, after Yemen, Nasser's next target would be Saudi Arabia. In a meeting with President Kennedy, he argued that the republicans would not survive without support from Cairo and Moscow. Openly casting doubts on Kennedy's claim that he could steer Nasser because of Egypt's dependence on US food aid, Faisal went on to confirm what the Americans suspected: his country would help the royalist leader Hassan. 'Not at all reassured' by his encounter with Kennedy, he left the United States a few days later. Before he did so, he had established one comforting fact from British diplomats at the United Nations in New York. Even if John F. Kennedy did not share his anxieties, on the other side of the Atlantic, Harold Macmillan did.[9]

* * *

Macmillan's perspective of the Yemeni coup was very different to Kennedy's, since it presented a direct threat to British interests. Successive imams of Yemen had laid claim to South Arabia and Aden, and Macmillan immediately appreciated that Nasser was likely to encourage the new regime in Sanaa to do the same. 'We are very much worried about the situation in the Yemen,' he told Queen Elizabeth. 'We have so far been able to maintain our position in the Gulf better than we had dared to hope ... But so much depends on Aden, and if we were to be driven out of Aden or faced with serious revolutionary troubles which might make the base useless, our whole authority over the Gulf would disappear.'[10]

The main reason why Macmillan was so anxious was because the coup had come when Britain's relationship with Aden was at a critical stage. Having once opposed turning the colony and the protectorates to its north into a Federation of South Arabia, the prime minister had recently changed his mind, having seen the role that Aden's military base had played during the 1961 Kuwait crisis. In the summer of 1962 the British government decided to pursue the merger and, by an uncanny coincidence, the Aden Legislative Council had voted in favour of the measure on the same day that the coup took place in Sanaa.

At first glance, the vote meant that the merger would go ahead, but the reality was far less certain. The Council had been set up by the British three years earlier to give the colony a semblance of democracy, and its composition meant that its approval was a foregone conclusion. The debate sparked rioting in Aden's streets – one man had died – and when after two and a half days' debate, the issue was put to a vote, only three of the ten Adeni representatives favoured the measure; the other seven had already walked out of the chamber. In other words it was the feeblest of endorsements.

With six months to go before the merger was due to take place, Macmillan and his colleagues realised that events in the Yemen might easily derail their plan. But they struggled to agree on what to do next. The prime minister himself was torn. Even though he complained that 'we should so often appear to be supporting out of date and despotic regimes and to be opposing the growth of modern and more democratic government', his instincts seem to have lain with the royalists even though he realised they were unlikely to succeed. In private he admitted that he was 'reminded of the Bonny Prince Charlie conflict in the Scotland of 1745; the Highlanders were more attractive, but one knew that the Lowlanders would win in the end'.[11]

When the cabinet discussed the question of recognition the foreign secretary Lord Home argued that there was little choice. Failure to recognise the new regime would antagonise Nasser, while its royalist opponents were so grotesque that active support for them would, as Macmillan was now forced to admit, be 'politically repugnant'. Following news of further setbacks for the royalists and Yemeni claims that they would not interfere in Aden, on 23 October (in the middle of the Cuban missile crisis) the cabinet agreed to recognise the new government in Sanaa 'in principle'. But tellingly, it did not set a date when it would do so.[12]

There was an important reason for that vagueness. A day earlier Macmillan had met the governor of Aden, Charles Johnston, and the cabinet's main advocates for and against recognition, Lord Home and Duncan Sandys, now secretary of state for the colonies. Although they all agreed that it was highly unlikely that the royalists could overthrow the new government, Johnston pleaded for more time. He wanted Hassan and Badr to be given one last chance to turn the tables so that he could show the Federation's sultans that Britain had done her best to help the royalists before the British government bowed to the inevitable and recognised the new regime. Macmillan commented in his diary: 'About a week seemed the time allowed.'[13]

A week also gave time for another scheme which Macmillan must have tacitly condoned. Soon after the coup his son-in-law, Julian Amery – now minister for aviation – had met King Hussein of Jordan at Claridges Hotel in London. 'Don't let your government recognise the Republicans,' Hussein had urged him. 'The Royalists are tough.' The two men agreed that another of Amery's old comrades from Special Operations Executive, Billy McLean, now the Conservative member of parliament for Inverness, should go on a mission to the country. His task would be to write an eyewitness report that showed how little of the country Sallal actually controlled, at a time when neither the Foreign Office nor MI6 could supply up-to-date information about what was going on. Hussein generously offered his CIA money to pick up McLean's tab.[14]

The 'epitome of cavalry dash and swagger', according to one friend, McLean had added a red cummerbund to his army uniform when he worked alongside Amery in Albania in the war; the two men had been friends ever since. Elected to parliament at the end of 1954, he saw his majority cut in the 1955 election and then started to believe that Scottish nationalists in his constituency were conspiring to kill him; a psychiatrist diagnosed paranoia brought on by excessive drinking. The result was that he only gave his maiden speech in March 1956, during the debate after the ousting of Glubb that went so disastrously for Eden and marked the moment when the then prime minister became determined to get rid of Nasser. McLean finished with an Arab proverb to warn the government against inaction: 'Well may you weep like a woman for what you could not defend as a man.' Eden apparently never spoke to him again.[15]

McLean blamed Nasser for Glubb's removal. During 1956 he and Amery used their friendship with Albania's exiled King Zog, who was close to King Farouq, to explore the possibility of restoring a member of Farouq's family to the throne in Egypt, by provoking a coup by disgruntled officers in the Egyptian army. Once MI6 had decided that killing Nasser would make him a martyr, it encouraged this project, and the two MPs had spent their summer shuttling between meetings with the Foreign Office and George Young of MI6, the Wafdists and exiled members of the Muslim Brotherhood in Geneva and the French Riviera, to where Zog had decamped. The Restoration Plot, as it became known, came to nothing; the fiasco that followed only made Amery and McLean all the more determined to get their revenge on Nasser.

There was a further reason why in autumn 1962 it was a good time for McLean to get away from London. In the small hours of 12 October, he was stopped by the police on suspicion of drink-driving. He had visited three clubs in St James's, he said. At the first, he had a vodka and tomato juice; at the second, a rum and lemon. Over dinner he had 'a glass, perhaps two glasses, of wine' and a glass of port. At the third, 'perhaps three or four glasses of port'. Then it was back to the first club, where he had two glasses of kummel. As he got into his car to drive home at 2.30 in the morning he recalled 'feeling well, but a bit tired'. At some red lights he was approached by the police, who told him that they had just watched him swerve to avoid some bollards and narrowly miss a car going in the opposite direction. When McLean denied this, they arrested him and charged him with being too drunk to drive. In the days before the breathalyser it would be the policemen's word against McLean's when the case eventually came to court the following January.[16]

Ten days after his arrest McLean found himself in the hotter and somewhat drier climes of Riyadh where he met King Saud, whose hands now shook as he spoke – a sign, the MP reckoned, of Parkinson's disease. The Saudis were reeling from the fact that the pilots of several plane-loads of weaponry that they had sent to the royalists had defected to the Egyptians. The Saudi air force was now grounded, and the king had called up a 20,000-strong tribal levy, the Jaysh al Abyad, because he no longer trusted his army. Sitting on a leopard skin-covered throne, Saud told McLean he was convinced that Egypt's intervention was the first phase of a much wider plot in which the Russians were also involved. Its aim was to disrupt Saudi Arabia, the Aden Protectorate and the Gulf sheikhdoms and later Jordan and Syria. The king was keen to restore diplomatic relations, which had been broken off following Suez. His message was that 'Saudi Arabia was on Britain's side'. It was the begin-ning of an important and, for British arms manufacturers, extremely lucrative, rapprochement.[17]

From Riyadh McLean flew on to Aden where the authorities put him on a plane to Beihan, the most northerly outpost in the Federation of South Arabia which lay on the frontier with Yemen. Crossing the border in a Land Rover he then drove north, following the ancient frankincense route along the western margins of the Rub al Khali through the once-great towns of Harib, Marib and Al Jawf to Najran in Saudi Arabia. 'During the whole of my journey', he later wrote, 'I do not remember seeing a single Yemeni over the age of ten who was not carrying a rifle and sporting a well filled bandolier of ammunition in which was stuck a great crooked dagger with a silver or brass handle.' Although he was unimpressed by the discipline or the training of the tribesmen, who greeted him by firing hundreds of rounds into the air, there was no question that their morale was excellent.[18]

After a further meeting with King Saud in Riyadh, McLean flew on to Amman to see King Hussein. From Jordan he returned home. The report he wrote up on his arrival back in London hammered home the argument desired by Amery: Sallal faced fierce resistance from the royalist-supporting tribes in a large part of the country. Since several journalists had by then published articles based on their visits to regime-held Sanaa, on 6 November McLean went public with his views. 'Apart from four Russian pilots shot down near Marib and captured Egyptian

soldiers, I was the first foreigner to have been with the forces supporting the imam in the mountains of the medieval Islamic kingdom of the
Yemen,' the opening of his article for the *Daily Telegraph* strikingly
began. The piece was widely read: that December McLean received a
card from Nasser, in which the Egyptian prime minister conveyed his
'best wishes for the New Year'.[19]

McLean's report and *Telegraph* article contained one blistering further detail that helped tip the argument against British recognition of
the new republican regime in Yemen. During his cross-country trek the
British MP had been introduced by the tribesmen to a captured Egyptian
parachutist. Confounding the official Yemeni claim that the new government would not interfere in Aden's politics, which was central to
the Foreign Office's argument for recognition, this prisoner-of-war
informed McLean that his unit had been told by Nasser that 'they were
being sent to the Yemen to fight the British'. In a cabinet meeting later
the same day, Home was noticeably more equivocal than he had previously been. Macmillan argued that there was a 'strong case' for delaying
recognition, at least until after a parliamentary debate on the merger
of the colony and the protectorate, due to take place in a week's time.[20]

* * *

While Macmillan procrastinated, the Americans tried to come up with
a compromise that might simultaneously please Nasser and the Saudis.
Once the Cuban Missile Crisis was over, Kennedy sent a message to
Crown Prince Faisal in Riyadh to tell him that he would publish a message restating American support for Saudi Arabia ahead of recognising
the new government in Sanaa.

Before Kennedy's message reached Riyadh, however, it was undone
by events on the ground in Yemen. While McLean was in the country the royalists had attacked republican positions in the north. On
2 November – the same day that Kennedy wrote to Faisal – Yemeni
republican and Egyptian forces retaliated. During this counter-offensive
Egyptian jets bombed Saudi territory.

The Americans bounced back from this setback. Correctly, they
appreciated that Nasser had thrown his forces into the Yemen because of
his struggle with Amer at home. Given that the Egyptian leader's future

depended entirely on the outcome of the conflict, they tried to offer him an escape route. In mid-November their ambassador to Riyadh suggested that the Saudis could stop helping the royalists in exchange for a commitment from Nasser to stop helping the Yemenis. When Crown Prince Faisal angrily rejected this one-sided proposal, slamming it and President Kennedy's letter on his desk in front of the American ambassador, the Kennedy administration decided to press ahead with recognition regardless. Bob Komer hoped that the move might jolt the Saudis to their senses, persuading them 'to abandon their futile war in Yemen, lest they end up being brought down themselves'. On 19 December the United States government recognised Yemen's republican regime, arguing that in doing so, it was trying to save King Saud and King Hussein from themselves.[21]

Across the Atlantic, McLean had just returned from another visit to Yemen. He and Amery met Macmillan in Downing Street on the same day that Washington recognised the Yemeni republic. During his visit, McLean had met Imam Badr and he now told the prime minister how amazed he had been both by the loyalty that Badr commanded despite his rackety reputation and the tribesmen's visceral hatred of the Egyptians, which was unlike anything he had witnessed in Albania. He argued that the situation in the country favoured the royalists and that 'the maximum possible support should now be given to the Imam'. McLean came armed with a map showing how the royalists had surrounded Sanaa, and a shopping list, which included 50,000 rifles, 10 million rounds of ammunition, radio sets, money, mines, Molotov cocktails and machine guns, and fifty experts who could train the tribesmen in their use. He also hand-delivered a letter addressed to the prime minister from the new imam. 'I am asking for your help, politically and militarily, and to make this help effective by any means you prefer, secretly or openly,' Badr's message read. Macmillan was convinced. 'It was one of the few turning points in history which I have witnessed,' Amery recalled later. His father-in-law delegated responsibility for the matter to him. Thereafter, whenever Yemen was on the cabinet's agenda, Amery was always present for the discussion.[22]

McLean's report was circulated around the cabinet in the first week of January 1963, a few days before its author was found not guilty of drink-driving. It provided the meat for a memorandum by the cabinet secretary that rehearsed, and then took apart, the Foreign Office's arguments for recognition of the new republican government in Sanaa. Although the dispute between the Foreign Office and the Colonial Office over the issue continued, the thorny question was never debated in cabinet again, and midway through February the Yemenis resolved the problem by severing diplomatic relations with London. Macmillan described the foreign secretary Lord Home as 'rather upset' at this development; the colonial secretary Duncan Sandys, on the other hand, was 'triumphant'. Privately, Macmillan reckoned it was 'the best thing in the short term'.[23]

President Kennedy continued to press Macmillan to recognise the Yemeni Republic. But provocative statements by Nasser and Sallal, an attack by Yemeni and Egyptian forces on British positions along the frontier of the Federation of South Arabia, and an inept airdrop by the Egyptians of weapons to arm dissidents inside Saudi Arabia soon convinced the British prime minister that he had made the right decision. He also thought that the Kennedy administration's willingness to trust Nasser was utterly naïve. 'The Kennedy administration consists of new men: very clever but very ignorant,' he told his colleagues, who agreed with him. 'For Nasser put Hitler and it all rings familiar,' Macmillan wrote in his diary on the same day that JFK held a meeting in Washington to try to find a new way to persuade the Saudis to disengage.[24]

Now that there were nearly 30,000 Egyptian troops in Yemen, and since the Egyptian airdrop of weapons in Saudi Arabia, the Kennedy administration was having second thoughts. 'What is ironical', Macmillan wrote, 'is that the Americans, who accepted the threat to Aden and the Federation with some equanimity (only an old colony!) are now tremendously excited and alarmed about Nasser going for Saudi Arabia and all the vast American oil interests involved.' While Washington was still keen to discourage the Saudis and the Jordanians from becoming embroiled in the war, the administration was equally quite happy for the British to take action.[25]

Macmillan feared that there was little more than they were already doing to help the royalists. But others were more optimistic. McLean and his allies shared the American analysis that Nasser was trapped in the Yemen. But far from trying 'to save Nasser from the consequences of his adventure', as they believed the Americans wished to do, these British diehards now intended to exploit his predicament, in an attempt to destroy him.[26]

SECRET WAR

After dinner one evening late in April 1963, the telephone rang at Jim
Johnson's Chelsea home. Johnson was now an insurance underwriter
at Lloyds. Brian Franks, the man on the other end of the line, was
a friend from a former life. Until the previous December Johnson
had commanded 21 SAS – the territorial regiment. Franks, a near-
legendary figure who had led the second of the two SAS regiments
in the war, was now the corps' colonel commandant. 'May I come
round and have a glass of brandy?' Franks asked. 'Of course,' Johnson
replied, intrigued.[1]

When Franks turned up a little later he explained that he had come
directly from a meeting at his club with the foreign secretary Lord
Home, Julian Amery, Billy McLean and the SAS's founder David
Stirling. McLean and Stirling were both just back from separate missions
to southern Arabia, where, on the surface, the news seemed bleak.

To gain the upper hand ahead of another American-led peace initiative, that spring Nasser had deployed more troops to Yemen and
attacked. During the 'Ramadan Offensive', Egyptian forces captured
the eastern towns of Marib, Harib and Al Jawf from the royalists – the
very towns that McLean had driven through the previous October.
Following some shuttle diplomacy between Cairo and Riyadh an
American mediator named Ellsworth Bunker had just announced that
he had secured a deal between the Egyptians and the Saudis, whereby
the Egyptians would begin a phased withdrawal while the Saudis
ended their support for the royalists. A 40km-wide demilitarised
zone along the Saudi/Yemeni border would be watched by the UN

and President Kennedy had reluctantly agreed to send a squadron of fighter jets to Saudi Arabia to deter the Egyptians from mounting further bombing raids on the Saudi side of the border. Following the Cuban missile crisis, the deployment made the president nervous. 'If we are going in there shooting down Egyptian bombers,' he reportedly said, 'I want to hear about it before we shoot.' To the Saudis' irritation, Nasser had announced that he was withdrawing his forces, presenting the move as a triumph.[2]

Franks, however, had just heard a different story from McLean, who had got back to London on 18 April. He urged Johnson not to believe anything he might have read in the papers. 'Don't believe the Americans about the Yemen. They don't understand the Middle East,' the maverick MP said. 'The resistance under the Imam is terrific.'[3]

McLean had reported that while King Hussein had largely abandoned the royalists following intense American pressure, the Saudi Crown Prince Faisal had no plan to follow suit, though he was frustrated by British inactivity so far. Inside Yemen itself the royalists' situation was much the same. But, under daily attack from Egyptian and Russian bombers and desperately short of arms and ammunition, they feared that they would have to withdraw from the Khawlan, the massif immediately east of Sanaa, from which they controlled the road to Marib, which the Egyptians were having to resupply by air. If the royalists abandoned the high ground, the Egyptians would be able to take over the road. Not only would they then be able to supply Marib far more easily, they would also consolidate their grip over the east of the country, disrupting the royalists' supply lines which for the time being were still open. McLean had been into the Khawlan by camel, passing within 5 miles of Marib. He had seen the situation for himself.

If the Khawlan was key to victory, the key to the Khawlan appeared to be the airstrip from which the Egyptian and Russian air attacks were being launched. It was this Franks had come to see Johnson about. 'Would you like to go in and burn all these aeroplanes?' he asked.[4]

'Well, yes,' replied Johnson. 'I've got nothing particular to do in the next few days. I might have a go.'

* * *

The Special Air Service had been set up by David Stirling twenty-two years earlier to conduct operations of precisely the type that Franks and Johnson envisaged. A year before Willkie's appearance in Cairo ahead of the decisive El Alamein battle, at a time when the North African desert war was still see-sawing back and forth along the Mediterranean coast, Stirling had created a force to raid the Axis airfields far behind enemy lines.

The purpose of Stirling's visit to the Middle East had been to see whether the same trick could be repeated in Yemen. Leaving London on 12 April he had flown to Aden, avoiding customs by leaving the air-field through a hole in the perimeter fence. Habit, rather than necessity, explained the manner of his exit, for his host was none other than the governor of Aden, Charles Johnston, with whom he had shared a riotous flat in wartime Cairo.

Johnston welcomed Stirling to Government House then, plead-ing tiredness, retired early to bed. His disappearance was probably diplomatic because it gave Stirling the opportunity to ask Johnston's aide-de-camp, Tony Boyle, if he could help with a deniable operation sanctioned at the top levels of the British government. Initially it would involve spiriting former members of his old regiment through Aden airport and onward into Yemen without documentation. Boyle read-ily agreed.

From Aden Stirling flew onto Bahrain where he met an old comrade from the war in the desert, Johnny Cooper. In 1943 the two men had been captured by the Germans, but while Stirling then spent the remain-der of the war in captivity, Cooper had managed to escape. 'We used to specialize in German airplanes on the ground. Get back behind their lines, get onto an airfield at night – do in a sentry, you know . . . and then attach pencil bombs to as many planes as we could get to,' he told an American journalist, euphoric after surviving a four-day trek across the desert to the Allied front line. The SAS had accounted for hundreds of enemy planes, he continued, 'before Jerry got onto that airport dodge'. Cooper had led one of the two squadrons on the Jebel Akhdar and, after being forced to retire from the SAS on grounds of age, joined the sultan's army in Oman. Cooper had been Stirling's youngest recruit. Now in his forties he signed up straight away to his old commanding officer's plan. In early June he arrived in London to meet Jim Johnson who, with the connivance of 22 SAS's colonel, had managed to recruit several other volunteers.[5]

Cooper did not spend long in London. On 5 June, after months of speculation, the sex scandal that was to destroy Macmillan's government erupted when the minister of war John Profumo issued a statement admitting that he had been lying when he claimed that there had been 'no impropriety whatsoever' in his 'acquaintanceship' with a call girl, Christine Keeler, and resigned his ministerial job and parliamentary seat. The news prompted a telephone call to Stirling from Duncan Sandys telling him to call the operation off. Sandys had been widely, though wrongly, rumoured to be the 'headless man' captured on Polaroid receiving a blow-job from the Duchess of Argyll: he did not want to be the cause of further trouble for Macmillan, who now looked as if he had either been colluding with Profumo, or was dreadfully naïve.[6]

Stirling passed the order on to Johnson, who decided to ignore it. He booked Cooper and the other volunteers onto overnight flights to Aden. Cooper's itinerary took him via Tripoli, where he had a narrow escape. Checking in for the connecting flight in the Libyan airport, one of his suitcases burst open, spilling rolls of plastic explosive wrapped up in paper. As security guards helped him cram the packages back into his case, Cooper explained away the telltale smell by claiming that he was a travelling marzipan salesman. On arrival in Aden a local man beckoned him and his colleagues from the plane, and ushered them into an old Dakota which took them to Beihan and the frontier. Riding camels by night and lying up by day they took the same route as McLean had done two months earlier to pass west of Egyptian-held Marib, to reach the camp of Abdullah bin Hassan in the Khawlan.

The son of Badr's erstwhile rival for the imamate, Abdullah bin Hassan was one of the few royalist leaders who had impressed McLean during his three visits to Yemen. A short, handsome and toothy-grinned youth wearing a white turban, and with a curved dagger thrust down the front of his belt, Abdullah had been educated at the American University in Beirut and had worked in Yemen's delegation at the UN. Not only was he clearly intelligent, he was also unquestionably brave. When the bombers came overhead, McLean noted approvingly, 'He made no move to take cover and showed no sign of fear.' Since Abdullah had accounted for about 500 Egyptian deaths in the first two months of the war, but was desperately short of arms, ammunition and money to pay his followers, McLean was careful to ensure he received some of the weaponry that the British had sent into Yemen that spring.[7]

Cooper must have reached Abdullah's camp by about 10 June. He soon realised that the sabotage expedition was a 'pipe-dream' because, as he told Stirling, 'a full-blown war is now in the making' in the area he would have had to cross to reach the airstrip. Instead he devoted the time to giving the tribesmen some basic training in the art of fire and manoeuvre, and how to use the Bren machine guns they had now received. The Khawlanis were 'pleasant, hospitable, polite, cheerful, in some ways childlike' people who 'like[d] guns and knives', recalled another of the mercenaries. Like Abdullah they all wore daggers in their belts, which they called 'sallal abyad' or 'white power' because of their steel blades, which they drew for the final stage of an attack. Another British visitor saw a man who had tucked an ivory handled table knife, a pair of scissors and a fountain pen into his belt next to the ever-present dagger. Given literacy rates in the country it is likely that the pen, unlike the sword, was just for show.[8]

To lure the Egyptians into the Khawlan, Cooper instructed the tribesmen to mine the main road in the valley opposite a wadi that climbed up into the massif before forking into two ravines. At the fork he discreetly marked out an ambush site above which he placed three parties of gunmen. 'At about 0900 hours the Egyptians moved into the wadi in great strength, with a parachute battalion up front and a force of T-34 tanks and light artillery bringing up the rear,' he later recalled. The tanks and the artillery stopped about halfway up the wadi, but the foot soldiers continued. 'As the enemy reached our markers, our men opened up with devastating effect, knocking down the closely-packed infantry like ninepins. Panic broke out in the ranks behind, and then their tanks opened fire, but their shells were exploding not on our positions, but among their own men. The light artillery also joined in, and most of the casualties they took during the ten-minute firefight were from their own guns.' Cooper counted eighty-five Egyptian corpses after the exchange. It was the first of many bloody encounters Cooper arranged before he returned to London that autumn to brief Stirling and Johnson on the situation.[9]

A few days after Cooper arrived in Yemen from the south, another man entered the country from the north. David Smiley bore accreditation organised by Julian Amery stating that he was the *Daily Telegraph*'s correspondent, but his only previous journalistic experience was as an inspector for the *Good Food Guide* in Scotland, the job he had taken on his retirement from the sultan of Oman's army. In May 1963 he received a call from an old friend. 'David?' enquired Billy McLean. 'How would you like to come with me to the Yemen?' Scotland in the 1960s was not known for its cuisine, and Smiley did not need asking twice. 'I ate more bad meals than good,' he recalled later, 'and thought it a pity that a country producing some of the best meat and fish in the world should cook it so atrociously.' It was to be useful training for Yemen, however, where he survived on tinned pineapple.[10]

Smiley's brief was to report to his former enemy, the Saudis, on what was happening in northern Yemen. The purpose of this report was two-fold: it was to show where the royalists could improve their tactics, and to provide evidence that Nasser was rotating rather than withdrawing his forces, which the Saudis could then put in front of the American ambassador. There was another reason why Smiley was ideal for this job. The UN secretary general, U Thant, had just announced that the United Nations Yemen Observation Mission, which was supposed to monitor the agreement brokered by Bunker, would be led by a Swedish general, Carl von Horn. Von Horn was a good friend of Smiley, and Smiley intended to use that friendship to put pressure on the UN to acknowledge that the Egyptians were not respecting the deal.

McLean and Smiley left London on the same day that von Horn arrived in Sanaa. In Jeddah, in his hotel lobby, Smiley saw a face that looked familiar. It was the imam of Oman's brother, Talib, one of the three men Smiley had spent several months of 1959 trying to kill. McLean warned Smiley away from introducing himself, but soon afterwards he was recalled to London to vote in a debate called by the Labour opposition on the Profumo affair. As a result Smiley entered Yemen a few days later on his own. A few days earlier Russian bombers operating from Aswan had hit the Saudi border town of Jizan. Now, as Smiley crossed the border, it was obvious that he was entering a war zone. 'At intervals a shell would land 50 or 100 yards away, to spur us on; from the northwest came the sound of rifle and machine-gun fire and the thud of bombs, and the sky was bright with parachute flares and the flash of bursting high explosive.'[11]

Having met the imam at the cave that doubled as his headquarters in Qara and completed a further tour of royalist positions south in the mountains which form the spine of the country, Smiley returned to Qara again. In June the Egyptian bombers had started using gas bombs, and the imam suggested that Smiley, on his way out of the country to report to the Saudis, might detour via a nearby village, Al Kawma, which had been hit, in order to investigate. Smiley photographed the sores and blisters of children and animals who had been exposed to the gas, and extracted some of the bomb casing from a crater. 'There was a pronounced smell of geranium, and suddenly I felt queer and almost fainted,' Smiley wrote later. 'There seemed little doubt that these were gas bombs.'[12]

The question was, what kind of gas? Smiley hurried to Jeddah with the bomb casing he had collected, some of which he gave to John Christie, the head of the new MI6 station in the city. He also wanted to present a sample to von Horn, but the Swedish officer was under instructions from the United Nations not to have any contact with him, so Smiley had to give it to one of his subordinates.

In the meantime, a real *Daily Telegraph* journalist, Dick Beeston, who was also in Yemen at the time, had received a tip-off that he too should visit al Kawma. His article was published on 8 July. In it he reported that the village sheikh had told him that the bomb had exploded letting off a cloud of brown smoke which had a 'dirty smell'. Soon afterwards his villagers started coughing up blood; seven of them, in all, had died. As Egypt depended on the Eastern Bloc for all its military supplies, Beeston speculated that the bomb was made in Czechoslovakia or Russia. The British government raised the issue with the United Nations the next day.[13]

The British allegation that Egypt was using chemical weapons in Yemen corroborated a similar claim made privately by the Israelis in April and three days after Beeston's article was published, the American ambassador in Cairo tackled Nasser. Nasser initially dismissed the *Telegraph* as biased and claimed that the bomb in question had not contained poison gas but napalm – an answer he may have hoped would discourage the Americans from pursuing the matter since they too were using napalm, in Vietnam. Given the eyewitness reports of the incident, however, the ambassador persisted, saying that the report he had received suggested that the bomb might have contained anything 'from phosphorous to mustard gas'. Nasser then conceded that 'a bomb' was being used but that 'he did not know the precise chemical content'. It must, he added, be 'relatively simple' since Egypt's expertise in this area was limited. The ambassador urged him never to use it again – advice that Nasser, as usual, ignored.[14]

Smiley returned to Britain thinking that he had found an issue that could be used against Nasser when the UN general assembly convened that October. But the British government was oddly unwilling to pursue the matter. Its own chemical and biological warfare laboratory at Porton Down analysed the casing which Smiley had given to MI6. While it found traces of tear gas, it concluded that the bomb was 'unlikely' to have contained a poison gas, which sits oddly with the eyewitness reports and what the CIA knew about the Egyptian chemical weapons programme. Since UNYOM's mandate did not permit it to visit royalist positions and its investigations in the rest of the country were being obstructed by the Egyptians, its own investigation was inconclusive. Von Horn realised he was wasting his time and resigned in September. At the UN, British and American diplomats were both quite happy to bury the matter because they thought that pursuing the issue would undermine their parallel effort to get Nasser to disengage.

* * *

Following Smiley's report and criticisms of the royalists' operation, that autumn the British reorganised themselves. At a meeting in Aden in September Stirling and Tony Boyle finalised a new set-up in which Cooper, who was about to return to Yemen, would command the 'British Field Liaison Force'. In this capacity Cooper would rejoin the young royalist Abdullah bin Hassan in the Khawlan, while his colleagues spread themselves across the country. Together they would attempt to coordinate the royalists' activities through better radio communication. They had ambitious ideas for airdrops of weapons into the country. In the meantime requests for supplies would be channelled through Tony Boyle in Aden. 'Everyone is freebooting,' observed an MI6 officer to his chief.

'Even the ADC to the governor-general in Aden.' But MI6 officers' doubts about the wisdom of the operation had little purchase, however, when the clandestine British effort was supported by the new prime minister.[15]

On 19 October 1963 Alec Douglas-Home succeeded Harold Macmillan as prime minister. Macmillan had been forced to resign because of bad health, his reputation ruined by the Profumo affair. Douglas-Home, whom Macmillan well described as 'steel painted as wood', had earlier advocated recognising Sanaa's republican government, but was now alarmed at the way the Soviets had taken advantage of decolonisation in Africa. Seeing the Yemen operation as a way to fight the pressures that would ultimately force Britain's withdrawal from Aden, he was willing to trade on his straight reputation to protect it. 'We are giving them nothing,' he lied when Kennedy directly asked him if Britain was supporting the royalists in Yemen.[16]

Wrong though it was, that was the answer Kennedy wanted, because he was hoping to get Nasser to honour his side of the disengagement agreement – something the Egyptian leader had so far conspicuously failed to do. The day after Douglas-Home became prime minister, Kennedy sent Nasser a pointed message accusing him of failing to keep his side of the deal brokered by Bunker. 'We are confident that the United Kingdom Government and the Saudi Arabian Government are honoring their assurances to us that they are not aiding the Royalists,' Kennedy continued, unwisely taking Douglas-Home at his word.[17]

Nasser resisted the pressure, and within the month Kennedy realised that he had been duped by Douglas-Home. One version of the story says that the president called up the prime minister directly over the scrambled line that connected the White House to Downing Street, and effectively accused him of lying by saying that the CIA knew the British were officially supporting the royalists. Douglas-Home replied that he would make enquiries and promised to get back to the president two days later, on 22 November. The conversation never happened because it was on the 22nd that Kennedy was assassinated in Dallas. What seems more likely is that the insinuation was made diplomatically. On 22 November the British ambassador in Washington reported that Kennedy felt that his prestige was at stake over Yemen – since his policy of supplying aid to Nasser was now being fiercely attacked in Congress – and that the sharif of Beihan (through whose territory all

British support was being funnelled) needed to be restrained. Soon after Lyndon Johnson succeeded Kennedy as president, the secretary of state, Dean Rusk, returned to the charge. On 3 December he told the ambassador in London that it would be most helpful if the British could 'clear the air' by 'making a more vigorous effort to circumscribe the freewheeling activities of the Sharif of Beihan'. Rusk told the ambassador, for his own personal information, that 'we remain unconvinced the Aden authorities are doing their utmost in this regard'.[18]

Douglas-Home took no notice because, so far as he was concerned, protecting Aden mattered more. Eleven days after Kenya attained her independence on 12 December, Nasser spoke in Port Said. 'We cannot accept ... that Britain continues to colonize a part of the Arab nation ... when she has abandoned her other colonies,' he declared, adding that he would do his utmost to drive the British out of Aden. In the Khawlan, Johnny Cooper responded three days later with a mortar attack on an Egyptian encampment guarding the road between Sanaa and Marib. 'The panic was fantastic,' he reported, of a bombardment in which another seventeen Egyptians were killed. By March the following year McLean reckoned that about 8,000 Egyptian soldiers had been killed. He calculated that the war was costing Nasser about $500,000 every day.[19]

* * *

By now the Israelis were doing what they could to increase the Egyptian casualty rate. Since 1956, when Eden would not deal with the Israelis directly, relations between Israel and Britain had improved considerably. The thaw was undoubtedly helped by Britain's surreptitious sale of heavy water to the Israelis in 1958 – an ingredient that would help them build a nuclear bomb and which in turn led the United States to supply conventional weapons to Tel Aviv in an attempt to ensure they did not use it. When McLean raised the possibility of working with Tel Aviv during 1963, he was put in touch with Dan Hiram, the Israeli military attaché in London. That autumn Smiley flew out to Israel to discuss the possibility that the Israelis might help drop in supplies to the royalists. The Israelis had converted a Boeing Stratocruiser for just this type of job, and willingly agreed.

In the Khawlan Cooper found a flat piece of ground that would serve as a drop zone and communicated its location to London via Aden. He remembered the arrival of the first consignment in the spring of 1964 vividly. 'The Israelis had muffled the engines and it was very quiet ... the huge aircraft came in for the actual drop and as it passed 60 parachutes spewed out of the back. It really was excellent dropping, real professional stuff.' Abdullah bin Hassan was delighted; Cooper, deeply impressed: 'The source of these weapons was brilliantly concealed,' he later wrote. 'Every serial number had been scored out, the parachutes were of Italian origin and even the wood shavings used in the packing had been imported from Cyprus. Even the most expert intelligence analyst would have had a job to unravel that one.'[20]

The Israelis' efforts to conceal their involvement were successful, those of the British less so. The Conservative government's deepening unpopularity, and the internal disagreement over how deeply Britain should be involved in Yemen, both encouraged a leak. On 18 February 1964 a Labour MP asked Douglas-Home if he was aware of the existence of copies of receipts for the export of 20,000 Lee Enfield rifles to Yemen during 1963. 'I know quite well that no rifles have been exported to the Yemen,' Douglas-Home replied, not quite answering the question. A few days later the director of the British company involved, Robert Turp, said he had subcontracted a Saudi order to a Belgian firm which had then purchased weapons that the Belgian government had earlier bought from the British. In line with export licensing requirements the shipment was made after the Saudis stated that the weapons would not be re-exported. 'The rifles were not destined for the Yemen, and to the best of our knowledge they are still in use by the Saudi Arabian forces,' claimed Turp of this deliberately byzantine arrangement.[21]

Journalists covering the conflict could see that the tribesmen were often equipped with British rifles and they were well aware of the British presence in Yemen even if they were bound not to report it. In March the US secretary of state Dean Rusk summoned the British ambassador to register his concern at new reports that British mercenaries were present in the royalists' camps. The ambassador claimed that his government was trying 'to discourage this private enterprise, which was a very amateur operation, because they realised that infiltration from the Federation led to retaliation'. Knowing that this was nonsense, when he reported the exchange to London he asked that 'vigorous action' now be taken to stop British involvement in the war 'in order to avoid feeding American suspicions of our motives'.[22]

The Egyptians were also well aware that the British were supplying the royalists. On 13 March Egyptian jets bombed two encampments inside the Federation of South Arabia, killing camels and burning down tents. The incident left the British government in an awkward position. To retaliate would certainly land it in hot water at the UN, but to do nothing would cause outrage in the Federation, where the British High Commissioner (as the governor was now known since the merger of Aden and the Federation) warned that a failure to protect the Beihani tribes might lead them to defect to the Yemeni side.

In the first instance Rab Butler followed his officials' advice and decided only to protest to Sanaa. But 'anger and dismay' from Aden at this feeble response led him and his colleagues to decide that further overflights had to be answered with violence. This policy was then put to the test when the High Commissioner reported on 27 March that an Egyptian helicopter had machine-gunned a military outpost in Beihan. The 27th was Good Friday and the news reached London 'about tea time' – which seems to have meant that the officials who had argued for moderation were not present when Douglas-Home, Butler, Sandys and the minister of defence Peter Thorneycroft agreed to retaliate during a phone call that evening. Harib fort, then occupied by the Egyptians, was picked as a target. Ten people died and several more were injured when British aircraft bombed it the following day.[23]

In sanctioning the reprisal, Douglas-Home and his colleagues accepted that they would face censure at the UN. But they calculated that the Americans would have to back them, because, as Sandys put it, sooner or later Washington would face a similar dilemma either in Cuba or Vietnam and would need London's support.

Sandys's intuition was correct. When the Arabs tabled a resolution attacking the British at the UN a few days later, the American permanent representative at the UN, then Adlai Stevenson, called Rusk and told him that if the United States failed to support a resolution condemning Britain's action, 'no one would respect the US moral position any longer'. But Rusk disagreed. As Sandys had guessed he would, he said that if the United States voted against the British, 'it would undermine reasonable and moderate elements in London and make it difficult to get British help on other matters.'[24]

Kennedy's successor as president, Lyndon Johnson, felt the same way. Having decided to escalate American involvement in Vietnam, he was pleased to have the British share some of the international opprobrium he might otherwise have faced alone. A few days earlier he had reassured Douglas-Home that he would support Britain's ongoing presence in Aden, which the Americans realised was key to the security of the Gulf. He agreed with Rusk that the vote also offered an opportunity to signal to Nasser that American patience with him was now wearing very thin. And so, when the resolution was put to the vote in New York, Stevenson, on instructions from Washington, abstained. But Johnson warned Douglas-Home afterwards that, 'On the merits, in a future case, it would be hard for me to make the same decision again.'[25]

The furore over the bombing of Harib reinvigorated Douglas-Home's appetite for clandestine methods. Wondering whether 'we have exhausted all the possibilities open to us as regards attributable and unattributable action', he ordered a review of British policy in Yemen. Butler, alarmed by the rough ride his diplomats had had in New York, wanted to limit support to the frontier tribesmen; Sandys by contrast produced a long list of actions to escalate the war, which included the sabotage of Egyptian military facilities and the assassination of Egyptian intelligence officers in Yemen. Neither of these measures was approved, but, in line with Douglas-Home's desire to 'make life intolerable' for Nasser, the government redoubled its efforts to help the royalists during the summer of 1964.[26]

At the end of April Butler went to Washington to see Rusk. Having told him openly that the British government was not willing to let Yemen get away with what it was doing, and that it would support the royalists covertly through Saudi Arabia, he then asked the secretary of state to help them force Nasser to quit Yemen, a step Rusk refused to take. At the National Security Council, Bob Komer argued that British efforts to prise Nasser out of Yemen had only made him more determined to hold on. 'Butler says they'd stay covert', he reported, 'but this is impossible in the Middle East (we know). The whole affair will soon leak as Cairo trades legitimate charges of subversion with London.'[27]

And so it proved. In early May Nasser told the American ambassador to Cairo that he had 'completely reliable and convincing evidence' that the British were supplying arms, money and advice to the royalists across the Federation border. That evidence came in the form of several intercepted letters which were then published the same month in the Egyptian newspaper *Al Ahram*. The British press initially believed that the Egyptian report was propaganda and it was only after the *Sunday Times* Insight team had investigated more thoroughly that it became clear this was not the case. On 5 July 1964 the paper printed copies of five letters the Egyptians had acquired, including one to Cooper from his bank, two from Tony Boyle that mentioned parachutes and drop zones and another offering its recipient 'Abdullah' (Cooper's *nom de guerre*) 'congrats on the mineing [*sic*]'. The subsequent military career of its author, Peter de la Billière, might not have been so golden had his signature been legible.[28]

So ended Britain's secret war in Yemen. Exposed in the press, and then orphaned in Whitehall when the Labour Party won that October's general election, the mercenaries would fight on until 1967, by which time they had helped cost Nasser about 20,000 men. But their cover had been blown, and with it went much of their usefulness. Now that it was clear who was orchestrating opposition to the Egyptians in Yemen, Nasser was able to confront the threat. In April 1964 on a surprise visit to Sanaa he vowed publicly to 'return aggression by force', and expel Britain from the Arabian peninsula. Although it was to be a pyrrhic victory, the next three years would see him do just that.[29]

FALLING OUT

On Christmas Day 1964, Inspector Fadhli Khalil of the Aden police paid a visit to the qat market in Crater, a district of the port. Qat played an extraordinary part in the South Arabian economy. Like the Yemenis next door, many Adeni men chewed the mildly narcotic green leaf from after lunch until the early evening; the trade was worth something like £2.5 million a year, at a time when the government of Aden's annual budget was only twice as much. That helped explain why qat, which had once been banned, had recently been unbanned so that it could be subjected to a swingeing tax instead. The ban and the tax meant that its dealers were well acquainted with the criminal networks now also being used by terrorists to smuggle weaponry into the port. And that was what brought Khalil to the market.[1]

What terrorism the authorities had seen so far in Aden had been notable for its incompetence. One rebel had blown his own feet off when he pulled the pin from his grenade, only to hurl it, and not the bomb, at his target. But the campaign had now taken a much uglier turn. Only the day before there had been a grenade attack on a children's Christmas party on the Khormaksar airbase: the sixteen-year-old daughter of the Middle East Command's chief medical officer was killed. Little did Fadhli Khalil know that he was about to become the terrorists' next victim. Before he had even got out of his car to go into the market, another car slowed down alongside him. There was a burst of machine-gun fire, and a smoke grenade went off. The unknown assailants screeched away, and Inspector Khalil was dead.[2]

* * *

Ten months had passed since Nasser had declared his intention to drive the British out of Aden, but the professionalism of the violence that was now punctuating daily life in the port suggested that he had been planning his campaign for rather longer. In the summer of 1962 he had helped the general secretary of Aden's trade union congress, Abdullah al-Asnag, set up the People's Socialist Party to encourage industrial unrest. A year on, having begun to think that his protégé was showing unwelcome signs of moderation, Nasser then established a competitor, the National Liberation Front, which would be run out of the Yemeni city of Taiz by 'a small chubby man whose appearance belied his revolutionary nature', Qahtan al-Shaabi.[3]

Established along cellular lines to ensure security, just as the Free Officers' movement in Egypt had been, the National Liberation Front trained its recruits for guerrilla warfare and simple acts of sabotage, like breaking air-conditioning units in government offices and pouring sugar or earth into the fuel tanks of British officials' cars, and quickly penetrated South Arabia's local government. While the People's Socialist Party's activities were focused on Aden, the NLF's remit was much more wide-ranging. Ultimately it aimed to destroy the chances of the Federation succeeding by pitting the tribesmen and the Adenis against one another. By the autumn of that year a rebellion directed by the NLF had broken out in the Radfan, a wild and hilly district due north of Aden, through which ran the main road to Yemen. The British wrongly interpreted the disturbance as tribal trouble.[4]

With al-Shaabi now breathing down his neck, al-Asnag responded by trying to organise a 'spectacular'. An ex-employee of Aden Airways, he convinced a former colleague who still worked for the airline to try to kill the British high commissioner, Sir Kennedy Trevaskis, as he flew home to discuss the future of the Federation of South Arabia. On 10 December 1963 a grenade was thrown at Trevaskis in the airport terminal. A woman died instantly and twenty-four others were injured. The high commissioner survived but his deputy George Henderson was not so lucky. Hit by a splinter as he tried to shield his boss, he died in hospital seventeen days later.

Trevaskis immediately declared a state of emergency, but his decision to use his powers to round up well over 100 trades unionists and nation-alists went down badly in London. Stung by the implication that he was 'acting too drastically', he insisted that 'strong action at the outset is the course best calculated to stop the rot and to prevent the public in general and indeed our weaker friends going over to the other side'.[5]

Trevaskis was not deterred by the reaction in London. An enthusiastic supporter of the war in Yemen, he now proposed similar methods to deal with the threat of terrorism in South Arabia. Eight days after the attempt on his life, he told his boss Duncan Sandys of his plan to 'bring about a clash between the PSP and SAL [South Arabian League] which will encourage them to slit each other's throats'. His reference to the South Arabian League – the original nationalist organisation long overtaken by the PSP – and his seeming ignorance of the existence of the NLF are telling; his enthusiasm for the targeted assassination of key terrorists was dismissed by MI5 in London, whose experts knew that fighting terror with terror was unlikely to work unless it was part of a bigger political strategy. It was only in March the following year that Trevaskis received permission to spend £15,000 'penetrating their organizations, suborning their key figures, stimulating rivalries and jealousies between them, encouraging dissension and the emergence of splinter groups and harassing them generally, for example by breaking up public meetings'.[6]

In the meantime, the British tried to re-establish the government's authority in the Radfan. In January British and Federal Army forces embarked on Operation Nutcracker, a show of force that had a neg-ligible effect. After more than a dozen vehicles were blown up along the road from Aden into the restive province that spring, the British decided to crack nuts on a bigger scale. Having failed to understand that the insurgency was being led by the NLF, they hoped that it would be possible to deal it a terminal blow by driving the dissidents out of the fertile Danaba Basin in the hills, and destroying the crops there so that the valley became useless as a base. But a lack of good intelligence meant that the campaign was flawed from the outset.

Before the British force could scorch the earth of the Danaba Basin, it would first have to capture the surrounding hills. When it was decided that 120 men of the Parachute Regiment should drop in to do this, Peter de la Billière, an SAS officer who had served on the Jebel Akhdar cam-paign and then as Tony Boyle's successor in Aden, successfully lobbied for his own unit to go in first to find a drop zone, when it might more usefully have been employed in an intelligence-gathering role. De la Billière picked one of his captains, Robin Edwards, to lead eight men on the operation: they were flown into the hills at the end of April. Within twenty-four hours, however, they were in deep trouble.

After the radio operator, Nick Warburton, went down with food poisoning, the patrol was forced to abandon its hunt for the drop zone and lie up for the day in a pair of stone enclosures on a hillside, waiting for nightfall when they intended to escape. There they were discovered by a goatherd, whom they shot, but not before he had alerted a woman who ran down the hillside to alert the nearby village. Within ten minutes the SAS were under attack and radioed de la Billière to ask him to call in the fast jets on standby at Khormaksar airport. Airstrikes helped reduce the pressure but, by the time night finally fell and the patrol got away, both Warburton and Edwards were dead. Their heads appeared on spikes in Taiz, the NLF's headquarters in Yemen, and their decapitated bodies were only recovered several weeks later. The Radfan campaign continued to the end of June, but it was inconclusive because the NLF simply withdrew to their sanctuary on the other side of the Yemeni border.

In the last days of the Conservative government that summer Sandys convened the constitutional conference which had been delayed after the attempt on Trevaskis's life. When the South Arabian delegates then requested a date for independence not later than 1968 and proposed reaching a defence agreement with Britain that would enable her to retain her Aden base, Sandys announced that Her Majesty's Government was in complete agreement.

It was the old formula – Britain would trade independence for a military base – and it was not one that the Tories' Labour opponents felt the country was in a position to afford. After Labour squeaked home with a majority of four in the October 1964 general election, the 'Economic Situation' was the ominous first item on the cabinet's agenda when it met for the first time on 18 October. The country's financial position was 'worse than expected', the new prime minister Harold Wilson told his colleagues, before handing over to his new secretary of state for economic affairs George Brown, who described the scale of the balance of payments deficit that Labour had inherited. Little could be done in the short term, Brown admitted. But if the government was to protect the welfare spending that was so dear to its supporters, it would need to make deep cuts elsewhere. The new defence secretary, Denis Healey, was directed to slice 16 per cent from his department's budget. Empire would be sacrificed for welfare.[7]

Although Wilson and his colleagues claimed the opposite in public, Aden was in their sights from the outset. 'Something must be done to equalise the burden we carry east of Suez on behalf of others,' Wilson insisted a few weeks later. What he meant was that the Gulf sheikhs should pay for their own defence. But the task was harder than it sounded. 'All these bases were necessary because of our political commitments – our responsibility for defending our dependent territories or our treaty obligations to other sovereign states,' Healey later explained. 'We could not give them up until our colonies had become independent or we had renegotiated our treaties with our allies.'[8]

To start that process of disentangling Britain from her political commitments the new colonial secretary, Arthur Greenwood, paid a visit to Aden that November, after the attacks in the port had started. Following a series of talks, the federal and Aden ministers he had spoken to together announced their ambition to establish 'a unitary sovereign state on a sound democratic basis', which they would pursue at yet another conference scheduled for March the following year. This was an attempt to assuage the Adenis' fears about the powers the tribal sheikhs would wield in a federal state. When Trevaskis, who was the architect of the federal plan, said that he could not abide this new departure, Greenwood pushed him into an early retirement.[9]

Trevaskis's distaste for the new policy was understandable given that its chances of succeeding would depend on the man who had tried to kill the high commissioner a year earlier, the People's Socialist Party leader Abdullah al-Asnag. As general secretary of the Aden Trades Union Congress al-Asnag had previously had contacts with Labour when the party was in opposition. When he agreed to abandon his ambition to unite the Federation with Yemen, Greenwood and his colleagues, failing to realise that the People's Socialist Party's influence was largely confined to Aden, naively began to hope that the Adeni trade unionist might be able to sell their plan.

Al-Asnag hoped to use his channel to the British to help him unite the nationalist movement under his leadership, but this strategy quickly foundered. Although key members of the Arab League supported him, Nasser and Yemen's President Sallal did not. And so the National Liberation Front refused to accept al-Asnag's leadership. His credibility took a further knock when it became clear that his willingness to talk to the British bought him no influence. When he and the federal government tried to insist that three states in the richer eastern protectorate be invited to take part in the London conference to discuss the future state, the British disagreed. They feared that any newcomers would reopen issues that had already been settled. Tainted and impotent, al-Asnag lost his job as secretary-general of the Aden Trades Union Congress midway through 1965, thanks to manoeuvring by the NLF behind the scenes.

The National Liberation Front was all the time gaining ground. At the same time as it fought a political battle with al-Asnag and his People's Socialist Party, it was trying to destroy Britain's already limited ability to counter its terrorism, a campaign in which the murder of Inspector Khalil in Crater's qat market was just the start. The NLF targeted Arab officers in the Special Branch, abducting and murdering them, then dumping their bullet-riddled bodies in the Arab districts of Crater and Sheikh Othman in Aden, with messages attached announcing that they had been 'executed by the NLF'. These tactics were terribly effective. By June 1965 the High Commission admitted that 'Aden Special Branch has now virtually no Arab element and will take considerable time to re-establish on an Arab basis even if Arabs can be found to serve in it. There is no likelihood of this happening in the foreseeable future.' The British were reduced to relying on expatriate recruits with no grasp of Arabic instead.[10]

Despite mounting evidence to the contrary, the British had managed to convince themselves that a smooth transition of power by 1968 might be possible. Two high-profile murders forced them to confront the reality. Sir Arthur Charles, the speaker of the Aden Legislature, invariably played tennis every Wednesday afternoon. As he walked back to his car after his game on 1 September 1965 an Arab man called out to him and, when Charles responded, shot him dead. Three days later the deputy head of Aden's Special Branch Harry Barrie was murdered on his drive to work, as he came to a halt at a junction near his office.

Such was the fear of retribution that no member of the legislature was willing to condemn Charles's murder publicly. The high commissioner, now Sir Richard Turnbull, immediately ordered a curfew. Following an order from London, he then suspended the constitution: that meant that the assembly was dissolved; the high commissioner now had powers of direct rule.

Turnbull's suspension of the constitution on 25 September 1965 marked a turning point. It was effectively a vote of no-confidence in the system of government. Now the onus was on the British. To rebuild confidence so that they could restore self-government and avoid a very messy exit from the colony, they first had to defeat the terrorists.

There were few signs that the British were up to this challenge. The port's dependence on a daily tide of about 60,000 workers made checks at the perimeter difficult. Inside the town security was lax: 'The white face and a smile open too many doors in Aden,' observed a visiting Special Branch officer with long experience of colonial counter-terrorism. There was infighting between the different agencies. Meanwhile, the NLF's devastating campaign of targeted assassination was working. Once it became clear that collaborating with the British brought a substantial risk of violent death, the quality of intelligence – on which successful counter-terrorism relied – collapsed.[11]

Finally, there was no sign of commitment from the British government in London, indeed quite the opposite. Denis Healey had just paid a fleeting visit to both Aden and the Federation and came away convinced that the entire project was unworkable. 'Back in the noise and stench of Aden's crowded slums it was impossible to imagine that its marriage to the sheikhdoms could survive,' he later wrote, admittedly with the benefit of hindsight. He found Turnbull pessimistic. 'When the British Empire sank beneath the waves of history,' the high commissioner told him, 'it would leave behind only two monuments: one was the game of Association Football, the other was the expression, "Fuck off".'[12]

* * *

American efforts to frustrate Britain's withdrawal and disagreement among Wilson's ministers in London both delayed a final decision on Aden until December 1965. At a time when the United States was consumed by the war in Vietnam, the Johnson administration interpreted British noises that they might have to withdraw from Aden and Singapore as profoundly unhelpful. When the chancellor of the Exchequer Jim Callaghan visited Washington in the summer to seek funds to stave off another sterling crisis, the US defence secretary, Robert McNamara, warned him that any British retrenchment 'between Aden and Hong Kong' would oblige the United States to reconsider 'all aspects of its relations with the UK'. Johnson's national security adviser went further, suggesting tying a promise of financial support to a British commitment to Vietnam. A 'battalion would be worth a billion', he suggested to one of Harold Wilson's advisers. But ultimately the British, though weak, had the upper hand. Knowing Johnson would support the pound because a devaluation of sterling would disadvantage American exporters, Wilson was able to insist that 'no clear link' could be made between American efforts to bolster sterling and a common approach to foreign policy. He said he would not send troops to Vietnam in exchange for American support for the pound.[13]

McNamara's treatment of Callaghan did nothing to improve Anglo-American relations. George Brown complained that Britain was being treated 'like a banana republic', while the Americans' sudden change of heart struck Healey as deeply cynical. 'The United States, after trying for thirty years to get Britain out of Asia, the Middle East, and Africa, was now trying desperately to keep us in; during the Vietnam war it did not want to be the only country killing coloured people on their own soil,' he wrote much later.[14]

Both Brown and Healey were determined to be shot of the base as fast as possible, realising that, like Palestine and Egypt before it, Aden was now 'more of a liability than an asset'. But the Foreign Office took a different view. It was concerned, justifiably, that a sudden announcement of withdrawal would have a calamitous effect on relations with Saudi Arabia and Iran. It might even trigger a war between Iran, Iraq and Saudi Arabia over the rich but vulnerable Gulf states. The fact that Nasser was also now clearly looking for an escape route from Yemen provided another argument for staying put. And so, when the cabinet finally discussed foreign policy, the foreign secretary, Michael Stewart, admitted that the situation was untenable but envisaged 'a gradual and orderly withdrawal from the Middle East'. In line with Wilson's desire to 'equalise the burden' a year earlier, Stewart said his staff had made some progress, by promoting cooperation between the Gulf rulers so that they might rely more on their own resources.[15]

The 'gradual and orderly withdrawal' proposed by Stewart was nothing like fast enough for Healey. On 12 and 13 October *The Times* ran a pair of articles by its defence correspondent on Britain's role in the Middle East, which reflected the defence secretary's thinking. The first, entitled 'Wasted Years in South Arabia', questioned the value of the Aden base if all the troops stationed there were required for its protection and argued that a satisfactory political settlement – for which the government was supposedly holding out – was unattainable. The second argued that the British presence in the Gulf could be smaller, since its role was only to act as a deterrent, preventing the larger states from absorbing the smaller ones, and so preserving a large number of independent states which kept the oil price competitive.[16]

* * *

In Washington the State Department could see which way the wind was blowing and suspected that the forthcoming UN general assembly might prove the final straw for the British. American diplomats expected a delegation from Aden to condemn the British government's suspension of the constitution and demand the immediate liquidation of the base. With their British counterparts admitting that they had 'no specific plans for solving the Aden crisis beyond the hope that suspension of the constitution will enable them to restore order and regain control of the situation', US officials decided to do what they could to back up their ally in the UN, because 'any precipitate withdrawal from the Aden area at this time would result in a chaotic situation in South Arabia harmful to general Western interests'. But American support failed to stop a motion censuring the British being passed by an overwhelming majority in UNGA on 3 November.[17]

In London, a day after the vote in the UN, the cabinet's defence and oversea policy committee concluded that the base was not worth having, and Wilson broke the bad news to President Johnson in person when he visited Washington in December. The prime minister, who only in July had implied that Britain would hang on east of Suez while the United States was fighting the Vietnam War, now told Johnson that Aden 'could not be regarded as a long-term base' but softened the blow by adding that the British would maintain a presence in the Gulf. Johnson must have realised immediately that Wilson's decision would be seized on by opponents of the Vietnam War, but ultimately there was nothing he could do about it. As his treasury secretary, Henry Fowler, put it, forcing Britain to maintain commitments she did not want to make would only cost the United States more money. 'A weak ally is of no use to us East of Suez, in Europe, in the international financial set-up, or anywhere else.'[18]

The British government then broke the news to the Federal Supreme Council in February 1966, shortly before it published the Defence White Paper on the 22nd. The news that the British would evacuate the colony by 1968 came as a profound shock to the shopkeepers, taxi drivers and local officials whose livelihoods depended on the British presence. Nasser had committed himself to withdrawing from Yemen, but when he heard the news he changed his mind. In a speech at Cairo University he bought himself time by declaring that he would not pull out his troops until a transitional government had been formed in Yemen. 'Should we surrender to Faisal or should we sit ten years in Yemen?' he asked rhetorically. 'I say, we shall sit for twenty.'[19]

*　*　*

By setting an end-date on their presence in the country, the British might have hoped to make the situation better. In fact, their announcement made matters worse. In January 1966, al-Asnag had achieved what he had long been hoping for: an alliance between his People's Socialist Party and Qahtan al-Shaabi's National Liberation Front, to be called the Front for the Liberation of South Yemen. Backed by Nasser, FLOSY would use violence to evict the British. The alliance only lasted until December. With the British going to leave, al-Asnag and al-Shaabi turned against each other, having realised that they were rivals in the race to lead the newly independent state.

The British hoped that they might simply be bystanders in this internecine war, just as they had been in Palestine twenty years earlier. But that did not happen either. The bomb attacks and shootings continued. At the end of February 1967 the NLF persuaded a young servant working for a British intelligence officer, Tony Ingledow, to plant a jumping mine in a bookcase in Ingledow's flat before a drinks party. The bomb went off at nine o'clock that evening when the party was in full swing, killing two women whose husbands also worked in intelligence. An NLF representative explained the reason for the violence to the veteran British diplomat Sam Falle, who visited in April 1967 on a mission to speak directly to the terrorists and see if some deal to halt the violence could be done. 'If we were to make a deal with you,' the man explained, 'Al-Jabhat al-Hurria [FLOSY] would proclaim that we were the running dogs of the imperialists and that they were the only true representatives of South Arabia. There must be no doubt in anyone's mind that Al-Jabhat al-Qomia [NLF] has achieved the freedom of South Arabia by force of arms, unaided by Al-Jabhat al-Hurria, the Egyptians, or anyone else.'[20]

In May Turnbull was succeeded by the former ambassador to Egypt and Iraq Humphrey Trevelyan, who had been called out of retirement for one final job. By the time he arrived, security was so poor that he was helicoptered from Khormaksar airport to his new and misnamed home, Government House. His job was to try to restore peace and order in South Arabia before the British left. On arrival at Government House, he called on all parties to talk to him. 'What we should like to achieve is a central caretaker government, broad-based and representing the whole of South Arabia,' he declared. Trevelyan's aim in issuing this statement was to put the onus on the NLF and FLOSY, the British journalist Tom Little recorded: 'If they did not want the existing federal government, they should come along and help to change it by agreement.'[21]

Trevelyan's job was soon made harder after Radio Cairo claimed, during the Six-Day War, that Britain was covertly supporting the Israelis. But if he and his colleagues were not to leave South Arabia in flames on their departure, he had to confront the lawless situation that the two terror groups had created and which magnified their power. 'The investigation of bank robberies, by which the terrorists financed their operations, had become impossible,' Little wrote on his return to London. 'The people walked through the streets, seeing nothing, hearing nothing, and above all saying nothing. Most magistrates and Adeni judges would not sit in court.'[22]

By now George Brown had replaced Stewart as foreign secretary. On 20 June 1967 he announced that the British government would provide

£9 million to help the new government, more modern arms including self-loading rifles to replace the old Lee Enfields, armoured cars and field artillery, and Hunter aircraft. Britain would station naval forces in the vicinity and V-bombers on Masirah Island, off the Oman coast. He also said that trial by jury would be suspended, while the proscription of the NLF would be ended because it was a bar to useful negotiation.

The impression that the British government was gripping the situation was instantly undermined by events in Aden the same day. There the army had mutinied, after four colonels complained that tribal ties had influenced promotion. No longer trusting their own men, the federal government called in British troops to crush the rebellion, which they did, but at a heavy cost with seventeen dead and twenty-two wounded. When news of the clash reached the armed police barracks in Crater, the police hurriedly armed themselves. The assistant commissioner of police was supposed to go to try to calm them, but he was secretly a senior figure in the NLF and he may have stoked the tensions. Certainly by the time a British army patrol arrived to assess the situation it found the shops shut, streets deserted and barricades improvised from furniture. The British were soon cut to pieces by heavy crossfire. A helicopter pilot who flew over the scene described seeing 'two Land Rovers and bodies all around'. Then his own kneecap and ankle were smashed by Kalashnikov bullets fired up at him from the ground and he was forced to crash land. 'Crater was in the hands of the enemy,' recalled Lt Col Colin Mitchell, commanding officer of the 1st Battalion, the Argyll and Sutherland Highlanders and one of the two men who had the task of identifying the mutilated corpses.[23]

'Mad Mitch', as Colin Mitchell would soon be better known, was an angry man. A 42-year-old career soldier who had fought in Italy and Korea, he had extensive experience of counter-insurgency from tours in Palestine, Cyprus and Kenya, where he had reached the conclusion that 'the controlled use of tough methods without brutality can prevent loss of life'. He was furious at the higher authorities' failure to sanction a rescue mission to Crater, which he blamed on a culture in which 'political expediency ... dominated military judgement'.[24]

Mitchell had just started his tour and was itching to recapture Crater as soon as possible. Trevelyan, however, was much less keen. He regarded Mitchell as a 'first class battalion commander' but no more, and feared the strong-arm tactics the Scotsman was proposing would inflict heavy casualties on the police force, which might trigger another mutiny. Trevelyan also had to consider the safety in those circumstances of the 100 or so British officials and advisers up-country. Other officials were already negotiating with the NLF through the assistant police commissioner in the hope of reaching a peaceful outcome, and Trevelyan and the Middle East Command wanted to see whether these approaches might succeed.[25]

It soon became clear that the terrorists had no particular desire to end the stand-off. Not only were they locked in a struggle with each other for control, but the seizure of one of the key districts of the British colony also represented a useful way to save face, two weeks after the Arabs' drubbing in the Six-Day War.

The Arabs were not the only ones who needed to save face, however, and both Trevelyan and the general in overall command of British forces approved Mitchell's plan to retake the district. On the evening of 3 July, with a piper playing the regimental charge, the Argylls re-entered Crater. Mitchell had tipped off the press, playing up the difference of opinion that existed between him and the top brass.

On arrival in Crater, Mitchell imposed what he called 'Argyll's Law'. 'They know that if they start trouble we'll blow their bloody heads off,' Mitchell told a journalist. The dark reality of what sounded like bravado only became apparent later. Soldiers under Mitchell's command were awarded a Robertson's Jam Golliwog sticker for each Arab that they killed.[26]

Mitchell in due course was reprimanded and reined in. It was not long before the grenade and gun attacks resumed, targeting the Argylls in particular. Mortars were fired at the High Commissioner's residence. Trevelyan's efforts to broker a political agreement got nowhere. Beyond Aden, the federation started to implode when the National Liberation Front seized power in five of its seventeen constituent states in August; all that the British could do was to arrange for the sultans and their families to flee into exile.

Trevelyan left on 28 November, sent on his way by a military band that played 'Fings Ain't Wot They Used T'Be'. The last British troops departed the following day – the same day that Nasser's last remaining troops left Yemen.

'All we could say at the time was that it might have been much worse,' wrote Trevelyan some years later as he reflected on the British legacy.

And in the end, another little independent Arab country came into being, desperately poor and probably destined to go through periods of violence and revolt. The mark of the British on it was light and will soon have disappeared save for the great barracks, the airport, the disused churches and a few half-obliterated direction signs to the NAAFI or the sergeants' mess. Our period of occupation did the country little permanent good, for all the selfless work of many devoted Englishmen and so many good intentions. Whatever the rights or wrongs of the way we left, whatever was to come after us, the time for us to be there was over. And if we were to go, it was better not to linger on.[27]

EPILOGUE

While Egypt's defeat during the Six-Day War destroyed Nasser's reputation, the closure of the Suez Canal and the Arabs' oil embargo put Britain under severe financial strain yet again. Over the next three years, the need to buy dollar-denominated oil cost the country £175 million it could ill afford. A mixture of anger and fear that the government might introduce capital controls led Arab investors to pull about the same amount from British banks. Harold Wilson had been loath to devalue the currency, believing that was what had done for the last Labour government's credibility. But by the autumn of 1967 he no longer had a choice. On 19 November – ten days before the last troops pulled out of Aden – the government devalued the pound by forty cents and the chancellor, Jim Callaghan, resigned.

Devaluation was not enough. Further cuts to public expenditure would be necessary, at a time when, according to opinion polls, the government was haemorrhaging support. The government had already been thinking about quitting the Gulf by 1975; on 4 January 1968, Wilson and his ministers agreed to bring the departure date forward to 1971.

The foreign secretary, George Brown, now had the unenviable task of breaking this news to the Americans, and he left for Washington under no illusions about how the government's decision would go down. President Johnson, who was still then planning to stand for re-election in November that year, was preparing his State of the Union address, and Brown had already been warned by the American ambassador to London that, 'The appearance of our being deserted, in the midst of our Vietnamese involvement, by a Government assumed to be our most reliable ally, headed by a Prime Minister who had repeatedly declared himself an "East of Suez Man" was unwise, provocative and totally unacceptable.'[1]

By the time Brown met Dean Rusk on 11 January, Rusk already knew what he had come to say, because Denis Healey, who was annoyed by Wilson's handling of the matter, had quietly given an American diplomat in London his version of the 4 January cabinet discussion. Brown, however, presented the matter as if there was still some possibility of a change of heart. Although Rusk told him that he smelled 'the acrid aroma of a fait accompli', he asked him to report his deep concerns to Wilson. The State Department's version of the meeting reports him saying that he was 'profoundly dismayed' and 'particularly disturbed' by the British government's intention. 'For God's sake act like Britain', Brown reported Rusk as saying, on his arrival back in London.[2]

The appeal had no effect. On 12 January 1968, after Brown had described his conversation with Rusk, Wilson and his colleagues decided not to change course. 'The time had come', the minutes of the meeting state, 'for a decisive break with our previous policies. We should no longer adopt policies merely because the United States wished us to adopt them and out of fear for the economic consequences if we did not do so. The friendship of the United States had been valuable to us; but we had often paid a heavy price for it. Both countries now faced balance of payments difficulties. The United States were dealing with theirs by a policy based mainly on self-interest. They could not complain if we did the same.'[3]

* * *

Before the British departed, there were loose ends to tie up. Although the spread of communism to the Middle East had long been prophesied, it was only in 1968 that it came to pass, when the short war that followed Britain's exit from Aden resulted in the establishment of the region's first and only Marxist state, the People's Republic of South Yemen. Although the Russian, Chinese and Cuban advisers who soon replaced the British never made much headway in Yemen, their impact was quickly felt in the neighbouring, isolated Dhofar region of western Oman.

Whereas South Yemen saw rapid economic improvements following an influx of Russian money, neighbouring Dhofar did not. Cut off by monsoon cloud and fierce surf for part of the year, the mountainous Dhofar was a fertile and yet extraordinarily poor place even by the low standards of Oman, peopled by herders who fed their cattle dried fish. 'To a man', a British soldier wrote, 'they were alert, aggressive, quick-witted and possessed of keen power of argument.' An independence movement backed initially by the Saudis – the Dhofar Liberation Front – had operated there since the mid-1960s and nearly succeeded in assassinating the sultan in 1966. Chastened, the sultan retreated to his palace in Salalah and thereafter conducted the business of government, and his campaign against modernity, with underlings by radio telephone. He had started to receive a cut of revenues from the oil that had finally begun to flow in 1967, but refused to share the wealth, arguing that it was important to build up financial reserves first. The British grew increasingly unpopular by association.[4]

The establishment of communist South Yemen next door in 1967 gave the Dhofari insurgency a new and more sinister momentum. South Yemen provided a safe haven for the rebels; Chinese, then Russian, advisers banned prayers and indoctrinated them in Marxist thinking, and supplied weaponry and training in guerrilla warfare. By 1969 the Dhofaris commanded the heights that dominated the coastline, had inflicted a series of defeats on the sultan's forces and, crucially, controlled the road that linked Salalah with Muscat and the oilfields in the north. In a sign of their ultimate ambition, they renamed themselves the People's Front for the Liberation of the Arabian Gulf.

With the 1971 deadline looming, and having promised the Americans that they would assure an orderly transfer of power, the British were forced to intervene. Having identified the sultan's son Qaboos as a suitable replacement – he had trained at Sandhurst and then done work experience with Bedfordshire County Council – they encouraged him to overthrow his father, which he did on 23 July 1970.

Today, the Foreign Office says that its file 'Oman: Politics 1970' has somehow been lost. But the British attempt to deny any involvement in the overthrow of the sultan has been undermined by the discovery of a memorandum, written hours before the coup took place, which set out the travel arrangements for the sultan once he had been ousted.

The sultan – who shot himself in the foot while trying to defend himself – spent the remainder of his life in a suite at the Dorchester Hotel on London's Park Lane. It was said that whenever anyone mentioned Oman to him, he roared with laughter. His son Qaboos transformed the country, and is still in power today.[5]

A few weeks earlier Harold Wilson had lost a general election; his successor Edward Heath left open the possibility that a Conservative government might reverse Labour's decision to withdraw from the Gulf. That depended, significantly, on the attitude of the shah of Iran, the man whom the British had once dismissed as unreliable and indecisive, but who was helping the Omanis fight their Dhofar insurgency, and had recently expressed an interest in buying a large number of British tanks.

In Britain's departure the shah saw an opportunity – to press his country's long claim to Bahrain and a number of disputed islands in the Gulf. When Heath's foreign secretary, the former prime minister Alec Douglas-Home met him, it was evident that the Iranian ruler was not going to be easily persuaded to change his mind. That November, just before they left the Gulf, the British acquiesced to Iran's seizure of what one man called 'a rock with a few snakes and three Indians with a lighthouse'.[6]

It was in South Arabia that Britain's reputation best stood the test of time. Oman – Britain's oldest ally in the region – remains her strongest. The terrible post-colonial experience of Yemen next door encourages some rosy recollections of the pre-1967 era. When I visited, forty years later, in the spring of 2006, one man asked me if the British might like to come back. I am still unsure that he was joking.

ACKNOWLEDGEMENTS

Extracts from *The Second World War* by Sir Winston Churchill and *Arabian Sands* by Wilfred Thesiger are reprinted by permission of Curtis Brown Ltd; *The Macmillan Diaries* by permission of Pan Macmillan. Quotations from Crown Copyright records held in all of the archives I consulted appear by permission of Her Majesty's Stationery Office.

Efforts have been made to contact every copyright holder for material contained in this book. If any owner has been inadvertently overlooked, the publisher would be glad to hear from them and to make good in future editions any errors or omissions brought to their attention.

* * *

I must credit Colin Midson with the idea that evolved into this book, which many other people then helped me to research and write. I would like to thank the archivists and staff of the National Archives, the British Library, the London Library, and everyone at the Middle East Centre at St Antony's College, Oxford, especially the archivist, Debbie Usher. I am particularly grateful to King's College London. My visiting fellowship at King's has given me free access to a wide range of electronic resources, newspaper databases in particular, which would otherwise be beyond the means of an independent historian. And I would like to thank whoever in the State Department's Office of the Historian got its website search engine up and running in time for me to check all the references relating to material from the *Foreign Relations of the United States* series, on which I have drawn extensively.

I had a delightful day on the Sussex coast with Bill Woodburn and Sir Jeremy Thomas discussing Buraimi, and a cup of tea in Parliament with Lord Wright, who talked about his time as a young diplomat in Beirut and his recollections of John Slade-Baker, whose diaries have provided vital material in this book. I am also grateful to Steve Boyle for introducing me to Monty Woodhouse's son and grandson, Lord Terrington and Jack Woodhouse, and to Shashank Joshi, Ian Kikuchi, Guy Laron, Jan Morris, Andrew Mussell, Ilan Pappé, Steven Wagner and Sir Harold Walker for insight and other help. Sophie Keynes and Greg Holyoke provided vital help in the closing stages, and John Hick generously read and commented on the first draft. Sir James Craig, Hugh Leach and Ivor Lucas also shared their memories of this era. Alas, I failed to write this book fast enough for any of these unforgettable men to see it.

Finally, I would like to thank my agent Catherine Clarke, my editors Mike Jones and Iain MacGregor and the team who turned my manuscript into this book: Melissa Bond, Charlotte Chapman, Matt Johnson, Kaiya Shang and Sue Stephens, as well as Martin Lubikowski, who drew the maps. My greatest debt is to my wife, Anna, without whose love and support, for me and our two wonderful children, there would have been no manuscript at all.

NOTES

List of abbreviations used in the notes

CAC – Churchill Archives Centre, Cambridge
FRUS – Foreign Relations of the United States
HC Deb – House of Commons, Debates
IOR – India Office Records, London
JTA – Jewish Telegraphic Agency
MEC – Middle East Centre Archive, Oxford
SHAT – Service Historique de l'Armée de Terre, Paris
TNA – The National Archives, London
USIME – US Intelligence on the Middle East (see Online Archives and Sources)

Chapter 1   The Beginning of the End

1   A good example of chiasmus. All the quotes from Churchill's speech '"Great Design" in Africa', *The Times*, 11 November 1942.
2   Churchill, *The Second World War*, Vol. IV, p. 344.
3   HC Deb, 2 July 1942, Vol. 381, c. 528. The speaker was Aneurin Bevan.
4   Hassall, *Edwin Marsh*, p. 484.
5   Willkie, *One World*, p. 4; *FRUS*, 1942, Vol. IV, p.72, Kirk to Hull, 16 February 1942. This was an incomplete explanation, as the Germans had cracked the cypher used by the US military attaché, who was wiring reports of British plans to Washington (TNA, FO 1093/238, Stockholm to FO, 13 August 1942).
6   Mangold, *What the British Did*, p. 6.
7   Willkie, *One World*, p. 16.
8   Evans, ed., *The Killearn Diaries*, pp. 215, 218, 4, 5 February 1942.
9   Willkie, *One World*, p. 5; TNA, PREM 4/27/1; 'Willkie at the Front', *Collier's Magazine*, 24 October 1942.
10   Willkie, *One World*, pp. 14–15.
11   Churchill, *The Second World War*, Vol. II, p. 500. Churchill's letter was dated 8 December 1940.

12   Neal, *Dark Horse*, pp. 187–8.
13   Beschloss, *Kennedy and Roosevelt*, p. 200; Winston Churchill, *The Second World War*, Vol. III, p. 23.
14   Gilbert, *Churchill and America*, p. 41; Meacham, *Franklin and Winston*, p. 51; Churchill, *The Second World War*, Vol. III, p. 23; 'Willkie in Air Raid, Forgets his Tin Hat', *The Republic*, 28 January 1941.
15   TNA, PREM 4/26/6, memorandum, 6 June 1941.
16   Churchill, *The Second World War*, Vol. III, p. 23.
17   Neal, *Dark Horse*, pp. 196–7; Meacham, *Franklin and Winston*, p. 75.
18   'Willkie, Home, Sees Peace for Us in Help to Britain', *New York Times*, 10 February 1941; 'Mr Churchill on Next Phase of War', *The Times*, 10 February 1941.
19   'Verbatim Testimony of Wendell Willkie in Answer to Questions Put to Him by Senators', *New York Times*, 12 February 1941.
20   Neal, *Dark Horse*, pp. 208–9.
21   Churchill, *The Second World War*, Vol. III, p. 617.
22   'Mr Churchill on a Symbolic Meeting', *The Times*, 25 August 1941; HC Deb, 9 September 1941, Vol. 374, c. 69.
23   *FRUS*, 1944, Vol. III, p. 62, Hull to Roosevelt, 30 September 1944.

Chapter 2   The Old Imperialistic Order

1   Fielding, *One Man in His Time*, p. 27; Cooper, *Cairo in the War*, p. 82.
2   Willkie, *One World*, p. 27; 'One World', *Life*, 26 April 1943, Willkie, *One World*, p. 21.
3   SHAT, 4H 314, Proclamation du Général Catroux, faite au nom du Général de Gaulle, chef des Français Libres, 8 June 1941; 'One World', *Life*, 26 April 1943.
4   Mott-Radclyffe, *Foreign Body in the Eye*, p. 109.
5   TNA, FO 1093/238, Menzies (SIS) to Loxley, 17 November 1942.
6   TNA, FO 608/107/2, 'The strategic importance of Syria to the British Empire', 9 December 1918.
7   Segev, *One Palestine Complete*, p. 147.
8   Willkie, *One World*, pp. 23–4.
9   Cowles, *Mike Looks Back*, p. 78.
10   MEC, Slade-Baker Papers, diary, 22 October 1954; Harvey, ed., *The War Diaries of Oliver Harvey*, p. 319, 4 November 1943; TNA, FO 1093/373, Menzies (SIS) to Sargent, 19 February 1948.
11   Crum, *Behind the Silken Curtain*, p. 154; Willkie, *One World*, p. 19.
12   Willkie, *One World*, p. 30.
13   Willkie, *One World*, p. 30.
14   HC Deb, 29 September 1942, Vol. 383, c. 667.
15   TNA, PREM 4/27/1, 'Note of What Mr Wendell Willkie said to Mr AJ Toynbee at Mr TW Lamont's House in New York on the 27th October 1942'; Neal, *Dark Horse*, p. 251.

16 Neal, *Dark Horse*, p. 260.

17 TNA, PREM 4/27/1, US Office of War Information, Willkie's Report to the people, 26 October 1942.

18 TNA, FO 371/61856. Official US figures estimated the Jewish population in 1941 at 4,893,748.

19 'On Red Prisoners and Poles', *Life*, 23 February 1942.

20 Oren, *Power, Faith and Fantasy*, p. 444.

21 'Palestine Project Pushed by Senator', *New York Times*, 2 November 1942.

22 TNA, PREM 4/27/1, minute by Churchill, 5 November 1942.

23 'Old Imperialistic Order', *The Times*, 18 November 1942; TNA, PREM 4/27/1, Halifax to Eden and Churchill, 19 November 1942.

Chapter 3   Heading for Trouble

1   JTA, 'Biltmore Declaration Will Be Principal Zionist Demand at Peace Conference', 27 November 1942; TNA, CAB 66/37/46, Casey, 'Palestine', 21 April 1943.

2   Rathmell, *Secret War in the Middle East*, p. 12.

3   Rhodes, James, *Chips: the diaries of Sir Henry Channon*, p. 396, 7 November 1944; Eden, *Another World*, pp. 132–3.

4   CAC, Amery Papers 2/2/19, Moyne to Amery, 16 February and 21 January 1943.

5   *FRUS*, 1941, Vol. III, p. 643, Roosevelt to Jones, 18 July 1941; Anderson, *Aramco, the United States, and Saudi Arabia*, p. 33.

6   CAC, Amery Papers 6/3/101, Moyne to Birdie Amery, 30 December 1942; Morton, *Buraimi*, p. 10.

7   Magnes, 'Toward Peace in Palestine', p. 248.

8   Thomas, *The Diplomatic Game*, p. 10.

9   'Supply Centre', *The Economist*, 13 March 1943; TNA, CAB 66/9/2, Middle East War Council, conclusions, 19 May 1943.

10 *FRUS*, 1943, Vol. IV, p. 772, Pinkerton to Hull, 17 April 1943; TNA, CAB 66/37/46, Casey, 'Palestine', 21 April 1943.

11 TNA, CAB 66/37/46, Casey, 'Palestine', 21 April 1943.

12 TNA, CAB 66/37/46, Casey, 'Palestine', 21 April 1943.

13 *FRUS*, 1943, Vol. IV, pp. 781–85, Hull to Roosevelt, 7 May 1943, enclosing Summary of Lieutenant Colonel Harold B Hoskins' Report on the Near East.

14 TNA, CAB 66/39/2, Casey, 'British Policy in the Middle East', 12 July 1943.

15 Davis, 'Keeping the Americans in Line?', p. 107; *FRUS*, 1943, Vol. IV, p. 856, Kirk to Hull, 18 January 1943.

16 Yergin, *The Prize*, p. 397; Davis, 'Keeping the Americans in Line?', p. 111.

17 *FRUS*, 1943, Vol. IV, pp. 778–80, Hurley to Roosevelt, 5 May 1943.

18 Medoff, *Militant Zionism in America*, p. 90; O'Sullivan, *FDR and the End of Empire*, p. 86.

19 Dockter, *Churchill and the Islamic World*, pp. 235–6.
20 *FRUS*, 1943, Vol. IV, pp. 773–5, King Abdul Aziz Ibn Saud to Roosevelt.
21 *FRUS*, 1943, Vol. IV, pp. 786–7, Hull to Kirk, 26 May 1943, enclosing Roosevelt to King Ibn Saud.
22 'The King of Arabia', by Noel Busch, *Life*, 31 May 1943.
23 Randall, 'Harold Ickes and United States Foreign Petroleum Policy Planning', p. 375.
24 *FRUS*, 1943, Vol. IV, p. 793, Memorandum by Weizmann, 12 June 1943.
25 TNA, CAB 66/36/50, Eden, 'Palestine', 10 May 1943.
26 TNA, CAB 195/2, meeting of 2 July 1943.
27 TNA, CAB 195/2, meeting of 14 July 1943.
28 TNA, CAB 195/2, meeting of 14 July 1943.

Chapter 4 Sheep's Eyes

1 Field, 'Trade, Skills and Sympathy', p. 6.
2 Crossman, *Palestine Mission*, p. 181.
3 Hart, *Saudi Arabia and the United States*, p. 38; *FRUS*, 1943, Vol. IV, p. 931, Hull to Roosevelt, 6 July 1943.
4 *FRUS*, 1943, Vol. IV, p. 796, Hull to Hoskins, 7 July 1943.
5 *FRUS*, 1943, Vol. IV, p. 936, Kirk to Hull, 27 July 1943.
6 Killearn, diaries, 18 August 1943; Roosevelt, *Arabs, Oil and History*, p. 212.
7 'US Post-War Policy', *The Times*, 1 October 1943.
8 Congressional Record – Senate, 28 October 1943, p. 8864.
9 'American Resources after the War', *The Times*, 6 November 1943.
10 *FRUS*, 1943, Vol. IV, p. 942, Hull to Ickes, 13 November 1943.
11 Harvey, ed., *The War Diaries of Oliver Harvey*, p. 332, 19 February 1944.
12 Yergin, *The Prize*, p. 401.
13 *FRUS*, 1944, Vol. III, pp. 100–1, Churchill to Roosevelt, 20 February 1944.
14 *FRUS*, 1944, Vol. III, pp. 101–3, Roosevelt to Churchill, 22 February 1944, Churchill to Roosevelt, 24 February 1944, Roosevelt to Churchill, 3 March 1944, Churchill to Roosevelt, 4 March 1944.

Chapter 5 A Pretty Tough Nut

1 Wagner, 'Britain and the Jewish Underground', p. 65.
2 TNA, FO 921/229, Killearn to Peterson, 18 February 1944; Killearn to Moyne, 29 March 1944.
3 Ritchie, *James M. Landis*, p. 121.
4 Ritchie, *James M. Landis*, pp. 124–5.
5 Landis, 'Anglo-American Co-operation', pp. 69, 67.
6 Roosevelt, *Countercoup*, pp. 35–6; TNA, FO 921/229, Killearn to Peterson, 16 March 1944.
7 TNA, FO 921/229, Moyne to FO, 29 March 1944.

8   IOR, R/15/1/377, 'Conversations with Mr Wallace Murray Regarding the Middle East'.

9   TNA, CAB 110/185, 'Note for Discussion: Future Regional Economic Organisation in the M.E.', 26 May 1944; CAB 195/2, meeting of 14 July 1944; CAC, Amery Papers 2/2/19, Moyne to Amery, 19 June 1944.

10 Hinds, 'Anglo-American Relations in Saudi Arabia', p. 136.

11 *FRUS*, 1944, Vol. V, p. 697, Hull to Winant, 1 May 1944.

12 TNA, FO 921/192, Moyne to FO, 5 July 1944.

13 Vitalis, *America's Kingdom*, p. 79.

14 TNA, FO 921/192, Jordan to Eden, 6 September 1944; Moyne, minute, 13 September 1944.

15 TNA, CAB 110/185, minutes of meeting, 10 October 1944.

16 'Talks in Cairo', *Daily Express*, 27 October 1944.

17 TNA, CAB 110/185, minutes of a meeting on 11 October 1944; 'List of Commodities for which MESC recommendations should continue in the Middle East', n.d.

18 Wilmington, *The Middle East Supply Centre*, p. 165; Ritchie, *James M. Landis*, p. 127.

Chapter 6   'The Jewish Problem'

1   O'Sullivan, *FDR and the End of Empire*, p. 120; TNA, FO 141/1001, Clayton, memorandum, 14 November 1944.

2   *FRUS*, 1945, Vol. VIII, p. 2, memorandum of conversation between Ibn Saud and Roosevelt, 14 February 1945.

3   Brands, *Inside the Cold War*, p. 166.

4   *FRUS*, 1945, Vol. VIII, p. 2, memorandum of conversation between Ibn Saud and Roosevelt, 14 February 1945.

5   'Texts of Letters Exchanged by Ibn Saud and Roosevelt', *New York Times*, 19 October 1945.

6   Crum, *Behind the Silken Curtain*, p. 16; *FRUS*, 1945 Vol. VIII, p. 707, Truman to Abdullah, 17 May 1945.

7   Ovendale, 'The Palestine Policy of the British Labour Government', p. 413; Ottolenghi, 'Harry Truman's Recognition of Israel', p. 969.

8   Report of Earl G. Harrison on his 'Mission to Europe to inquire into the conditions and needs of those among the displaced persons in the liberated countries of Western Europe and in the SHAEF area of Germany – with particular reference to the Jewish refugees – who may possibly be stateless or non-repatriable,' n.d.

9   Harris, *Attlee*, p. 390.

10 Cohen, 'The Genesis of the Anglo-American Committee on Palestine', p. 190.

11 *FRUS*, 1945, Vol. VIII, pp. 737–40, Truman to Attlee, 31 August 1945, and Attlee to Truman, 14 and 16 September 1945.

12 'Palestine "Pledge" denied by Truman', *New York Times*, 27 September 1945.

13 'Palestine "Pledge" denied by Truman', *New York Times*, 27 September 1945.
14 *FRUS*, 1945, Vol. VIII, p. 764, Henderson, memorandum, 10 October 1945.
15 *FRUS*, 1945, Vol. VIII, p. 769–70, Byrnes to Eddy, 13 October 1945, enclosing a message from Truman to Ibn Saud.
16 TNA, KV, 3/443–2, extract from CX report No. 54, 17 October 1945; *FRUS*, 1945, Vol. VIII, p. 777, memorandum of a conversation between Byrnes and Halifax, 19 October 1945.
17 TNA, CAB 195/3 part 2, meeting of 13 November 1945.
18 MEC, Crossman Papers, 'The Palestine Report', speech to RIIA, 13 June 1946.
19 Crum, *Behind the Silken Curtain*, p. 130.
20 Crossman, *Palestine Mission*, p. 126.
21 Crum, *Behind the Silken Curtain*, pp. 25, 9.
22 Crum, *Behind the Silken Curtain*, pp. 213, 170; Crossman, *Palestine Mission*, p. 42.
23 TNA, CAB 129/9, Report by the Anglo-American Committee of Inquiry, 20 April 1946.
24 TNA, CAB 195/4, meeting of 29 April 1946.
25 'Text of President Truman's Statement on Report by Committee on Palestine', *New York Times*, 1 May 1946.
26 'Government Studying the Palestine Report', *The Times*, 2 May 1946.
27 Rose, *'A Senseless Squalid War'*, p. 93.
28 'Sabotage and Violence in Palestine', *The Times*, 25 July 1946; Crossman, *Palestine Mission*, p. 139, 11 March 1946; MEC, Crossman Papers, Singleton, 'Public Security', 9 April 1946.
29 Hoffman, *Anonymous Soldiers*, p. 267.
30 Cesarani, *Major Farran's Hat*, p. 39.
31 Hoffman, *Anonymous Soldiers*, pp. 282–3.
32 'Firm British Action in Palestine', *The Times*, 2 July 1946.
33 'Jerusalem Bomb Kills 41 in Attack on British Offices', 'Bombed Hotel Property of New York Corporation', *New York Times*, 23 July 1946.
34 MEC, Crossman Papers, Shaw to Crossman, 2 August 1946.
35 TNA, CAB 195/4, meeting of 23 July 1946.

Chapter 7 Fight for Palestine

1 TNA, CO 537/1738, *New York Post*, 29 July 1946.
2 'Divided Palestine is urged by Anglo-US Cabinet Body, delaying entry of 100,000', *New York Times*, 26 July 1946.
3 'Statement by Mr Truman', *The Times*, 24 July 1946.
4 TNA, CO 537/1738, press advertisement, 2 July 1946.
5 TNA, FO 371/52595, Halifax to Foreign Office, 6 March 1946.
6 'Gillette Blames Policy', *New York Times*, 24 July 1946.
7 Barr, *A Line In The Sand*, p. 329.

8 Oren, *Power, Faith and Fantasy*, p. 488.

9 Medoff, *Militant Zionism in America*, p. 152.

10 Hoffman, *Anonymous* Soldiers, p. 323; 'Two Plays to Hold Premieres Tonight', *New York Times*, 5 September 1946.

11 TNA, CO 537/1738, MI5 to Trafford-Smith, 4 October 1946.

12 Ottolenghi, 'Harry Truman's Recognition of Israel', p. 970; 'The Palestine Outlook: Mr Bevin on U.S. "Pressure"', *The Times*, 26 February 1947.

13 TNA, CAB 195/5, meeting of 15 January 1947.

14 Rose, '*A Senseless, Squalid War*', p. 135.

15 HC Deb, 18 February 1947, Vol. 433, cc. 988–9.

16 TNA, CAB 195/5, meeting of 14 February 1947.

17 HC Deb, 25 February 1947, Vol. 433, c. 2007.

18 TNA, FO 1093/420, 'Proposals for action to deter ships' masters and crews from engaging in illegal Jewish immigration traffic', 19 December 1946.

19 TNA, CAB 195/5 meeting of 19 December 1946; TNA, FO 1093/420, 'Proposals for action to deter ships' masters and crews from engaging in illegal Jewish immigration traffic', 19 December 1946, 'C' to Hayter, 19 December 1946.

20 TNA, CAB 195/5, meeting of 20 March 1947.

21 TNA, CO 537/2314, 'Build Dov Gruner's Memorial'; Medoff, *Militant Zionism in America*, p. 176.

22 TNA, CO 537/2314, FO to Washington, 22 May 1947; 'Halt in Palestine Agitation Here Requested by Truman', *New York Times*, 6 June 1947.

23 TNA, CO 967/103, Robey to Bromley, 9 September 1947; Eveland, *Ropes of Sand*, p. 32; Roosevelt, *Arabs, Oil and History*, p. 194.

24 '3 Slain on Zionist Vessel as Refugees fight British', *New York Times*, 19 July 1947.

25 'British Statement to UN on Palestine', *The Times*, 27 September 1947.

26 Hecht, *A Child of the Century*, p. 612.

27 Truman, *Memoirs*, Vol. II, pp. 168–9.

28 TNA, CAB 195/6, meeting of 22 March 1948.

Chapter 8   Eggs in One Basket

1 Seale, *The Struggle for Syria*, p. 13.

2 TNA, CAB 195/5, meeting of 22 January 1947; Pappé, 'Sir Alec Kirkbride and the Anglo-Transjordanian Alliance', p. 127.

3 FRUS, 1947, Vol. V, p. 741, Marshall to Gallman, 14 February 1947.

4 FRUS, 1947, Vol. V, p. 742, Gallman to Marshall, 17 February 1947; p. 744, Marshall to Gallman, 3 March 1947; p. 746, Editorial Note.

5 FRUS, 1947, Vol. V, pp. 748–9, Marshall to Baghdad Embassy, 12 June 1947; p. 749, note 3.

6 Wilford, *America's Great Game*, p. 114.

7 Roosevelt, *Arabs, Oil and History*, pp. 249, 6, 9.

8 Roosevelt, *Arabs, Oil and History*, p. 101; Wilford, *America's Great Game*, p. 79.

9 Roosevelt, *Arabs, Oil and History*, p. 119.

10 Roosevelt, *Arabs, Oil and History*, p. 122.

11 HC Deb, 14 July 1947, Vol. 440, c. 9; Roosevelt, *Arabs, Oil and History*, p. 122.

12 Roosevelt, *Arabs, Oil and History*, p. 75.

13 Roosevelt, *Arabs, Oil and History*, p. 127.

14 *FRUS*, 1947, Vol. V, p. 759, Editorial Note.

15 Roosevelt, 'Triple Play for the Middle East', p. 366.

16 Little, 'Pipeline Politics', p. 273; TNA, FO 371/75528, Syria, Political Summary for the Months of January and February 1949, n.d.

17 Little, 'Cold War and Covert Action', p. 55; Wilford, *America's Great Game*, p. 101.

18 Wilford, *America's Great Game*, p. 72; 'US Attaché Fights Off Gunmen', *New York Times*, 10 March 1949.

Chapter 9 Exploring the Wilder Areas

1 MEC, Philby Papers, 2/3/2/6, Philby to Mrs Astley, 27 January 1948.

2 Morton, *Buraimi*, p. 19.

3 Morton, *Buraimi*, p. 15.

4 IOR, R/15/1/238 Ambassador Cairo to Political Resident Bushire, 1 April 1945.

5 Thesiger, *Arabian Sands*, p. 41.

6 TNA, FO 371/68777, Burrows to Trott, draft, 20 February 1948.

7 Thesiger, *Arabian Sands*, p. 156.

8 Thesiger, *Arabian Sands*, p. 203.

9 MEC, Philby Papers, 2/3/2/6, Philby to Mrs Astley, 27 January 1948.

10 IOR, R/25/599, Bird to Jackson, 17 April 1948; MEC, Paxton Papers, Bird to Lermitte, 13 June 1948, 'Note on Mr Thesiger'.

11 IOR, R 15/2/599, Bird to Jackson, 17 April 1948.

12 MEC, Paxton Papers, Bird to Lermitte, 13 June 1948, 'Note on Mr Thesiger'.

13 Thesiger, *Arabian Sands*, p. 272; Morton, *Buraimi*, p. 48; Thesiger, 'A Further Journey Across the Empty Quarter', p. 40.

14 Morton, *Buraimi*, p. 48; Thesiger, 'A Further Journey Across the Empty Quarter', p. 39; Thesiger, *Arabian Sands*, p. 314.

15 Morton, *Buraimi*, p. 76.

16 MEC, Paxton Papers, Bird to Lermitte, 28 April 1949.

17 IOR, R/15/2/465, FO to Bahrain, 7 May 1949; MEC, Paxton Papers, Bird to Longrigg, 10 April 1949.

18 IOR, R/15/2/549, memorandum, 4 May 1949.

19 MEC, Paxton Papers, Henderson to Lermitte, 20 March 1950.

20 IOR, R/15/6/250, Hay to Bevin, 25 April 1950.

Chapter 10   Going Fifty–Fifty

1   *FRUS*, 1950, Vol. V, p. 11, Funkhouser, memorandum of conversation, 10 January 1950.
2   *FRUS*, 1949, Vol. VI, p. 1624, Editorial Note; 1950, Vol. V, p. 1147, Childs, memorandum of conversation, 23 March 1950; 1950, Vol. V, p. 25, Note 2.
3   *FRUS*, 1950, Vol. V, p. 1128, Truman to Ibn Saud, n.d.
4   McGhee, *Envoy to the Middle World*, p. 186.
5   Grafftey-Smith, *Bright Levant*, p. 267.
6   *FRUS*, 1950, Vol. V, p. 52, Acheson to US Embassy, Saudi Arabia, 1 June 1950; p. 56, Childs to Acheson, 13 June 1950.
7   *FRUS*, 1950, Vol. V, p. 52, Acheson to US Embassy, Saudi Arabia, 1 June 1950.
8   *FRUS*, 1950, Vol. V, p. 63, Childs to Acheson, 25 July 1950.
9   McGhee, *Envoy to the Middle World*, pp. 320–21.
10   Yergin, *The Prize*, p. 159; TNA, CAB 195/4, meeting of 3 June 1946; Louis, *The British Empire in the Middle East*, p. 56.
11   Churchill, *The World Crisis 1911–14*, p. 132; Abdelrehim, 'Oil Nationalisation and Managerial Disclosure', p. 126.
12   Marsh, 'HMG, AIOC and the Anglo-Iranian Oil Crisis', p. 147; Hardy, *The Poisoned Well*, p. 109.
13   Abdelrehim, 'Oil Nationalisation and Managerial Disclosure', pp. 117–21, 126.
14   Elm, *Oil, Power and Principle*, p. 37.
15   TNA, CAB 195/9, meeting of 23 April 1951: Philip Noel Baker made the remark. Elm, in *Oil, Power and Principle*, p. 102, estimates that AIOC's Iranian assets represented 10 per cent of the company's overall assets of £286 million.
16   *FRUS*, 1950, Vol. V, p. 580, Douglas to Acheson, 12 August 1950.
17   McGhee, *Envoy to the Middle World*, pp. 323–4.
18   *FRUS*, 1950, Vol. V, pp. 106–9, Funkhouser, memorandum of conversation, 6 November 1950.
19   *FRUS*, 1950, Vol. V, p. 1190, Truman to Ibn Saud, 31 October 1950; *FRUS*, 1951, Vol. V, p. 277, Funkhouser, memorandum of conversation, 10 January 1951; *FRUS*, 1951, Vol. V, p. 283, Acheson to Certain Diplomatic and Consular Posts, 25 January 1951.

Chapter 11   An Unfortunate Turn

1   *FRUS*, 1950, Vol. V, p. 512, 'The Present Crisis in Iran', n.d.
2   Falle, *My Lucky Life*, p. 76; McGhee, *Envoy to the Middle World*, p. 390.
3   Elm, *Oil, Power and Principle*, p. 70.
4   Kinzer, *All the Shah's Men*, p. 75.
5   Elm, *Oil, Power and Principle*, p. 76.
6   TNA, CAB 129/44/28, Bevin, 'Persia', 22 January 1951.

7   'Iranian Intrigue', *Wall Street Journal*, 4 October 1952; *FRUS*, 1952–54, Iran 1951–54, p. 126, Richards, 'Recent Increase in Political Prestige of Ayatollah Kashani', 20 August 1951; TNA, CAB 129/54/25, Eden, 'Political Developments in Persia', 5 August 1952, circulating Middleton's letter of 28 July 1952.

8   Elm, *Oil, Power and Principle*, p. 74.

9   Elm, *Oil, Power and Principle*, p. 78.

10 Goodman, *The Official History of the Joint Intelligence Committee*, p. 357.

11 McGhee, *Envoy to the Middle World*, p. 327, Falle, *My Lucky Life*, p. 80 (the verdict was Middleton's).

12 *FRUS*, 1951, Vol. V, p. 290, Fritzlan to State Department, 26 March 1951.

13 Thorpe, *Eden*, p. 363; McGhee, *Envoy to the Middle World*, p. 333; TNA, CAB 195/9, meeting of 5 April 1951.

14 Falle, *My Lucky Life*, p. 79.

15 Louis, 'Britain and the Overthrow of Mosaddeq', in Gasiorowski and Byrne, eds, *Mohammad Mosaddeq and the 1953 Coup in Iran*, p. 156; McGhee, *Envoy to the Middle World*, p. 333.

16 USIME, CIA, National Intelligence Estimate: Iran's Position in the East-West Conflict, 5 April 1951; *FRUS*, 1952–54, Vol. X, p. 33, Rountree, memorandum of conversation, 17 April 1951; TNA, CAB 129/45/39, Morrison, 'Persian Oil', 20 April 1951.

17 *FRUS*, 1952–54, Vol. X, p. 33, Rountree, memorandum of conversation, 17 April 1951.

18 TNA, CAB 129/45/39, Morrison, 'Persian Oil', 20 April 1951.

19 TNA, CAB 195/9, meeting of 30 April 1951.

20 *FRUS*, 1952–54, Iran 1951–1954, p. 117, CIA, 'Effects of Closing Down the Iranian Oil Industry', 11 July 1951.

21 *FRUS*, 1952–54, Iran 1951–1954, p. 90, Memorandum for the Record, 16 May 1951.

22 Catterall, ed., *The Macmillan Diaries*, Vol. I, p. 75, 7 May 1951; HC Deb, 29 May 1951, Vol. 488, cc. 41–2.

23 *FRUS*, 1952–54, Vol. X, pp. 58–9, Stutesman, memorandum of conversation, 31 May 1951.

24 Kinzer, *All the Shah's Men*, p. 93.

25 TNA, CAB 195/9/1, meeting of 25 June 1951; TNA, CAB 195/9, meeting of 2 July 1951.

26 *FRUS*, 1952–54, Vol. X, p. 112, Harriman to State Department, 24 July 1951.

27 Elm, *Oil, Power and Principle*, p. 135; TNA, CAB 195/9/1, meeting of 27 September 1951.

28 TNA, CAB 195/9/1, meeting of 27 September 1951.

29 *FRUS*, 1952–54, Vol. X, p. 191, Gross to Hickerson, 2 October 1951; Dorril, *MI6*, p. 562.

30 *FRUS*, 1951, Vol. IV, pp. 974–5, Perkins to Acheson, 26 September 1951.

31 *FRUS*, 1952–54, Vol. X, p. 244, Walters, memorandum of conversation, 28 October 1951.

Chapter 12   Second Fiddle

1   Catterall, ed., *The Macmillan Diaries*, Vol. I, p. 79, 11 June 1951, p. 180, 13–15 August 1952.

2   *FRUS*, 1952–54, Vol. VI, part 1, p. 740, Bradley, notes, 5 January 1952; Thornhill, *Road to Suez*, p. 36.

3   Colville, *The Fringes of Power*, p. 596; HC Deb, 7 November 1951, Vol. 493, c. 193.

4   *FRUS*, 1952–54, Vol. X, p. 280, Acheson to State Department, 10 November 1951; p. 257, Acheson, memorandum of conversation, 4 November 1951; Shuckburgh, *Descent to Suez*, p. 27, 4 November 1951.

5   Shuckburgh, *Descent to Suez*, p. 27, 4 November 1951.

6   *FRUS*, 1952–54, Vol. X, p. 280, Acheson to State Department, 10 November 1951, p. 257.

7   *FRUS*, 1952–54, Vol. VI, p. 1082, memorandum of a meeting between Eisenhower and Churchill, 25 June 1954; Brands, 'The Cairo-Teheran Connection', p. 443; *FRUS*, 1952–54, Vol. X, p. 280, Acheson to State Department, 10 November 1951; p. 257.

8   Thornhill, *Road to Suez*, p. 43; TNA, CAB 195/10, meeting of 12 November 1951.

9   TNA, CAB 195/10, meeting of 12 November 1951.

10 *FRUS*, 1951, Vol. V, p. 431, Note 2; p. 431, Caffery to State Department, 6 December 1951.

11 TNA, CAB 129/48/40, Eden, 'Egypt', 6 December 1951; TNA, CAB 195/10, meeting of 7 December 1951.

12 Shuckburgh, *Descent to Suez*, p. 29, 16 December 1951.

13 *FRUS*, 1951, Vol. V, p. 443, Note 2.

14 *FRUS*, 1952–54, Vol. VI, part 1, p. 721, Gifford to State Department, 28 December 1951.

15 *FRUS*, 1952–54, Vol. VI, p. 731, Acheson, memorandum, 8 January 1952; Shuckburgh, *Descent to Suez*, p. 32, 5 January 1952.

16 Thornhill, *Road to Suez*, p. 55; *FRUS*, 1952–54, Vol. VI, pp. 737–8, Acheson, memorandum, 8 January 1952.

17 Catterall, ed., *The Macmillan Diaries*, Vol. I, p. 133, 17 January 1952.

18 Thornhill, *Road to Suez*, p. 58.

19 Thornhill, *Road to Suez*, p. 64.

20 TNA, FO 141/1453, Hamilton, minute, 13 February 1952.

21 TNA, CAB 195/10, meeting of 14 February 1952; Catterall, ed., *The Macmillan Diaries*, Vol. I, pp. 163–4, 30 May 1952.

22 Lucas and Morey, 'The Hidden "Alliance"', p. 97.

23 O'Sullivan, *FDR and the End of Empire*, p. 61; Grafftey-Smith, *Bright Levant*, pp. 238, 236; MEC, Slade-Baker Papers, diary, 21 August 1952.

24 Lucas, 'Divided We Stand', p. 17.

25 Lucas and Morey, 'The Hidden "Alliance"', p. 19; *FRUS*, 1952–54, Vol. IX, p. 1839, Byroade to Acheson, 21 July 1952.

26 Thornhill, *Road to Suez*, p. 88.

27 Thornhill, *Road to Suez*, p. 88.

28 MEC, Slade-Baker Papers, diary, 19 September 1952.
29 Roosevelt, 'Egypt's Inferiority Complex', p. 357.
30 MEC, Slade-Baker Papers, diary, 19 September 1952.
31 MEC, Slade-Baker Papers, diary, 8 September 1952; Brands, 'The Cairo-Teheran Connection', p. 446; Lucas, 'Divided We Stand', p. 21; Lucas and Morey, 'The Hidden "Alliance"', p. 98.
32 Catterall, ed., *The Macmillan Diaries*, Vol. I, p. 186, 27 September 1952.

Chapter 13   Plotting Mosaddeq's Downfall

 1 Maclean, *Eastern Approaches*, p. 274.
 2 Elm, *Oil, Power and Principle*, p. 235.
 3 TNA, CAB 129/54/25, Eden, 'Political Developments in Persia', 5 August 1952, circulating Middleton's letter of 28 July.
 4 TNA, CAB 195/10, meeting of 29 July 1952.
 5 Rahnema, *Behind the 1953 Coup in Iran*, p. xviii.
 6 TNA, CAB 195/10, meeting of 7 August 1952.
 7 Dobson, *Anglo-American Relations in the Twentieth Century*, p. 116.
 8 Rahnema, *Behind the 1953 Coup in Iran*, p. 25.
 9 'Iranian Intrigue', *Wall Street Journal*, 4 October 1952.
10 Brands, *Inside the Cold War*, p. 267.
11 Rahnema, *Behind the 1953 Coup in Iran*, p. 25; USIME, CIA, 'Prospects for Survival of Mossadeq Regime in Iran', 14 October 1952, and 'Probable Developments in Iran Through 1953', 13 November 1952; Shuckburgh, *Descent to Suez*, p. 55, 20 November 1952.
12 Shuckburgh, *Descent to Suez*, p. 47, 5 November 1952.
13 Talbot, *The Devil's Chessboard*, pp. 200-3; Ferrell, ed., *The Eisenhower Diaries*, p. 237, 14 May 1953; Thornhill, *Road to Suez*, p. 122.
14 Hoopes and Brinkley, *FDR and the Creation of the UN*, p. 56.
15 Catterall, ed., *The Macmillan Diaries*, Vol. II, p. 22, 20 March 1957; Lucas, *Divided We Stand*, p. 37; Dulles, 'Policy for Security and Peace', p. 355.
16 TNA, CAB 195/11, meeting of 30 December 1952.
17 Eisenhower, *Crusade in Europe*, pp. 69-70; Ferrell, ed., *The Eisenhower Diaries*, pp. 222-4, 6 January 1953.
18 Ferrell, ed., *The Eisenhower Diaries*, pp. 222-3, 6 January 1953.
19 Colville, *The Fringes of Power*, pp. 620, 629.
20 Shuckburgh, *Descent to Suez*, p. 71, 7 January 1953.

Chapter 14   The Man in the Arena

 1 *FRUS*, 1952-54, Vol. X, pp. 662-3, Dulles to US Embassy London, 10 February 1953; USIME, CIA, 'Mossadeq Plans to Announce End of Oil Negotiations', 17 February 1953.
 2 *FRUS*, 1952-54, Vol. X, pp. 689-90, CIA, memorandum for the president, 1 March 1953.

3   *FRUS*, 1952–54, Vol. X, pp. 693, 698, memorandum of discussion at the NSC, 4 March 1953; Wevill, *Diplomacy, Roger Makins and the Anglo-American Relationship*, p. 107.

4   USIME, CIA, 'The Iranian Situation', 8 March 1953.

5   *FRUS*, 1952–54, Vol. X, p. 713, memorandum of discussion at the NSC, 10 March 1953.

6   Wilber, *Clandestine Service History: Overthrow of Premier Mossadeq of Iran, November 1952–August 1953*, p. 2.

7   Wilber, *Iran: Past and Present*, p. 90.

8   Wilber, *Clandestine Service History*, p. 9.

9   Wilber, *Clandestine Service History*, p. 6.

10 Roosevelt, *Countercoup*, p. 19.

11 Wilber, *Clandestine Service History*, p. 14; Woodhouse, *Something Ventured*, p. 125.

12 Roosevelt, *Countercoup*, p. 18.

13 Roosevelt, 'Propaganda Techniques of the English Civil Wars', p. 373.

14 Brands, *Inside the Cold War*, p. 272; TNA, FO 371/82393, Rothnie, minute, 19 March 1953.

15 Roosevelt, *Countercoup*, p. 52; Dorril, *MI6*, p. 588.

16 Kinzer, *All the Shah's Men*, p. 9.

17 Wilber, *Clandestine Service History*, p. 27.

18 TNA, FO 371/104569, note by Gandy, 17 August 1953; O'Connell, *King's Counsel*, p. 19; Rahnema, *Behind the 1953 Coup in Iran*, p. 99; Talbot, *The Devil's Chessboard*, p. 229.

19 O'Connell, *King's Counsel*, p. 19.

20 Roosevelt, 'Citizenship in a Republic', 23 April 1910.

21 Wilber, *Clandestine Service History*, p. 51; TNA, FO 371/104569, Makins to FO, 17 August 1953.

22 TNA, FO 371/104569, unsent FO response, 18 August 1953; CIA, *Clandestine Service History*, p. 59.

23 Kinzer, *All the Shah's Men*, p. 175.

24 *Saturday Evening Post*, 6 November 1954, cited in Woodhouse, *Something Ventured*, p. 129.

25 Kinzer, *All the Shah's Men*, p. 181.

26 Wilber, *Clandestine Service History*, pp. 78–9.

27 Roosevelt, *Countercoup*, p. 207.

28 Elm, *Oil, Power and Principle*, p. 277.

29 *FRUS*, 1952–54, Iran 1951–1954, p. 781, Editorial Note.

Chapter 15   The Gift of a Gun

1   *FRUS*, 1952–54, Vol. IX, pp. 11–12, memorandum of conversation, 11 May 1953, p. 21, memorandum of conversation, 12 May 1953.

2   *FRUS*, 1952–54, Vol. IX, p. 25, Caffery to State Department, noon, 13 May 1953; p. 27, Caffery to State Department, 1 p.m. 13 May 1953.

3   *FRUS*, 1952–54, Vol. IX, p. 406, Dulles to Certain Diplomatic Missions, 30 July 1953; Vol. IX, p. 395, memorandum of discussion at the NSC, 9 July 1953.

4   Lucas, *Divided We Stand*, p. 26.

5   Petersen, 'Anglo-American Rivalry in the Middle East', p. 76.

6   Thornhill, *Road to Suez*, p. 163; *FRUS*, 1952–54, Vol. IX, p. 9, memorandum of conversation, 11 May 1953; Catterall, ed., *The Macmillan Diaries*, Vol. I, p. 231, 12 May 1953.

7   *FRUS*, 1952–54, Vol. IX, p. 10, memorandum of conversation, 11 May 1953; MEC, Slade-Baker Papers, diary, 19 January 1954.

8   *FRUS*, 1952–54, Vol. IX, p. 2140, Caffery to State Department, 24 September 1953.

9   *FRUS*, 1952–54, Vol. IX, p. 2219, Dulles to Embassy in the UK, 15 July 1953; MEC, Slade-Baker Papers, diary, 15 January 1954; Thornhill, *Road to Suez*, p. 173.

10 Thorpe, *Eden*, p. 420.

11 *FRUS*, 1952–54, Vol. VI, Part 1, p. 1024, Dulles, memorandum of dinner conversation, 12 April 1954; Mott-Radclyffe, *Foreign Body in the Eye*, pp. 214–15; TNA, CAB 195/12, meeting of 22 June 1954.

12 Thornhill, *Road to* Suez, p. 194; Lucas, *Divided We Stand*, p. 37.

13 TNA, CAB 195/12, meeting of 7 July 1954.

14 Thornhill, *Road to Suez*, p. 207.

15 Copeland, *The Game of Nations*, pp. 176–8; Eveland, *Ropes of Sand*, p. 102.

16 Beeston, *Looking for Trouble*, p. 19; MEC, Slade-Baker Papers, diary, 8 November 1955.

Chapter 16   Baghdad Pact

1   TNA, CAB 129/68/31, Lloyd, 'Future Defence Arrangements with Iraq', 31 May 1954.

2   Nasser described his deal to Slade-Baker, who worked for MI6. MEC, Slade-Baker Papers, diary, 31 July 1954.

3   Shuckburgh, *Descent to Suez*, p. 224, 15 July 1954.

4   TNA, CAB 129/65/4, Eden, 'United States Project to Associate Military Aid to Pakistan with Middle East Defence', 5 January 1954; Sanjian, 'The Formulation of the Baghdad Pact', p. 240.

5   Seale, *The Struggle for Syria*, p. 217; MEC, Slade-Baker Papers, diary, 18 March 1955, 2 February 1956.

6   MEC, Slade-Baker Papers, diary, 2 February 1956; Hart, *Saudi Arabia and the United States*, pp. 235–6.

7   Heikal, *Cutting the Lion's Tail*, p. 75.

8   TNA, FO 371/115493, Stevenson to FO, 'Discussion between the Secretary of State and Egyptian Leaders', 21 February 1955; Lucas, *Divided We Stand*, p. 41.

9   Heikal, *Cutting the Lion's Tail*, p. 77.

10 Thornhill, *Road to Suez*, p. 209; TNA, CAB 195/13, meeting of 15 March 1955.

11   *FRUS*, 1955–57, Vol. XIV, p. 118, memorandum of conversation, 24 March 1955.

12   Ashton, 'The Hijacking of a Pact', p. 132.

13   Wilford, *America's Great Game*, pp. 192–93; Tuhami to Nasser, 18 June 1955, http://digitalarchive.wilsoncenter.org/document/112263.

14   Lucas, *Divided We Stand*, p. 48.

15   *FRUS*, 1955–57, Vol. XIV, p. 237, Byroade to State Department, 9 June 1955.

16   Lucas, *Divided We Stand*, p. 52.

17   Lucas, *Divided We Stand*, p. 52; MEC, Slade-Baker Papers, diary, 5 November 1955.

18   Catterall, ed., *The Macmillan Diaries*, Vol. I, p. 480, 22 September 1955.

19   USIME, Joint Chiefs of Staff, 'Comparative Cost of US Equipment to Egypt as opposed to the Cost of USSR Equipment', 5 October 1955.

20   Copeland, *The Game of Nations*, p. 134.

21   *FRUS*, 1955–57, Vol. XIV, pp. 520–21, State Department to Mission, UN, 27 September 1955.

22   Catterall, ed., *The Macmillan Diaries*, Vol. I, p. 507, 13 November 1955.

23   Shuckburgh, *Descent to Suez*, p. 281, 26 September 1955.

24   Catterall, ed., *The Macmillan Diaries*, Vol. I, p. 489, 2 October 1955.

25   *FRUS*, 1955–57, Vol. XIV, p. 519, memorandum of conversation, 26 September 1955; p. 526, Dulles to State Department, 27 September 1955.

26   *FRUS*, 1955–57, Vol. XIV, p. 543, memorandum of conversation, 3 October 1955.

27   TNA, CAB 195/14, meeting of 4 October 1955.

28   Lucas, *Divided We Stand*, p. 53; TNA, CAB 195/14, meeting of 4 October 1955; TNA, CAB 128/29/34, meeting of 4 October 1955.

Chapter 17   Overreach

1   'Michael Weir', *Daily Telegraph*, 14 August 2006.

2   TNA, DO 35/6313, Samuel, 'Buraimi', 30 September 1955.

3   'Breakdown of Arbitration over Buraimi', *The Times*, 17 September 1955; TNA, DO 35/6313, 'The Buraimi Dispute', 4 October 1955.

4   TNA, DO 35/6313, Samuel, 'Buraimi', 30 September 1955.

5   TNA, CAB 129/78/2, Macmillan, 'Middle East Oil', 13 October 1955; TNA, CAB 128/29/35, Cabinet, conclusions, 18 October 1955; Catterall, ed., *The Macmillan Diaries*, Vol. I, p. 493, 20 October 1955.

6   Shuckburgh, *Descent to Suez*, p. 293, 26 October 1955.

7   Catterall, ed., *The Macmillan Diaries*, Vol. I, p. 508, 20 November 1955; 'Aramco, Disputed by British and Arab Interests, Courts Favor in Saudi Arabia and Gains Profits', *Wall Street Journal*, 28 June 1956, estimated the Saudi share of Aramco's profit at $270 million; Vassiliev, in his *History of Saudi Arabia*, believes that the figure was much higher: $348 million; Philby, 'The Scandal of Arabia – II', *Sunday Times*,

30 October 1955; TNA, CAB 129/78/2, Macmillan, 'Middle East Oil', 14 October 1955; CIA, 'Saudi Arabia: A Disruptive Force in Western-Arab Relations', 18 January 1956.

8   Catterall, ed., *The Macmillan Diaries*, Vol. I, p. 508, 20 November 1955.

9   TNA, FO 371/115954, Turton, memorandum, 12 October 1955.

10 Yeşilbursa, *The Baghdad Pact*, pp. 143–4.

11 *FRUS*, 1955–57, Vol. XIV, p. 821, Dulles to Macmillan, 5 December 1955; Shuckburgh, *Descent to Suez*, p. 307, 2 December 1955.

12 Gorst, '"A Modern Major General": General Sir Gerald Templer, Chief of the Imperial General Staff', in Kelly and Gorst, eds, *Whitehall and the Suez Crisis*, p. 32; Horne, *But What Do You Actually Do?*, pp. 44–5; French, *The British Way in Counter-Insurgency*, p. 1.

13 MEC, Slade-Baker Papers, diary, 13 January 1956.

14 Catterall, ed., *The Macmillan Diaries*, Vol. I, p. 516, 11 December 1955.

15 MEC, Slade-Baker Papers, diary, 13 January 1956.

16 Catterall, ed., *The Macmillan Diaries*, Vol. I, p. 525, 12 January 1956.

17 'British Assessment of Middle East', *Observer*, 8 January 1956.

18 TNA, FO 115/4547, Gardener, letter, 27 January 1956; *FRUS*, 1955–57, Vol. XIII, p. 567, memorandum of conversation, 30 January 1956; TNA, FO 115/4547, minute of the meeting of 30 January 1956; Lucas, *Divided We Stand*, p. 90.

19 TNA, FO 115/4547.

20 TNA, CAB 195/14, meeting of 9 February 1956; 'Palace Brains Trust Angers Desert Rebels', *Daily Express*, 13 February 1956.

21 Glubb, *A Soldier with the Arabs*, p. 300.

22 Asseily and Asfahani, eds, *A Face in the Crowd*, 30/11 'The Situation in Jordan', n.d., 33/11, 'Report from Amman', 11 March 1956.

23 MEC, Slade-Baker Papers, diary, 6 March 1956; Beeston, *Looking for Trouble*, p. 21.

24 TNA, CAB 195/14, meeting of 5 March 1956; Shuckburgh, *Descent to Suez*, p. 341, 3 March 1956.

25 Shuckburgh, *Descent to Suez*, p. 345, 7 March 1956; Thorpe, *Eden*, p. 466.

26 Shuckburgh, *Descent to Suez*, p. 346, 12 March 1956.

27 Shuckburgh, *Descent to Suez*, p. 345, 8 March 1956.

Chapter 18   Ditching Nasser

1 Von Tunzelmann, *Blood and Sand*, p. 100.

2 *FRUS*, 1955–57, Vol. XV, p. 307, Anderson to Dulles, 6 March 1956.

3 Ferrell, ed., *The Eisenhower Diaries*, p. 318, 8 March 1956; Lucas and Morey, 'The Hidden "Alliance"', p. 103.

4 TNA, CAB 195/14, meeting of 21 March 1956.

5 Nutting, *No End of a Lesson*, p. 34. Originally Nutting said that Eden had told him he wanted Nasser destroyed; after Eden's death he said that the word Eden had used was 'murdered'.

6   TNA, CAB 195/14 meeting of 21 March 1956.
7   Ferrell, ed., *The Eisenhower Diaries*, p. 323, 28 March 1956.
8   Wilford, *America's Great Game*, p. 220.
9   Eveland, *Ropes of Sand*, p. 169; Cavendish, *Inside Intelligence*, p. 195; Dorril, *MI6*, p. 569.
10   Eveland, *Ropes of Sand*, p. 170.
11   Young, *Who Is my Liege?*, p. 31.
12   Eveland, *Ropes of Sand*, p. 171.
13   Wilford, *America's Great Game*, p. 224.
14   Heikal, *Cutting the Lion's Tail*, p. 118.
15   Eveland, *Ropes of Sand*, p. 181; Wilford, *America's Great Game*, p. 224.
16   Eveland, *Ropes of Sand*, p. 189.
17   Eveland, *Ropes of Sand*, p. 190.
18   'US to Reshuffle Envoys to Bolster Role in Mideast', *New York Times*, 16 July 1956.
19   Ferrell, ed., *The Eisenhower Diaries*, p. 318, 8 March 1956.
20   TNA, AIR 19/0163, Mclean, 'Notes on Conversation with King Saud, Riyadh', 22 October 1962; Vitalis, *America's Kingdom*, p. 164; MEC, Slade-Baker Papers, diary, 6 March 1955, 3 July 1956.
21   MEC, Slade-Baker Papers, diary, 28 June 1956.
22   Asseily and Asfahani, eds, *A Face in the Crowd*, p. 157, 131/13,'Report on Development of Arab political activities in Lebanon in relation to the opposition to and support of the Turkish Alliance', n.d.
23   MEC, Slade-Baker Papers, diary, 10 February 1957.
24   TNA, CAB 129/82/34, Lloyd, 'Egypt', 20 July 1956.
25   Lucas, *Divided We Stand*, p. 136.
26   *FRUS*, 1955–57, Vol. XV, p. 867, memorandum of a telephone conversation, 19 July 1956; Kyle, *Suez*, p. 129; Lucas, *Divided We Stand*, p. 137.
27   *FRUS*, 1955–57, Vol. XV, p. 873, memorandum of telephone conversation, 19 July 1956; MEC, Slade-Baker Papers, diary, 21 July 1956.

Chapter 19   A Sort of Jenkins' Ear

1   Thorpe, *Eden*, p. 101.
2   'Suez Canal Company', *The Times*, 18 June 1956.
3   Von Tunzelmann, *Blood and Sand*, p. 28.
4   MEC, Slade-Baker Papers, diary, 26 July 1956.
5   Horne, *Macmillan*, Vol. I, p. 395.
6   Owen, *In Sickness and in Power*, p. 121.
7   Lane, 'The Past as Matrix: Sir Ivone Kirkpatrick, Permanent Under-Secretary for Foreign Affairs', in Kelly and Gorst, eds, *Whitehall and the Suez Crisis*, p. 209.
8   Shuckburgh, *Descent to Suez*, p. 178, 26 April 1954; Lucas, *Divided We Stand*, p. 142.

9 TNA, CAB 195/15, meeting of 27 July 1956.
10 *FRUS*, 1955–57, Vol. XVI, p. 9, Eden to Eisenhower, 27 July 1956.
11 *FRUS*, 1955–57, Vol. XVI, pp. 61–2, Murphy to Dulles and Hoover, 31 July 1956.
12 CIA, Intelligence Estimate, 'Nasser and the Middle East Situation', 31 July 1956; *FRUS*, 1955–57, Vol. XVI, p. 70, Eisenhower to Eden, 31 July 1956.
13 *FRUS*, 1955–57, Vol. XVI, pp. 98–9, memorandum of conversation, 1 August 1956.
14 TNA, CAB 195/15 meeting of 1 August 1956. Dulles used 'disgorge' in a meeting with Eisenhower on 31 July, and again in his meeting with Lloyd before his lunch with Eden on 1 August (*FRUS*, 1955–57, Vol. XVI pp. 64, 95).
15 Kyle, *Suez*, p. 163.
16 *FRUS*, 1955–57, Vol. XVI, p. 119, Note 3.
17 HC Deb, 2 August 1956, Vol. 557, cc. 1603, 1608.
18 'Channel Race Ban on Egyptians', *The Times*, 3 August 1956; 'One Man's War Breaks Out in Mayfair', *Daily Express*, 3 August 1956.
19 Catterall, ed., *The Macmillan Diaries*, Vol. I, p. 586, 9 August 1956; TNA, CAB 195/15, meeting of 14 August 1956; MEC, Slade-Baker Papers, diary, 22 August 1956. Slade-Baker's connection to MI6 is clear from his diary entries of 28 August and 12 September 1952.
20 Lucas, *Divided We Stand*, p. 180.
21 Lucas, *Divided We Stand*, p. 186.
22 *FRUS*, 1955–57, Vol. XVI, pp. 402–3, Eden to Eisenhower, 6 September 1956.
23 Lane, 'The Past as Matrix' in Kelly and Gorst, eds., *Whitehall and the Suez Crisis*, p. 209 ; TNA, CAB 195/15, meeting of 11 September 1956.
24 HC Deb, 12 September 1956, Vol. 558, c. 11.
25 Kyle, *Suez*, p. 246.
26 HC Deb, 13 September 1956, Vol. 558, c. 304.
27 MEC, Slade-Baker Papers, diary, 15 September 1956.

Chapter 20   The Suez Miscalculation

1 Von Tunzelmann, *Blood and Sand*, p. 138.
2 Barr, *A Line in the Sand*, pp. 286–93, 336–48.
3 Lucas, *Divided We Stand*, p. 227; Shlaim, 'The Protocol of Sevres', p. 512.
4 Kyle, *Suez*, p. 296.
5 Von Tunzelmann, *Blood and Sand*, p. 134; Onslow, 'Unreconstructed Nationalists and a Minor Gunboat Operation', p. 81.
6 TNA, CAB 195/15 meeting of 18 October 1956.
7 Lucas, *Divided We Stand*, p. 208.
8 Kyle, *Suez*, p. 256.
9 Shuckburgh, *Descent to Suez*, p. 317, 5 January 1956.
10 TNA, CAB 195/15, meeting of 18 October 1956.
11 Von Tunzelmann, *Blood and Sand*, p. 46.

12 TNA, CAB 195/15, meeting of 23 October 1956.
13 Heath, *The Course of my Life*, p. 169; TNA, CAB 128/30/74, Cabinet, 74th Conclusions, 25 October 1956.
14 TNA, CAB 138/30/74, Cabinet, 74th Conclusions, 25 October 1956.
15 MEC, Slade-Baker Papers, diary, 23 January 1957.
16 *FRUS*, 1955–57, Vol. XVI, p. 798, Special Watch Report, 28 October 1956.
17 *FRUS*, 1955–57, Vol. XVI, p. 818, Aldrich to State Department, 29 October 1956.
18 *FRUS*, 1955–57, Vol. XVI, p. 818, Aldrich to State Department, 29 October 1956.
19 *FRUS*, 1955–57, Vol. XVI, p. 807, memorandum of a telephone conversation, 28 October 1956.
20 *FRUS*, 1955–57, Vol. XVI, p. 807, memorandum of a telephone conversation, 28 October 1956.
21 *FRUS*, 1955–57, Vol. XVI, pp. 815–16, Dulles to Embassy in France, 29 October 1956.
22 Hennessy, *The Prime Minister*, p. 236; Lane, 'The Past as Matrix', in Kelly and Gorst, eds, *Whitehall and the Suez Crisis*, p. 213.
23 Shuckburgh, *Descent to Suez*, p. 362, 1 November 1956; Von Tunzelmann, *Blood and Sand*, p. 215.
24 *FRUS*, 1955–57, Vol. XVI, p. 849, Eisenhower to Eden, 30 October 1956.
25 TNA, CAB 195/15, meeting of 2 November 1956, at 4.30 p.m.
26 Von Tunzelmann, *Blood and Sand*, p. 297.
27 CAB 195/15, meeting of 4 November 1956.
28 HC Deb, 5 November 1956, Vol. 558, c. 1966; Kyle, *Suez*, p. 452.
29 *FRUS*, 1955–57, Vol. XVI, pp. 985–6, Eden to Eisenhower, 5 November 1956.
30 *FRUS*, 1955–57, Vol. XVI, p. 1001, memorandum of a conference with the president, 5 November 1956.
31 Thorpe, *Eden*, p. 529.
32 TNA, CAB 128/30, Cabinet, conclusions, 2 November 1956, 4.30 p.m. meeting; CAB 195/16, meeting of 8 January 1957; Horne, *Macmillan*, p. 441.
33 Thorpe, *Eden*, p. 538; Lucas, *Divided We Stand*, p. 311.
34 Smith, *Ending Empire in the Middle East*, p. 65; TNA, CAB 195/16, meeting of 28 November 1956.

Chapter 21   Failed Coups

1 Eveland, *Ropes of Sand*, p. 227; Lucas and Morey, 'The Hidden "Alliance"', p. 112; Little, 'Cold War and Covert Action', p. 67.
2 Hahn, 'Securing the Middle East', p. 39.
3 Johnston, *The Brink of Jordan*, p. 80.
4 Johnston, *The Brink of Jordan*, p. 54.
5 *FRUS*, 1955–57, Vol. XIII p. 89, Mallory to State Department, 29 March 1957; Wilford, *America's Great Game*, p. 267.

6 Wilford, *America's Great Game*, p. 267; Shlaim, *Lion of Jordan*, p. 131.

7 MEC, Slade-Baker Papers, diary, 11 April 1957.

8 MEC, Slade-Baker Papers, diary, 23, 30 April 1957; Johnston, *The Brink of Jordan*, p. 67.

9 *FRUS*, 1955–57, Vol. XIII, p. 109, Editorial Note.

10 Seale, *The Struggle for Syria*, pp. 281, 319.

11 Rathmell, *Secret War in the Middle East*, p. 138.

12 Asseily and Asfahani, eds, *A Face in the Crowd*, 144/12, report dated 30 May 1957; Rathmell, *Secret War in the Middle East*, p. 136.

13 MEC, Slade-Baker Papers, diary, 6 August 1957; Little, 'Cold War and Covert Action', p. 70.

14 Rathmell, *Secret War in the Middle East*, p. 137.

15 *FRUS*, 1955–57, XIII, p. 642, Dulles to Eisenhower, 20 August 1957.

16 Little, 'Cold War and Covert Action', p. 72; *FRUS*, 1955–57, Vol. XIII, p. 648, Dulles to Lloyd, 21 August 1957.

17 Goodman, *The Official History of the Joint Intelligence Committee*, p. 396; Catterall, ed., *The Macmillan Diaries*, Vol. II, p. 55, 27 August 1957.

18 Catterall, ed., *The Macmillan Diaries*, Vol. II, pp. 57–8, 7 September 1957.

19 Kirk, 'The Syrian Crisis of 1957', p. 60; *FRUS*, 1955–57, Vol. XIII, p. 702, memorandum of NSC discussion, 12 September 1957.

20 Asseily and Asfahani, eds, *A Face in the Crowd*, p. 143, 173/12, 'The Situation in Syria'; TNA, CAB 195/16, meeting of 8 October 1957.

21 *FRUS*, 1955–57, Vol. XIII, p. 718, Strong to Rountree, 16 October 1957.

Chapter 22 The Year of Revolutions

1 *FRUS*, 1955–57, Vol. XIII, p. 745, Hare to State Department, 11 December 1957.

2 MEC, Slade-Baker Papers, diary, 12 February 1958.

3 Eveland, *Ropes of Sand*, p. 271; Seale, *The Struggle for Syria*, p. 323.

4 Yapp, *The Near East Since the First World War*, p. 104.

5 Johnston, *The Brink of Jordan*, p. 88.

6 MEC, Slade-Baker Papers, diary, 13 February 1958; Yaqub, *Containing Arab Nationalism*, p. 194.

7 MEC, Slade-Baker Papers, diary, 15 February 1958.

8 MEC, Slade-Baker Papers, diary, 28 March 1958.

9 Yaqub, *Containing Arab Nationalism*, p. 197; MEC, Slade-Baker Papers, diary, 27 April 1959.

10 Yaqub, *Containing Arab Nationalism*, p. 209.

11 *FRUS*, 1958–60, Vol. XI, p. 47, memorandum of conversation, 13 May 1958.

12 TNA, CAB 195/17, meeting of 13 May 1958; Catterall, ed., *The Macmillan Diaries*, Vol. II, p. 116, 13 May 1958.

13 Ionides, *Divide and Lose*, p. 189; MEC, Slade-Baker Papers, diary, 7 October 1957.

14   Falle, *My Lucky Life*, p. 108.
15   Falle, *My Lucky Life*, pp. 106–7, 118–19.
16   MEC, Slade-Baker Papers, diary, 6 March 1958.
17   Falle, *My Lucky Life*, p. 113; MEC, Slade-Baker Papers, diary, 13 March 1958; TNA, CAB 195/17, meeting of 18 March 1958.
18   Shlaim, *Lion of Jordan*, p. 158.
19   Falle, *My Lucky Life*, p. 141; Beeston, *Looking for Trouble*, p. 52.
20   TNA, CAB 195/17, meeting of 14 July 1958 at 7.30 p.m.; Ovendale, 'Great Britain and the Anglo-American Invasion', p. 291.
21   Catterall, ed., *The Macmillan Diaries*, Vol. II, p. 134, 14 July 1958; TNA, CAB 195/17, meeting of 14 July 1958 at 11 p.m.
22   Beeston, *Looking for Trouble*, p. 48.
23   Catterall, ed., *The Macmillan Diaries*, Vol. II, p. 135, 16 July 1958.
24   Catterall, ed., *The Macmillan Diaries*, Vol. II, p. 136, 17 July 1958.

Chapter 23   Rebels on the Jebel

1   Parris and Bryson, *Parting Shots*, p. 330.
2   Mangold, *What the British Did*, p. 29; Hart, *Saudi Arabia and the United States*, p. 75.
3   Morris, *Sultan in Oman*, p. 10.
4   TNA, CAB 195/16, meeting of 18 July 1957.
5   TNA, CAB 195/16, meeting of 18 July 1957.
6   TNA, CAB 195/16, meeting of 23 July 1957; 'US–British Rift Denied', *Washington Post*, 24 July 1957.
7   *FRUS*, 1955–57, Vol. XIII, p. 233, Editorial Note.
8   Catterall, ed., *The Macmillan Diaries*, Vol. II, p. 54, 13 August 1957.
9   'Britain's Burden in Arabia', *The Times*, 22 August 1957.
10   'New Ideas on the Tide of Oil', *The Times*, 21 August 1957.
11   Thesiger, *Arabian Sands*, pp. 316–17.
12   Allfree, *Warlords of Oman*, p. 98.
13   Bailey, *The Wildest Province*, p. 252.
14   MEC, Smiley Papers, Smiley, letter, 5 December 1959.
15   Mott-Radclyffe, *Foreign Body in the Eye*, p. 232; Smiley, *Arabian Assignment*, p. 18.
16   Catterall, ed., *The Macmillan Diaries*, Vol. I, p. 448, 14 July 1955; Morton, *Buraimi*, p. 37.
17   Smiley, *Arabian Assignment*, pp. 41–2 ; 'New Ideas on the Tide of Oil', *The Times*, 21 August 1957.
18   Smiley, *Arabian Assignment*, pp. 49–50.
19   Smiley, *Arabian Assignment*, p. 65.
20   Smiley, *Arabian Assignment*, p. 66.
21   Smiley, *Arabian Assignment*, p. 68.
22   MEC, Smiley Papers, Smiley to Amery, August 1958.
23   TNA, CAB 131/20, Lloyd, 'Muscat and Oman', 1 October 1958.

24   TNA, CAB 131/20, Report by the Working Party on Oman Policy, 7 November 1958, Annex A, 'Outline Concept of Special Operations in Oman'; Smiley, *Arabian Assignment*, p. 70.

25   MEC, Smiley Papers, Smiley, letter, 28 October 1958.

26   MEC, Graham Papers, Deane-Drummond, '22 Special Air Service Operations in Muscat & Oman 1958/59', n.d.

Chapter 24   Iraq and Kuwait

1   TNA, CAB 129/87/38, Lloyd, 'Persian Gulf', 7 June 1957.

2   TNA, CAB 129/87/38, Lloyd, 'Persian Gulf', 7 June 1957, Annex I.

3   TNA, CAB 195/17, meeting of 31 July 1958.

4   The coup's mastermind was Rashid Ali al Gailani. By then the CIA had close links with Nazi German intelligence officers, who had encouraged Gailani to try to overthrow the government in Iraq in 1941. Trevelyan, *Public and Private*, p. 44; MEC, Slade-Baker Papers, diary, 24 February 1959; *FRUS*, 1958–60, Vol. XII, p. 445, memorandum of discussion at the NSC, 30 April 1959.

5   Trevelyan, *Public and Private*, p. 45; MEC, Slade-Baker Papers, diary, 10 July 1959.

6   Trevelyan, *Public and Private*, p. 45; Worrall, 'Coping with the Coup d'Etat', p. 189.

7   Trevelyan, *Public and Private*, p. 46.

8   MEC, Slade-Baker Papers, diary, 24 February 1959; Trevelyan, *Public and Private*, pp. 42, 46; Falle, *My Lucky Life*, p. 145; MEC, Slade-Baker Papers, diary, 19 December 1959.

9   MEC, Slade-Baker Papers, diary, 16 February 1959; MEC, Slade-Baker Papers, diary, 17 February 1959; MEC, Slade-Baker Papers, diary, 14 March 1958.

10   Mobley, 'Gauging the Iraqi Threat', p. 21; Catterall, ed., *The Macmillan Diaries*, Vol. II, p. 137, 18 July 1958.

11   Bower, *The Perfect English Spy*, p. 237.

12   Trevelyan, *The Middle East in Revolution*, p. 188.

13   TNA, FO 371/164266, Baghdad to Foreign Office, 20 January 1962; CAB 131/25, Cabinet Defence Committee, minutes, 29 June 1961; Winger, 'Twilight on the British Gulf', p. 666.

14   TNA, CAB 195/19, meeting of 3 July 1961.

15   Bower, *The Perfect English Spy*, p. 238.

16   Wolfe-Hunnicutt, 'The End of the Concessionary Regime', p. 51.

17   Wolfe-Hunnicutt, 'The End of the Concessionary Regime', pp. 49–50.

18   Lakeland Oral History Interview (Seeley G. Mudd Manuscript Library, Princeton), p. 43.

19   *FRUS*, 1961–1963, Vol. XVIII, p. 343, note 1; Aburish, *A Brutal Friendship*, p. 140.

Chapter 25 Pandora's Box

1 Hart-Davis, *The War That Never Was*, p. 5; HC Deb, 13 November 1962, Vol. 667, c. 247.
2 MEC, Slade-Baker Papers, diary, 5 June 1956; TNA, CAB 195/17, meetings of 14, 15 April 1958.
3 'New Wind in an Old Quarter?', *The Times*, 21 September 1962; Beeston, *Looking for Trouble*, p. 41.
4 Adams Schmidt, *Yemen*, p. 45.
5 TNA, AIR 19/1063, McLean, 'Report on Visit to the Yemen, 4 December – 16 December 1962', n.d.; TNA, AIR 19/1063, Report of Visit to the Yemen 27–30 October 1962 by Lt Col Neil McLean.
6 Ferris, *Nasser's Gamble*, p. 24.
7 Bass, *Support Any Friend*, pp. 100, 77, 89.
8 *FRUS*, 1961–63, Vol. XVIII, p. 177, Komer to Talbot, 12 October 1962.
9 Hart, *Saudi Arabia and the United States*, p. 115.
10 Taylor Fain, 'John F. Kennedy and Harold Macmillan', p. 109.
11 Clark, *Yemen*, p. 91; Bower, *The Perfect English Spy*, p. 248.
12 TNA, CAB 128/36, 59th Conclusions, 9 October 1962; TNA, CAB 128/36, 61st Conclusions, 23 October 1962.
13 Catterall, ed., *The Macmillan Diaries*, Vol. II, p. 509, 22 October 1962.
14 Bower, *The Perfect English Spy*, pp. 244–5.
15 Fielding, *One Man in his Time*, p. xii; HC Deb, 7 March 1956, Vol. 549, c. 2146.
16 'MP Not Guilty on Drinking Charge', *Guardian*, 16 January 1963.
17 TNA, AIR 19/1063, Report of Visit to the Yemen 27–30 October 1962 by Lt Col Neil McLean.
18 TNA, AIR 19/1063, Report of Visit to the Yemen 27–30 October 1962 by Lt Col Neil McLean.
19 'With the Loyalists in the Yemen', by Neil McLean, *Daily Telegraph*, 6 November 1962; Hart-Davis, *The War That Never Was*, p. 35.
20 TNA, AIR 19/1063, Report of Visit to the Yemen 27–30 October 1962 by Lt Col Neil McLean; TNA, CAB 128/36, 66th Conclusions, 6 November 1962.
21 *FRUS*, 1961–63, Vol. XVIII, p. 238, Komer to Kennedy, 21 November 1962.
22 TNA, AIR 19/1063, 'Report on Visit to the Yemen, 4 December–16 December 1962'; Bower, *The Perfect English Spy*, p. 247.
23 TNA, CAB 129/112, 'The Yemen', 10 January 1963; Catterall, ed., *The Macmillan Diaries*, Vol. II, p. 541, 17 February 1963.
24 TNA, CAB 195/22, meeting of 3 January 1963; Catterall, ed., *The Macmillan Diaries*, Vol. II, p. 538.
25 Catterall, ed., *The Macmillan Diaries*, Vol. II, p. 544, 7 March 1963.
26 Bower, *The Perfect English Spy*, pp. 246–7.

Chapter 26   Secret War

1   Hart-Davis, *The War That Never Was*, p. 12.
2   Bass, *Support Any Friend*, p. 101.
3   Hart-Davis, *The War That Never Was*, p. 12.
4   Hart-Davis, *The War That Never Was*, p. 12.
5   Macintyre, *SAS*, pp. 185–6.
6   HC Deb 22 March 1963, Vol. 674, c. 810.
7   TNA, AIR 19/1063, McLean, 'Report on Visit to the Yemen, 4 December – 16 December 1962'.
8   Hart-Davis, *The War That Never Was*, pp. 55, 50, 64; TNA, AIR 19/1063, McLean, 'Report on Visit to the Yemen, 4 December–16 December 1962'.
9   Walker, *Aden Insurgency*, p. 57.
10   Smiley, *Arabian Assignment*, p. 104.
11   Smiley, *Arabian Assignment*, p. 124.
12   Smiley, *Arabian Assignment*, p. 150.
13   Adams Schmidt, *Yemen*, p. 258.
14   *FRUS*, 1961–63, Vol. XVIII, p. 640; Badeau to State Department, 11 July 1963.
15   Bower, *The Perfect English Spy*, p. 248.
16   Aldrich and Cormac, *The Black Door*, p. 244; Mawby, 'The Clandestine Defence of Empire', p. 119.
17   *FRUS*, 1961–63, Vol. XVIII, p. 752, Rusk to Badeau, message from Kennedy to Nasser, 19 October 1963.
18   *FRUS*, 1961–63, Vol. XVIII, p. 822, Rusk to London Embassy, 3 December 1963.
19   Ferris, *Nasser's Gamble*, p. 220; Hart-Davis, *The War That Never Was*, pp. 125, 160.
20   Jones, 'Where the State Feared to Tread', p. 731.
21   HC Deb, 18 February 1964, Vol. 689, c. 1024; 'Firm Denies Yemen Arms Deal', *The Times*, 25 February 1964.
22   Smith, *Ending Empire in the Middle East*, p. 107; Hart-Davis, *The War That Never Was*, p. 131.
23   TNA, FO 371/174629, T.F. Brenchley, 'Yemen: The Harib Incident', 14 April 1964.
24   *FRUS*, 1964–68, Vol. XXI, p. 624, Bundy to Johnson, 9 April 1964.
25   *FRUS*, 1964–68, Vol. XXI, No. 330, Johnson to Douglas-Home, 12 April 1964.
26   Smith, *Ending Empire in the Middle East*, p. 108.
27   *FRUS*, 1964–68, Vol. XXI, p. 633, Komer to Bundy, 28 April 1964.
28   *FRUS*, 1964–68, Vol. XXI, p. 638, Badeau to State Department, 8 May 1964; 'The Story Behind These Five Captured Letters', *Sunday Times*, 5 July 1964.
29   'Surprise Visit to Yemen by President Nasser', *The Times*, 24 April 1964.

Chapter 27   Falling Out

1   Little, *South Arabia*, pp. 69, 125.
2   Clark, *Yemen*, p. 83.
3   Little, *South Arabia*, p. 182.
4   Clark, *Yemen*, p. 83.
5   French, *The British Way in Counter-Insurgency*, p. 58.
6   Andrew, *The Defence of the Realm*, p. 474.
7   TNA, CAB 195/24, meeting of 18 October 1964.
8   TNA, CAB 195/24, meeting of 26 November 1964; Healey, *The Time of my Life*, pp. 278–9.
9   Little, *South Arabia*, p. 115.
10 Walker, *Aden Insurgency*, p. 141; French, *The British Way in Counter-Insurgency*, p. 25.
11 French, *The British Way in Counter-Insurgency*, p. 26.
12 Healey, *The Time of my Life*, pp. 282, 283.
13 *FRUS*, 1964–68, Vol. XII, No. 250, Bundy to Johnson, 10 September 1965; Pham, *Ending 'East of Suez'*, p. 38.
14 Healey, *The Time of my Life*, p. 281.
15 Smith, *Ending Empire in the Middle East*, p. 113; TNA, CAB 128/39, CC(65) 49th Conclusions, 23 September 1965; Pham, *Ending 'East of Suez'*, p. 39.
16 'Wasted Years in South Arabia', *The Times*, 12 October 1965.
17 *FRUS*, 1964–68, Vol. XXI, p. 152, circular airgram from State Department to certain posts, 15 October 1965.
18 *FRUS*, 1964–68, Vol. XII, p. 511, memorandum: 'visit of Prime Minister Wilson', n.d.; *FRUS*, 1964–68, Vol. XII, p. 542, Fowler to Johnson, 18 July 1966.
19 Ferris, *Nasser's Gamble*, p. 250.
20 Falle, *My Lucky Life*, p. 170.
21 Little, *South Arabia*, p. 168.
22 'Aden Struggle Over Who Will Succeed the British', *The Times*, 21 June 1967.
23 Walker, *Aden Insurgency*, p. 248; Mitchell, *Having Been a Soldier*, p. 13.
24 Mitchell, *Having Been a Soldier*, pp. 115, 1.
25 Trevelyan, *Public and Private*, p. 73.
26 'Lt Col CC "Mad Mitch" Mitchell', *Daily Telegraph*, 24 July 1996; French, *The British Way in Counter-Insurgency*, p. 151.
27 Trevelyan, *Public and Private*, p. 75.

Epilogue

1   Smith, *Ending Empire in the Middle East*, p. 119.
2   TNA, CAB 128/43, CC (67) 6th Conclusions, 12 January 1968; *FRUS*, 1964–68, Vol. XII, p. 604, memorandum of conversation, 1 January 1968.

3 TNA, CAB 128/43, CC (67) 6th Conclusions, 12 January 1968.
4 Akehurst, *We Won a War*, p. 8.
5 The missing file is FO 1016/795.
6 Buchan, *Days of God*, p. 167.

BIBLIOGRAPHY

1. Archive Sources

Churchill College, Cambridge
Amery, L.

India Office Records, London
L/PS Series files (India Office: Political and Secret Department Records
    1756–*c.* 1950)
R/15 Series files (Gulf States: Records of the Bushire, Bahrain, Kuwait,
    Muscat and Trucial States Agencies 1763–1951)

Middle East Centre Archives, Oxford
Crossman, R.
Deane-Drummond, A.
Graham, J.
Paxton, J.
Philby, H.
Slade-Baker, J.
Smiley, D.

National Archives, London
Files from series:
AIR 19 (Air Ministry: Private Office Papers)
CAB 66 (Cabinet: Second World War Memoranda)
CAB 67 (Second World War Memoranda)
CAB 110 (War Cabinet and Cabinet Office: Joint American Secretariat:
    Correspondence and Papers)
CAB 128 (Cabinet Post-War Conclusions)
CAB 129 (Cabinet Post-War Memoranda)

CAB 131 (Cabinet: Defence Committee: Minutes and Papers)

CAB 134 (Cabinet: Miscellaneous Committees: Minutes and Papers)

CAB 195 (Cabinet Secretary's Notebooks)

CAB 301 (Cabinet Office: Cabinet Secretary's Miscellaneous Papers, 1936–1952)

CO 537 (Colonial Office: Confidential General and Confidential Original Correspondence)

CO 733 (Colonial Office: Palestine Original Correspondence)

CO 967 (Colonial Office: Private Office Papers)

DO 35 (Dominions Office and Commonwealth Relations Office: Original Correspondence)

FO 115 (Foreign Office: Embassy and Consulates: United States: General Correspondence)

FO 141 (Foreign Office: Embassy and Consulates: Egypt: General Correspondence)

FO 248 (Foreign Office: Embassy and Consulates: Iran: General Correspondence)

FO 371 (Foreign Office: Political Departments: General Correspondence)

FO 800 (Foreign Office, Private Offices, Various Ministers' and Officials' Papers)

FO 898 (Political Warfare Executive and Foreign Office: Political Intelligence Department: Papers)

FO 921 (War Cabinet: Office of the Minister of State Resident in the Middle East: Registered Files)

FO 1093 (Permanent Under-Secretary's Department: Registered and Unregistered Papers)

HS 3 (Special Operations Executive: Africa and Middle East Group: Registered Files)

KV 3 (Security Service: Subject Files)

PREM 4 (Prime Minister's Office: Confidential Correspondence and Papers)

PREM 11 (Prime Minister's Office: Correspondence and Papers, 1951–1964)

T 220 (Treasury: Imperial and Foreign Division: Registered Files)

2. Online Archives and Sources

Aid, Matthew M., ed., US Intelligence on the Middle East 1945–2009, http://primarysources.brillonline.com/browse/us-intelligence-on-the-middle-east

Eddy, W., *FDR meets Ibn Saud*, http://susris.com/wp-content/uploads/2014/02/100222–fdr-abdulaziz-eddy.pdf

Foreign Relations of the United States, Volumes covering 1941–1971, https://history.state.gov/historicaldocuments

Lakeland, W., interview (Seeley G. Mudd Manuscript Library, Princeton), http://models.street-artists.org/wp-content/uploads/2010/07/Lakeland-interview-final.pdf

Stutesman, J., oral history interview, http://www.adst.org/OH%20TOCs/Stutesman,%20John%20H.toc.pdf

Reports by H. Tuhami for Nasser: http://digitalarchive.wilsoncenter.org/document/112263; http://digitalarchive.wilsoncenter.org/document/112262

Wilber, D., *Clandestine Service History: Overthrow of Premier Mossadeq of Iran, November 1952–August 1953*, March 1954, https://nsarchive2.gwu.edu/NSAEBB/ciacase/Clandestine%20Service%20History.pdf

3. Books, Theses and Articles

Abdelrehim, N, 'Oil Nationalisation and Managerial Disclosure: The Case of Anglo-Iranian Oil Company, 1933–1951', PhD thesis, University of York 2010

Aburish, S., *The St George Hotel Bar*, London 1989

Adams Schmidt, D., *Yemen: The Unknown War*, London 1968

Akehurst, J., *We Won a War: The Campaign in Oman, 1965–75*, Wilton 1982

Aldrich, R., *The Hidden Hand: Britain, America and Cold War Secret Intelligence*, London 2002

Aldrich, R., 'Policing the Past: Official History, Secrecy and British Intelligence Since 1945', *The English Historical Review*, Vol. 119, No. 483 (September 2004), pp. 922–53

Aldrich, R., and Cormac, R., *The Black Door: Secret Intelligence and 10 Downing Street*, London 2016

Allfree, P., *Warlords of Oman*, London 1967

Anderson, I., *Aramco, the United States, and Saudi Arabia: A Study of the Dynamics of Foreign Oil Policy, 1933–1950*, Princeton 1980

Anderson, P., '"Summer Madness": The Crisis in Syria, August–October 1957', *British Journal of Middle Eastern Studies*, Vol. 22, No. 1/2 (1995), pp. 21–42

Andrew, C., *The Defence of the Realm : The Authorized History of MI5*, London 2009

Ashton, N., 'The Hijacking of a Pact: The Formation of the Baghdad Pact and Anglo-American Tensions in the Middle East, 1955–58', *Review of International Studies*, Vol. 19, No. 2 (April 1993), pp. 123–37

Ashton, N., 'A Microcosm of Decline: British Loss of Nerve and Military Intervention in Jordan and Kuwait, 1958 and 1961', *The Historical Journal*, Vol. 40, No. 4 (December 1997), pp. 1069–83

Asseily, Y., and Asfahani, A., eds, *A Face in the Crowd: A Selection from Emir Farid Chehab's Private Archives*, London 2007

Bailey, R., *The Wildest Province: SOE in the Land of the Eagle*, London 2008

Baram, P., *The Department of State in the Middle East 1919–1945*, Univ. of Pennsylvania Press 1978

Barger, T., 'Middle Eastern Oil Since the Second World War', *Annals of the American Academy of Political and Social Science*, Vol. 401, America and the Middle East (May 1972), pp. 31–44

Barr, J., *A Line in the Sand*, London 2011

Bass, W., *Support Any Friend*, New York 2003

Beeston, R., *Looking for Trouble: The Life and Times of a Foreign Correspondent*, London 1997

Beschloss, M., *Kennedy and Roosevelt: The Uneasy Alliance*, New York *c.* 1980

Bew, J., *Citizen Clem: A Biography of Attlee*, London 2016

Blackwell, S., 'A Desert Squall: Anglo-American Planning for Military Intervention in Iraq, July 1958–August 1959', *Middle Eastern Studies*, Vol. 35, No. 3 (July 1999), pp. 1–18

Bower, T., *The Perfect English Spy: Sir Dick White and the Secret War, 1935–90*, London 1995

Bradshaw, T., 'History Invented: The British–Transjordanian "Collusion" Revisited', *Middle Eastern Studies*, Vol. 43, No. 1 (January 2007), pp. 21–43

Brands, H. W., 'The Cairo-Teheran Connection in Anglo-American Rivalry in the Middle East, 1951–53', *International History Review*, Vol. 11, No. 3 (August 1989), pp. 434–56

Brands, H. W., *Inside the Cold War: Loy Henderson and the Rise of the American Empire, 1918–1961*, New York 1991

Brecher, F., 'US Secretary of State George C. Marshall's Losing Battles against President Harry S. Truman's Palestine Policy, January–June 1948', *Middle Eastern Studies*, Vol. 48, No. 2 (March 2012), pp. 227–47

Brinkley D., and Facey-Crowther, D., eds, *The Atlantic Charter*, Basingstoke 1994

Buchan, J., *Days of God*, London 2012

Burrows, B., *Footnotes in the Sand*, Salisbury 1990

Catterall, P., ed., *The Macmillan Diaries*, Vols I and II, London 2003, 2011

Cavendish, A., *Inside Intelligence*, London 1997

Cesarani, D., *Major Farran's Hat: Murder, Scandal and Britain's War against Jewish Terrorism 1945–48*, London 2009

Chamoun, C., *Crise au Moyen Orient*, Paris 1963

Charmley, J., 'Churchill and the American Alliance', *Transactions of the Royal Historical Society*, Sixth Series, Vol. 11 (2001), pp. 353–71

Churchill, W. S., *The World Crisis 1911–1914*, London 1923

Churchill, W. S., 'Europe's Plea to Roosevelt', *Evening Standard*, 10 December 1937

Churchill, W. S., *Great Contemporaries*, London 1939

Churchill, W. S., *The Second World War*, Vols. I–VI, London 1948–54

Citino, N., 'Internationalist Oilmen, the Middle East, and the Remaking of American Liberalism, 1945–1953', *Business History Review*, Vol. 84, No. 2 (Summer 2010), pp. 227–51

Clark, V., *Yemen: Dancing on the Heads of Snakes*, New Haven 2010

Cohen, M., 'The British White Paper on Palestine, May 1939. Part II: The Testing of a Policy, 1942–1945', *The Historical Journal*, Vol. 19, No. 3 (September 1976), pp. 727–57

Cohen, M., 'American Influence on British Policy in the Middle East during World War Two: First Attempts at Coordinating Allied Policy on Palestine', *American Jewish Historical Quarterly*, Vol. 67, No. 1 (September 1977), pp. 50–70

Cohen, M. 'The Genesis of the Anglo-American Committee on Palestine, November 1945: A Case Study in the Assertion of American Hegemony', *Historical Journal*, Vol. 22, No. 1 (March 1979), pp. 185–207

Colville, J., *The Fringes of Power: Downing Street Diaries, 1939–1955*, London 1985

Conway, E., *The Summit*, London 2014

Cooper, A., *Cairo in the War, 1939–45*, London 1989

Copeland, M., *The Game of Nations*, New York 1969

Corera, G., *The Art of Betrayal*, London 2011

Cowles, G., *Mike Looks Back*, New York 1985

Crossman, R., *Palestine Mission*, London 1947

Crum, B. C., *Behind the Silken Curtain: A Personal Account of Anglo-American Diplomacy in Palestine and the Middle East*, New York 1947

Davidson, L., 'Truman the Politician and the Establishment of Israel', *Journal of Palestine Studies*, Vol. 39, No. 4 (Summer 2010), pp. 28–42

Davis, S., 'Keeping the Americans in Line? Britain, the United States and Saudi Arabia, 1939–45: Inter-Allied Rivalry in the Middle East Revisited', *Diplomacy & Statecraft*, Vol. 8, No. 1 (March 1997), pp. 96–136

de Moraes Ruehsen, M., 'Operation "Ajax" Revisited: Iran, 1953', *Middle Eastern Studies*, Vol. 29, No. 3 (July 1993), pp. 467–86

Deane-Drummond, A., *Arrows of Fortune*, London 1992

Dilks, D., ed., *The Diaries of Sir Alexander Cadogan, 1938–45*, London 1971

Dobson, A., *Anglo-American Relations in the Twentieth Century*, London 1995

Dockter, W., *Churchill and the Islamic World: Orientalism, Empire and Diplomacy in the Middle East*, London 2014

Dodge, B., 'American Educational and Missionary Efforts in the Nineteenth and Early Twentieth Centuries', *Annals of the American Academy of Political and Social Science*, Vol. 401, America and the Middle East (May 1972), pp. 15–22

Doran, M., *Ike's Gamble: America's Rise to Dominance in the Middle East*, New York 2016

Dorril, S., *MI6: Fifty Years of Special Operations*, London 2000

Dulles, J. F., 'Policy for Security and Peace', *Foreign Affairs*, Vol. 32, No. 3 (April 1954), pp. 353–64

Easter, D., 'Spying on Nasser: British Signals Intelligence in Middle East Crises and Conflicts, 1956–67', *Intelligence and National Security*, Vol. 28, No. 6 (2013), pp. 824–44

Eden, A., *Another World 1897–1917*, London 1976

Eisenhower, D., *Crusade in Europe*, New York 1948

Elm, M., *Oil, Power and Principle*, Syracuse 1994

Evans, T. E., ed., *The Killearn Diaries, 1934–1946: The Diplomatic and Personal Record of Lord Killearn (Sir Miles Lampson), High Commissioner and Ambassador, Egypt*, London 1972

Eveland, W., *Ropes of Sand: America's Failure in the Middle East*, New York 1980

Evensen, B., 'Truman, Palestine and the Cold War', *Middle Eastern Studies*, Vol. 28, No. 1 (January 1992), pp. 120–56

Falle, S., *My Lucky Life*, Lewes 1996

Ferrell, R., ed., *The Eisenhower Diaries*, New York 1981

Ferris, J., *Nasser's Gamble*, Princeton 2013

Field, J., 'Trade, Skills and Sympathy: The First Century and a Half of Commerce with the Near East', *Annals of the American Academy of Political and Social Science*, Vol. 401, 'America and the Middle East' (May, 1972), pp. 1–14

Fielding, X., *One Man in his Time: The Life of Lieutenant-Colonel NLD ('Billy') McLean, DSO*, London 1990

French, D., 'Duncan Sandys and the Projection of British Power after Suez', *Diplomacy & Statecraft*, Vol. 24, No. 1 (March 2013), pp. 41–58

French, D., *The British Way in Counter-Insurgency, 1945–1967*, Oxford 2011

Gandy, C., 'A Mission to Yemen: August 1962–January 1963', *British Journal of Middle Eastern Studies*, Vol. 25, No. 2 (1998), pp. 247–74

Gasiorowski, M., and Byrne, M., eds, *Mohammad Mosaddeq and the 1953 Coup in Iran*, Syracuse 2004

Gibson, J., *Jacko: Where Are You Now? A Life of Robert Jackson, Master of Humanitarian Relief; The Man Who Saved Malta*, Richmond 2006.

Gilbert, M., *Churchill and America*, London 2005

Glubb, J., *A Soldier with the Arabs*, London 1957

Goodman, M., *The Official History of the Joint Intelligence Committee*, Vol. I, London 2014

Gorst, A., and Lucas, W. S., 'The Other Collusion: Operation Straggle and Anglo-American Intervention in Syria, 1955–56', *Intelligence and National Security*, Vol. 4, No. 3 (1989), pp. 576–95

Grafftey-Smith, L., *Bright Levant*, London 1970

Grob-Fitzgibbon, B., *Imperial Endgame*, Basingstoke 2011

Hahn, P., 'Securing the Middle East: The Eisenhower Doctrine of 1957', *Presidential Studies Quarterly*, Vol. 36, No. 1 (March 2006), pp. 38–47

Harbutt, F., 'Churchill, Hopkins, and the "Other" Americans: An Alternative Perspective on Anglo-American Relations, 1941–1945', *International History Review*, Vol. 8, No. 2 (May 1986), pp. 236–62

Hardy, R., *The Poisoned Well: Empire and its Legacy in the Middle East*, London 2016

Hare, R., 'The Great Divide: World War II', *Annals of the American Academy of Political and Social Science*, Vol. 401, America and the Middle East (May 1972), pp. 23–30

Hare, P., *Diplomatic Chronicles of the Middle East: A Biography of Ambassador Raymond A. Hare*, Lanham 1993

Haron, M., 'The British Decision to Give the Palestine Question to the United Nations', *Middle Eastern Studies*, Vol. 17, No. 2 (April 1981), pp. 241–8

Harris, K., *Attlee*, London 1982

Hart, P., *Saudi Arabia and the United States: Birth of a Security Partnership*, Bloomington 1998

Hart-Davis, D., *The War That Never Was*, London 2011

Harvey, J., ed., *The War Diaries of Oliver Harvey*, London 1978

Hassall, C., *Edward Marsh, patron of the arts*, London 1959

Healey, D., *The Time of my Life*, London 1989

Heath, E., *The Course of my Life: My Autobiography*, London 1998

Hecht, B., *A Child of the Century*, New York 1955

Heikal, M., *Cutting the Lion's Tail: Suez through Egyptian Eyes*, London 1988

Hennessy, P., *The Prime Minister: The Office and its Holders Since 1945*, London 2000

Hinchcliffe, P., *Without Glory in Arabia*, London 2006

Hinds, M. 'Anglo-American Relations in Saudi Arabia, 1941–1945: A Study of a Trying Relationship', PhD thesis, London School of Economics 2012

Hoffman, B., *Anonymous Soldiers: The Struggle for Israel 1917–1947*, New York 2015

Hoopes, T., and Brinkley, D., *FDR and the Creation of the UN*, New Haven and London 1997

Horne, A., *Macmillan: The Official Biography*, Vol. I, London 1989

Horne, A., *But What Do You Actually Do?*, London 2011

Hudson, M., 'To Play the Hegemon: Fifty Years of US Policy toward the Middle East', *Middle East Journal*, Vol. 50, No. 3 (Summer 1996), pp. 329–43

Innes, N., *Minister in Oman*, Cambridge 1987

Ionides, M., *Divide and Lose*, London 1960

James, L., *Churchill and Empire*, London 2013

Johnston, C., *The Brink of Jordan*, London 1972

Jones, C., '"Where the State Feared to Tread": Britain, Britons, Covert Action and the Yemen Civil War, 1962–64', *Intelligence and National Security*, Vol. 21, No. 5 (2006), pp. 717–37

Jones, C., 'Military Intelligence, Tribes, and Britain's War in Dhofar, 1970–1976', *Middle East Journal*, Vol. 65, No. 4 (Autumn 2011), pp. 557–74

Jones, M., 'The "Preferred Plan": The Anglo-American Working Group Report on Covert Action in Syria, 1957, *Intelligence and National Security*, Vol. 19, No. 3 (2004), pp. 401–15

Kelly S., and Gorst, A., eds, *Whitehall and the Suez Crisis*, London 2000

Kinzer, S., *All the Shah's Men: An American Coup and the Roots of Middle East Terror*, New York 2003

Kirk, G., 'The Syrian Crisis of 1957 – Fact and Fiction', *International Affairs*, Vol. 36, No. 1 (January 1960), pp. 58–61

Kyle, K., *Suez*, New York 1991

Landis, J., 'Restoring World Trade', *Proceedings of the Academy of Political Science*, Vol. 21, No. 3 (May 1945), pp. 175–82

Landis, J., 'Anglo-American Co-Operation in the Middle East', *Annals of the American Academy of Political and Social Science*, Vol. 240, Our Muddled World (July 1945), pp. 64–72

Lesch, D., 'When the Relationship Went Sour: Syria and the Eisenhower Administration', *Presidential Studies Quarterly*, Vol. 28, No. 1, Wheeling and Dealing in the White House (Winter 1998), pp. 92–107

Levey, Z., 'Britain's Middle East Strategy, 1950–52: General Brian Robertson and the "Small" Arab States', *Middle Eastern Studies*, Vol. 40, No. 2 (March 2004), pp. 58–79

Little, D., 'Cold War and Covert Action: The United States and Syria, 1945–1958', *The Middle East Journal* (Winter 1990), Vol. 44, No. 1, pp. 51–75

Little, D., 'Pipeline Politics: America, TAPLINE and the Arabs', *Business History Review*, Vol. 64, No. 2 (Summer 1992), pp. 255–85

Little, T., *South Arabia: Arena of Conflict*, London 1968

Louis, W. R., *The British Empire in the Middle East, 1945–51*, Oxford 1984

Louis, W. R., and Shlaim, A., eds, *The 1967 Arab–Israeli War: Origins and Consequences*, Cambridge 2012

Lucas, I., 'The Middle East and the Cold War', *Cambridge Review of International Affairs*, Vol. 7, No. 1 (1993), pp. 12–20

Lucas, I., *A Road to Damascus: Mainly Diplomatic Memoirs from the Middle East*, London 1997

Lucas, S., 'Divided We Stand: The Suez Crisis of 1956 and the Anglo-American "Alliance"', PhD thesis, LSE 1991

Lucas, S., *Divided We Stand: Britain, the US and the Suez Crisis*, London 1991

Lucas S., and Morey, A., 'The Hidden "Alliance": The CIA and MI6 Before and After Suez', *Intelligence and National Security*, Vol. 15, No. 2 (2000), pp. 95–120

McGhee, G., *Envoy to the Middle World*, New York 1983

Macintyre, B., *SAS: Rogue Heroes: The Authorized Wartime History*, London 2016

Maclean, F., *Eastern Approaches*, London 1991

Magnes, J., 'Toward Peace in Palestine', *Foreign Affairs*, Vol. 21, No. 2 (January 1943), pp. 239–49

Mangold, P., 'Britain and the Defence of Kuwait, 1956–71', *The RUSI Journal*, Vol. 120, No. 3 (1975), pp. 44–8

Mangold, P., *What the British Did*, London 2016

Marsh, S., 'The Special Relationship and the Anglo-Iranian Oil Crisis, 1950–4', *Review of International Studies*, Vol. 24, No. 4 (October 1998), pp. 529–44

Marsh, S., 'HMG, AIOC and the Anglo-Iranian Oil Crisis', *Diplomacy & Statecraft*, Vol. 12, No. 4 (December 2001), pp. 143–74

Mawby, S., 'The Clandestine Defence of Empire: British Special Operations in Yemen 1951–64', *Intelligence and National Security* (2002), Vol. 17, No. 3, pp. 105–30

Meacham, J., *Franklin and Winston: An Intimate Portrait of an Epic Friendship*, New York 2003

Mead, W. R., 'The New Israel and the Old: Why Gentile Americans Back the Jewish State', *Foreign Affairs*, Vol. 87, No. 4 (July–August 2008), pp. 28–46

Medoff, R., *Militant Zionism in America: The Rise and Impact of the Jabotinsky Movement, 1926–1948*, Tuscaloosa 2002

Mejcher, M., 'Saudi Arabia's "Vital Link to the West": Some Political, Strategic and Tribal Aspects of the Transarabian Pipeline (TAP) in the Stage of Planning 1942–1950', *Middle Eastern Studies*, Vol. 18, No. 4 (October 1982), pp. 359–77

Mitchell, C., *Having Been a Soldier*, London 1969

Mobley, R., 'Gauging the Iraqi Threat to Kuwait in the 1960s', *Studies in Intelligence*, Fall/Winter 2001, pp. 19–31

Moe, R., *Roosevelt's Second Act: The Election of 1940 and the Politics of War*, New York 2013

Morris, J., *Sultan in Oman*, London 1957

Morton, H. V., *Atlantic Meeting*, London 1944

Morton, M. Q., *Buraimi: The Struggle for Power, Influence and Oil in Arabia*, London 2013

Mott-Radclyffe, C., *Foreign Body in the Eye: A Memoir of the Foreign Service Old and New*, London 1975

Nachmani, A., '"It is a Matter of Getting the Mixture Right": Britain's Post-War Relations with America in the Middle East', *Journal of Contemporary History*, Vol. 18, No. 1 (January 1983), pp. 117–40

Neal, S., *Dark Horse: A Biography of Wendell C. Willkie*, New York 1984

Nutting, A., *No End of a Lesson: The Story of Suez*, London 1967

O'Connell, J., *King's Counsel*, New York 2011

Onslow, S., 'Unreconstructed Nationalists and a Minor Gunboat Operation: Julian Amery, Neil McLean and the Suez Crisis', *Contemporary British History*, Vol. 20, No. 1 (March 2006), pp. 73–99

Oren, M., *Power, Faith and Fantasy: America in the Middle East, 1776 to the Present*, New York 2007

O'Sullivan, C., *FDR and the End of Empire: The Origins of American Power in the Middle East*, Basingstoke 2012

Ottolenghi, M., 'Harry Truman's Recognition of Israel', *Historical Journal*, Vol. 47, No. 4 (December 2004), pp. 963–88

Ovendale, R., 'The Palestine Policy of the British Labour Government, 1945–46', *International Affairs*, Vol. 55, No. 3 (July 1979), pp. 73–93

Ovendale, R., 'Great Britain and the Anglo-American Invasion of Jordan and Lebanon in 1958', *International History Review*, Vol. 16, No. 2 (May 1994), pp. 284–303

Owen, D., *In Sickness and in Power*, London 2008

Pappé, I., 'Overt Conflict to Tacit Alliance: Anglo-Israeli Relations 1948–51', *Middle Eastern Studies*, Vol. 26, No. 4 (October 1990), pp. 561–81

Pappé, I., 'Sir Alec Kirkbride and the Anglo-Transjordanian Alliance, 1945–50', in Zametica, J., ed., *British Officials and British Foreign Policy, 1945–50*, Leicester 1990

Parris, M., and Bryson, A., *Parting Shots*, London 2010

Pearson, I., 'The Syrian Crisis of 1957, the Anglo-American "Special Relationship", and the 1958 Landings in Jordan and Lebanon', *Middle Eastern Studies*, Vol. 43, No. 1 (2007), pp. 45–64

Penkower, M., 'Eleanor Roosevelt and the Plight of World Jewry', *Jewish Social Studies*, Vol. 49, No. 2 (Spring 1987), pp. 125–36

Petersen, T. T., 'Anglo-American Rivalry in the Middle East: The Struggle for the Buraimi Oasis, 1952–1957', *International History Review*, Vol. 14, No. 1 (February 1992), pp. 71–91

Petersen, T. T., 'Transfer of Power in the Middle East', *International History Review*, Vol. 19, No. 4 (November 1997), pp. 852–65

Pham, P., *Ending 'East of Suez': The British Decision to Withdraw from Malaysia and Singapore, 1964–68*, Oxford 2001

Podeh, E., *The Decline of Arab Unity: The Rise and Fall of the United Arab Republic*, Brighton 2015

Porath, Y., 'Nuri al-Sa'id's Arab Unity Programme', *Middle Eastern Studies*, Vol. 20, No. 4 (October 1984), pp. 76–98

Rahnema, A., *Behind the 1953 Coup in Iran*, Cambridge 2015

Randall, S. J., 'Harold Ickes and United States Foreign Petroleum Policy Planning, 1939–1945', *Business History Review*, Vol. 57, No. 3 (Autumn 1983), pp. 367–87

Rathmell, A., *Secret War in the Middle East*, new edn, London 2014

Rhodes James, R., *Chips: The Diaries of Sir Henry Channon*, London 1967

Ritchie, D. A., *James M. Landis: Dean of the Regulators*, Cambridge, MA 1980

Roberts, A., *Masters and Commanders*, London 2008

Roosevelt, T., 'The Man in the Arena', Speech at the Sorbonne, France 1910

Roosevelt, K., 'Propaganda Techniques of the English Civil Wars and the Propaganda Psychosis of Today', *Pacific Historical Review*, Vol. 12, No. 4 (December 1943), pp. 369–79

Roosevelt, K., 'The Arabs Live There Too', *Harper's Magazine*, October 1946, pp. 289–94

Roosevelt, K., 'Egypt's Inferiority Complex', *Harper's Magazine*, 1 October 1947, pp. 357–64

Roosevelt, K., 'The Partition of Palestine: A Lesson in Pressure Politics', *Middle East Journal*, Vol. 2, No. 1 (January 1948), pp. 1–16

Roosevelt, K., 'Triple Play for the Middle East', *Harper's Magazine*, April 1948, pp. 359–69

Roosevelt, K., 'The Middle East and the Prospect for World Government', *Annals of the American Academy of Political and Social Science*, Vol. 264 (July 1949), pp. 52–7

Roosevelt, K., *Arabs, Oil and History*, London 1949

Roosevelt, K., *Countercoup: The Struggle for the Control of Iran*, New York 1979

Rose, N., *'A Senseless Squalid War': Voices from Palestine 1945–1948*, London 2009

Rubin, B., 'Anglo-American Relations in Saudi Arabia, 1941–45', *Journal of Contemporary History*, Vol. 14, No. 2 (April 1979), pp. 253–67

Rubin, B., *The Great Powers in the Middle East 1941–1947*, London 1980

Sanjian, A., 'The Formulation of the Baghdad Pact', *Middle Eastern Studies*, Vol. 33, No. 2 (April 1997), pp. 226–66

Seale, P., *The Struggle for Syria*, London 1965

Segev, T., *One Palestine, complete: Jews and Arabs under the British mandate*, London 2000

Shlaim, A., 'The Protocol of Sevres, 1956: Anatomy of a War Plot', *International Affairs*, Vol. 73, No. 3 (July 1997), pp. 509–30

Shlaim, A., *Lion of Jordan*, London 2007

Shuckburgh, E., *Descent to Suez: Diaries 1951–56*, London 1986

Slonim, S., 'Origins of the 1950 Tripartite Declaration on the Middle East', *Middle Eastern Studies*, Vol. 23, No. 2 (April 1987), pp. 135–49

Smiley, D., *Arabian Assignment*, London 1975

Smith, S., *Ending Empire in the Middle East: Britain, the United States and Post-war Decolonisation*, London 2012

Sweet Escott, B., *Baker Street Irregular*, London 1965

Tal, L., 'Britain and the Jordan Crisis of 1958', *Middle Eastern Studies*, Vol. 31, No. 1 (January 1995), pp. 39–57

Talbot, D., *The Devil's Chessboard: Allen Dulles, the CIA and the Rise of America's Secret Government*, London 2016

Talhamy, Y., 'American Protestant Missionary Activity among the Nusayris (Alawis) in Syria in the Nineteenth Century', *Middle Eastern Studies*, Vol. 47, No. 2 (2011), pp. 215–36

Taylor Fain, W., '"Unfortunate Arabia": The United States, Great Britain and Yemen, 1955–63', *Diplomacy & Statecraft*, Vol. 12, No. 2 (June 2001), pp. 125–52

Taylor Fain, W., 'John F. Kennedy and Harold Macmillan: Managing the "Special Relationship" in the Persian Gulf Region, 1961–63', *Middle Eastern Studies*, Vol. 38, No. 4 (October 2002), pp. 95–122

Thesiger, W., 'A New Journey in Southern Arabia', *The Geographical Journal*, Vol. 108, No. 4/6 (October–December 1946), pp. 129–45

Thesiger, W., 'Across the Empty Quarter', *The Geographical Journal*, Vol. 111, No. 1/3 (January– March 1948), pp. 1–19

Thesiger, W., 'A Further Journey Across the Empty Quarter', *Geographical Journal*, Vol. 113 (January–June 1949), pp. 21–44

Thesiger, W., 'Desert Borderlands of Oman', *The Geographical Journal*, Vol. 116, No. 4/6 (October–December 1950), pp. 137–68

Thesiger, W., 'Buraimi Oasis', *Illustrated London News*, 3 July 1954

Thesiger, W., *Arabian Sands*, London 1991

Thomas, J., *The Diplomatic Game*, n.d.

Thornhill, M., *Road to Suez: The Battle of the Canal Zone*, Stroud 2006

Thorpe, D. R., *Eden: The Life and Times of Anthony Eden, First Earl of Avon, 1897–1977*, London 2003

Trevelyan, H., *The Middle East in Revolution*, London 1970

Trevelyan, H., *Public and Private*, London 1980

Truman, H., *Memoirs* , Vols I and II, London 1955 and 1956

Twitchell, K., *Saudi Arabia: With an Account of the Development of Its Natural Resources*, Princeton 1958

Tydor Baumel, J., 'The IZL Delegation in the USA 1939–1948: Anatomy of an Ethnic Interest/Protest Group', *Jewish History*, Vol. 9, No. 1 (Spring 1995), pp. 79–89

Vassiliev, A., *The History of Saudi Arabia*, London 1998

Vitalis, R., *America's Kingdom*, London 2009

Von Tunzelmann, A., *Blood and Sand*, London 2016

Wagner, S., 'Britain and the Jewish Underground, 1944–46: Intelligence, Policy and Resistance', MA thesis, University of Calgary 2010

Walker, J., *Aden Insurgency: The Savage War in Yemen 1962–67*, Barnsley 2011

Walton, C., *Empire of Secrets: British Intelligence, The Cold War, and the Twilight of Empire*, London 2013

Wevill, R., *Diplomacy, Roger Makins and the Anglo-American Relationship*, Farnham 2014

Wilber, D., *Iran: Past and Present*, Princeton 1958

Wilford, H., *America's Great Game*, New York 2013

Willkie, W., *One World*, London 1943

Wilmington, M. W., *The Middle East Supply Centre*, Albany 1971

Winger, G., 'Twilight on the British Gulf: The 1961 Kuwait Crisis and the Evolution of American Strategic Thinking in the Persian Gulf', *Diplomacy & Statecraft*, Vol. 24, No. 4 (2012), pp. 660–78

Wolfe-Hunnicutt, B., 'The End of the Concessionary Regime: Oil and American Power in Iraq, 1958–72', PhD thesis, Stanford University 2011

Woodhouse, C. M., *Something Ventured*, London 1982

Woodward, L., *British Foreign Policy in the Second World War*, Vols I–V, London 1970–76

Worrall, R., '"Coping with the Coup d'Etat": British Policy towards Post-Revolutionary Iraq, 1958–63', *Contemporary British History*, Vol. 21, No. 2, pp. 173–99

Wright, D., 'Ten Years in Iran – Some Highlights', *Asian Affairs*, Vol. 22, No. 3 (1991), pp. 259–71

Yapp, M., *The Near East Since the First World War*, London 1996

Yaqub, S., *Containing Arab Nationalism: The Eisenhower Doctrine and the Middle East*, Chapel Hill 2004

Yergin, D., *The Prize*, New York 2003

Yeşilbursa, B., 'The American Concept of the "Northern Tier" Defence Project and the Signing of the Turco-Pakistani Agreement, 1953–54', *Middle Eastern Studies*, Vol. 37, No. 3 (July 2001), pp. 59–110

Yeşilbursa, B., *The Baghdad Pact: Anglo-American Defence Policies in the Middle East 1950–1959*, London 2005

Young, G. K., *Who Is my Liege?*, London 1972

Zadka, S., 'Between Jerusalem and Hollywood: The Propaganda Campaign in the USA on Behalf of the Palestinian Jewish Insurgency in 1940s', *Revue Européenne des Études Hébraïques*, No. 3 (1998), pp. 66–82

INDEX